M000209362

Hirohito and War

上奏関係綴 其一

大本営

自昭和十六年十月
至〃十二月

38

Hirohito and War

Imperial Tradition and
Military Decision Making
in Prewar Japan

•

Peter Wetzler

University
of Hawai'i Press
Honolulu

© 1998 University of Hawai'i Press
All rights reserved
Printed in the United States of America
98 99 00 01 02 03 5 4 3 2 1

Library of Congress Cataloging-in-Publication Data
Wetzler, Peter.
Hirohito and war : imperial tradition and military decision making
in prewar Japan / Peter Wetzler.
p. cm.
Includes bibliographical references and index.
ISBN 0-8248-1925-X (alk. paper)
1. World War, 1939-1945—Japan. 2. Hirohito, Emperor of Japan,
1901-   . 3. Japan—Intellectual life—20th century. 4. Japan—
Politics and government—1926-1945. 5. Military planning—Japan.
I. Title.
D767.2.W67 1998
940.54'0952—dc21   97-29981
                                        CIP

University of Hawai'i Press books are printed on acid-free
paper and meet the guidelines for permanence and dura-
bility of the Council on Library Resources

Frontispiece: Title page of *Jōsō kankeisetsu sono ichi* (Writings related
to imperial audiences, no. 1) by Daihon'ei (Imperial Headquarters).
Bōeichō Bōeikenkyūjo Toshokan (The National Institute of
Defense Studies Library).

Designed by Omega Clay

To John and Dee,
who were always there

Contents

Preface

At the end of 1926 the term "Shōwa"—enlightenment and peace—was chosen as the name of Emperor Hirohito's reign. The irony escapes few, Japanese and non-Japanese alike, as the first half of the era (1926–1989) was marked by disharmony and war. The dispute about the emperor's role in starting the war in the Pacific, moreover, cast a dark shadow over the period following the fall of Imperial Japan in August 1945 until Hirohito's death more than forty-three years later.

This study was begun in 1984, five years before the Shōwa emperor died, when I was asked my opinion of David Bergamini's book, *Japan's Imperial Conspiracy*. I realized then that although I had spent many years studying Japanese language and history, I knew little about one of Japan's most important institutions—the imperial house. As a teacher of modern Japanese history, I noted that, with the exception of David A. Titus' fine study of Hirohito's wartime political adviser, Lord Keeper of the Privy Seal Kido Kōichi, there was at that time little solid information available on the role of the imperial house in prewar developments in Japan. Since then I have spent most of my free time investigating the subject. A number of books and articles on the Shōwa emperor have appeared while this work was being researched and written. They have contributed to my thinking, but the conclusions offered in the following pages are my own.

This study focuses on two topics: Emperor Hirohito's role in military decision making; and the intellectual background that formed the foundation of the emperor's participation in these decisions. I chose the first topic because I saw an opportunity to contribute to an all-but-ignored area of studies about the emperor and the prewar years. The second was addressed because it seemed necessary to understand Hirohito's role in military planning. This topic too has been neglected, and preliminary research revealed that, contrary to expectations, the crown prince's education was totally consistent with his subsequent active participation in wartime decision making.

The imperial house has long had a special mystique for the Japanese, if not always an aura of respect or political importance. This can be seen in simple matters such as the way in which the emperor is referred to: even in the modern era, the emperor and the immediate members of his family have no surname. (In modern times princes and princesses receive a family name when they marry and establish a house outside the imperial palace.) Until recently, in fact, the emperor himself was not referred to by name. He was "the honorable emperor" *(tennō heika)*. His given name, Hirohito, was often used in Western books and articles, but as late as the mid-1960s it was all but unknown among ordinary Japanese living in Japan. The name "Shōwa" refers to his reign and was usually not used with respect to him personally until after he died. Thereafter Hirohito became the "Shōwa Tennō." Throughout this work he is referred to as Hirohito, Emperor Hirohito, and the Shōwa emperor interchangeably.

Personal names of other Japanese appear in their Japanese order—family name preceding given name—with one exception: references to Japanese authors of works in Western languages appear in the Western order. Chinese names are given in Wade-Giles spelling because those appearing in this work are, with few exceptions, well known in this form.

While doing research on this topic I neither solicited nor accepted financial support of any kind. Nevertheless, a number of people have been very helpful to me over the years. Especially I wish to thank Professor Bernd Martin of the University of Freiburg. This was originally a "Habilitation" project in the Seminar for Modern History at that university, and without Professor Martin's advice I surely would not have been able to complete it. Dr. Gerhard Krebs, presently at the Institute for Military History Research in Potsdam, was very helpful as well, referring me to sources and discussing issues during our visits. Professor Klaus Antoni at Trier University offered encouragement at important times. Dr. Rainer Krempien, director of the East Asia Department in the German National Library in Berlin, became a good friend and was ever ready to assist in finding materials. The library staff at the National Institute for Defense Studies (NIDS) in Tokyo was extremely helpful as well: their assistance in tracking down references and locating information was invaluable. Professor K. Tashiro at the National Institute of Multimedia Education, a long-standing friend, patiently discussed issues in modern Japanese historiography. Professor N. Yaegashi, also a longtime friend, introduced me to the mysteries of *kambun* many years ago as well as the problems of doing research in premodern Japanese history. Ishida Ichirō, professor emeritus at Tōhoku University, offered sage advice throughout many years. Delmer M. Brown, professor emeritus at the University of California, Berkeley, was an early supporter of my efforts in Japanese history. Professor Titus of Wesleyan University spent many hours going over an earlier version of this work. His suggestions were extremely useful, and I owe him a special note of thanks. Finally, Patricia Crosby, my editor at the University of Hawai'i Press, must be mentioned. Without her effort, patience, and encouragement this project might never have come to fruition.

While all of these persons have contributed to what this study has become, they are not of course responsible for what it is not. I greatly appreciate the help I received but am solely responsible, for better or worse, for what follows.

Only where love and need are one,
And the work is play for mortal stakes . . .

Hirohito and Japan, the contradictions of the man and the confusion surrounding the island nation, are expressed succinctly in these lines by the American poet Robert Frost. Certainly Frost had neither the Land of the Rising Sun nor its emperor in mind when he wrote them, but such is the universalistic appeal of good poetry and the particularistic challenge of Japan.

I

·

Introduction

Emperor Hirohito (1901–1989) was the titular head of the Japanese government when the Imperial Army set up a puppet state in Manchuria in 1931–1932, when the war with China began in 1937, when the Japanese attacked Pearl Harbor and other targets in Southeast Asia without warning in late 1941 and early 1942, when Japan surrendered unconditionally in 1945, and when he visited Disneyland in the United States many years later. Of course, "titular head" meant different things to different people before and after the war. Accordingly, the debate about Emperor Hirohito's accountability for imperial government decisions and military operations up to the termination of World War II began before the end of the war and has continued even after his death in 1989. It is my contention that the debate is based on a false conception of the emperor's role in prewar decision making and how responsibility is to be assigned for those decisions. Supporters maintain that "the Emperor regarded his sanctioning of the war decision in 1941 as an act of political integrity required of a constitutional monarch."[1] He therefore shared in the collective responsibility for the war, but only in a "formal legal sense." Critics assert that Hirohito personally approved the decision and is personally responsible for the war in the Pacific.[2] Irokawa Daikichi, in a work recently translated into English, presents a more complicated picture: the emperor was not without authority, and on occasion he exercised it decisively. But due to his concern about constitutional monarchy, the emperor was "in a tragic position: the more he attempted to adhere to the principle of constitutional monarchy, the more he departed from the actual political situation and compromised his ability to lead."[3] Each of these explanations contains an element of truth. But they all ignore a more important factor: contemporary concern about the survival of the imperial house and its position in the body politic.

Most conclusions about the Shōwa emperor's role in the prewar decision-making process are based on inferences drawn from postwar political policies and ideological preconceptions unrelated to those activities. Irokawa is to some extent an exception. My work agrees in part with his evaluations—but not with his assessment of Hirohito's advisers or the way Irokawa assumes political and military decision making took place in the prewar years.[4] I propose instead another decision-making process and alternative conclusions derived from primary source materials intimately related to the emperor's activities.

The Emperor and the Pacific War

Historian Carol Gluck wrote shortly after Hirohito's death: "Placing the Showa emperor in national history means dealing with the war."[5] Nevertheless, few have dealt with the war and the emperor, including Gluck and the other scholars who contributed to the volume she and Stephen Graubard edited about this era. Indeed, the special issue of *Daedalus*, "Showa: The Japan of Hirohito," and the book of the same title are examples of what for the most part has been left undone— research into primary sources to ascertain what the emperor did and did not do in prewar Japan. Masataka Kosaka's comment is typical:

> Though the emperor himself was not responsible for the failure to change the [prewar] political order, it is undeniable that many of the acts that led to tragedy were carried out in his name, however painful they were to him.[6]

That is, Hirohito was officially responsible for the tragedy, meaning the war, but not personally accountable for it. This is a compromise— neither fact nor fiction—that is profoundly unsatisfying because it exempts the emperor's role in prewar Japanese decision making from detailed analysis.

The debate about Hirohito's war responsibility revolves around the issues of war versus peace and constitutional monarchy versus direct imperial rule. Despite this trend, one cannot analyze Hirohito's actions only in terms of constitutionalism or militarism. Obviously these were significant issues for the emperor, but something else was even more important to him: the Japanese imperial house. The well-being and continued existence of Japan's imperial house were among the themes most often repeated by his teachers of ethics and history; were an overriding consideration of his two early advisers, Prince Saionji and Count Makino; and were of the utmost importance to the Shōwa emperor himself.

Hirohito affirmed the supreme importance of the imperial house by emphasizing his descent from the gods, even after Japan's defeat and occupation. Before his famous renunciation of divine status, the emperor told his vice-grand chamberlain, Kinoshita Michio (1887–1974):

> It is permissible to say that the idea that the Japanese are descendants of the gods is a false conception; but it is absolutely impermissible to call chimerical the idea that the emperor is a descendant of the gods.[7]

Though Hirohito disavowed the divine origins of the Japanese people, he reaffirmed the special symbolic relation between the imperial house and Japan's gods.[8] This folk belief was fundamental to Japan's war effort. It also coincided with the folkish ideals esteemed by the "war premier," General Tōjō Hideki (1884–1948). And it was these two very different men, Emperor Hirohito and Prime Minister Tōjō, who led Japan into a war it obviously could not win.[9]

The Imperial Line, Imperial Legitimacy, and the Imperial Will

The Shōwa emperor shared in the collective responsibility for the war, and not merely in a formal legal sense. He individually did not and could not approve starting a war with China, the United States, or anyone else, but he was actively involved in the decision to go to war reached in the fall of 1941, as well as in many other political and military decisions before the attack on Pearl Harbor. He participated in these decisions because he was the head of state, and head of the imperial line, but his powers, while noted in the constitution, were not based on that document.

The emperor's legitimacy in the prewar era was based on three pillars: his descent from the Sun Goddess; his possession of the imperial regalia (sword, jewel, and mirror); and the performance of ceremonies honoring the Sun Goddess. The importance of these factors for the state in prewar Japan has been described by Ernst Lokowandt:

> Princely sovereignty, for example, as per the divine right of kings, meant in Europe that a monarch received his right to rule from God; thereby he was, if worst came to worst, the basis of the state power apparatus. In Japan, by contrast, the emperor was as a descendant of the highest goddess (demonstrated by his possession of the imperial regalia), and as proprietor of the highest spiritual authority in Shintō, not just the basis of the state power apparatus. He was, what is more, the basis of the state in an all-encompassing sense, including the people themselves.... The Tennō was the state, and another higher instance surpassing him was not to be seen.[10]

In other words: in prewar Japan the state and national polity *(kokutai)* were, devoid of the emperor, inconceivable.

With respect to religion, David Titus has written about Shinto, the religion in which the emperor is the highest "shaman-priest": "In taking the welfare of the nation as its primary principle, Shinto differs from other religions, which seek the salvation of all mankind."[11] The emperor's position is based on mythology (his descent), possession of sacred objects, and ceremonies (honoring the imperial line), not military or political power or financial wealth. His concern is for the Japanese people, not all men and women.[12] The emperor's significance, in summary, was very specific in prewar Japan—limited to the Japanese polity. But he was indispensable to that community. The imperial house as an institution was essential to the continued existence of native Japanese religion, the Japanese folk, and state. For this reason the preservation of the imperial house was of great importance to Hirohito personally, his immediate advisers, and also many lesser persons.

The significance of the emperor for prewar Japanese culture has also been related to his status as a "god manifest." This, of course, had nothing to do with the all-powerful, omniscient god found in the world religions originating in the Middle East—Christianity and Islam, for instance. Gods in Japan are of a different character. According to a Japanese authority, Watsuji Tetsurō, in Japan "the emperor is the god who bears sacred authority as the offspring of the gods of heaven *(amatsukami)*. . . . Gods are gods because their divinity is always bestowed from a beyond reaching to infinity. Therefore, only as mediums do gods become gods, and they are mediums to the revelations of infinity, not of an ultimate source." The emperor is one of a number of gods who are worshiped *(matsurareru)* and also who worship *(matsuru)*. These gods "have personae as mediators with indeterminant gods, as routes for sacred commands."[13] This means that the emperor is a god in that he is a medium between the gods of the Japanese pantheon, the imperial line, and the Japanese people. Thereby the people become a united folk. "Rites themselves," says Watsuji, "are nothing less than expressions of how a people is conscious of its entirety. . . . Therefore, for the founding god of the imperial family and the august gods manifest [emperors past and present] to express the folk entirety is for them to express the absolute entirety as mediums for the folk entirety."[14] Watsuji continues: "Purity or pollution of the heart meant obedience to or disobedience of the emperor. This was not submission or nonsubmission to the rule of power; it was belief or non-belief in the sacred authority of the entirety."[15] The emperor was unlike a Western (or Near Eastern) god and equally unlike a commander in chief in one of these cultures. He revealed and stood for the unity of the Japanese people, but he did not ordain or issue orders.

Watsuji offers an authoritative explanation of the imperial tradition —the legitimacy of the imperial line as titular leaders of Japan, a legitimacy based on early mythology and the history of that institution since the ninth century. Emperors reigned but did not rule. At the beginning of the fourteenth century there was one short-lived exception when an emperor sought with some success to rule directly—the Kemmu Restoration. Another exception came much later—between 1926 and 1945.

The Meiji Constitution of 1889, a combination of Prussian constitutional theory and Japanese imperial line mythology based on Western principles, legitimized the modernization of the emperor's powers. Article 1 stated: "The Empire of Japan shall be reigned over and governed by a line of Emperors unbroken for ages eternal." The emperor was pronounced "sacred and inviolable" (Article 3). He "combined in his being the supreme rights of rule" (Article 4) and "exercised supreme command over the Army and Navy" (Article 11).[16] As Titus concludes: "The emperor thus became the source of executive, legislative, and judicial powers, and all government acts were issued in his name."[17] At the same time, interpreters of this constitution strove to protect the emperor from personal responsibility for government acts. In particular, Article 55 of the constitution called for the various ministers of state to advise and assist the emperor within their respective areas of responsibility. This meant that they, not the emperor, were accountable for government acts. As Titus has observed about the refurbished titular head of state: "The traditional role of the emperor for 'ages eternal' as a medium between the Japanese people and the gods was therefore adopted as the basis of sovereignty in the Meiji Constitution."[18] Titus continues: "The emperor was not to be the captive of inner court anachronisms but a modern symbol of old virtues."[19] Japanese tradition—the emperor reigns but does not rule—was translated into modern terms: with respect to political policy, the emperor's personal will, which admittedly was fallible, was not identical with the imperial will. The imperial will was defined in theory as the will of the imperial ancestors extending into the past, and into the future, to infinity; in practice it was promulgated by government leaders. But this does not mean the emperor, in particular the Shōwa emperor, did not attempt to impress his personal will on the imperial will in prewar times.

The problem of Hirohito's war responsibility is related to questions about the imperial will, the legitimacy of the imperial house, and the nature and extent of his efforts to influence prewar political and military policy. Are these activities to be interpreted exclusively in the light of imperial line tradition as outlined here or in terms of constitutional monarchy—or was the emperor the state? In fact all three extremes, taken separately, are incorrect. They must be considered together. Even if the "emperor had not been sovereign for almost 1000 years" and the Meiji political system was an "aberration,"[20] between 1868 and 1945 the emperor "was the superintendent of the supreme right of rule—he was *perceived* as the locus of final political authority."[21] Because of this widely shared view, the lacunae between the three positions—medium, sovereign, and constitutional monarch—gave rise to the possibility that the first and third ideals would be used to service the "sovereignty" of less exalted persons: civil and military leaders who assumed the right to declare to the Japanese people what the imperial will was in a given situation. Especially the militarists appealed to the former (emperor as medium), and civil authorities to the latter (emperor as constitutional monarch), in the 1930s and early 1940s.

Besides the military, certain politicians and high-ranking bureaucrats sought to appropriate for themselves the authority of the imperial will. This is well known. Less well known is the fact that Emperor Hirohito, who was personally fallible, was far more predisposed to acting behind the scenes to influence formation of the imperial will than he and his advisers acknowledged publicly. Therefore the question of his responsibility for political and military policies cannot be easily resolved. One must examine old and newly revealed sources to determine what in fact Hirohito did and did not do in prewar Japan. Moreover, the influences on these activities must be looked at anew.

Military Planning and Decision Making

With respect to the emperor's role in military planning, documents available at the Bōeichō Kenkyūjo (National Institute for Defense Studies, or NIDS) in Tokyo and studies by scholars there provide three new revelations. First, the emperor was regularly and extensively informed about military planning for at least six years before the attack on Pearl Harbor.[22] Second, he was given a detailed explanation of the plan to attack Pearl Harbor by surprise one month before its execution.[23] Third, he did not question military plans in imperial conferences because they were top secret and because he demanded the opportunity to suggest revisions in private before official approval.[24] In short, handwritten records from the Imperial Army and Navy general staffs illustrate that the emperor was consulted about military planning, on occasion demanded and achieved revisions of specific plans, but was not able to dictate plans or basic strategy.

Hirohito's actions may be compared with Watsuji's interpretation of the position of the Sun Goddess, Amaterasu Ōmikami, on the plain of high heaven: "Amaterasu decided all matters in accordance with conferences of the myriad gods, and usually carried out her actions in concert with other gods. . . . She neither decided nor acted on her own volition."[25] The records show that audiences with the army and navy chiefs of staff were very similar. At the same time one should not discount the emperor's prerogatives in the Meiji Constitution or the principles of consensus decision making in Japan: the former gave the emperor the right to be consulted about these plans; the latter meant that once a policy was discussed and decided in chambers, disagreements were not to be aired in public.

The emperor was not the ultimate or the only decision maker; he was part of the decision-making process. Since he did not follow, in chambers, the advice of Saionji and Makino to avoid participating in these decisions, he was equally responsible with other leaders for them. Therefore, as titular head of the deciding body he might be expected to "take responsibility" for the decisions reached.[26] The times when Hirohito did not act were as important as when he did. Both were expressions of his personal will. Absolute consistency with respect to a particular principle or set of ideals was, as in most political processes, impossible. But he did do his best to preserve the central position of the imperial house in this process.

Tōjō and Hirohito

Another prominent person who contributed much to preserving the central position of the imperial house was General Tōjō Hideki, although he is not always examined in this light. A model army bureaucrat and prime minister when war broke out in the Pacific, Tōjō is often regarded as one of the most active and influential proponents of war in late 1941 and contrasted with the peace-loving emperor.[27] But important similarities between Tōjō and Hirohito have been overlooked. In fact, his political ideals were quite compatible with the imperial tradition Hirohito embodied and was intent on preserving. Tōjō was much less a warlord than a man with powerful convictions who readily acted in strict accord with them. This can be seen not only in his well-known assumption, during the Tokyo war crimes trials, of responsibility for starting the Pacific War—thus shielding the emperor from charges of war responsibility. Diaries and statements by persons serving close to him during the war reveal unequivocally his devotion to the imperial house. This allegiance took on a historical-spiritual dimension on account of his esteem for Kusunoki Masashige, the

samurai who sided with Emperor Godaigo during his attempted imperial restoration at the beginning of the fourteenth century. And Tōjō's
unswerving devotion is no doubt one reason for his bitterly uncompromising suppression of opposition during the war: he identified his
policies as prime minister with the imperial institution. Hirohito may
not have known about these convictions when he appointed Tōjō prime
minister,[28] but he did come to know the general through their many
audiences. Their mutual convictions provided a basis for working together, and this is one reason for the emperor's continuing support of
Tōjō long after he became unpopular in government circles.

Hirohito's Mentors

Prior to these political and military developments, Crown Prince Hirohito received a lengthy education in Japanese imperial ethics *(teiōgaku)*
and history. Both of his teachers, Sugiura Shigetake and Shiratori Kurakichi, addressed a broad range of topics, but their presentations were
reactionary at best. Their lectures demonstrated the inimitable sublime nature of the imperial line and the absolute necessity of preserving it. Moreover, their methodology in explaining the "unique" Japanese imperial line was of a dubious character. Both used arbitrarily
Western precedents and Japanese authorities from the past to legitimize
ancient Japanese myths supporting the preeminence of the imperial
house in modern Japanese society. Hirohito was greatly influenced by
these men.

While Hirohito is well known for the scholarly skepticism and scientific methods he brought to his biological research, it is doubtful that
these attitudes influenced his views about the position of the imperial
house in Japanese society. Hirohito's appeals to English constitutional
monarchy were not only inconsistent but similar in method to those
of Sugiura and Shiratori: Western window dressing for the sake of making the imperial institution appear modern and justifying action or inaction in public. Old customs and practices—the emperor reigns but
does not rule—were given new clothes: English constitutionalism. At
the same time, the prerogatives newly assigned the emperor in the
Meiji Constitution were pursued in private, based on the emperor's
special character as a descendant of the gods, but with a tendency to
displace the ancient tradition of nonrule with Prussian-style authori-
tarianism.

Which is to say: an idealized view of English constitutional monarchy combined with imperial line folklore contributed to a separation
of the emperor's political activities into public and private spheres at
court. This separation is consistent with Titus' analysis of the place of

the palace in Shōwa politics in terms of "Emperor-in-Public" and "Emperor-in-Chambers."[29] These two concerns, Japanese-English constitutionalism and the imperial line, contributed to the conflation of ancient custom and modern precedent even before the Shōwa era, that is, in the formulation of late Meiji ideology, as has been documented by Carol Gluck.[30] But the authoritarian (Prussian) elements of the Meiji Constitution and the ensuing consequences for Hirohito's reign have not been thoroughly investigated. The prominent German scholar Bernd Martin, comparing developments in 1930s Japan with those in Europe, termed Imperial Japan "a 'folkish' imperial state" and the *kokutai* ideology a sort of "Japanese-style fascism" *(Facismus japanischer Prägung)*.[31] The term "fascism" may be objectionable to some if applied to the Shōwa emperor. But there were closer links between the emperor—as the incumbent head of the imperial line—and nationalist *kokutai* ideology and the military than is acknowledged by many.

The content and methodology of Hirohito's education in ethics and history contributed to his being much more insistent and arbitrary in asserting his will, in chambers, on government decisions than is generally known. In school the crown prince learned much about the imperial line, little about English constitutional monarchy, and the former influenced his actions much more than the latter. This assertion flies in the face of many commentaries that emphasize Hirohito's scholarly nature and devotion to constitutional monarchy. But it coincides well with the tenor of his activities as emperor from the late 1920s to the mid-1940s and is demonstrated by his participation in military planning prior to and including the attack on Pearl Harbor.

Another important influence on Hirohito's activities, in private as well as public, has been little studied: the advice and counsel of Count Makino Nobuaki. Makino was imperial household minister from 1921 to 1925 and lord keeper of the privy seal, the emperor's political adviser, from 1925 to 1935. Thus he served in two key court positions close to Hirohito from the time he became regent through the first nine years of his reign as emperor. Noted for his knowledge of the West and moderate politics, Makino was in fact not so moderate as is generally assumed. Although one cannot judge someone like Makino from outside Japan exclusively, during the prewar years many non-Japanese unknowingly did exactly that. And this was one source of misunderstanding between Japanese and foreign leaders.

This difference between foreign and domestic Japanese perspectives brings to light a related problem. Two of Hirohito's most important advisers, Makino and Prince Saionji, were frequently called, then and now, "liberal." What this means, however, is not entirely clear. Germaine Hoston has dealt authoritatively with the difference between Western and Japanese assumptions about liberalism, and Lesley Connors has written convincingly about Saionji.[32] Nevertheless, Hirohito's understanding of "liberal constitutional monarchy," Makino's actual disposition, and his influence on the young crown prince and emperor are in need of further examination.

Makino, like all prewar Japanese leaders, was devoted not just to constitutional monarchy but to the task of establishing Japan's equality with the Western powers. This goal included industrial and military development as well as government reforms. It also included, for a short time at least, human rights. In 1919 Makino strove mightily at the Paris Peace Conference to include a clause banning racial discrimination in the charter of the League of Nations. Makino personally represented the Japanese effort—and was rebutted, especially by the United States and Great Britain.[33] At least one European scholar maintains that this was an important factor in Japan's later decision to go to war in the Pacific.[34] Hirohito mentioned this in his "monologue" in 1946: "When we look for the causes of the Greater East Asia War, they lie in the past, in the peace treaty after World War I. The proposal on racial equality put forward by Japan was not something the Allies would accept."[35] And David Titus concurs that this rebuff was important.[36] Since the end of the war, however, in view of Japanese treatment of minorities at home and other Asians in lands occupied by the Imperial Army, some have begun to doubt the altruism of the Paris initiative. Might it have been an exercise in Western diplomacy, the defeat of which was foreseen, for home consumption? Makino, however, was not a representative of the Imperial Army or the ultranationalists, and he no doubt was personally frustrated by these developments. In the end, the rebuke weakened the position of those who opposed the use of military force to attain equality with the West. This no doubt carried over into Hirohito's moral and political preconceptions: Makino's influence—that of an experienced but frustrated diplomat and politician—on Hirohito's "worldview" had both pro-Western and anti-Western shades. Quite possibly the emperor's public advocacy of English constitutional monarchy and closer relations with the Anglo-Saxon nations was balanced in private by uncertainty. This skepticism is demonstrated by his handling of military planning.

In conclusion, then, it seems questionable that Hirohito was either the foremost constitutional monarch and "peacenik" of the twentieth century or a scheming warmonger. There is another way of approaching this issue, an approach closer to Japanese history and tradition. The avowed purpose of Japan's march into the outside world was to modernize (meaning industrialize) its society, as many have written. But these writers often neglect the Japanese drive to preserve their beloved traditional values and, moreover, the role of the military in this undertaking. Modern technology and institutions—military as well as civil—and their theoretical underpinnings were adopted to preserve tradition, not replace it. Thus Hirohito's advocacy of Western scientific learning and constitutional monarchy was fundamental to the perpetuation of Japan's imperial line, its supposedly unique polity, and especially the preeminent position of his family, the imperial house, in Japanese society. The same can be said for his participation in prewar military decisions. New values and new modus operandi were the means to old ends, not ends in themselves. This contraposition of means and ends is central to the Japanese confusing perception of themselves at home and their confounding image elsewhere. It is central, too, to understanding Hirohito's seemingly contradictory conduct in prewar Japan.

2

.

Imperial Navy Planning
and the Emperor

Japanese critics of Hirohito and the "emperor system" have long pointed out his obvious legal responsibility as official chief of state and commander in chief of the armed forces.[1] The Meiji Constitution, promulgated in 1889 and in force until shortly after the end of the war, made the emperor of Japan a living god—the pinnacle of the spiritual and political hierarchy. It is absurd, therefore, to argue against his legal responsibility for Japan's aggression in China and the Pacific.[2] Apologists for Hirohito emphasize his function as a constitutional monarch. They argue that practically speaking he knew little about the plans or operations of the army and navy—and in any case was in no position to resist their proposals. His role was to sanction, as a constitutional figurehead, what was laid before him. He was not expected to approve or disapprove policies as a political ruler participating in the decisions of state.[3]

Friendly chroniclers of Hirohito's reign also allude to the influence of Prince Saionji Kimmochi, the last elder statesman *(genrō),* and Count Makino Nobuaki, Hirohito's first political adviser. Makino will be treated extensively here, and there are a number of studies of Saionji. Although Saionji and Makino were staunch supporters of constitutional monarchy, a careful comparison of sources shows that prior to August 1945 neither the emperor, the prince, nor Makino was content with the purely ceremonial role of a constitutional monarch. This can be seen not only during the famous officers' revolt of 26 February 1936 but on numerous other occasions.[4]

After the war the supreme commander of the occupation forces, General Douglas MacArthur (1880–1964), in order to facilitate the occupation, promoted the assumption that Emperor Hirohito had nothing to do with Pearl Harbor. According to MacArthur, Hirohito was a figurehead monarch whose only military functions were ceremonial— riding about in a field marshal's uniform on a white horse to inspire his subjects and pro forma signing plans for sending them to war. This explanation has been accepted by many Japanese and Western authors and rejected by a few. But the polemics employed by most have clouded rather than clarified the issue.[5] In this chapter I will show that the emperor was indeed deeply involved in the war effort. He was well informed about the Imperial Navy's plans, for example, including the plan to attack Pearl Harbor. Moreover, contrary to accepted assertions about Hirohito's education, his conduct during this period was consistent with Sugiura's imperial ethics and Shiratori's oriental history: the emperor acted in the interests of first promoting and then preserving the Japanese national polity with the imperial house at its center.

Hirohito's Personal Views

Not long after Japan's surrender Hirohito described his situation in prewar Japan:

> It goes without saying that the war was unavoidable. Concerning the war, [We] attempted somehow to avoid it. I thought until totally exhausted; played every hand that was to be played.
>
> Even though I did everything in my power [to avoid hostilities], in the end my efforts were to no avail, and we plunged into war. This was indeed regrettable. With respect to this conflict, as I mentioned recently in a general way, the war came to an end because I stopped it. Because I did this a debate has arisen about why the war was not stopped before it began. Indeed, this argument seems logical. It sounds reasonable in some ways. However, this could not be done.
>
> Needless to say, our country has a constitution. Strictly speaking the emperor must act in accord with the provisions of the constitution. According to the constitution, responsibility for state affairs is borne by the ministers of state who are vested with due authority.
>
> The emperor is not allowed to willfully meddle, interfere, or intervene in the areas of responsibility of the ministers of state specified in the constitution.
>
> Therefore, with respect to internal affairs and foreign relations, there are persons designated by the constitution who are charged with carefully deliberating and formulating policy. If they do this, present the policy in accord

with the regulations, and request that it be approved *(saika)*, whether I am satisfied with it or not there is no way around agreeing and approving it.[6]

Grand Chamberlain Fujita Hisanori (1880–1970), who recorded this statement in February 1946, described the emperor's concern about the "misunderstanding" of the emperor's role in the Meiji Constitution.

Recently a unique source was published that supports the emperor's comments to Grand Chamberlain Fujita: "The Shōwa Emperor's Eight-Hour Monologue." In March and April 1946 Emperor Hirohito delivered a monologue using questions presented to him in advance. This is the only known commentary by Emperor Hirohito on the events surrounding World War II, but its uniqueness does not guarantee its objectivity. Indeed, Hirohito spoke not for history but for the version of Japanese history and ethics inculcated in him—meaning in his own defense—at a time when it was being debated whether the emperor should be tried as a war criminal.[7]

The Hirohito Monologue

During this monologue five persons were present: Imperial Household Minister Matsudaira Tsuneo (1882–1948), former Chief Secretary to the Privy Seal Matsudaira Yasumasa (1893–1957), Vice Grand Chamberlain Kinoshita Michio, Chief of the Palace Secretariat Inada Shūichi (1902–1973), and the first secretary of the Japanese Embassy in Washington, D.C., during the final negotiations between Japan and the United States in 1941, Terasaki Hidenari (1900–1951). In 1946 Terasaki acted as liaison officer of the imperial household (goyōkakari) during the conferences between the emperor and the occupation forces. He was the person who interpreted during the meetings between McArthur and Hirohito.

Less well known is the fact that during his stay in Washington Terasaki was also in charge of espionage in North and South America. Although an American intelligence officer, Ellis M. Zacharias, mentioned this in a book written immediately after the war,[8] he could not substantiate his charge because his information came from classified materials. Gerhard Krebs, however, followed up on this assertion many years later. Krebs notes that the Japanese, suspecting the Americans had uncovered Terasaki's extradiplomatic activities, ordered him to leave the United States at once. The English translation of the telegram with this order was declassified only at the end of the 1970s and can be found in the National Archives among the 150,000 pages titled "Magic."[9] Awaya Kentarō cites an FBI report from 18 November 1941 with a similar allegation.[10] In connection with this order a farewell party was given for Terasaki in the Japanese Embassy on the night of

6–7 December 1941. The disagreeable aftereffects from this party have been cited as one reason for the delay in translating, typing, and delivering the final note (which was not a formal declaration of war) to the secretary of state before the attack on Pearl Harbor.[11] Although Terasaki was not able to leave the United States as soon as he and the Japanese had hoped, his espionage activities remained all but unknown. The text of the monologue was found in Terasaki's personal effects long after his death and published in the December 1990 issue of the monthly journal *Bungei shunjū* with the permission of his daughter, Mariko Terasaki-Miller.[12]

The emperor spoke without using notes. He began with a short statement about the long-term cause of the war—the peace negotiations after World War I during which the Western Powers rejected public recognition of the equality of races. He concluded that in view of the U.S. oil embargo and the domestic political climate he was unable to "veto" the war proposal. Had he done so there would have been a bloody civil war.[13] Hirohito consistently described the few occasions when he did intervene in the political and military decision-making process: they were exceptions when he attempted to restrain the radical forces raging in Japan. The emperor emphasized that the army officers' revolt in February 1936, one such exception, had failed. But generally the aftermath of Prime Minister Tanaka Giichi's forced resignation in 1929, he said, had already prompted him to refrain from participating in government affairs regardless of his personal opinions.[14]

The incidents described in the emperor's 1946 monologue corroborate Hirohito's statement to Grand Chamberlain Fujita about his respect for the principles of constitutional monarchy. Both statements, however, appear more like timid postwar excuses for supposed inactivity than a defense of constitutional government. Both were made with an eye to prewar domestic developments and postwar eventualities—that is, war crimes trials. Like his teacher of morals, Sugiura Shigetake, Hirohito availed himself of modern methods to support ancient traditions. If necessary, the continued existence of the center of Japanese tradition, the imperial house, was to be defended in a Western court process using Western ideology—constitutional monarchy.

The fact that the emperor spoke in detail about political and military matters with Fujita contradicts the testimony of an earlier grand chamberlain, Admiral (retired) Hyakutake Saburō (1872–1963), given to interrogators from the U.S. Strategic Bombing Survey in November 1945. During this interrogation Hyakutake maintained on numerous occasions that "the Grand Chamberlain at no time interferes with or touches upon questions relating to military or political affairs; political and military matters are entirely outside the province of the Grand Chamberlain's work." Moreover, he said, the grand chamberlain was informed of this policy by the emperor personally.[15]

Thus there appears to have been a postwar effort to construct an image of the emperor's prewar activities that was consistent with one aspect of those activities and with which Western authorities could associate positively—the image of Emperor Hirohito as an English-style constitutional monarch and peace advocate. This was, in part, a deception with implicit contradictions: while openly advocating constitutional monarchy, Hirohito was actually intent on protecting the imperial line; and as an English-style constitutional monarch he could not actively participate in policymaking as he did, whether in favor of peace or not. In sum, then, the differences between constitutional monarchy in England, the Japanese imperial tradition of reigning without ruling, and the possibilities opened up to the emperor by the Meiji Constitution were conveniently ignored.

Postwar Testimonies

The statements made by Hirohito and Fujita coincide nicely with similar assertions made by high government, court, and military officials shortly after the war about the emperor's prewar activities. Admiral Yonai Mitsumasa, for example, testified to the Strategic Bombing Survey that the emperor in line with his peacemaking role acted decisively to end the war. Yonai called for informal meetings with the Supreme War Direction Council on 6 and 22 June 1945 to discuss continuing the war, and at that time Hirohito personally decided to terminate the war.[16] But, strictly speaking, as a constitutional monarch in Japan the emperor, acting alone, could not make such a decision. The situation was not so simple as Yonai would have one believe.

Prince Konoe Fumimaro reiterated the emperor's key role in ending the war, but with a rather different twist. In November 1945 he stated: "The only thing that the army leaders had in mind was a fight to the bitter end. So if it hadn't been for the decision made by the emperor, we would still be fighting." The emperor, according to Konoe, was the only person who could persuade the army to give up this idea. But the only way to influence the emperor was to first convince Lord Keeper of the Privy Seal Kido Kōichi, his political adviser, of the wisdom of this policy.[17] Konoe testified as follows to the Strategic Bombing Survey about ending the war:

> Q. Was Marquis Kido persuaded of the advisability of discontinuing the war prior to August 1st?

A. From what I heard, Kido gave his advice to the Emperor first around April of this year.

Q. Was it reluctance on the part of the Emperor to make this drastic decision which delayed it from April to August?

A. The Emperor wanted to end hostilities just as soon as possible, but the situation in the country as a whole was such that he evidently hesitated because of conditions.

Konoe concluded his testimony with an interesting statement about the position of the prime minister as well as the emperor in the body politic:

Q. After the war broke out, in view of the Emperor's desire for peace, and since the Premier during the period of the early Konoye cabinets had no access to the strategic plans and aims of the army and navy, then in an attempt to understand the governments of that period, would it be safe to say that both the Emperor and Primier [sic] were figureheads, with the final power resting with the army and navy?

A. There is no other conclusion than that. . . . [18]

The reliability of this assertion remains to be ascertained. Suzuki Kantarō, prime minister from 7 April to 17 August 1945, was of a much different opinion. During an interrogation by American officials he said:

The man who is responsible for events—political events—is the PREMIER. He is appointed and he himself in turn appoints all his various Cabinet members. All decisions relative to government policies and actions are made in different councils and decided upon by various groups inside the Government. Their decisions are then submitted for approval to the EMPEROR, so that all policies and actions taken by the Japanese Government are really the product of the Government itself, of which the PRIME MINISTER is the head. Political decisions cannot be regarded as the responsibility of the EMPEROR.

Ordinarily speaking, even though He himself may be opposed to the proposed plans or policies, the EMPEROR will approve them. Therefore I want it very clearly understood that the PRIME MINISTER throughout recent Japanese history is the man who is responsible for the actions of the Japanese Government.[19]

Hirohito could not have said it better himself. Nevertheless, it is impossible to render a blanket confirmation or denial of these statements or those by Hirohito in the monologue and elsewhere. Such is, however, not terribly important because, as we shall see, this is not how decisions were made in Imperial Japan. If this was not explained by these witnesses after the war, it is because the confusion obscured the actual role of the emperor in prewar politics and contributed to

relieving him of any war responsibility. Both Konoe and Suzuki, looking to the preservation of the imperial house, sought, in the name of
constitutional monarchy, to absolve the emperor from any war guilt.
Although their statements have very different implications for the
office of prime minister, these differences can be attributed to the
amorphous nature of the office and the characters of the two men.
More to the point, before the war could be terminated it had to begin.
And various sources on the events leading up to the outbreak of war in
December 1941 point in a totally different direction. They demonstrate the emperor's participation in these events.

The Emperor and the Imperial Navy's Plans

All modern Japanese emperors, Hirohito included, were systematically
informed of the plans of the Imperial Army and Navy. (See Appendix 1
for a tabular overview of the military activities the emperor sanctioned.) In 1906 it was decided the army would regularly present a
yearly operations plan to the emperor for his approval *(saika)*—for
example, the "Meiji 39 (1906) Imperial Japanese Army Operations
Plan Outline." In 1907 it was decided the army and navy would both
do this, but for unknown reasons the navy did not begin to draft and
submit to the emperor the required plan until 1914.

The mandate for military preparedness and operations was called
the "annual operations plan." The purpose of these plans, as expressed
in the 1907 National Defense Policy, was to unify the government and
high command with respect to the strength of the military. In wartime
they constituted a basic strategy and operations guide for the general
staffs. In peacetime they contained guidelines for armaments, organization, maneuvers, education, communications, intelligence, and the
like. In the event of war this plan was to be reviewed and the organization of the armed forces precisely delineated. This too was to be approved by the emperor.[20] The National Defense Policy was updated
three times: in 1918, 1923, and 1936. The yearly operations plans were
based on a "basic tactics outline" drawn up shortly after the National
Defense Policy was formulated. The changes in these policies reflected
the changing times. In 1936, for example, England is of increased interest; in the 1907 policy, due to the treaty relation between Japan and
England, the latter was not mentioned. The possibility of war with the
United States loomed large in every plan.[21]

The procedure for presenting the annual operations plan was very
formal. Each chief of staff presented the plan of his service, and it was
usually approved on the same day. In the Taishō era (1912–1926) these
yearly plans were generally presented to the throne and approved in

October or November. From the beginning of the Shōwa era they were approved in September and became effective on 1 April of the following year. Since customarily the emperor's chief aide-de-camp was from the army, there were differences between the presentations of the army and navy. Prior to officially requesting imperial approval, the chief aide-de-camp discussed the army's plan with the emperor to facilitate the process. The navy chief of staff made his presentation without benefit of this preliminary review. After the emperor approved the 1936 operations plans, in November 1935 the high commands of both services were informed that in the future the emperor desired more time for reviewing their plans: "In accord with the emperor's preferences, should the presentation to the throne not be immediately approved on that day, the chief of staff should retire taking his plan with him. On another day approval should be requested, and in the meantime if there are any questions the chief of staff should come to court and answer them."[22] Beginning in the fall of 1936, the army chief of staff reported directly to the emperor without first having the chief aide-de-camp review the plan with him. This no doubt shows Hirohito's growing concern about the activities of the military. This procedure was initiated with the approval of the 1937 plan after the attempted putsch in February 1936. But the imperial directive was issued before the officers' revolt and thus was not a result of it.

These plans were top secret. Those who participated in the drafting, as well as those to whom the finished product was distributed, were extremely limited in number. At the end of the Taishō era seven copies of the Navy Operations Plan were made: emperor, 2; navy minister, 1; army chief of staff, 1; Navy General Staff, 3. In the mid-1930s the number of copies was increased to ten, the additional three copies all going to the Navy General Staff.[23]

Imperial Navy Plans: 1936–1941

The Imperial Navy records now available to us were preserved by accident. After World War II an employee of a vault company was going through the burned-out ruins of the Navy General Staff office building and happened to salvage an old safe. When it was opened the documents were found: annual operations plans, National Defense Policy papers, basic tactics outlines, and more. These records were handed over to the Office of the Police Commissioner, stored there until August 1955, and then transferred to the Cabinet Archives and held there for some time because they contained secrets pertaining to foreign affairs. Researchers from the National Institute for Defense Studies were allowed access to them, and these records were transferred to that institute on 16 September 1968.[24] These are not the same materials used by Tsunoda Jun and his colleagues in their history. Nor were they consulted by Nobutaka Ike when he translated the notes from the imperial and liaison conferences. Tsunoda thought all navy records had been destroyed when he did his work, and Ike accepted Tsunoda's assertion to this effect.[25]

The earliest Navy Operations Plan that escaped destruction at the end of the war was that of 1936; the latest plan was that of 1941.[26] During the Pacific War, annual operations schedules were not drafted. This does not mean that no plans were made during the war or that the emperor was not informed of the military's proposed operations. On 5 November 1941 the emperor approved the "Imperial Navy Operations Plan for the War Against America, Great Britain, and the Netherlands." On 16 April 1942 he approved the "Second Stage of Operations for the Greater East Asia War, Imperial Navy Operations Plan." On 25 March 1943 Hirohito approved the "Third Stage of Operations for the Greater East Asia War."[27]

The yearly operations plans that survive illustrate the war-related information made available to the emperor and the nature of his participation in approving these plans. The 1936 annual Imperial Navy Operations Plan, for example, was divided into four sections:

1. General Provisions
2. War Against America
3. War Against the Soviet Union
4. War Against China

Section 1, General Provisions, included the items prescribed in the National Defense Policy. Sections 2 to 4 contained the following subheadings:

1. Operations Policy
2. Operations Outline
3. Defense
4. Protecting Sea Lanes
5. Transport and Supply

On 24 August 1935, Imperial Prince Fushimi Hiroyasu (1875–1939), navy chief of staff, met with Imperial Prince Kan'in Kotohito (1865–1945), army chief of staff, to discuss the items in this plan to be reported to the throne and their order of presentation. Emphasis was placed on the United States. The plan was presented to Hirohito by Navy Minister Ōsumi Mineo (1876–1941) on 3 September and approved the same day. The tone and description of the operations could not have given the emperor the impression that the proposed deployments were intended only as defense measures. This can be seen, for example, in the description of a possible war with the United States. In the sections dealing with the American-held Philippine Islands, taking these islands was the central aspect of the navy's plans. And while the Hawaiian Islands and other ports in the "American Pacific" were secondary, they were to be the object of offensive clandestine activities. One element of the navy's submarine fleet was to move into this area and serve as an outpost for the duration of the fighting in Asian waters. The enemy's strength and ship movements were to be spied out and, should the opportunity arise, its forces impaired.[28] The next annual plan, the 1937 Navy Operations Plan, was approved by the emperor on 3 September 1936. This plan differed little from the previous year's plan with one exception: a short section was added covering a possible war with Great Britain.[29]

Before the deadline for submitting the 1938 plan, war broke out in China, on 7 July 1937, and this led to complications. To assess the situation in China and the Soviet Union, an extension was requested in September 1937 and granted. Thus the plan was officially submitted to the emperor in September 1938, one year late. In the meantime, the emperor was kept abreast of developments through periodic reports. For example, due to the constantly changing situation in China it was finally deemed impossible to formulate a set plan of operations. In December Imperial Prince Fushimi petitioned the emperor for permission to submit a draft that left China operations open. It was to include sections on America, Russia, and England along the lines of the 1937 plan, while the section on China left room for changes depending on developments there. Imperial approval was granted on 9 December 1937.[30] This plan did not work as well as projected, however, because a new feud arose between the army and navy.

From the beginning of February 1938, members of the army and navy general staffs held consultations on the China War. During the deliberations it became clear that the army and navy were in basic disagreement about the consequences of engaging in war with still another country. The army demanded that plans be made for the contingency of war with a second country while the war with China was still in progress. The navy, however, opposed such a plan. Since 1913, navy planning had been limited to operations on a single front. If war with another country was opened while the conflict in China was still in progress, the navy predicted that hostilities could not be limited to just two countries. Japan would be at war with four countries: the Soviet Union, America, and England, in addition to China.[31] After approximately one month of talks, the dispute could not be resolved. This became grounds for requesting another delay in submitting the annual operations plan for imperial approval. The extension was requested and a basic explanation of the dispute was presented to the emperor on 12 March 1938. Approval was granted on 15 March.[32]

Here the often cited grounds for imperial intervention presented themselves—disunity in the government. War and peace with a number of countries were at stake, but the emperor did nothing. At this juncture, as on a number of other occasions, Hirohito disregarded his own postwar criteria for becoming active in the decision-making process—protracted indecision or disunity in government circles. Reasons for his inactivity can only be speculated upon. Perhaps he was satisfied since he was being consulted regularly; perhaps he himself was undecided about what to do. This debate continued until the middle of June. Finally it was decided in favor of the army and a brief outline of the naval yearly operations plan was submitted to the emperor on 23 June. This draft indicated that the forthcoming plan would include sections on wars against China and each of the three countries cited— for example, China and America—as well as a war against all four together. An explanation was appended that essentially repeated the crux of the March report: The China War would be a long drawn-out affair; therefore one must account for these contingencies; should war with one of the three countries break out while the China War was in progress, inevitably this will lead to war with all four countries, the United States, the Soviet Union, England, and China.[33] The draft also indicated that the finalized plan was to be submitted by the end of July or beginning of August. This deadline, however, could not be met. The plan was presented to the emperor on 5 September 1938 and approved the following day.[34]

In preparing the 1938 Navy Operations Plan, numerous other reports were completed for internal use by the general staff. Not all of them were shown to the emperor, but several are worth mentioning. Of special interest is the explanation of the official operations plan prepared for the chief of staff's use in presenting the plan to the emperor. This explanation, some twenty handwritten pages, as well as the preliminary reports from which it was drafted, have been preserved. Together they show the navy was extremely concerned about getting involved in a war with the United States. A long study was made of how the war was to be prosecuted, together with a comparison of U.S. and Japanese forces in the Pacific.[35] Studies of the war potential of the Soviet Union and England were also made.[36] And an eventual war with all four powers was reviewed. Here the navy was especially troubled because of the obvious superiority of combined U.S. and English forces.[37] These problems are noted in the statement prepared for the chief of staff's explanation to the throne, but it is peculiar that the navy's anxiety about a war with the United States and England is not emphasized as one might expect.[38] This may reflect the influence of the army. The navy was at pains not to appear to have less fighting spirit than the army. The report itself presents a tremendous amount of detail about the military strength of potential enemy forces.

The long delay in submitting the 1938 operations plan, as well as its wealth of details, give pause for reflection. A cursory examination of the navy's plans show they were unrealistic. The navy was to clear the seas of enemy forces in the Far East, secure the South and North Pacific, take the Philippine Islands, secure the China coast and lower Yangtze River valley, conduct reconnaissance around Hawai'i, and protect the home islands.[39] But the forces available for all these operations, compared with the navy's own estimates of probable opposition, were inferior to the combined British and American naval and air forces. Any rational evaluation of the situation shows the Japanese could not expect to sweep the seas clear of the enemy in a short time, if at all. The Navy General Staff's lack of enthusiasm for a war with the United States and Great Britain was not unwarranted. Whether the emperor was aware of these details and discussed them with his military advisers is unknown. In any case, long before the fall of 1941 Hirohito was confronted with one war in China, the possibility of another conflict with three additional countries, and the imponderabilities of military operations during a war.

The dispute between the army and navy in Japan was not unusual among policymakers in nations making the transition from "old school" military thinking to planning for the necessities of mechanized warfare. Similar differences are to be seen in Germany, for example, in the 1920s. Major General (later colonel general and chief of the Army Command) Hans von Seeckt represented the old "wilhelmian" school that emphasized the expansion of military power based on a traditional elite officer corps without accounting for the economic foundations prerequisite to such a buildup. Major (later general and prime minister) Kurt von Schleicher represented the modern school of thought. Schleicher proposed first to rebuild the economy along lines that would enable Germany to produce and maintain a modern army and navy. Only then could Germany hope to regain what it had lost in World War I and establish itself as a world power.[40]

In Japan during the late 1930s and early 1940s the issues between army and navy were similar. And the emperor was privy to information indicating the nature of these differences. The interim reports he received—not to mention the contents of the 1938 Navy Operations Plan itself—show that Emperor Hirohito was well informed about the activities, intentions, and disagreements of the Japanese Imperial Army and Navy. Moreover, the issue that emerged in 1937–1938—the navy's reluctance to fight a war with the United States versus the army's aggressive willingness to take on all comers—was much the same as that which precipitated the crisis between Prime Minister Konoe Fumimaro (1891–1945) and Army Minister Tōjō Hideki in 1941. In that crisis the army again insisted on pursuing a war against the Anglo-Saxon powers. And the navy, relying on more sophisticated estimates of the economic and material aspects of prosecuting a modern war, was again less enthusiastic.[41]

Whether or not the emperor was informed of the technical details behind these debates is unclear. Nor is it clear if he realized what these differences meant in terms of modern warfare. In any case, he did insist on his right as emperor of Japan to be consulted about military plans. The Meiji Constitution covered this right, and it was consistent with being a constitutional monarch in Japan. It accorded, too, with the aura and image of the imperial house propagated earlier by his ethics and history teachers. In his role as emperor, a sacrosanct figure in prewar Japan, Hirohito was consulted in the imperial palace, and there he sought to influence policy. But Hirohito did not make policy; he was one of the elites involved in policymaking.

The 1939 Navy Operations Plan was late as well. A brief summary of the proposed plan sent to the navy minister by the Navy General Staff states that the only difference between the 1938 and 1939 operations plans is a revision of the part concerning a possible war with England.[42] The revision was a subject of controversy due to the emperor's demand for changes in this part of the plan. The alterations, and the manner in which they were made, show that the emperor was not without knowledge and influence in military matters.

The Emperor's Amendments to the 1939 Plan

The problem originated in the 1939 Army Operations Plan. The army's plan included positioning troops for an attack on Singapore in the event of a war with England. To provide better air support for this attack the army proposed to occupy a small area near the upper end of the Malay peninsula. The place in question, however, the province of Songkhla, belonged to Thailand, and this plan would involve violating its neutrality.[43] The same operation was included in the navy's plan as part of its support for the army operation.[44] Drafts of these plans were first presented to Hirohito on 24 February. The emperor objected: "If the plan involves violating Songkhla's neutrality, it would be difficult to approve."[45] The exact phrases to which the emperor objected were then crossed out and the plan resubmitted to him for provisional approval, which he granted, on the same day.[46] But the planners in the army and navy were resourceful officers. The final revision they submitted on 27 February 1939 included the possibility of Thailand going over to England's or Japan's side in the event of war. In either case, stationing troops there and building an airfield would not violate Thailand's neutrality.[47] The emperor noticed this amendment and asked the chiefs of staff if they intended to demand diplomatic cover from the government. The answer was negative: they would limit themselves to what the foreign minister could arrange.[48] The operations plans were then approved by the emperor.

Despite the dispute about Songkhla and the neutrality of Thailand, the final plans were little affected. Instead of deleting the operation, the navy added the words *"the situation permitting,* a surprise attack on, and occupation of, the area of Songkhla Malaya will be made."[49] The military's unyielding attitude is self-evident. Yet one can see that the emperor was acquainted with surprise attack tactics and could act in a decisive manner when he wished. Not only did he know how to deal with circumventing tactics, but he could influence military planning. Although his choice of issues to question may seem dubious, one must recall the context of the time. Previously, as in Manchuria, he had been presented with faits accomplis as the army usurped his role in forming military policy on more than one occasion. Perhaps he tried to prevent such a situation from arising again in the case of Singapore.[50]

The final operations plan for 1939 contained the same provisions as before, but much more emphasis was placed on plans for an eventual war with England. It is noteworthy that Hirohito did not object to these plans, which included surprise attacks on British possessions in Singapore, Malaya, and Borneo. In 1939, however, he set limits on and finally blocked an alliance with Germany and Italy—apparently due to his predilection for England but officially because of disunity in the government over the alliance.[51] He even had a nasty quarrel over this issue with his brother, Prince Chichibu (1902–1953), who was visiting him three times a week to support the treaty.

The Emperor's Opposition to the Tripartite Pact

Hirohito's concern about the tradition of friendly relations with England is totally absent from the discussions about military planning.

Here is an obvious discrepancy between his actions concerning political and military matters: in July 1939, the same year he approved offensive military plans against English possessions in the Far East, he intervened to block a military pact with Germany, reportedly because of his affection for England. In August of the same year he influenced the formation of a cabinet for the same reason: due to his positive inclination toward England he reportedly went to exceptional lengths to influence the selection of General Abe Nobuyuki (1875–1953) as the next prime minister.[52] The emperor appears to have personally chosen Admiral Yonai in 1940 to be prime minister with the same thing in mind: the admiral opposed the Tripartite Pact.[53] The emperor has been criticized for his intervention, but this criticism has nothing to do with his differing positions vis-à-vis political and military matters. Some say he should not have acted at all; others contend he was not active enough.[54] In 1946, disregarding the contradiction between his predilection for Great Britain and his approval of the military's plans, all but unknown at the time, Hirohito said that something else influenced his attempts to block an alliance with Germany and Italy. He regarded the entire initiative on the army's part in 1938–1939 as a diversionary tactic. The army high command sought to divert the people's attention from their poor showing in China, he said, by presenting America and England as the main enemies of Japan. This was the reason for their renewed interest in the Tripartite Pact, and this was Hirohito's reason for blocking it.[55] Taking into account the contradiction between his open support of England and his covert approval of military operations against the same country, it appears that Hirohito was again asserting the position of the imperial house. Departing from the "Tanaka lesson," he acted in accord with his English inclinations and, more important, to assert imperial influence over the military.

Escalation in Naval Operations Plans

The 1940 Navy Operations Plan was similar to those for 1938 and 1939, except that a possible attack on U.S. forces in Hawai'i was briefly discussed. Before the 1940 plan was drawn up, the navy general staff ordered a significant revision in the 1939 plan regarding the organization of the Combined Fleet. This revision included apparent increases in the units that were to operate along the China coast and near the Philippines.[56] Moreover, the unit to be dispatched to Hawai'i and the American Pacific was upgraded from "one part of the Combined Fleet" to the Sixth Fleet. It is hard to determine exactly what this meant in terms of numbers and types of ships, but the units concerned with the

"American Pacific" in the event of a war with the United States were without doubt strengthened. The report to the throne on 15 November 1939 says specifically that the submarine squadron in the earlier plan is to be replaced by the Sixth Fleet, though this fleet would remain on paper only until the submission of the 1940 operations plan.[57] Obviously the possibility of war with the United States and England was becoming ever more critical in the navy's thinking. Hirohito was appropriately informed of this development. If he made any comment about this turn of events it was not recorded. He did not mention it after the war.

The changes in the navy's thinking are evident, too, in the copy of the 1939 operations plan that was used as a basis for the 1940 plan. As was the custom, the officers on the Navy General Staff responsible for drawing up the annual plan for imperial approval did not start from scratch each year. They used the previous year's plan, making additions, corrections, and deletions as needed. This "worksheet" includes the corrections just noted and shows that the Sixth Fleet was basically given a scaled-up version of the mission formerly assigned to the submarine squadron.[58]

The final draft of the 1940 plan, like those of the previous two years, was late. The emperor granted an extension on 11 September for reasons similar to those cited earlier.[59] The 1940 plan contained several noteworthy alterations. First, the section on "Operations Against England and China" was changed to "Operations Against England, France, and China." Second, the section on "Operations Against a Number of Nations" was more detailed. And third, in the section on "Operations in the Event War Breaks Out with America While Operations Against China are in Progress" the main interest was in the South China coast, the lower Yangtze River valley, and the Philippine Islands. Special emphasis was placed on destroying the air forces stationed on Luzon and other islands. But the navy was also showing signs of greater ambition. The second phase of the attack was to include thrusts into the Pacific along the U.S. West Coast and Hawai'i, should American forces elect not to sortie into Asian waters. Commercial shipping was to be disrupted, and control of the seas and sky in the "Western Pacific" was to be established.[60]

The proposed operations around Hawai'i and in the "American Pacific" had nothing to do with the surprise attack on Pearl Harbor. This strike was still only a glimmer in the mind of Admiral Yamamoto Isoroku (1884–1943). Yamamoto first mentioned the possibility of an attack on Hawai'i (to Vice Admiral Fukudome Shigeru) in the spring of 1940: "Kōkūbokan ni yoru Hawai kōgeki wa dekinai mono kanaa" ("Would an attack on Hawai'i using aircraft carriers really be impossible?").[61] Well before the Hawai'i attack plan was drawn up, the navy was preparing itself and the emperor for an escalation of its wartime operations. Not only is the expansionist evolution of the operations plans over the years obvious, but the emperor sanctioned these plans in fact as well as form, demonstrating in the process considerable knowledge of what was involved. Each year, besides the operations plan itself, a lengthy oral presentation was prepared by the two general staffs for the private audience with the emperor. During these sessions Hirohito asked pointed questions and discussed the issues in detail. If the emperor did not always achieve the acquiescence of his military leaders, he certainly was aware of what they were planning and he certainly influenced these plans on more than one occasion. To maintain otherwise is to disregard the imposing number of documents he personally read, discussed, and approved, as well as the nature of decision making in Japan generally.

The 1941 Navy Operations Plan was presented to the emperor on 17 December 1940 and approved the same day. Except for the original (presumably still in Imperial Household Agency archives), no other copy of this plan exists. According to one author, this plan was among the documents retrieved from the safe in the burned-out navy office building and handed over to Prime Minister Yoshida Shigeru's office. The completed plan then disappeared.[62] Only the 1940 plan, which was used to prepare the 1941 edition, is available to historians. As noted earlier, the officers on the Navy General Staff responsible for drafting the annual operations plans used the previous year's plan as a worksheet. This worksheet, not the final draft presented to the emperor, is the only document we have. The additions to the 1940 plan mainly concern possible coordination of operations with Germany and Italy in the event of war with the United States and its allies. There are notes concerning a possible war with Holland, not mentioned in previous plans, and France is deleted from the 1941 draft. Given the developments in Europe these supplements are natural. Planning with respect to the United States alone was only slightly altered, showing increased interest in attacking and occupying the Philippine Islands. The additions to the 1940 plan for 1941 are unfinished, however, and one can only surmise the contents of the final draft of the 1941 plan.[63]

The Emperor's Approval of Surprise Attacks

Although we have only a worksheet for the 1941 Navy Operations Plan, the operations plan for a war with the United States, England, and Holland, approved by the emperor on 5 November 1941, came through the war intact. In the general provisions of this plan, "The Imperial Navy Operations Plan for a War Against America, England, and Holland," it says this is a revision of the 1941 Navy Operations Plan.[64] Some thirty-two handwritten pages in length, it is principally a revision of Section 6 (Parts 1 and 2) of the 1941 operations plan, "Operations in Case War Breaks Out with the United States, Russia, England, and Holland While Operations Against China Are in Progress."[65]

Especially worthy of note here is the number of operations involving surprise attacks *(kishū)*. The word *"kishū"* appears no fewer than ten times in this draft. This revised "attack plan" calls for the elimination of American, English, and Dutch influence in the Far East and the destruction of their military forces stationed in China, the Philippines, Guam, Hong Kong, British Malaya, British Borneo, the Dutch East Indies, the Bismarck Islands, Timor, and elsewhere. The surprise attack on Hawai'i is mentioned as well. The various fleets in the Imperial Navy are listed with their respective assignments: the Sixth Fleet is responsible for overseeing the Hawai'i operation; the First Carrier Flotilla is to carry out the attack on Pearl Harbor.[66] The second paragraph of the text for the oral explanation to the throne also deals with the surprise attack on Pearl Harbor: it is to be carried out concomitant with similar actions in the Philippines and Malaya; the navy is to support landings by the army in the Philippines and Malaya; Borneo, the Celebes Islands, and Hong Kong are to be attacked and taken.[67] The emperor approved these plans. He voiced misgivings only about their chances of success.[68]

Hirohito expressed his doubts in a private audience with his chiefs of staff on 3 November 1941. The private audience, as recorded by Army Chief of Staff Sugiyama, concerned the operations projected in the plan against Hong Kong, Malaya, the foreign concessions in China, the Philippines, and Thailand, in order of appearance. The navy chief of staff made a special presentation about the proposed surprise attack on Pearl Harbor. (A detailed discussion appears in Chapter 3.) The audience was held to inform the emperor about the details of military planning before the upcoming imperial conference.

During this private audience the emperor interrogated both chiefs of staff extensively, questioning in particular the army's chances of success. He did not question the surprise attack on Pearl Harbor or similar plans for British Malaya. Imperial misgivings were not to be heard in the imperial conference of 5 November or on any other "public" occasion, but military affairs usually were not discussed in detail in imperial conferences. In any case, Hirohito had ample opportunity beforehand to make any dissatisfaction known. The surprise attacks on Pearl Harbor and British Malaya are mentioned in both the formal operations plan presented to the emperor by the naval chief of staff and in his oral explanation. Moreover, the occupation of Song-khla Thailand again found its way into army and navy planning. If the emperor protested, his protestations were not grave enough to warrant noting as in the past.

On 5 November 1941 Emperor Hirohito approved the navy's program of aggression calling for surprise attacks in numerous places at various times. Similar operations are to be seen in the Army Operations Plan approved the same day. The official written operations plans, the oral explanations made to the emperor with their formal presentation, the information provided to him in audience with the chiefs of staff—all indicate that Hirohito could not possibly have had any doubts about what the military was planning. His approval of these plans appears similarly self-evident but is still the subject of much debate.

Imperial Approval: What Did It Mean?

Hirohito's activities vis-à-vis the military—and his lack of activity—can be interpreted variously. During the five-year period preceding the war with the United States and its allies in the Pacific, Hirohito was kept well informed about the navy's proposed operations in the event of a war with these countries. The proposals made by the army and navy in the fall of 1941 contained nothing that deviated drastically from previous plans. The surprise attack on Pearl Harbor was new, but surprise attacks were not new to military planning in Japan. The emperor was not upset by the threat to peace these plans represented; he was only skeptical about the chances of quick success predicted by Army Chief of Staff General Sugiyama. He did not indicate that any aspect of the plans would be "difficult to approve," as he had done before on at least one occasion. Nor was the import of these plans lost on others. Hara Yoshimichi (1867–1944), president of the Privy Council, who usually asked questions for the emperor during imperial conferences, indicated during the 5 November imperial conference that war seemed inevitable.

"When the constitutionally responsible persons deliberate carefully and formulate some policy, present it in accord with the regulations, and request that it be approved (saika), whether I am satisfied with it or not there is no way around agreeing and approving it," Hirohito said in 1946. Is this why he approved these plans? Was Hirohito resigned to war after so many years of being prepared for it by the general staffs? Was he afraid there would be a military putsch if the plans were not approved? No one had forgotten the close call of February 1936. After the war Hirohito, in his first meeting with General MacArthur, said that he would have been placed in an insane asylum or killed had he not approved the decision for war. Had he not approved the war plans, he emphasized in his monologue of March and April 1946, there would have been a coup d'état.[69]

After the war this was no doubt the correct thing to say. Before the war, however, might not the emperor have regarded the Greater East Asia Co-prosperity Sphere as a risky adventure yet also an opportunity to expand the influence and power of Japan and the imperial house? Such a possibility is consistent with Hirohito's education in imperial ethics and oriental history—meaning his concern for the destiny of the unique Japanese *kokutai* in the world. This all but neglected topic (see Chapters 5 and 6) converges nicely with the right of self-preservation and self-defense *(jizon jiei)* referred to by military and political leaders who were concerned about the U.S. oil embargo of 1 August 1941.

Quite possibly a combination of these factors influenced Emperor Hirohito's thinking. He questioned the propriety of specific proposals and questioned their chances of success. But he did not question the correctness of a policy that clearly was expansionistic and inevitably would lead to military confrontation with one or more nations. The emperor said on more than one occasion that opposing the military was impossible, and no less an authority than Professor Emeritus Hayashi Kentarō (Tokyo University) agrees. After reviewing the Hirohito Monologue and numerous other sources he concludes that the Shōwa emperor was a tragic figure trapped between his personal good intentions and the principles of constitutional monarchy.[70] Presumably due to the latter, Hirohito could not act on the former.

Although one is tempted to accept this conclusion, careful comparison of this monologue and well-known sources like Privy Seal Kido Kōichi's diary with surviving army and navy records makes this impossible. Of course, one must remember that by illuminating the emperor's role in operations planning former army and navy officers, unlike General Tōjō, sought to relieve themselves and their services of responsibility for World War II. Still, these plans are handwritten documents and not susceptible to manipulation after the fact. More important, the parties involved from the military side during the war were only too ready then to take the initiative, responsibility, and credit for the operations.

Undoubtedly the emperor had reservations about specific military operations. But this does not mean he had nothing to do with them.

True, Emperor Hirohito did not attend the liaison conferences where decisions for and against war were made. But he was well informed about military planning, and during the audiences with the chiefs of staff he actively contributed to the formulation of these plans. His contributions indicate that he was neither a militarist nor a strong advocate of peace. Rather he was an opportunist. Given the constellation of contending forces, at home and abroad, the emperor sought to avoid a putsch or a civil war and to further the interests of his nation and family as best he could.

"The fiction that the Emperor himself 'made' decisions" may well be a fiction itself.[71] The emperor, as we have seen, participated in the policymaking process. To maintain that he was excluded from decision making because he did not mandate policy in the manner of an American president or European prime minister is to miss the point. No single person made decisions in prewar Japan. Informal groups of high officials participated in discussions that would lead to a consensus of opinion about an issue, and this constituted a "decision." On specific occasions some people had more influence than others. But all were equally responsible, and without responsibility, including the emperor. As Stephen Large says of prewar Japanese politics: "Elite pluralism potentially enhanced the court as an informal intermediary capable of helping to resolve disputes on national policy."[72] This does not, however, absolve the Shōwa emperor personally or officially from war responsibility. Rather, it means the emperor was a party to resolving disputes among government leaders, forming a consensus, and arriving at a policy for action. If individual military officers acted arbitrarily and illegally in pursuing a certain policy—by ignoring government policies, for example, or the emperor's prerogative of supreme command— then the emperor, among others, acted illegally in not fulfilling the duties of his "office" and calling them to account.[73] This may appear to be a simplistic rejoinder to those who would absolve the emperor from war responsibility because of his fears or lack of knowledge, but it demands an answer. More to the point, it reveals the fallacy of this entire line of argument. Deciding and enforcing policy in the manner of a Western commander in chief was not the emperor's role in Japan. His role was to participate as one of the elites in Japan's pluralistic politics. As these and other records show, the emperor was thoroughly informed of military matters. And comensurate with his position and Japanese methods of forming policies, he participated in making political and military decisions as the constitutional emperor of Imperial Japan and head of the imperial house.[74]

3

•

Pearl Harbor and Decision Making

The decision to start a war with the United States and its allies by attacking Pearl Harbor and a number of other bases in Southeast Asia, by surprise, was long in coming. It was a decision, contrary to many analysts' opinions, in which the emperor took part. Documentary evidence shows this conclusively. In Chapter 2, some of these documents from the Imperial Navy were introduced. We also have numerous records from the Imperial Army, which were not all destroyed as was thought for many years.[1]

The preservation of army records after the war, unlike those from the Imperial Navy, was not due to happenstance. Some were preserved by a Lieutenant Nakane with the approval of his superior officer. In August 1945 he transported them to his house and buried them in a steel drum. At the end of the same year they were retrieved and given to Lt. Col. Hara Shirō. To prevent their recognition and confiscation by the occupation forces he removed the cover sheets from the documents and burned them. Under the direction of Col. Hattori Taku-shirō, in December 1946 the records were divided among three persons to be preserved until after the occupation so that a history of the war based on reliable information could be written. In 1953 Hattori published his *Daitōa Sensō zenshi* (Complete History of the Greater East Asian War) based on these documents.[2] These war records have been systematically copied and edited since the establishment of the Self-Defense Agency Defense Research Institute, War History Office, in

1956 (now called in English the National Institute for Defense Studies). Since June 1960 they have been stored there permanently.[3] These are the documents on which Tsunoda and Ike based their works,[4] but they did not exhaust the resources of this institute. Since the publication of the works by Tsunoda and Ike, a number of scholars have made use of the various resources of the National Institute for Defense Studies (NIDS). But these materials have yet to be fully explored, and studies based on these documents have not always been free of controversy.

A case in point is the work of Hara Shirō (1911–1991), formerly of the War History Office. At the end of the war he was serving in Section 20, War Operations (Sensō shidō), of the Army High Command. As noted above he was instrumental in preserving these records. Later, drawing on them and other materials, he made a detailed study of the way military decisions were made by the imperial Japanese government, including the emperor's involvement. Hara wrote five thick volumes, "Particulars on the Beginning of the Greater East Asia War,"[5] and much later an accompanying commentary.[6] He intended to show how the Pacific War began and why Japan lost it. The five-volume compendium is an extremely detailed account of the decisions and the personalities behind them that finally led to Japan's attack on the U.S. fleet at Pearl Harbor. His documentation, citing innumerable diaries and official and unofficial records from that time, is overwhelming. Nevertheless, the publication of his manuscript was almost as problematic as the saving of the original records.

Hara completed his work between February and May 1964, and it was circulated for additions and corrections among the members of the War History Office from November 1964 until May 1967.[7] Then the work was withheld from publication until 1973–1974 due to protests from former members of the Imperial Navy who objected to his interpretations in some forty different places. Originally his work was to be titled "Imperial Headquarters, Army and Navy Departments, Particulars on the Beginning of the Greater East Asia War." The word "Navy" was eventually deleted to accommodate these objections and allow the work to be published.[8] Later Uchida Kazuomi, former navy chief of staff of the Self-Defense Forces, edited a two-volume work presenting the navy's viewpoint.[9] Hara's final book, a commentary on the events described in detail in the preceding five volumes, was published in 1987. His last study was published after Uchida's work but, like his earlier publications, is in no way a vindication of the army's role in what he describes as a political debacle that led to a military catastrophe.

During the time it took to resolve this dispute—a vestige of the rivalry between the Imperial Army and Imperial Navy—much speculation and misinformation about the war, especially the Shōwa emperor's role in it, was being published. Even after its publication, Hara's work has been all but ignored despite his thorough scholarship. This is a great pity because much ink has been wasted arguing issues he has already explicated. A pertinent example is Hirohito's knowledge of—as opposed to his role in—the planning of the surprise attack on Pearl Harbor.

Imperial Approval Before the Attack

Hara documents clearly that Navy Chief of Staff Nagano Osami (1880–1947) explained the Pearl Harbor attack plan to the emperor in an audience on 3 November 1941. Nagano personally inserted the explanation into a report prepared by the general staff for this audience:

> At the very outset of the beginning of hostilities, as nearly as possible coinciding with the first air attacks on the Philippines and Malaya, an air attack will be made on the main enemy force stationed in Hawai'i, using an expeditionary force with a nucleus of six aircraft carriers led by the commander in chief of the First Carrier Flotilla.
>
> This expeditionary force will set out after replenishing in the Kuriles a number of days before hostilities are to begin. It will approach Hawai'i from the north. One or two hours before sunrise some 200 nautical miles north of the island of Oahu the fully loaded planes—about 400—will be launched. The plan is to initiate a surprise attack *(kishū kōgeki)* on the aircraft carriers and battleships at their moorings as well as the aircraft there.
>
> This surprise attack operation *(kishū sakusen)* can even be compared with the battle of Okehazama. It is an extremely daring operation. Its success is dependent from the start on the fortunes of war, which can oscillate greatly. On the day of the surprise attack, depending on the enemy ships present, it will be possible to sink two or three battleships and aircraft carriers each.[10]

Nagano went on to explain why the attack should be made by citing the relative strengths of the American and Japanese fleets. He also had answers prepared for eventual questions from the emperor. If any were asked, they are not noted.

After the war the emperor steadfastly maintained he was only informed of military plans in a formal way after they had been completed.[11] Moreover, he reportedly told the chief prosecutor at the Tokyo war crimes trials, Joseph Keenan, that in late 1941 "he knew that war steps were being taken, but he didn't know the objective. He was not told. He didn't know that Pearl Harbor was going to be bombed."[12] Clearly if Hirohito said this to Keenan, either his memory was momentarily and unusually faulty or he lied. Hirohito was not just informed of the military's plans formally; he received extensive reports regularly that he discussed in detail. After the war he never mentioned this. It could have had dire consquences for the preservation of the imperial line, and this, no doubt, was more important than simple candor.

The outline of the attack on Pearl Harbor was sent on 8 November, as a top-secret report, to the emperor's chief aide-de-camp by the army and navy chiefs of staff. Perhaps this is why it is now to be found in a collection of top-secret Imperial Army documents and not among those of the Imperial Navy.[13] Although Hara included this information in his draft (1964),[14] and it appears unaltered in his book (1974), this unimpeachable source has so far remained all but unmentioned. The special report on the Hawai'i operation was sandwiched between explanations of first and second attack phases at the beginning of the war.[15] For reasons of secrecy Sugiyama did not include this information in his notes; nor did the emperor inform his political adviser Kido of the plan.[16] The content and style of Nagano's insertion, and the progress of the planning of the attack, indicate that it was probably the first time the emperor had heard of the Hawai'i operation.

The idea, as noted earlier, was that of Commander in Chief of the Combined Fleet Admiral Yamamoto Isoroku. In January 1941 he began a secret investigation of the project. At that time he sent an assessment of the world situation to the minister of the navy, Admiral Oikawa Koshirō (1883–1958), in which he recommended engaging the American fleet in Hawai'i in a decisive battle *(kessen)* at the beginning of a war. Essentially Yamamoto's concepts were based on the battle in the Straits of Tsushima in 1905 where Tōgō Heihachirō defeated the Russian fleet. In a similar manner a crippling blow was to be dealt U.S. forces. It was assumed that since the U.S. fleet could not be lured into such a trap, it had to be attacked in Hawai'i.[17] John J. Stephan says Yamamoto had such an attack plan as early as 1928 "in the back of his mind." Then, while serving at Kasumigaura air base, he received a paper from a subordinate, Lt. Comdr. Kusaka Ryūnosuke, proposing an attack on Hawai'i.[18] Another writer, William H. Honan, maintains the idea came even earlier to Yamamoto from a novel published in 1925 by an English journalist and specialist on naval warfare, Hector C. Bywater. His novel, *The Great Pacific War: A History of the American-Japanese Campaign of 1931–1932*, describes a war between the two "Pacific-powers" started by a Japanese surprise attack on U.S. bases in Hawai'i. Japan eventually lost this fictional war too, but the defeat aroused more consternation than caution in Japan at that time.[19]

In 1941, from April onward, Yamamoto consulted with officers in the Imperial Navy Ministry about the feasibility of such an attack.

Eventually the air attack on Pearl Harbor was part of the navy's offensive in Southeast Asia, but it was so secret, and controversial, that it was noted only briefly in the final plans.[20]

At the end of July plans for the push south were sent in an internal communiqué from the Navy Ministry to the Combined Fleet. The surprise attack on Hawai'i was not included in it. Likewise army-navy joint maneuvers on 15–16 August and navy maneuvers on 3–5 September did not include this operation. Plans for the strike south were approved by the Navy Ministry in conferences held 8–10 September. Hawai'i was still not part of these operations. From 11 to 20 September large-scale maneuvers were held at the Imperial Naval Academy led by Yamamoto and his staff. Based on the internal communiqué, Yamamoto and part of his staff had prepared plans for an air attack on Hawai'i. During these exercises, on 16 September, a special session was held that included only the participants in the proposed attack. At that time it was decided the surprise attack should take place on Sunday, 16 November (U.S. time). Nevertheless, general planning for operations in the south, completed on 20 September, did not include Hawai'i. On 24 September a special meeting was held in Vice Admiral Fukudome's office, the First Operations Department. It ended inconclusively.[21]

By the end of September 1941 the Imperial Navy still had not adopted Yamamoto's plan, and it became a major issue of contention between the Combined Fleet and the Navy Ministry. Maneuvers were again held in Kagoshima, between 4 and 6 October, centering on the naval air operations planned in the south. Similar exercises were held in Yamaguchi prefecture between 9 and 13 October that included the Combined Fleet's plan to attack Hawai'i by air. After the maneuvers in Kagoshima, the date was set for the opening of hostilities: 8 December (Japan time). On 19 October, Admiral Nagano, chief of staff, finally decided in favor of Yamamoto's plan over the objections of the First Operations Department of the Navy Ministry.[22]

Hara did not cover all these details, but he did note that this was Yamamoto's special project and was put into effect only through his perseverance. Others say he threatened to resign if the plan was not adopted.[23] Finally, on 29 October, the Combined Fleet received an "Operations Plan for the Imperial Navy" that included the surprise attack on Pearl Harbor, but without a specific timetable.[24] This was, no doubt, the document cited earlier: "Tai Bei, Ei, Ran sensō Teikoku Kaigun sakusen keikaku" (War Against the United States, England, and Holland, Imperial Navy Operations Plan).

Following these preparations the audience on 3 November, with the special report on the Hawai'i surprise air attack, was held as a precursor to the imperial conference on 5 November. Hirohito had at this time an opportunity behind the scenes to object to these war plans. If changes were to be made, clearly they had to be made before the impending imperial conference where open disagreements were to be avoided. Either the emperor did not object to this surprise attack, or his objections were not strong enough to warrant noting by those present. In the imperial conference, as Hirohito must have expected, Nagano and Sugiyama referred to the audience of 3 November, naming various theaters of operation without mentioning Hawai'i. The emperor remained silent, "approving" the proceedings.[25] The contemporary document just cited, long available but overlooked, shows that the emperor at least knew about the plan to attack Pearl Harbor well before it took place. Whether his lack of action indicates his approval of the operation is still a matter of controversy.

Imperial Conferences

The authority of an imperial conference is still unclear. The lack of clarity is due to two factors: first, the documents we have are ambiguous; second, that which constituted "imperial approval" is disputed—especially the role of imperial conferences.

In modern Japanese history imperial conferences are a relatively new "institution." They were first convened during the Meiji era and then discontinued. The first such conference during the Shōwa era was convened on 30 January 1938 to discuss the China War. By the end of 1941 there had been a total of eight such conferences. During these eight meetings the emperor spoke only once: at the famous 6 September 1941 conference. In 1946 Emperor Hirohito said the imperial conferences were very strange affairs *(okashii)*. He emphasized that he had no authority to influence what took place in them,[26] but the reliability of this postwar statement must be reexamined. Stephen Large cites contemporary authorities to show that "the purpose of the imperial conferences was not to make policy decisions but, rather, to ritually endorse the policy decisions of the liaison conferences through the formal bestowing of the 'imperial will' symbolized by the mere presence of the Emperor."[27] Herbert Bix marshals similar authorities to support the opposite view: "Although the imperial conferences . . . were very formal, this formality did not mean that the topics discussed were unknown to the emperor, nor that he lacked opportunity for his 'imperial will' to be reflected in national policy."[28] Large's position, as Bix points out and Large himself illustrates on occasion, overlooks what went on behind the scenes prior to these conferences.[29]

Fujiwara Akira lists the eight imperial conferences, the reasons for calling them, and the decisions reached:

1. 11 January 1938: "Basic Policy for Managing the China Incident." Decision: If the people's government does not pursue peace, it will not be acknowledged; rather, a new political authority will be established.

2. 15 June 1938: decision about the campaigns in Wuhan and Kwantung.

3. 30 November 1938: "Regulating Policy for the New Relation Between China and Japan." Decision: Due to establishing the new order in East Asia a policy for cooperation between Japan, Manchuria, and China, also for North China and the lower Yangtze River, was set.

4. 13 November 1940: agreement with Wang Cheng-ch'uan on the "Basic Pact Between Japan and China."

5. 2 July 1941: "Imperial Government National Policy in Response to the Changing Situation." Decision: Prepare for hostilities in the north (USSR) and at the same time a war with the United States and England in connection with the push south, which [it was assumed] cannot be avoided.

6. 6 September 1941: "Outline for Executing Imperial Goverment National Policy." This is the famous conference where Hirohito read the poem by his grandfather, Emperor Meiji. Decision: Complete preparations for war with the United States, England, and Holland by the end of October.

7. 5 November 1941: after reviewing the "Outline for Executing Imperial Government National Policy," it was decided to go to war at the beginning of December if no significant changes were achieved through diplomacy.

8. 1 December 1941: decision to commence "War Against the United States, England, and Holland."[30]

Fujiwara then notes that—considering the discussions that went on behind the scenes prior to these conferences and the liaison conferences that preceded them—the thesis that the "emperor as an organ of responsibility" could not reverse cabinet decisions is a myth *(shinwa)* fabricated after the war.[31] Fujiwara does not present enough evidence to document this conclusion, but the process of sanctioning Imperial Army and Navy annual operations plans, as we have seen, emphatically supports it. Moreover, the emperor was briefed behind the scenes on the plan to attack Pearl Harbor in this manner.

In short, Hirohito made use of informal but important audiences with military leaders to discuss and amend their plans. Imperial Army and Navy records indicate that political and military decisions, and the responsibility for them, were a matter of consensus. Establishing individual responsibility for specific decisions was not as clear-cut a matter in prewar Japan as General MacArthur and the occupation authorities led everyone to believe. Decisions were formulated by the general staffs and in the liaison conferences. But the fact that Hirohito did not attend these meetings does not mean he did not participate in the decisions. Responsible officials had private audiences with the emperor at the palace while these decisions were being reached. The emperor used these audiences to make his opinions known and persuade others to adopt them. For an example of how the emperor was consulted in this way, consider the review of national policy that took place at the end of October 1941—just prior to the private audience with the two chiefs of staff on 3 November and the seventh imperial conference, recommending war, two days later.

The Political Crisis of October 1941

If Hirohito's role in the decision-making process that led to the Pearl Harbor attack is to be fairly evaluated, one must look at the alternatives presented to him, his use of the information he received, and his responses to the proposals presented to him by Lord Privy Seal Kido, Prime Ministers Konoe and Tōjō, Navy Chief of Staff Nagano, Army Chief of Staff Sugiyama, and others. This task will be undertaken here by examining the events just prior to and following General Tōjō Hideki's appointment as prime minister.

Shortly before Tōjō was appointed prime minister, perhaps the last opportunity to avoid war presented itself and was rebuffed. The debate about war versus peace precipitated many lengthy conferences on Japan's rights in China and Japan's lack of material resources. Finally, on 6 September 1941, an imperial conference formulated Japan's minimum demands and set a timetable. If no positive results were reached through diplomatic negotiations by 10 October, military force was to be used. It was assumed that under the circumstances war with the United States was inevitable and that due to the oil embargo the longer Japan waited the worse its chances would be. Until the 10 October deadline war preparations were to be carried out secretly to avoid endangering the negotiations. After this date military preparations were to take precedence. They were to be completed during the last ten days of October.[32]

The resolution of 6 September stipulating this course of action made war with the United States and Great Britain inevitable because decisions made at imperial conferences were, in theory, irrevocable. Though everyone present at this imperial conference was well aware of this custom, only after the war policy was finalized did it become clear that the navy was in no way ready for a confrontation with the United States. Despite its lack of confidence, the navy was not prepared to say this publicly for reasons of pride and budget appropriations—such an admission would result not only in a loss of face but also a loss of funds to the army.[33] Tōjō, who was army minister at the time, realized this and said as much to the director of the Planning Board, Suzuki Teiichi (b. 1888), for communication to Prime Minister Konoe Fumimaro.[34] By mid-September it became clear that the navy wanted Konoe, who was against the war, to take responsibility for reexamining (and possibly negating) an imperial conference decision.[35] Konoe was unwilling to do this. He was also unwilling to preside over the beginning of a war. But Tōjō, a self-assured officer who was a stickler for proper procedure, insisted that war preparations must proceed as decided.

This stalemate precipitated a serious policy disagreement between Prime Minister Konoe and Army Minister Tōjō, who did not like one another anyway. It became clear that the cabinet would fall. But despite their differences of opinion, the two adversaries did agree on who should lead the next cabinet: Prince Higashikuni (1887–1990), an uncle to Hirohito's wife, Empress Nagako. Konoe and Tōjō both thought that only someone from the imperial house could conduct such a review, unite the feuding army and navy, and hold the army in check if the decision went against war. And this, a number of scholars believe, was the only real chance available to the emperor to avoid a war. (This supposition is not unassailable. Higashikuni was known to be sympathetic to right-wing militarists and may have gone along willingly with the pro-war faction in the government.)[36]

On 15 October a number of discussions took place between leading members of the government and the imperial court concerning this possibility—discussions that have been cited by various historians to prove various things. The next section presents a detailed consideration of the treatment of these events in two important secondary sources. These two books illustrate the problem of ascertaining the emperor's position vis-à-vis war.

Tōjō's Appointment

According to one of the most highly acclaimed secondary sources on the beginning of the Pacific War, Tsunoda Jun and Fukuda Shigeo's *Nichibei kaisen* (The Beginning of Hostilities Between Japan and America), Konoe proposed Prince Higashikuni personally to the emperor in a private audience on the afternoon of 15 October. That evening, with Kido's understanding *(ryōkai)*, Konoe met with Higashikuni to procure his consent. He appealed to the prince:

> It is without precedent to appropriate a Prince's influence, but there is no other way to abrogate the previous [imperial conference] decision and

return to a clean slate. I have told Kido that the leader of the next Cabinet must be an Imperial Prince; Kido has related this to the emperor, and the emperor agrees *(dōi)*.[37]

Here Tsunoda cites the records of the International Military Tribunal Far East (IMTFE).[38] According to Tsunoda, the emperor had been informed of the Higashikuni option personally. His political adviser, Lord Keeper of the Privy Seal Kido, was also informed. Both agreed to the proposal.

But another historian, citing what seems to be essentially the same materials, though in English, comes to the opposite conclusion. A lesser known but no less informative work in German by Peter Herde was published in 1980. *Pearl Harbor: 7. Dezember 1941* is an extremely detailed and well-documented chronicle of the events leading up to the opening of the war in the Pacific. Herde too cites the IMTFE records, saying the emperor and Kido were informed and Konoe talked with Higashikuni. But he portrays the positions assumed by Hirohito and Kido very differently. From the beginning Kido was allegedly skeptical of a plan that would involve a member of the imperial family directly in political decision making. The emperor adroitly sidestepped the controversy: he cleverly answered Konoe's appeal with the rejoinder that an imperial prince could only decide in favor of peace. Would the army be satisfied with that?[39]

In the end Herde has the emperor rejecting the suggestion made by Tōjō and Konoe basically because Kido opposed it. In Tsunoda's account Kido rejects the proposal on his own, explaining the danger to the imperial house. This is an important difference. While Herde has the emperor making the decision, Tsunoda saddles Kido with this responsibility. Neither side, however, cites a specific document substantiating its conclusion. The documents say, in typical impersonal Japanese fashion, that the proposal was rejected without specifying who made the decision.[40] It appears that Tsunoda assumes the emperor unquestioningly accepted the advice of his court adviser as emperors supposedly have done since Heian times (794–1185). Herde, on the other hand, transforms the situation between Kido and the emperor into that of a Western monarch being informed by, and delegating responsibilities to, a court-appointed minister. Both sides have Hirohito acting as a shadowy figure in the background. He seems well informed, supports a maneuver in favor of peace, but does not actively assert himself.

Kido's Views

Both authors concur that Emperor Hirohito, whether he made the decision himself or not, left it to the privy seal to formulate an opinion and put the decision into effect. Yet Kido's explanation for the decision has nothing to do with the issue at hand: war or peace. Kido rejected the appointment of Prince Higashikuni as prime minister for the purpose of reexamining the war issue, on the grounds that impossible issues were not to be left to the imperial house to decide. Later, if things did not go well, this course could endanger the position of the imperial house in the minds of the people.[41] Before telling others of the decision he told Planning Board Director Suzuki on the morning of 15 October that he was afraid some people in the army wanted to use Higashikuni once he was prime minister to further their pro-war aims. Kido requested that Suzuki ask Tōjō if peace was to be decided upon beforehand and a member of the imperial family was necessary to enforce this among dissidents in the military. Or was an imperial prince being called upon to preside over the decision making itself? Tōjō replied that if the decision went against war and Prince Higashikuni could not keep the military under control, who could? Tōjō could not say if he himself could do this.[42]

That settled the issue for Kido. After the war he repeated his previous concern that having Higashikuni preside over such a decision was not permissible because the imperial house would then carry full responsibility for the war. Upon request he amplified on his earlier statement: if the "impossible issue" was that of war or peace, this could not be decided in a cabinet led by a member of the imperial family.[43] The reason this was not acceptable, however, was only tangentially related to the issues of war, peace, or constitutional monarchy. Kido was concerned about the consequences of losing a war, not war itself. He was afraid the future existence of the imperial house would be endangered if one of its members were associated with a decision for a war that eventually was lost. Kido was not the only person bothered by this fear.

Kido's phraseology in his diary, as well as his statements during his interrogation prior to the Tokyo war crimes trials in 1946, support the interpretation that he, not the emperor, made this decision for the reasons just given. But a close examination of other records shows that Hirohito too had something on his mind in mid-October 1941 which was more important to him than war or peace, that both Kido and Konoe were well aware of this concern, and that this concern lay behind what appears in public to be Kido's initiative.

The Emperor's Position

On the afternoon of 15 October, after Suzuki had informed Kido of Tōjō's position, Prime Minister Konoe went to the palace, conferred with Kido, and had an audience with the emperor. He explained the political crisis that had arisen over the disagreement between the army and navy and between himself and his army minister. He then appealed for Higashikuni's appointment as the next prime minister in order to pursue the peace initiative. At this point the emperor commented:

> I actually thought Prince Higashikuni suitable as chief of staff of the army. But I think the appointment of a member of the imperial house to a political office must be considered very carefully. Above all, in times of peace this is fine; but when there is a fear that there may even be a war, then, more importantly, considering the welfare of the imperial house, I wonder about the wisdom of a member of the imperial family serving [as prime minister].[44]

Clearly the emperor was worried about having the imperial house appear responsible for the war decision and, of course, the consequences for the continued existence of his house. For Konoe, however, his statement meant: "The emperor did not seem absolutely opposed [to his suggestion]." Here is the cause of the confusion about the emperor's position on this issue: Konoe's dubious interpretation of this imperial comment. The Higashikuni diary also includes Konoe's statement telling the prince that Kido and the emperor agree with this plan.[45] Since Konoe's loose rendition of Hirohito's statement—implying imperial approval where there was none—appears in both sources, it apparently went unquestioned, misleading even a fine scholar like Tsunoda. Herde did not have access to these documents, however, and he clearly misconstrued the order of events. He has the emperor reaching a decision after lengthy discussions with Kido and others, but Hirohito seriously questioned Higashikuni's selection from the very beginning.

Konoe and Kido were informed of the emperor's misgivings. The discussions about an imperial cabinet centered not on war or peace but on the possibility of responsibility for the war being attributed to the imperial house.[46] Finally, Hirohito's statement is a vivid expression of the emperor's priorities at that time, which have been all but ignored: for Hirohito war and peace were of considerable import, but the welfare of the imperial house was his paramount consideration. This position was consistent with his early training and education. And the episode was not unique. Emperor Hirohito's actions before and during World War II were systematically atuned to his concern for the well-being of his house.

Hirohito's Postwar Recollections

In the spring of 1946 Hirohito mentioned this dilemma in a manner confirming such an interpretation. He recapitulated this event, but in

1946 he interpreted it slightly differently. In the debate over war versus peace, three important figures were in favor of war: Army Minister Tōjō, Army Chief of Staff Sugiyama, and Navy Chief of Staff Nagano. Three other persons were opposed to war: Prime Minister Konoe, Navy Minister Oikawa Koshirō, and Foreign Minister Toyoda Teijirō (1885–1961). Moreover, most members of the imperial house were in favor of war.[47] Those in the navy who were against the war argued that in two years the country's resources would be depleted making naval operations impossible. Here they reversed Navy Chief of Staff Nagano's argument in the 6 September imperial conference, according to which, since oil was running out, the sooner the war started the better.[48] In any case the decision, even though it involved military matters, should be made by the prime minister and not the service ministers. This position they maintained in a self-serving manner to avoid being held responsible for reversing an imperial conference decision. Bound by the 6 September resolution and confronted with this debate, Konoe resigned.

According to Hirohito in 1946, it was the stress caused by the situation, not a confrontation with the army, that led Konoe to resign. Then a new prime minister had to be selected from among those privy to the decision of 6 September. Only those present at that imperial conference could be considered, and it had to be someone who could control the army. Tōjō, Oikawa, and Toyoda were the only candidates. When the navy refused to allow one of its members to become prime minister in this situation, that left only Tōjō. (Toyoda was also a navy admiral.) Referring to the prince's diary, the emperor also mentioned the controversy surrounding the candidacy of Imperial Prince Higashikuni. Hirohito said that although Higashikuni was recommended by the army, he himself was against members of the imperial house assuming offices with political responsibility. He had Kido talk to Tōjō about preserving peace at any price, but Tōjō would not agree. The emperor reiterated that if war were to begin while a member of the imperial house was prime minister, the imperial house would have to carry the responsibility, and this he opposed.[49] Then he chose, at Kido's recommendation, the man who refused to preserve peace at any price as his next prime minister: Tōjō Hideki.

In mid-October 1941 the emperor was clearly undecided about the best course to take. His selection of his new prime minister, and his subsequent orders to him, reflect this. It was a complex situation and Hirohito compounded it.

Tōjō on war

When Emperor Hirohito ordered General Tōjō Hideki to form a cabinet on 17 October 1941, he commanded Tōjō to reexamine the decision of the imperial conference on 6 September. At the same time the emperor informed the army and navy of this directive. General Tōjō was known for his efficiency, directness, and unswerving loyalty to the throne. Indeed, he was selected for the office of prime minister because of these qualities. But some believe Kido did not properly evaluate him and the situation before recommending him to the emperor. According to these critics, Tōjō was by nature "full of fighting spirit" and not given to deep reflection. He would not consider the sweeping implications for the Japanese people that this decision would have, nor would he conduct the review impartially.[50] Others believe that Kido's main interest was not the policy review, but controlling the military, and Tōjō was the best man for this dangerous assignment.[51] As we have seen, Kido was concerned not with two but three problems: reviewing the war decision, controlling the army, and preserving the imperial house.

The emperor too must have been well informed about Tōjō's position. Tōjō told Planning Board Director Suzuki on 13 October, shortly before he forced the fall of the third Konoe cabinet, that such a review was out of the question.[52] This information was transmitted to Kido and the emperor. Moreover, Konoe and Kido had no doubt told Hirohito of Tōjō's position earlier: on 4 and 9 October Konoe briefed the emperor on the diplomatic impasse developing between the United States and Japan; on 13 October Kido had a long audience with the emperor in which the situation was discussed in detail. On the previous evening, 12 October, Chief Cabinet Secretary Tomita Kenji (1897–1977) had informed Kido of the results of a conference at Prime Minister Konoe's residence in Ogikubo, noting specifically the attitudes of the army and navy ministers. Although it is not expressly mentioned in his diary, Kido more than likely informed Hirohito of the dispute between Prime Minister Konoe and Army Minister Tōjō that came to a head at the Ogikubo conference. Finally, Tōjō's position was underlined in Konoe's letter of resignation presented to the emperor on 16 October.[53]

Hirohito had long been aware of Tōjō's opposition to a policy of peace at any price. He also must have known about Tōjō's opposition to a new review of the military and diplomatic situation, disregarding the decision of the 6 September imperial conference, before he ordered his new prime minister to do just that. Furthermore, the emperor was aware of the controversial nature of the review and knew that the decision of 6 September could probably not be reversed without active support from the emperor himself. Lord Privy Seal Kido intimated as much to the emperor on 20 October. According to Kido, the emperor indicated that all along he had understood the gravity of the situation:

> As regards changing the cabinet and the great effort involved, I received some gracious comments from the emperor and was truly awed. With this cabinet change it is feared that should there be a single misstep we will be plunged into a senseless war. I believe as the result of careful deliberations this [Tōjō's nomination as prime minister] is the sole way to develop a new policy and therefore petitioned his majesty accordingly, explaining my position in detail. The emperor understood extremely well and said, "It's just as they say, if you do not enter the proverbial tiger's lair, you can't catch his cubs."[54]

But in the end, having entered the lair, Hirohito would have us believe he only watched the tigers at play. Because he was a constitutional monarch he supposedly could not do otherwise—meaning he could not actively support the peace faction at court or in the government. He did, however, look after the interests of the imperial house. He appointed a prime minister whose loyalty was well known to all, including quite possibly the emperor,[55] and that finally meant more than the policy issues at hand.

The Policy Review

General Tōjō had been a leader of the pro-war faction, but he was also an ardent supporter of the imperial tradition. He embarked on the review ordered by the emperor in his usual earnest manner. His contemporaries noted the unexpected change in his attitude toward the war issue, and at least one person (besides the emperor), Admiral Oka Takazumi, understood the reason for this change. When General Mutō Akira (1892–1948), chief of the Military Affairs Bureau, asked his counterpart, the chief of the Naval Affairs Bureau, Admiral Oka, about Tōjō's apparent change in attitude, putting peace and war on an equal footing, the latter responded: "Perhaps it is because he is supposed to embody *(taiken)* the wishes of the emperor."[56] Indeed it appears that Tōjō did change his position, his official position in any event, in response to the emperor's wishes. Despite his personal feelings Tōjō conscientiously carried out his assigned task.

Immediately after his audience with the emperor and before officially taking office as prime minister, Tōjō ordered Col. Ishii Akiho (b. 1900) of the Military Affairs Bureau to prepare an outline for such a review. Ishii worked all night, conferred with the general staffs of the army and navy on the morning of 18 October, and presented Tōjō with a draft at noon. Tōjō approved this draft. That evening, after forming his cabinet, he presented copies to the ministers concerned—navy, foreign affairs, finance, and the director of the Planning Board. (The army is not mentioned because Tōjō continued to serve as army minister. Prime Minister Tōjō had himself simultaneously appointed army minister and interior minister so he could control matters should the decision go against war.)[57] Work was to begin without delay. The review consisted of eleven points:

1. What is the outlook for the war in the European Theater? (Reviewing authorities: Foreign, Supreme Command)

2. In a war with the United States, Great Britain, and Holland, what is the outlook in the initial stages and over a number of years? In this case, what are the chances of the United States and Great Britain deciding to use the unoccupied part of China for military activities? (Supreme Command)

3. With respect to opening hostilities in the south [Southeast Asia] this fall, what sort of related developments can be expected in the north [the Soviet Union]? (Army, Navy, Foreign, Supreme Command)

4. What is the outlook in a war with the United States, Great Britain, and Holland after three years with respect to shipping—requirements and losses? (Supreme Command)

5. With respect to the above, what is the volume of our domestic civilian shipping requirements and the supply and demand of important commodities? (Planning)

6. What is our financial strength based on the magnitude of the imperial government's calculations in connection with a war with the United States, Great Britain, and Holland? (Finance)

7. What level of cooperation can be expected through an agreement with Germany and Italy in connection with a war with the United States, Great Britain, and Holland? (Foreign, Army, Navy)

8. Could one limit the war adversaries only to Holland or only to Great Britain and Holland? (Foreign, Supreme Command)

9. Should the commencement of the war be delayed until around March of next year, what are the advantages and disadvantages in Foreign Affairs? (Foreign, Army, Navy, Supreme Command)

What is the outlook with respect to the supply and demand of important commodities? (Planning, Army, Navy)

The advantages and disadvantages for military operations? (Supreme Command)

With the above in mind, how should one decide on the time to initiate hostilities? (Army, Navy, Foreign, Supreme Command)

In connection with the above, what is our appraisal of the possibility, advantages, and disadvantages of abandoning plans for a war with the United States, Great Britain, and Holland and through increasing production of synthetic oil and so forth to maintain the present situation? (Planning, Army, Navy)

10. What is the outlook for attaining in a short period of time our minimum demands as decided in the imperial conference of 6 September if we continue diplomatic negotiations with the United States? (Foreign, Army, Navy, Supreme Command)

What is the outlook for a compromise if we modify to some extent our minimum demands? Would this be acceptable to Imperial Japan? (Foreign, Army, Navy, Supreme Command)

If we accept completely the terms of the U.S. note of 2 October, how would the international position of Imperial Japan change, especially in China, as compared with the situation before the China Incident? (Foreign, Army, Navy, Supreme Command) [The 2 October note reiterated the United States' basic position that Japan must demonstrate its willingness to withdraw from China and Indochina.

11. In a war with the United States, Great Britain, and Holland, how could the resolve of the Chungking government be influenced? (Foreign, Army, Navy)[58]

In his memoirs, Colonel Ishii noted that the Army General Staff opposed this review. There had been enough study and discussion; now was the time for action. The navy's position was more complex. Chief of the Naval Affairs Bureau Oka was especially interested in the second topic and "the chances of the United States and Great Britain deciding to use the unoccupied part of China for military activities." He was more willing to compromise, and the Navy Ministry appeared indecisive compared to the army.[59] Navy Chief of Staff Admiral Nagano, on the other hand, was firmly against the review: "There is no room for changing the decision of the imperial conference," he stated on 21 October.[60]

Some have maintained that the military's intransigence or indecision was due to the fact that Privy Seal Kido had failed to directly inform the Supreme Command of this imperial wish.[61] But as we have seen they were appropriately informed. The military's apparent "foot dragging" had to do with individual military priorites or differences in personalities, not bureaucratic formalities. Compared with Navy Minister Oikawa, for example, Navy Chief of Staff Nagano was said to be more headstrong and given to quick changes of mind.[62]

The Emperor's Participation

Ostensibly this review was conducted without being swayed by the emperor. Although the extent of his influence remains to be ascertained, Hirohito appears to have been more than a passive observer as he and others later maintained. Tōjō, the emperor's new prime minister and subsequent first line of defense, is the key to the emperor's role (and its ambiguity later). At the time, Tōjō made sure that the emperor was regularly informed of the progress of these liaison conferences and other decisions made by his cabinet. One person in a position to know commented decisively on Hirohito's role in these policymaking activities. The chief of the General Affairs Section of the Prime Minister's Office, Inada Shūichi, remarked to Tōjō's private secretary, Akamatsu Sadao:

> There has never been a cabinet in which the prime minister, and all the ministers, reported so often to the throne. In order to effect the essence of genuine direct imperial rule *(tennō shinsei)* and to relieve the concerns of the emperor, the ministers reported to the throne matters within the scope of their responsibilities as per the prime minister's directives. With important problems, the direction of such and such an investigation in progress was reported in [unfinished] form to the emperor. It was entirely different from the time of party politics. Then, after a decision was made, it was written on thick paper and presented as a bound book.
>
> In times of intense activity [during the Tōjō cabinet], typed drafts were presented to the emperor with corrections in red. First draft, second draft, final draft, and so forth, came as deliberations progressed one after the other and were sanctioned *(gokyo)* accordingly by the emperor. Nevertheless, with important matters secrecy was preserved.[63]

This statement utterly contradicts the assertions that the emperor was purposely left uninformed of important military matters or that he, with the exception of the surrender at the end of the war, was always presented with polished resolutions after a consensus had been achieved. But this does not mean that the emperor's critics—who maintain he plotted and directed the war from behind the scenes—have been right all along. Emperor Hirohito never claimed he was totally ignorant of what the army and navy were doing. Rather, he said he was only informed of military plans in a formal, general way; opposition to the military was impossible; and in any case, as a constitutional monarch, he was supposed to sanction the measures laid before him regardless of his personal feelings.[64] The emperor's assertions, however, were less than candid. As we have seen, Hirohito was much better informed about military matters than he ever admitted. And quite another decision-making process was involved. It was pluralistic in nature, entailed building a consensus among high civilian and military officials, and the emperor personally took part in this process. The correctness of Hirohito's participation in these decisions was self-evident to Tōjō and other prewar Japanese leaders. Given this pluralistic, consensus-oriented decision-making process, despite Hirohito's statements about upholding the principles of English constitutional monarchy, his actions must be examined in the light of Japanese conventions—the context in which he actually operated. Then quite another perspective emerges.

At least one author, Fujiwara Akira in his book *Tennōsei to guntai* (The Emperor System and the Military), recognizes the inherent complexity of this issue. He notes that the emperor, due to his position according to tradition and in the Meiji Constitution, did exercise political influence on occasion. After the demise of the Meiji-era elder statesmen, the emperor was the only authority who could bring the civil and military elements of the government together. Perhaps, Fujiwara says, Hirohito did attempt to refrain from active participation in politics, adapting to the role of an English constitutional monarch. He reminds us that Prime Minister Konoe complained about the emperor's lack of engagement in political affairs during the crisis following the 6 September imperial conference. Yet Konoe may have intended only to relieve himself of responsibility. He was noted for his indecisiveness. Fujiwara concludes that although the military dominated politics during this period, the emperor's will could not be ignored. Unfortunately, he fails to clarify the manner in which this will was manifested. Finally, Fujiwara does not absolve the emperor from responsibility. But he does not examine all the evidence available either and comes to no conclusions about Hirohito's role in the decision-making process in the fall of 1941.[65]

At least one member of the Army General Staff expected that Tōjō's literal sense of loyalty would lead to a type of direct imperial rule. Colonel Ishii, who drafted the outline of the review, received a communication on 16 October from the throne to the army minister saying they should drop the idea of stationing troops in China and that an imperial command (to form a cabinet) was conceivable. Ishii quickly wrote a reply justifying the necessity of stationing troops in China and gave it to Tōjō for his audience with the emperor on the afternoon of 17 October. Whereupon Tōjō told Ishii: "If the emperor said it should be so, then that's it for me. One cannot recite arguments to the emperor. You may keep your finely phrased memorandum." Colonel Ishii concluded to himself: "If Army Minister Tōjō receives an imperial command to form a cabinet, I have an insight into his attitude of absolute obedience [to the emperor]."[66] The author who cited Ishii, Hara Shirō, notes that this attitude must have been known to Kido and Konoe—and, moreover, that it could be expected that Tōjō would carry out the review impartially in accord with the emperor's wishes.

In fact, the "clean slate" reappraisal of Japan's international and military situation in late October 1941 was carried out in a manner designed to forge a consensus among Japan's leaders, including the emperor. This can be deduced from Shūichi Inada's description of policymaking in the Tōjō Cabinet and other records from that time. The reexamination of the "Essentials for Carrying Out the Empire's Policies" took place between 24 October and 1 November 1941, and Hirohito was regularly informed about the progress of these conferences. The emperor had an audience with Prime Minister Tōjō on 24 October. Finance Minister Kaya met with Hirohito on 25 October. The head of the Planning Board Suzuki and again Prime Minister Tōjō met with him on 29 October. All discussed the liaison conferences with the emperor. On 30 October the emperor talked over the conference with Kido for forty minutes and on the same day Foreign Minister Tōgō came for an audience. On 31 October Hirohito again discussed the matter with Kido, and Tōjō came for an audience to report on the progress of the deliberations. Finally on 2 November Tōjō reported the results of the review to the emperor. During this time the emperor also had audiences with a number of other officials and may have discussed the topic.[67] Although it is not specifically recorded that on this particular occasion Tōjō and the other officials who consulted with the emperor presented position papers, as generally was the case, Kido specifically notes that the impending decision was discussed in all but the first of these meetings. One might reasonably assume that the emperor, as on numerous other occasions, indicated his preferences during these meetings.

At this time, moreover, Army Imperial Headquarters was continuously communicating with the throne in detail about the military situation. On 8 October 1941 Chief of Staff Sugiyama signed a report to the throne *(sōjōan)* outlining in minute detail plans for the advance into Southeast Asia: "Matters Relating to All Operations in the South."[68] Here, in forty-seven handwritten pages, the general staff provided the emperor with a massive amount of information about the planned operations. From this document one can see that—contrary to what Hirohito told Keenan, general prosecutor in the Tokyo war crimes trials after the war, and steadfastly maintained until his death —the emperor knew very well what the objectives of the operations were. These objectives were clearly stated near the beginning of the document:

> Important bases of the English and Americans in East Asia *(tōa)* will be destroyed and needed areas occupied *(senryō)*. At the same time the Dutch East Indies will be attacked, and thereafter the above areas secured *(kakuho)*. Thereby a self-sufficient self-defense *(jizon jiei)* arrangement will be established. In conjunction with, and using the results of, these operations the subjugation of China is planned.

Hirohito was given a detailed description of the total amount and types of forces involved, the order of attack, even the number of forces to be employed for specific objectives. The enemy's buildup of defenses was outlined, and the importance of attacking quickly was emphasized.

The emperor was not just a disinterested onlooker in these proceedings. In a fifty-one-page document dated the last third of October, "Materials in Reply to the Throne: The Operational Outlook in a War with America, England, and Holland," Hirohito again was given—at his request—a thorough appraisal of the situation in the West Pacific.[69] The report begins with a direct statement of the operational goals that repeats almost exactly the report cited earlier: "The important bases in East Asia of the United States, Great Britain, and Holland will be destroyed, and strategic areas in the south will be occupied and secured. For this purpose the army has around eleven divisions and two air groups ready." Points of attack were listed: the Philippines, Malaya, Guam, Hong Kong, English Borneo, and so on. Close coordination between the army and navy was called for. The order of attack was specified as well: first British and American bases in Singapore and Manila, respectively, then the Dutch East Indies, especially Java. For the most important objectives, the report listed the expected duration of the respective campaigns: Hong Kong, around a month; Singapore, about 100 days; Manila, 40 to 50 days. The emperor was told the U.S. Navy had about 40 percent of its forces in the West Pacific; even with the opening of hostilities they must leave some forces in the Atlantic to oppose the German navy; therefore the Japanese in terms of comparative military power would have an advantage.

In the event of an extended war, the outlook is extremely problematic, the report says at the beginning, though it is more optimistic in the middle. Some of the statistics in this report vary slightly from those cited earlier, but the main difference is an increased emphasis on the timing of the attack. The plans in Southeast Asia are completely based on beginning with a surprise attack *(sensei kyūshū)* and swiftly overcoming the enemy. And it is necessary to begin soon—before the Americans and British supplement their forces to such an extent that the balance of military power shifts in their favor. The report recommends the first ten days in December.

At present, the emperor was assured, the Imperial Army with respect to organization, equipment, quality, force of arms, and so forth is absolutely superior. Then the report presents a detailed inventory of the important military equipment available in August 1941. For example:

> Airplanes: about 4,400 are practically ready for use. Based on an increase in production efficiency, 3,500 more would be made operational in 1941, some 5,500 in 1942, and some 7,000 in 1943. Thus even if a northern offensive begins while the campaign in the south is in progress, supplying planes for the north should be no problem.
>
> Tanks: about 1,800 are available in August 1941; 1,200 more are projected for this year, 1,500 in 1942, and 1,800 in 1943. The report makes the same comment about a possible offensive in the north.

Ammunition for ground operations, bombs, fuel (aviation gasoline and gas for land vehicles), and shipping are similarly enumerated. These figures—and the optimistic, if not unrealistic, projections about war production in the future—are followed with a synopsis of how the operations in the south will proceed. Briefly, as stated in the beginning, English and American possessions in the Far East will be secured and shipping to these areas from the home countries will be interdicted. Militarily, then, Imperial Japan will secure an invincible position. In China Japan will continue its present offensive against Chiang Kai-shek unabated, and shifting some troops to the south will not adversely affect progress there. While the operations in the south continue, stern warnings will be imparted to the Soviet Union, but at the same time Japan will maintain its policy of avoiding a conflict. The war between Germany and the Soviet Union will be closely monitored, watching for a reduction of the threat from the Soviet Union. Cooperation between China and the Soviet Union against Japan, especially after next spring, will be prevented. There will be hardships militarily and materially in 1942 and 1943. But with the determined resolve of its people Japan will prevail—in the south, in China—and with German cooperation the Soviet Union can be destroyed.[70]

These reports to the throne were part of the ongoing work in both the army and navy ministries. During this period they also produced a general plan for military policy through joint discussions at the section chief *(kachō)* level. This "General Guidance Plan for War Against

America, Great Britain, and Holland," which is very similar to the presentation to the throne on 3 November mentioned earlier,[71] places great emphasis on self-sufficiency and self-defense. It shows that in mid-October 1941 the army and navy were still working on achieving a consensus about the best course of action in a war. And assuming that he read at this important juncture the military reports he requested and received, the emperor must have known this.

The details of the two reports to the throne—one from the chief of staff to the emperor, the other in answer to questions from the emperor—indicate that Hirohito was not only actively involved with his civilian leaders during the policy review at the end of October 1941. He was also engaged in a dialogue with the military.[72] Neither the information presented to the emperor nor the dialogue was new. Consistent with practices outlined in Chapter 2, he was informed about the issue of fuel and oil reserves at the end of July and about the navy's reluctance to go to war. David Titus emphasizes that, at that time, "the emperor did not simply keep himself informed; he also pressured his officials in regard to the correctness and consistency of their policies."[73]

The documents preclude any conclusions about the extent of imperial influence on specific army plans. The documents do show, however, that the army consistently attempted to influence the emperor to decide for war. Hirohito was presented with a great amount of information by the general staffs about the military situation in East Asia. These preparations were purposely designed to make it difficult for him to oppose their plans. General Mutō Akira, for example, chief of the Military Affairs Bureau, told his staff after the crucial 6 September imperial conference: "The [army] minister and chief of staff cannot pressure the emperor and bring him to [favor] war. The emperor himself, from the bottom of his heart, must conclude that this is all but unavoidable and make an imperial decision for war. We must adopt measures such that imperial consent is granted."[74] The army's efforts, however, do not absolve the emperor from responsibility for going along with their plans. Not only was the emperor well informed, he was given ample opportunity to make his concerns known in private before decisions were officially promulgated.

This is the pluralistic type of decision making referred to by Stephen Large and others. The style is well known in Japan: those responsible for forming a consensus—arriving at a policy to be endorsed officially by the head of state or, nowadays, the head of a large firm—discuss the issues with him beforehand in private talks. During these sessions he often tries to mediate between persons with conflicting views and intimates his own opinions. In a similar manner Hirohito actively worked to achieve a consensus among his ministers and military leaders. This also conforms to the traditional role of the emperor in the Japanese history and ethics lessons taught to Hirohito. The imperial institution was the spiritual center around which the leaders of the Japanese folk consolidated. Hara reiterates that the emperor's policy of reigning but not ruling *(Kunrin suredomo, tōji sezu)* prevented him from reversing the policy decided upon in the 6 September imperial conference.[75] This is a supposition, however—a supposition based on "misinformation" propagated by the emperor and his advisers, not on documentary evidence. In fact, Hirohito acted contrary to this often cited convention but consistent with his role in the consensus-building process.

At the beginning of November 1941, Tōjō and his associates came to the conclusion, again, that war was inevitable. The prime minister reported this to Hirohito who protested but sanctioned the decision. Everyone concerned, including the emperor, seemed unaware or unconcerned that the entire reexamination revolved around the questions of natural resources, war materials, and tactics—under the circumstances could the war could be won? This, not war or peace, was the vital question.

Certainly no one wants to lose a war. But in Japan's case something more than material destruction had to be considered: the continued existence of the imperial house. If Japan lost the war, the victors might dictate the end of the imperial line. Hirohito did not mention this concern in 1946. He did not mention peace either. In 1946 he said the focal point of the discussions was oil: "The oil embargo had driven Japan into a corner."[76] The question of whether or not war should be pursued at all was strictly secondary.[77] Nevertheless, Tōjō claimed to have been impressed by the emperor's aversion to war. On 1 December, after the final decision had been made, Tōjō related to his secretary:

> Because the emperor decreed that the slate should be wiped clean and negotiations between Japan and the United States be reexamined anew, I set out to do this in all sincerity. Since we came to the conclusion that war was inevitable, I requested the emperor's sanction *(gokyo)*. However, this sanction was not readily forthcoming. Then in the end he said it could not be avoided. The emperor truly loves peace. I could see with my own eyes that the emperor highly values peace. Inexcusably in one way or another I had to request the imperial sanction. It was extremely regrettable. In a quiet voice the emperor talked about the treaty between Japan and England [1902] and the warm reception he received on his visit to England [1921]. I prayed in my heart that never again would I fall into this predicament and

have to request such a sanction. In the Imperial Edict proclaiming war the sentence, "Indeed, this is not my will," was not in the original draft. It was explicitly added at the emperor's command.[78]

This statement agrees with Tōjō's well-known disclaimer during the Tokyo war crimes trials (May 1946–April 1948).[79] It agrees, too, with less well known statements made in private at that time:

> The Emperor did everything possible to prevent the war. That it finally came to war and that war was considered unavoidable in the end was the result of my advice. That responsibility—formal as well as practical—is mine alone.[80]

These statements, however, do not correctly reflect the mechanics of decision making in prewar Japan. As we have seen, not only Tōjō but also the emperor and a number of other high officials were formally and practically responsible for the decision to go to war with the United States and its allies in late 1941.

The Road to War

Over the years the emperor was informed thoroughly about the thinking and planning of army and navy leaders. Records of private audiences with Hirohito show he often discussed military matters in an animated fashion. He was decisive but inconsistent. He pointedly raised the issue of Songkhla's neutrality in 1938–1939; he blocked a military alliance with Germany and Italy in the summer of 1939; and his comments on the appointment of General Tōjō as prime minister, as well as numerous other examples dating back to Prime Minister Tanaka Giichi's dismissal following the murder of Chang Tso-lin in 1928, indicate that the emperor was far from being a mere rubber stamp for the imperial government. One might assume, therefore, that Hirohito indeed was a strong peace advocate. Yet the war resolution of 1941 was consistent with operations plans he had been reading, discussing, and approving for at least five years. The decision to start a war with the United States, Great Britain, and the Netherlands could not have come to him as a surprise. Nor was it a decision in which he was not involved.

Rather than repeatedly questioning whether the emperor had a hand in these decisions, or rhetorically asking if he could have vetoed the decision for war, there is a more appropriate approach: let us acknowledge the former and ask what he was prepared to risk to achieve the latter. Given his inconsistent conduct—censuring aggression while approving the aggressive operations plans of his military leaders—it appears he was undecided. Certainly he was not ready to risk his own position or that of his family at the pinnacle of Japanese society. Neither his education nor his advisers had prepared him to take such a risk. During Hirohito's years of schooling, the sublime quality of the Japanese folk was treated extensively. The future emperor was instructed in ethics and history and the supreme position of the imperial line. From his early teachers and later advisers he learned about the importance of preserving his house—not only its existence but its position in society. He also learned about the fragile position of the emperor. The imperial house had been relegated to a position of economic penury and political insignificance for centuries. Certain emperors had even been replaced. The Meiji Constitution changed this. But while the position of the head of the imperial line was officially "sacred and inviolable," an emperor's power and influence were not. In the power struggles at the top of the prewar Japanese polity both the existence and position of the imperial house were in danger. An unsuccessful war might mean the end of the imperial line. An ill-considered political posture might mean the end of the emperor's power and influence. Hirohito did not wish to risk either. He was undecided about the prospects for success of the military's plans, chose to deal with the immediate threat of losing power, and did not vigorously oppose the decision for war.

Ensuring Japan's operational readiness for a war and deciding to start one, of course, are two different things. So too are preparations for offensive versus defensive military operations. For over five years Hirohito had been receiving operations plans that included offensive options. The plans to attack Singapore, Hong Kong, and finally Pearl Harbor by surprise could hardly be construed as defensive—except in the sense that the best defense is a good offense. At the end of October and beginning of November 1941, everyone in the Japanese military and government was discussing how to go to war, and the chances of winning, not how to avoid one. Hirohito was no exception.

Aftermath

Many have contended that after the war Tōjō knew his fate was sealed and sought, successfully, to deflect war crimes charges against the emperor. But perhaps the emperor and Tōjō were not trying to deceive anyone. Simple "deception" would have been beneath their sense of dignity. More to the point, they were only doing what was natural to preserve Japan's paramount institution: the imperial house.

There was no grand conspiracy to make war. Nor was there a great cabal to cover up the emperor's wartime activities. There were misunderstandings about Hirohito's war responsibility based on a certain amount of deception regarding his role in military planning and a lack of knowledge in the West about how political and military decisions were reached in prewar Japan. Moreover, the emperor's priorities while participating in these decisions have not been accurately depicted. The Shōwa emperor was not a saint or a soldier. He was a family man intent on preserving his family line and tradition.

Although the topic will not be pursued here, it appears that Hirohito's manner of approving army and navy operations plans before the war coincides with his activities after the war began. On 12 February 1942, for example, shortly before the fall of Singapore, he told Prime Minister Tōjō:

> I believe you [Prime Minister Tōjō] have reflected sufficiently such that no opportunities will be lost with respect to bringing the war to a conclusion. For the sake of peace for all mankind, a useless prolongation of the war and an increase in serious destruction is undesirable. If [the war] is prolonged, quite naturally there will be a deterioration in the quality of the military. This of course will also be a problem for our adversaries. It depends on the moves made by the Americans and English from now on, and we must also watch closely changes involving Germany and the Soviet Union. In addition, should the procurement of natural resources in Southeast Asia not be well managed, it would be distressing. Reflect carefully on these points and formulate a policy that omits nothing![81]

Obviously Hirohito was well informed about the military requirements of wars in general and this war in particular. After it began he voiced concern about the inhumane character of war and advocated bringing the conflict to a quick end. At the same time, consistent with promoting his heritage and protecting his lineage, he was not reticent about offering advice on the military aspects of achieving Japan's goals during the war.[82]

Before turning to the content and character of Hirohito's introduction to his imperial heritage, we shall address a related question: how and why Emperor Hirohito and Prime Minister Tōjō Hideki, who have been portrayed as such different personalities, were able to work together so well in leading Japan to war. One historian has argued that "Tōjō Hideki was completely subservient in the presence of the emperor," and this, he says, was the basis of their mutual understanding.[83] But the situation was not so simple. To understand how the academic emperor and his belligerent "warlord" managed the war effort, one must examine the role of the imperial tradition in Tōjō Hideki's thinking and its significance for his relation to the emperor, who esteemed that same tradition. This examination will include a look at Tōjō's use of the military police (Kempeitai) to enforce his policies, a review of the importance of the imperial house to Tōjō and to Hirohito's prewar activities, and a questioning of the relevance of the controversy surrounding his war responsibility.

4

·

Tōjō and the Emperor:
Mutual Political Convictions

Tōjō Hideki (1884–1948) was prime minister of Japan from October 1941 to July 1944.[1] For the Allied Nations he was "the war premier," and he was treated accordingly after the war. Tōjō was hanged as a war criminal on 23 December 1948, the birthday of Crown Prince Akihito, the present emperor.

During his long tenure as prime minister Tōjō appeared to have a special relation with the emperor. Although Hirohito appointed him to office with reservations, he soon gained the emperor's trust and the emperor supported him, despite mounting criticism, until the very end. Some say it was Tōjō's subservience to the emperor that pleased Hirohito. Others have said it was Tōjō's unaffected direct manner, which allowed Hirohito as seldom before to gain a clear picture of civil and military activities.[2] In any event, an unexpected degree of mutual respect grew up between the man who was to be known as the war premier and the man who wanted to be known as the peace emperor. An important reason for this respect was a little-examined personal trait common to both: their appreciation of traditional Japanese values and like interpretations of the proper role of the imperial house in Japanese society. Indoctrination in the importance of the imperial line in Japanese history and society was integral to the training of all military men in Japan. It was an important part of Hirohito's education as well. The well-being of the imperial house was one of the emperor's principal concerns when considering military and political policy. This mutual concern, then, formed a basis of communication between prime minister and emperor.

The difference between Tōjō and his colleagues in high office in the 1940s was that while others mouthed the expected platitudes for reasons of career and public consumption, Tōjō genuinely believed in the unique Japanese national polity *(kokutai)*. In his public statements, he too said what was expected. But his private records reveal his personal convictions quite clearly. From these materials, in fact, one gains clear insight into the nature of his beliefs and their significance for the relation between Tōjō and Hirohito. Here it will be shown how the constellation of tradition, emperor, and prime minister contributed to the formation of Japanese political policy immediately before and during the war.

On 12 October 1881 the Japanese government decided that the constitution, promulgated in 1889, would be modeled after the Constitution of Prussia. In the words of a prominent German scholar: "The beginnings of an antimodern agrarianism were . . . consciously promoted at that time by the military in order to block further development of constitutionalism in Japan even before the constitution had been publicly announced" (or drawn up for that matter).[3] Later in the 1930s this antimodern agrarianism came to fruition as the so-called young officers in the army demanded a "Shōwa Restoration." As Bernd Martin observes: "The demand for a 'Shōwa Restoration' implied the complete overthrow of the existing social order and the establishment of a 'folkish' imperial state. . . . The *kokutai,* the theory of being Japanese centered on the emperor, . . . was raised . . . to the status of a state doctrine and used as a palliative against foreign subversive influences by the military, whose opinions carried ever more weight in society."[4] Although Tōjō was a prominent member of the military establishment, he was not among those who favored a Shōwa Restoration. A study of his career reveals important information about the development of militarism in Japan, but it would be an oversimplification to see him only as a militaristic leader and opinion maker. Insofar as one can speak of Japanese militarism, Tōjō himself was a product, a champion, and finally a victim of the intrigues he helped foment.

Tōjō the Product

Tōjō was the first son of a respected army career officer, Tōjō Hidenori (1855–1913). But Hidenori was not from a family with a long military (samurai) tradition. He came from a house of Nō actors specializing in subordinate characters *(waki-kata)*. The main line went back to the time of the third shogun, Tokugawa Iemitsu (1604–1651; shogun 1623–

1651). The specific line of actors to which Tōjō's ancestors belonged, the Hōshō-ryū, is noted for its severe style. In 1832 the head of one branch of this school, Jōnosuke, was invited to Nanbu-han (Morioka) where Nō was supported by the local lord. He was given a status comparable to a retainer *(kashin)* and a stipend of 160 *koku* of rice.[5] Jōnosuke had no heirs and his only daughter was married to the third son of a local retainer, Tōjō Hideki's grandfather, Hidemasa, who was to continue the Hōshō tradition in Morioka. After an uprising in 1853, in which more than twenty thousand peasants took part, a new lord *(hanshu)* was appointed who was not inclined to support Nō. Many artists returned to Edo, but Hidemasa was from a local vassal house and was able to keep his retainer status. In 1856, he was subsequently ordered to relinquish the name Hōshō and take the name Tōjō. This was the name of a school of Neo-Confucian scholars, the Tōjō Ichidō, which the new lord had studied in Edo. It had been suppressed in Edo, and he wanted to revive it in Morioka.[6] Hidemasa became a scholar, and Tōjō Hideki's father, Hidenori, was actually raised in this minor Neo-Confucian house of learning.

In the fighting prior to the Meiji Restoration, Nanbu fought on the losing side. Nanbu even fought on after the other lords in the northeast capitulated to the restoration army, surrendering only after the start of the Meiji era. In retaliation the restoration government immediately reduced the size of the fief to 130,000 *koku* of rice. The Tōjō family lost its status and stipend, and Hidemasa attempted to survive through teaching both Nō and Neo-Confucianism in Morioka. With six children, this turned out to be a hard existence. Looking for something better, the eldest son Hidenori went to Tokyo in 1873 where he eventually entered the Army Academy (Rikugun Shikan Gakkō) when it opened in 1875.[7] He was a student of the Prussian officer, Major Jacob Meckel (1842–1906), who taught there and greatly influenced the structure and strategy of the Imperial Army.[8] Meckel's training reportedly enabled the Japanese to win the Sino-Japanese War in 1894–1895. Ten years later Mekel's students were again victorious in the Russo-Japanese War (1904–1905), though his strategy resulted in enormous casualties for the Japanese. After graduating Hidenori was sent to Germany to study, later taught at the Army Academy, served on the general staff during the Sino-Japanese War, and was chief editor of the history of that conflict *(Nisshin senshi)*. He was promoted to the rank of lieutenant general *(chūshō)* when he retired.

Tōjō followed in his father's footsteps. He too attended the Army Academy (seventeenth graduating class), the Army Staff College, and served as a military attaché in Switzerland and Germany (1919–1922).

Prior to becoming army minister in July 1940 and then prime minister in October 1941, he built a reputation as a hardworking and very efficient staff officer. He favored technical innovation and modernization over emphasis on the unique spiritual qualities of the Japanese soldier. Tōjō was one of the "new" officers who had not experienced the humiliations of the early and middle Meiji period. And while he was not a member of the Imperial Way faction *(kōdōha)* whose adherents placed the *kokutai* above "mere" technical considerations, Tōjō was among the influential officers in the Imperial Army who favored direct military action to "protect" Japanese interests in China. Whatever their factional affiliation, Tōjō and his army colleagues were highly educated in the modern technology of war and equally well indoctrinated in the ideology of *kokutai* and the supposed superiority of the Japanese spirit *(yamato-damashii)*. They advocated sweeping changes in Japanese society to prepare for total war—a war they were sure they would win.

In the mid-1920s Tōjō participated in a weekly discussion group with men like Nagata Tetsuzan who wanted total mobilization, Suzuki Teiichi who advocated a new state in Manchuria separate from China's administration, and Kōmoto Daisuke who would have disenfranchised the Chinese there. Also present was the well-known right-wing officer Ishiwara Kanji.[9] Tōjō and these officers were members of the Futaba-kai (named after a restaurant in Shibuya where they met). They opposed the conservative army leadership that was dominated by the Chōshū clique. Tōjō's group met at the end of 1928 with another society, the Kokusaku Kenkyūkai (National Policy Study Association), and heard Ishiwara on "The Nature of War" and debated policy in Manchuria and Mongolia. The two groups merged formally on 19 May 1929 to form the Issekikai, an officer's society for the purification and militarization of Japan. Important members included Ishiwara, Nagata, Suzuki, Kōmoto, Tōjō, Doihara Kenji, Okamoto Yasuji, and Yamashita Tomoyuki.[10] Some say they supported in one way or another one of their colleagues, Kōmoto, who successfully managed the plot to kill Chang Tso-lin in 1928.[11] But they are not to be equated with those who advocated fighting with "human bullets" *(nikudan)* rather than those of metal. This comes from the thinking of General Araki Sadao, as seen especially in his *Kōgun no hongi* (Basic Principles of the Imperial Army), issued in 1928. He inaugurated the use of the term "emperor's army" *(kōgun)* and had words such as "surrender," "retreat," and "defense" removed from this manual. His new *Tōsui kōryō* (General Principles of Strategic Command) "became the official doctrine of the 'imperial army' and remained so until 1945. Araki's efforts ensured the priority of morale over equipment."[12]

Tōjō's basic thinking agreed with the militarism advocated by these men but not their unrealistic reaction to "Japan's 'insufficient numbers of troops and scant resources.' " His bent can be seen in his subsequent activities. Just prior to the second Manchurian Incident in 1931, for example, Tōjō was made chief of the Organization and Mobilization Section in the Imperial Army General Staff. At that time he objected to the last sentence of a proposed directive from the Army Ministry to the commander of the Kwantung Army, a sentence that said: "Your military action should be confined within limits prescribed by the need to maintain public order."[13] Tōjō and Imamura Hitoshi, chief of the General Staff Operations Section, wanted it eliminated. But Army Vice Minister Sugiyama Hajime said the sentence represented the army minister's thinking correctly and must be retained.[14] Not only does the objection by Tōjō and Imamura reflect the prevailing sentiments of most field officers in the Imperial Army at that time; it also shows Tōjō's impulsive predilection for using force to settle issues.

Many years later, during his term as prime minister, Tōjō was often charged with willfully using his power in a brutal manner. These charges, as we shall see, are not without grounds. At the same time, while acknowledging the importance of his military training, his aggressive attitudes, and those of his fellow officers, one cannot deny that the emperor and Japanese tradition were at the center of his considerations—and that with respect to the imperial tradition he always acted in good conscience. Yet his conscience was not infused with traditional classical concepts of right and wrong. What this means—and the meaning of Japan's historical tradition to Tōjō—can be seen in one of the private sources on Tōjō: the diary of his secretary, Col. Akamatsu Sadao.

Tōjō and the Imperial Tradition

Slightly less than a week after Tōjō resigned all his offices in the summer of 1944 he visited five of the most important prewar monuments to the imperial tradition: Ise Shrine, Kashiwara Shrine, the imperial tomb at Fushimi-Momoyama, Minase Shrine, and the ruins of Sakurai Station.[15] A series of monologues by Tōjō at this time was recorded by Akamatsu, and they reveal the character and depth of his convictions. Before taking up these monologues, one must first consider the significance of these places in prewar Japanese culture. Their importance was due to their role in symbolizing specific aspects of the imperial tradition—the same tradition Hirohito was taught to embody and protect. The following synopsis is important to understanding the common ground of conviction shared by Tōjō and the emperor.

The first monument, Ise, is the most holy shrine in Japan. Here the Sun Goddess Amaterasu Ōmikami, the highest god of the Shinto pantheon, is enshrined. According to classical Japanese mythology her grandson descended to earth and founded the Japanese empire. The shrine was founded in prehistoric times; the exact date is unknown. The *Nihon Shoki*, a history of Japan completed in 720, records that the shrine was founded in the year 5 B.C. during the reign of Emperor Suinin (29 B.C.?–A.D. 70?).[16] As noted in Chapter 5 the dates and events from this era are totally fictitious, but it is unlikely that many people in Imperial Japan before the end of August 1945 questioned them.[17] After the Meiji Restoration in 1868, Ise was called simply "the Shrine" *(jingū)*, denoting its importance. Other shrines were always referred to by their individual names—for example, Kashiwara Shrine or Meiji Shrine. Only Ise was called "the Shrine," and only after the Meiji Restoration. There are no earlier precedents for this practice in Japanese history.

The Kashiwara Shrine, the second monument, is the place where, according to Japanese tradition, the first emperor Jimmu-Tennō (660–585 B.C.?) ascended the throne. (Japanese emperors are "crowned" in a sort of communion ceremony, the *daijōsai*.)[18] Although it is a holy memorial built in the memory of this mythological figure and his spouse, the shrine is not a monument with origins reaching back into the dark recesses of prehistory. It was first completed in 1889, the year the Meiji Constitution was promulgated. The cult surrounding Emperor Jimmu was intimately associated with the ideology about the imperial house propagated by Japanese government leaders after 1868. From the Meiji period until the end of World War II, Jimmu's enthronement day, 11 February according to the *Nihon Shoki*, was a national holiday, Foundation Day *(Kigensetsu)*.[19] For obvious reasons this holiday was canceled by occupation authorities after the war. But it was reinstituted in 1966 by the government as National Memorial Day *(Kokka Kinenbi)* despite strong protests and demonstrations against it.[20] Fushimi-Momoyamaryō, the third monument, is where the Meiji emperor is buried. The emperor was (and for many still is) the symbol of Japan's modernization and rise to international prominence. He was Hirohito's grandfather and appears to have stamped the conservative character of his grandson's education. In going there Tōjō may have underlined his devotion to the imperial line.

These three places were among the foremost religious centers in

Japan up to the end of the Pacific War. But visiting them did not necessarily make Tōjō a religious man or a nationalistic fanatic. He was simply doing what was expected of a statesman in Imperial Japan when withdrawing from public life. Although one cannot say whether these pilgrimages were important to him, reflecting his own convictions, the other two memorials he visited—Minase Jingū and Sakurai Station—had without doubt great meaning for him personally. This is clear, not only from what they represented, but from what he said during the visits. Minase Shrine is a memorial to three emperors from the middle ages: Gotoba (1180–1239, r. 1183–1198), Tsuchimikado (1195–1231, r. 1198–1201), and Juntoku (1197–1242, r. 1210–1221). All three emperors were treated very poorly by the military leaders of that day and finally were banished from Kyoto by them. Sakurai Station, the fifth monument, is a memorial to the failed supporter of another emperor, Godaigo (1288–1339, r. 1318–1339), who was banished and later forced to abdicate by the foremost military man of his day, Ashikaga Takauji (1305–1358). It may seem strange that Tōjō would honor such figures. But Tōjō, as we shall see, was an army officer who was devoted to the Japanese imperial house, not the military. Gotoba, Godaigo, and his supporter Kusunoki Masashige were all involved in imperial restorations that failed. Only the Meiji Restoration succeeded. No doubt Tōjō's interest in these figures stems from this situation, and they are treated at length here to illustrate the nature of Tōjō's devotion to the throne.

Emperor Gotoba: Japan's First Imperial Restoration

Emperor Gotoba was on the throne when Minamoto no Yoritomo (1147–1199) was granted his long-sought title, Seiitai Shōgun, the first shogun who effectively ruled all Japan.[21] This took place in 1192 when Gotoba was only twelve years old. Up to this time his grandfather, Goshirakawa (1127–1192, r. 1155–1158), who as retired emperor had manipulated political affairs from behind the throne, had been able to resist granting Yoritomo this title and official authority.[22] After the death of the retired emperor, though, his grandson Gotoba was unable to deny the overlord in Kamakura his prize. The position of the imperial house was especially weak because the emperor was still very young and his regent, Kujō no Kanezane (1149–1207), supported Yoritomo's claim. Kanezane, who led the Fujiwara clan, hoped in this way to improve the political position of his house. Moreover, the Minamotos had defeated their archrivals among the military clans, the Taira, and no one was strong enough to oppose the wishes of Yoritomo.

In 1198 Gotoba, intent on correcting what had been forced on him as a youth, abdicated and placed his three-year-old son, Tsuchimikado, on the throne in an effort to increase his political influence as his grandfather had done. Yoritomo was not pleased by this move.[23] He well understood what the emperor was attempting to do, but he died before he could act. His fears proved to be well founded, as Gotoba indeed sought in 1221 to "restore" imperial rule. At this time he felt the time was right to dislodge the Hōjōs who had succeeded the Minamoto in Kamakura. This proved to be a major miscalculation. The emperor found almost no support for his campaign and was quickly defeated by the Hōjōs.[24] Gotoba, his son, and his grandson were then sent into exile far from Kyoto. This was the ultimate punishment for a noble in the middle ages because life began and ended for them in the capital. Outside of Kyoto there was no culture or "Japanese civilization" as such. They had no social life, no friends, and were often all but forgotten in Heian society. Banishment was therefore tantamount to a sentence of death. (For this reason, perhaps, among the nobility there was no death sentence for crimes or rebellions. Banishment from the capital was sufficient.)

Eight centuries later General Tōjō Hideki, who had just resigned all his offices after ruling Imperial Japan almost single-handed for nearly three years, was moved by the fate of these medieval aristocrats. Colonel Akamatsu, Tōjō's secretary, who accompanied him on these visits, has described his chief's mood at the shrine commemorating the ill-fated Gotoba and his immediate progeny:

> Tōjō's own thoughts seemed to return to the sad fate of these three emperors in the middle ages. Inside the shrine there is an elegant tea room that was built in the time of Retired Emperor Gomizuno-o [1596–1680, r. 1611–1629]. Also there is a pond in the form of the Chinese character for heart (*kokoro*). In the garden were some withered China-aster chrysanthemums. [*Miyakowasure* in Japanese, an alternative word for *noshingiku*, China-aster chrysanthemum. The reading "*miyakowasure*," translated literally, means "forget the capital."][25]

In retrospect the imperial insurrection of 1221 appears at once spectacular and pathetic. This is probably what aroused Tōjō's sympathy. Still it is noteworthy that he was not proud of the founders of Japan's military tradition but, rather, sympathetic to the dishonored imperial house. The parallels between his own recent experience, that of the three sovereigns of the thirteenth century, and the popular name of the flowers in the garden are not to be overlooked. At the same time one should not assume that he was comparing himself with these emperors. For him the imperial house was sacrosanct. As the imperial tradition embodied the holy origins of the Japanese empire, such a comparison would have been sacrilegious.

Tōjō's religiouslike devotion to the imperial house was demonstrated many times before these shrine visits. His agenda while prime minister included an unusual number of visits to Ise, Yasukuni, and other Shinto shrines associated with the imperial house, illustrating his belief in the imperial tradition.[26] He also expressed this conviction privately on numerous occasions. For example:

> The emperor is a holy being *(shinkaku)*. We subjects, regardless of how important we become, cannot overcome our existence as human beings *(jinkaku)*. [Compared with the emperor] even the prime minister is unimportant.[27]

The imperial house was untouchable, unattainable, and unfathomable for ordinary people. This conviction can be clearly seen during his next visit, to the Sakurai Station.

Emperor Godaigo: Japan's Second Imperial Restoration

The Sakurai Station is connected in popular folklore with another imperial insurrection at the beginning of the fourteenth century. As a text from that day, the *Taiheiki*, informs us, the reigning emperor Godaigo proclaimed an imperial restoration in 1331.[28] Although he had more support than his predecessor in 1221, in the end he too was defeated. The main opponent of this restoration was the founder of the next shogunate, Ashikaga Takauji. During this conflict the emperor was obliged to leave Kyoto a number of times. On one occasion he was banished to the island of Oki in the Sea of Japan.

The emperor's primary supporter was one Kusunoki Masashige (d. 1336), a warrior from a relatively unknown and unimportant family. Inspired by a vision, he rallied to Godaigo's side. Kusunoki was able to turn the tide temporarily in favor of the emperor, winning a number of battles, including a major victory at Chihaya Castle in 1333.[29] He was finally defeated in a battle on the banks of the Minato River, however, and obliged to commit seppuku. Prior to this defeat, which was a foregone conclusion, he supposedly said farewell to his son at the Sakurai Station before following the emperor's orders and going into a battle he was certain to lose. Shortly thereafter Emperor Godaigo was forced to turn over the three imperial regalia to a successor, Emperor Kōmyō (1321–1380, r. 1336–1348), who had been chosen by the victor, the new shogun. Barely seven months after Kusunoki's death Godaigo fled the capital for the final time and established a rival court in the Yoshino

Mountains about 80 kilometers south of Kyoto. This was the beginning of the period of northern and southern courts, which lasted until 1392.

Kusunoki's loyalty to the imperial house in the fourteenth century was often held up in the twentieth as a fine example of devotion to the imperial house and government.[30] No doubt this was the reason for Tōjō's interest in Kusunoki and the Sakurai Station. The preceding outline follows the story found in the accepted authoritative text, the *Taiheiki*. The issue here is not its historical accuracy but its importance for people like Tōjō in Imperial Japan.

Kusunoki: Model of Loyalty

The Kusunoki tradition was widely taught and accepted in Japan prior to the end of 1945. The tales in the *Taiheiki*, especially the one about Emperor Godaigo's stalwart samurai, enjoyed increasing popularity during the Tokugawa period (1603–1868), and Kusunoki became a model of loyalty to the imperial house to be emulated even then.[31] It was propagated by, among others, the famous haiku poet Matsuo Bashō (1644–1694). It was further popularized during the years before and after the restoration in 1868, for obvious reasons, and continued to be propagated thereafter. The broad acceptance of the Kusunoki tradition is demonstrated by the variety of persons supporting it: the educator and founder of Keiō University, Fukuzawa Yukichi, for example, and General Nogi Maresuke. Fukuzawa was a leading intellectual; General Nogi was the army hero of the Russo-Japanese War, universally respected as a model of military discipline during the late Meiji period.

This hallowed tradition was not to be questioned. Two professors were censured during the Meiji period, for example, for challenging its historicity. These two Tokyo Imperial University scholars, Shigeno Yasutsugu (1827–1910) and Kume Kunitake (1839–1931), were out of step with the times. Shigeno opposed the use of history for moralizing; Kume emphasized the need for objective research on old documents; both pointed out that the *Taiheiki* story about Kusunoki could not possibly be true because Masashige's son in the famous farewell scene must have been well over ten years old. For his trouble Professor Shigeno was dubbed "Dr. Debunker" (Massatsu Hakushi) by his colleagues,[32] and both were eventually forced by Shinto nationalists to resign their positions.[33]

Kume, at least, was not totally oblivious to his intellectual surroundings. He claimed he only wanted to provide Shinto with a modern theoretical base so it could weather the storm of modernization.

And as we shall see, this trend among a few sophisticated scholars was adopted by Hirohito's ethics teacher as well as his teacher of history. Indeed, Hirohito supported constitutional monarchy for similar reasons—to legitimate in a modern way the imperial tradition. Such debates, to be sure, were confined to academicians. It is unlikely that Tōjō even knew about them. Tōjō was acquainted with the Kusunoki tradition because the warrior was a highly venerated figure in late Meiji Japan when Tōjō was a youth. Moreover, Tōjō appears to have had personal reasons for his admiration of Kusunoki. His father is reported to have been known as a Kusunoki scholar.[34]

Kusunoki ideology was pushed to extremes between 1868 and August 1945. The ideal was widely accepted in the Shōwa emperor's Japan because, among other reasons, it had a prominent position in the school textbooks that were standardized and distributed by the central government beginning in 1903.[35] These were the texts studied by the adults of the early Shōwa period when they were children. Once again, the purpose of this instruction was to "spread the faith," not teach history.

This purpose can be seen in what was taught, how it was taught, and the texts selected to do the teaching. Although the author of the classical text describing the insurrection at the beginning of the thirteenth century, Jien, was a contemporary of the principals—Shogun Minamoto no Yoritomo, Retired Emperor Gotoba, his opponents the Hōjōs—and in addition was the younger brother of Regent Kujō Kanezane, his description of these events was ignored by the imperial government. Jien wrote his history by way of advising Gotoba not to try what he finally in fact attempted with such a spectacular lack of success: an imperial restoration. Jien was openly critical of the imperial house of his day and the idea of imperial dominion. This stance was not approved of by the custodians of imperial rule in Imperial Japan, especially in the 1930s and 1940s.

By contrast, the same leaders found the text from the fourteenth century, the *Taiheiki*, very much to their liking. Although its authors were not much concerned with Kusunoki's role in Godaigo's insurrection, they praised the emperor and his plans. Accordingly, the few places where Kusunoki is mentioned were cited with ever increasing frequency and in a variety of ways in official schoolbooks after 1903.[36] Although the content of the schoolbooks between 1890 and 1900 when Tōjō was in grade school varied from place to place,[37] it is clear that instruction was slanted in this imperialist direction. In other words: Tōjō was indoctrinated with teachings about the preeminent position of the imperial house in Japan much as Hirohito later would be. And these common convictions laid the foundation for their mutual respect and cooperation in the future.

Tōjō's exposure to the Kusunoki tradition began at home with his father and probably was reinforced by the public education system. Certainly many young people were similarly educated without becoming a Tōjō Hideki, but there are certain similarities between the traditional description of Kusunoki's activities and the role Tōjō was to play during and immediately after the war. At the time of his "pilgrimage" to the Sakurai Station, Tōjō had this to say about Kusunoki:

> I believe that Prince Kusunoki is the most superlative person in the world. Napoleon and others cannot be compared with him. With the imperial house above, he always evaluated the overall state of affairs in the world correctly. As a tactician he was number one among us mortals, and as a statesman he was number one among us mortals. Naturally the emperor is not included here [since for Tōjō he was not an ordinary mortal]. I am only speaking about the emperor's subjects. . . . In the difficult battle at Chihaya Castle he fulfilled the role of a brilliant military tactician, but Prince Kusunoki not only defended the castle as a military tactician. With conviction he gathered loyal troops from all over the land for this battle to the death, and they fought hard. I believe that Kusunoki fought as a statesman for a great principle.[38]

The great principle for which Tōjō thought Kusunoki fought may be seen in Articles 1 and 3 of the Meiji Constitution:

> Article 1. The Empire of Japan shall be reigned over and governed by a line of Emperors unbroken for ages eternal.
>
> Article 3. The Emperor is sacred and inviolable.[39]

Kusunoki's loyalty to the imperial house was an ideal to be exemplified. Like Kusunoki, Tōjō came from a military family, but both were military men by choice and became prominent due to their own talents and achievements. Both were thoroughly convinced of the sublime nature of the imperial house. Tōjō, for example, was head of the military police (Kempeitai) in Manchuria in February 1936 when the young officers attempted their putsch—proclaiming a Shōwa Restoration against the express wishes of the emperor. Before waiting to see which way the wind would blow, according to the historian Robert Butow, Tōjō arrested all known sympathizers in his area of jurisdiction.[40] But before praising Tōjō's loyalty or legalism too highly, one must remember that the situation was rather more complicated. Apparently those investigated and later arrested were almost all from the Imperial Way faction, which Tōjō opposed.[41] Even so, there are parallels between Tōjō's forthright actions and those of the historical figure he admired.

Kusunoki rallied to Godaigo's cause in 1331 (Eighth Month) when the emperor first escaped from the capital. In 1333, when the battle at Chihaya Castle against the Kamakura regime's forces was prolonged by Kusunoki's skilled tactics, other military lords including Ashikaga Takauji, sensing an opportunity to increase their power, turned against their former lords and allies and sided with the emperor. Later Takauji turned again—against the emperor. He was initially defeated and driven to Kyūshū in 1336 (Second Month), and Kusunoki entered the capital with Godaigo who celebrated a complete victory. Kusunoki was at the height of his power and fame. Sensing, however, that Takauji would again raise troops and try to defeat the emperor's forces in order to become shogun, Kusunoki tried to negotiate a peace with him. Takauji rejected his offers. Several months later, on the 25th Day, Fifth Month, 1336, he defeated Kusunoki decisively at the Minato River engagement, subsequently drove Godaigo from the capital, and placed his own emperor on the throne.

There is no direct connection, of course, but one notes that in a similar manner the emperor and Tōjō were celebrated late in 1941 and early in 1942 when the Imperial Army and Navy experienced their rash of successes at the beginning of the Pacific War. Later, after Tōjō had been driven from office (July 1944) and Japan was for all intents and purposes defeated, everyone turned against him. In the face of this adversity he remained faithful to the imperial house. He went through a war crimes trial whose outcome was a foregone conclusion.[42] Like a modern Kusunoki, and unlike the others who were similarly indicted, he asserted unequivocally his personal responsibility for wartime decisions and protected the emperor from implication and possible prosecution.

One might assume that Tōjō, along with the emperor, was devoted to constitutional monarchy and only accepted responsibility for his actions as prime minister within that framework. In view of his education, career, and professed beliefs, however, it seems unlikely that the principles of British, or Prussian, constitutional monarchy were the source of Tōjō's convictions and his resolve. Tōjō was schooled in the use of Western military tactics to protect Imperial Japan. He had not been schooled in the use of Western political theory to protect himself or anyone else.

Others less sympathetic to Tōjō portray him quite differently. He was known as an efficient officer and as an extremely willful man who was able to prevail over others. Tōjō was not called "The Razor" *(kami-sori)* without reason.[43] During Tōjō's tenure as army minister in the third Konoe cabinet, for example, General Sugiyama was army chief of staff. According to Hara Shirō, a former member of the Imperial Army general staff and military historian, the relative influence of these two leading officers, army minister and chief of staff, was very much dependent on the incumbents themselves. In 1940–1941 one would normally expect Sugiyama to have had more power than Tōjō, who was five years his junior. Tōjō should have deferred to Sugiyama—his *sempai*, his elder associate. This, however, was not the case, due to Tōjō's willful nature.[44]

Tōjō was also known for his flinty tenacity outside of army circles. His obstinacy was the main reason for the discord between him and Konoe during his term of office in Konoe's cabinet. His reverence for the imperial tradition led him to identify his own policies with it, which in turn sparked extremely aggressive behavior and, on occasion, merciless suppression of anyone who opposed him. A prominent contemporary critic who saw him simply as a ruthless general and politician wrote of his conduct as prime minister: "Accustoming oneself to power [as Tōjō did] is a terrible thing."[45] These two aspects of Tōjō's character—identifying his will with the imperial will and ruthless treatment of his opponents—were especially apparent during his term as prime minister.

Tōjō the Champion

When Tōjō Hideki was appointed prime minister he was, like most men in a similar situation, moved by the new responsibilities that had been thrust upon him. He had not sought the office. Having caused the fall of the last Konoe cabinet in which he had served as army minister, he expected a quick end to his political career. Instead the emperor and his political adviser, Kido Kōichi, selected him to succeed Konoe as the only person eligible for the office who might be able to control the military. ("Controlling the military" did not necessarily mean avoiding war. It meant that Tōjō was to uphold the constitution and the imperial dignity: the army and navy were not to act unilaterally without securing imperial approval as had happened in the past.) Tōjō, suitably impressed with the weight of his new office, went immediately to pray at three important shrines in Tokyo: Meiji Jingū, Tōgō Jinja, and Yasukuni Jinja.[46] According to critical contemporary observers, this humility was just a passing phase and he soon became dictatorial:

After the first great successes of the [Pacific] war Tōjō became very high-handed. He only had very banal people around him, base fellows from the Kempeitai, and he gradually became a military autocrat.[47]

These critics cite the following episode as an example. In June 1942 the Japanese fleet was defeated in the Battle of Midway. Tōjō decided, against the recommendations of his advisers, that the defeat should not be revealed to the public. General Tanaka Ryūkichi, head of the Army Administrative Department, reportedly said to Tōjō at the time:

It is better not to hide the truth. It should be told to the people. The Japanese people, for better or worse, are in their grief a courageous folk. Telling the truth is the best way to build up the people's spirit.[48]

Tōjō is supposed to have answered this suggestion cynically:

The people are stupid. If told the truth, in fact it would discourage them.[49]

Tanaka was an outspoken enemy of Tōjō's who actively worked against him during the war crimes trials in Tokyo. He wrote these words after the war, and the reliability of such descriptions is questionable.[50] On the day after the defeat at Midway, Monday, 8 June 1942, Tōjō's appointment calendar shows he went with the navy minister to the Meiji and Yasukuni shrines.[51] The reason for the visits is not noted, but one can well imagine that at the first shrine they apologized to the Meiji emperor's spirit for the defeat and at the second they prayed for the souls of those killed in battle. Afterward he went to the Army Ministry—he was concomitantly minister of the army—and later had lunch with the chief of staff and other army leaders. No mention is made of the confrontation with General Tanaka, and no mention is made about concealing the defeat from the public.

This does not mean Tōjō did not issue such orders. The Tōjō Agenda is more an appointment book than a diary, and the subjects discussed during his appointments are not systematically recorded in it. Moreover, many others shared Tanaka's opinion about Tōjō. The commander of the Tokyo Kempeitai cited earlier wrote, for example, that Tōjō was an autocratic prime minister. He believed the people simply had to accept the government's explanations. When they resisted he insisted that they should be pressured and made to conform. In short, he governed in a manner that clearly had nothing to do with constitutional monarchy. And, further, he availed himself of dubious help in pursuing his policies:

In 1943 and 1944 covert whispers in the Army Ministry told of the "three intriguers" *(sankan)* and "four blockheads" *(shigu)*. They were the leaders who stood by Tōjō. As for the three intriguers, they changed from time to time, but Suzuki Teiichi and Lieutenant General Katō, chief of the General Affairs Department, were continually in attendance. The third person was usually either Hoshino [Naoki 1892–1987, cabinet secretary] or the commander of the Tokyo Kempeitai, Colonel Shikata [Ryōji].[52]

Using these unscrupulous characters Tōjō supposedly pressured his political opponents or simply had them removed from the scene. A good example of the latter tactic is the case of Nakano Seigō (1886–1943), a journalist, right-wing politician, and founder of the Tōhōkai (Far Eastern Society).[53]

Tōjō versus Nakano

On 20 December 1942, Nakano made a speech at the public hall in Hibiya Park. In it he warned his audience about a worsening of the war and criticized the lack of control over government bureaucrats. He did this despite an official ban on all antigovernment speeches. On New Years Day 1943, Nakano went even further. He published in one of the leading newspapers in Japan, the *Tokyo Asahi Shimbun,* a strong criticism of Tōjō entitled "The Problem with the Wartime Prime Minister" (Senji saishōron). The newspaper was confiscated immediately. In the article he said:

> The crisis-time prime minister must by all means be strong. But the strength of one individual has its limits. In order, as prime minister, to truly play the role of a strong man, he empathizes with the patriotic zeal of the people. Sometimes it is necessary to inspire them; at other times he is encouraged by them. . . . The Great Empire of Imperial Japan has at its peak an incomparable imperial house. Being grateful, the crisis-time prime minister must not lack exemplary courage, and he must fulfill his obligations. Also, even if the crisis-time prime minister of Japan is exceptionally dedicated he may not willfully take advantage of his high reputation. The crisis-time prime minister of Japan should put the endangered fatherland above all else. If he completely disregards his own interests, courage will come of itself.[54]

At the beginning of the article Nakano quotes the statesmen Clemenceau, Hindenburg, Ludendorff, Lenin, Napoleon, and others to show that a wartime prime minister must be very strong. Indirectly he refers to two figures well known in Japan: Chu Ko Liang (also known as K'ung Ming, 181–234) and Katsura Tarō (1847–1913). Chu Ko Liang was a faithful public official in Shu (China) during the Three Dynasties period, and with his oblique reference Nakano was advising Tōjō that he should tell the truth, acknowledge his responsibility for the shortcomings of his administration, and withdraw from public life. Katsura Tarō was a general and politician during the Meiji era. After noting

Katsura's outstanding leadership during the Russo-Japanese War, Nakano remarked that although some thought Katsura was arrogant, in fact he was deeply loyal and self-effacing. These references, however indirect, were understood as a sharp attack on Prime Minister Tōjō.

Later, as other statements of opposition became linked with Nakano's name, Tōjō decided to punish him. Such is obvious from a description of a meeting held on 24 October 1943 in the prime minister's official residence. Although this meeting is described in Tōjō's appointment book (the source followed here), Ōtani Keijirō, a former high-ranking Kempeitai officer, offers a detailed account of the conference that is much more critical of Tōjō. (See Appendix 3 for a comparison of sources.) Briefly Nakano, who was a Diet member, had been arrested because Tōjō thought his criticism of the government played into the enemy's hands. Tōjō was doing his best for all the people, and Nakano's continuing interference could not be tolerated any longer. Finally, after three to four hours of acrimonious debate, it was decided that the matter should be investigated further. (Ōtani says it was agreed that Nakano should be released if he could not be brought to confess in the course of the following morning. After the conference ended Tōjō asked a police inspector and Kempeitai Colonel Shikata once again if there was not some way to bring down Nakano. When the inspector demurred, Tōjō turned to the colonel, who gave him a clear answer: "Leave it to me!")[55]

Nakano was kept under arrest. The following day, after the interrogation had been concluded, Nakano asked the attending Kempeitai officer to be allowed to speak with his superior. Nakano then met with Colonel Shikata and told him he would cease his opposition so that one could present the enemy with a united front. He asked Colonel Shikata to "put the beads on the abacus back to the starting point." The colonel replied that he would consider the proposal. Nakano then was allowed to leave. A Kempeitai officer accompanied him on his way home, and Nakano asked the officer about the prospects of his request. Well aware of Tōjō's attitude, the man answered that he could not say anything definite but things did not look good. Nakano was taken aback and on the same night he committed suicide.[56]

No one can say for certain why Nakano took his own life. The investigating Kempeitai officer said, according to Ōtani, that during the interrogation Nakano was concerned about his second son. Perhaps he was worried because, as a Diet member, the authorities might not be able to touch him but could draft his son into the army. There, as the son of an opponent of the military, he would be subject to considerable repression and most certainly would receive a dangerous front-line assignment. Supporting this supposition is the fact that Colonel Shikata later maintained that the Kempeitai had brought Nakano to this extreme. He was proud, he said, to accept the responsibility for causing the anxiety that prompted Nakano to commit suicide.[57]

Tōjō the Autocrat and Servant of the Emperor

Behind the Kempeitai colonel, Tōjō stood in the wings. According to his critics, if the prime minister had not persecuted Nakano, Shikata and the Kempeitai would not have pursued him. But these two sources —notes kept by one of Tōjō's confidants and a book by a Kempeitai officer who clearly belonged to an opposing faction in the army—show that it is easier to condemn a historical figure than it is to get the record straight. Probably there is an element of truth as well as exaggeration in both accounts. Tōjō was known for his forthright manner. That was what the emperor valued in him. No doubt the same manner appeared "autocratic" to others. One should not forget that the emperor and Tōjō's critics saw him from very different perspectives. He stood above many of those who feared and criticized him. Since Tōjō at that time was not only prime minister but also army minister, opposing colleagues had reason to be afraid of him. The emperor did not.

Tōjō no doubt felt threatened politically by Nakano. But his personal justification for repressing opposition leaders like Nakano was the need to present the enemy with a united front. This meant, ultimately, protecting the imperial line. Quite possibly, then, his extreme measures can be traced back to his belief in the emperor, meaning the emperor system.[58] He never expressed these convictions in public. Only with the war crimes trial in Tokyo were they brought to light. The records of his secretaries during the war, however, indicate that his was not a new set of beliefs found, for whatever reason, after the war.

Tōjō described the role of a loyal Japanese politician to his secretaries a number of times. Colonel Akamatsu recorded his words on one such occasion:

> The emperor is behind everything, and standing in his noble light, we first come to be respected by the people. I have heard that in conducting politics it used to be important for a statesman to apprehend the will of the people, to formulate this will, and to move in the direction indicated. But this is not sufficient in Japanese politics. This means that since our people are like the children of the emperor it is important to disseminate the imperial will to all corners [of the land]. At the same time the feelings *(kokoro)* of the people, who are children, must be bound together and united with the emperor. This is certainly an important duty of the prime minister and the other ministers.[59]

These private records show that Tōjō's personal beliefs accorded with the positions he maintained in public. Although he did not write them, he did approve and issue under his name "Army Internal Ordinances" setting forth direct loyalty to the throne and unquestioning obedience to the superiors of Imperial Army officers.[60]

In 1950 the psychoanalyst Erik Erikson wrote about the German Nazis: "Hitler and his cronies used in an extremely merciless way a nation's struggle for its identity while they were the undisputed political and military leaders of this large, industrious, ambitious Folk."[61] Some say the same about Tōjō and his advisers. Others respect him as a man who did his duty and upheld Japanese tradition—the same tradition that the crown prince's teachers of ethics and history deftly transmitted to Hirohito. It is not hard to imagine that later the emperor appreciated Tōjō's efforts. Likewise one can assume that he was not totally informed of his prime minister's methods, some of which he may not have approved.

Tōjō the Victim

After the war Tōjō assumed total responsibility for Japan's wartime decisions, especially the decision to attack the United States and its allies in 1941.[62] Many think he did this because he knew his fate was sealed and therefore wished to relieve the emperor from responsibility. This policy was welcomed by the American prosecuting attorney, but it was not accepted by all of the judges sitting on the bench.[63] The Americans wanted to use the emperor for purposes that made questions of war guilt irrelevant—to ensure the obedience of the people; to make the occupation easier; to contain communism in Japan.[64] According to this theory, the American victors and a key leader of Japan's defeated military conspired together to save the emperor. But it is doubtful that Tōjō thought of himself as participating in some sort of American-made conspiracy. His actions required great resolve and self-control. And they were completely in line with his beliefs about Japan.

While Tōjō was being held in Sugamo Prison awaiting trial he told his former cabinet secretary, Hoshino Naoki, what he believed about past events and future eventualities:

> Japan's going to war was unavoidable. It was never something we wanted. Therefore, prosecuting the war should not be treated as a crime.
>
> But if the victorious powers want to treat this as a crime, all responsibility lies with me only and no one else.
>
> The emperor did everything possible to avoid the war. That it finally

came to war and war was unavoidable was due to my recommendations. That responsibility, formal as well as practical, lies with me alone.

Other persons also voiced various opinions up until the final decision was made. But the person who finally made the decision and advised the emperor accordingly was none other than I myself.

The result was a war, a war that ended with Japan's total defeat. If one believes that the fatherland has suffered damage and shame, and somehow someone must be called to account, naturally I must submit myself [for judgment].

As my last service to the nation I wish to take advantage of this opportunity and clearly state to the world that Japan never wanted to go to war.[65]

General Tōjō Hideki served the emperor faithfully before and during the war. Following Japan's defeat he did not question his own beliefs or his actions. Like Kusunoki Masashige five hundred years earlier, he defended the honor and continued existence of the emperor to the death. For Tōjō the emperor was a "holy being." He was not moved so much by the emperor's legal status in the Meiji Constitution as by his religious-historical role. Tōjō himself was not just a prime minister of a constitutional state. He acted in accord with the precedent of one of Japan's most famous, highly revered folk heroes. Like Kusunoki, Tōjō "gathered loyal troops from all over the land for this battle to the death." He believed that Kusunoki fought as a statesman for a great principle—"the emperor . . . sacred and inviolable"— and he did the same. Which is to say: Tōjō sincerely believed in the traditions concerning the imperial line propagated in prewar Japan, and he acted accordingly. This folklore meant much to him personally. In doing what he did after the war he not only defended the imperial house and the emperor, he also sought to preserve the only form of existence left to him—his memory in Japanese history.

Tōjō's War Responsibility

Loyalty was central to discussions about politics, personal relations, and individual ethics in prewar Japan. Tōjō's loyalty to the imperial house and the meaning of this loyalty to him have been described here in an effort to understand why, from a perspective amenable to his personal convictions, he did what he did. This description is not an excuse for his actions. Certainly Tōjō's unswerving devotion to duty, and to the emperor, is laudable in one sense. But insofar as "unswerving" also meant a lack of consideration for the consequences of his actions, Tōjō was irresponsible, perhaps even criminally negligent. As an army officer not only did he not question the use of force, he assumed that fighting in and of itself was good for the morale of the troops, perhaps even the nation. Moreover, he approached civil government arrogantly. As a general and prime minister he equated his policies with the imperial will, and he was determined to prevail whatever the costs. Compromise was regarded as retreat. And retreat, according to the military's code of honor, was a disgrace. Courting disaster was preferable. As Army Minister Tōjō told Prime Minister Konoe when confronted in the autumn of 1941 with a choice between humiliation (withdrawal from China) and possible defeat in a war with the Allies: "Sometimes a man has to jump from the veranda of Kiyomizu Temple with his eyes closed."[66] Tōjō jumped. But he neglected to consider the consequences for those who were obliged to jump with him.

On 1 September 1934 the Army Ministry published a pamphlet entitled "On the Essence and Improvement of National Defense" (Kokubō no hongi to sono kyōka no teishō). It begins with the statement, "War is the father of creation and the mother of civilization."[67] This epigram, which comes from Clausewitz' *On War (Vom Kriege)*, trenchantly describes the moral climate in prewar Japan: there were no social values that effectively opposed militarism.[68] General Tōjō Hideki contributed mightily to this trend—as did the emperor, as we shall see, consistent with his education and training.

5

•

Scientism, History, and Confucianism:

An Emperor's Education

The Shōwa emperor acted in prewar times not as a British constitutional monarch but as the head of the Japanese imperial line and the Japanese imperial state. In discussing his activities with respect to military planning it was indicated that they were consistent with his early education and training. In effect I am painting a picture of the prewar emperor that is different from conventional portraits. Having sketched in the foreground—the emperor's role in prewar military decision making—it is time to address the background that provided the context for this role.

Hirohito was first confronted with Japanese imperial tradition while still a baby. Born on 29 April 1901, he was entrusted just seventy days later to the care of "foster parents," Count Kawamura Sumiyoshi (1836–1904) and his wife, as was the custom in the imperial family. Kawamura, sixty-five years old at the time, was from Satsuma. A former vice admiral in the Imperial Navy and an adviser to the Privy Council, he was a military man with thoroughly Confucian convictions.[1] Hirohito remained in the Kawamura house for only three years —until 1904 when Kawamura died—and was then moved with his brother to the Eastern Palace Grounds (Tōgū-gosho) at Aoyama. At this time Kido Takamasa, the father of Kido Kōichi, Emperor Hirohito's political adviser from 1940 to 1945, was made responsible for his training at home. Retired General Nogi Maresuke (1849–1912) was eventually put in charge of the primary school he attended.

At an early age Hirohito became acquainted with the trappings of modernization as conceived in Meiji Japan—namely militarism and nationalism. Indeed many early photographs show him dressed in military uniform, and one shows him waving a Rising Sun battle flag.[2] The theoretical significance of this early indoctrination for the development of his personal character must be left to the speculation of psychologists. Here I shall confine my account to the nature and content of Hirohito's early education and training to become emperor.

Crown Prince Hirohito's education has been described as broad and comprehensive by the historian Stephen Large.[3] It has been depicted as a normal middle school education at the time, with the exception of horsemanship and military studies, by a Japanese author.[4] In fact, the future Shōwa emperor's rounded education was heavily colored by patriotic tradition. This tradition came from Japan's ancient history—that is, from histories written at the end of the seventh and beginning of the eighth centuries to glorify the origins of the imperial family and legitimize its claim as the hereditary ruling house of Japan.

In Japan ancient history is not just history. From the point of view of a modern Western observer, it has a surprising importance for contemporary politics and social ethics: the origins of houses and customs in Japan contribute significantly to their contemporary authority. For this reason, special attention is paid to ancient history in the schools —inculcating in students an acceptance of the existing order. This was especially so in Imperial Japan, and Hirohito was no less an object of this indoctrination because of his imperial status. Indeed, Japanese history and ethics were a central part of his education, and considerable time was devoted to them. Thus Hirohito's instruction in these subjects and their "modern" interpretations, a topic that has not been fully explored to date, deserves our attention.

A great deal of time and money has been spent worldwide on studies of education. The assumption is that educational content has some relation to the political and social values that influence the decisions people make as adults. According to the eminent authority S. N. Eisenstadt:

> The general societal functions of educational activities and institutions are twofold. One is the transmission of the cultural heritage of a society from generation to generation and the participation with the family in the process of socialization of the new generations. The other is the channeling and differential placement of people to those positions in society that are allocated on the basis of achievement.[5]

Beyond its obvious importance to specific studies on education, this assumption is fundamental to the consideration of broader historical issues. It is basic, for example, to the highly praised work of Carol Gluck on Meiji ideology and the works of other historians writing about Japan.[6] Scholars dealing with Meiji Japan, like the leaders of that era, are convinced of the value of education in modernizing Japan and recognize its potential as a means of indoctrination. But close examination of Hirohito's education presents us with a dilemma. Either the assumption that the values learned in school have something to do with future adult activities is erroneous or Emperor Hirohito was a striking exception to the rule.

Hirohito spent his entire childhood in the presence of military tutors and heroes. His education was planned and administered by military figures. The content was ostensibly modern, meaning in this case nationalistic and militaristic. Yet from the time he became emperor in 1926, we are told, the adult Shōwa emperor wanted nothing more than to be an English-style constitutional monarch and consistently opposed Japan's jingoistic army and navy leaders. He was especially opposed to their right-wing propaganda at home and their imperialistic ventures overseas.

At least this is what the authors of the postwar chronicles about the emperor's prewar activities would have us believe.[7] The apparent contradiction between Hirohito's training as future emperor and his activities as emperor is the starting point of this chapter. I shall demonstrate that the content of Hirohito's instruction in ethics and history was infused with conservative interpretations of ancient Japanese history and Confucian ethics—and, moreover, that these interpretations vary considerably from the sources from which they are drawn. In the following chapter I will show how foreign institutions, ancient and modern, were made to serve and enhance nationalism in Imperial Japan. With respect to the convictions and goals of the men who educated the crown prince, it is well to remember "that Japanese were not attempting to adapt themselves to the new knowledge of the West, but rather to understand and incorporate that knowledge into their received knowledge and institutions."[8]

A School for the Crown Prince

Hirohito's secondary school, called the Tōgū Gogakumonjo (Honorable Place of Learning in the Eastern Palace), usually shortened to Ogakumonjo, was established in May 1914 and disbanded in March 1921 (when the crown prince was nearly twenty). Immediately after "graduating," Hirohito departed on the battleship *Katori*, accompanied by a second warship *Kashima*, for a six-month trip to Europe. By the time he returned his father's mental debility had worsened, and in November

1921 Hirohito was formally appointed regent to the reigning emperor. He was twenty years old.

The Ogakumonjo existed for seven years for a single purpose: the education of the future emperor.[9] Altogether there were six students, Crown Prince Hirohito and five of his elementary school classmates chosen for their aristocratic birth and academic prowess. The school was founded according to principles laid down by the former army general Nogi Maresuke. General Nogi was one of the two heroes of the Russo-Japanese War (1904–1905). Despite appalling losses, his Third Army took the Russian stronghold at Port Arthur in a siege that lasted 155 days. Some 130,000 Japanese troops were involved in the fighting, of which 59,000 lay dead or wounded when it was over. The famous third assault on Hill 203 alone is said to have cost 17,000 men. Among those who died were both of Nogi's sons. When his oldest son was killed he reportedly wrote his wife, "Rejoice that Katsusuke died a glorious death in battle."[10] Nogi was known as a disciplinarian and for his devotion to the Meiji emperor. In 1907 the emperor personally appointed him head of the Peers School (Gakushūin), where Hirohito received his primary school education. His task was to instill proper discipline in the effete children of the nobility and, as well, the future emperor. He and his wife created quite a controversy when in the old samurai tradition they followed their lord in death, committing suicide on the day of Emperor Meiji's funeral ceremony.[11]

General Nogi's influence on Hirohito is widely acknowledged. The emperor himself related in 1941 an incident confirming his continuing respect for Nogi. One day on his way home from primary school he met Director Nogi by chance. Nogi asked him how he commuted to and from school, and the imperial prince answered that he walked when the weather was good and traveled by carriage when it rained. To this Nogi replied, "Even on days when it rains, put on a cloak and walk!" And the emperor commented, "I was taught at that time that luxury was not permissible, and I learned to be frugal and courageous."[12] Several days before the Meiji emperor's funeral Nogi visited Hirohito, the newly appointed crown prince. He exhorted Hirohito to study even more diligently now that he had become crown prince: "As your Highness will become a great supreme commander *(gensui)*, this area of studies must also be pursued earnestly." His suicide a scant two days later must have made a deep impression on Hirohito, who was only eleven.

The first and only director of the Ogakumonjo was the other hero of the war with the Russians, Fleet Admiral Tōgō Heihachirō (1848–1934). He commanded the Japanese force that "crossed the T" in the

Straits of Tsushima and destroyed the Russian fleet, weary from its long journey from the Baltic Sea. Tōgō had studied naval tactics in England from 1871 to 1878, and his flagship in 1905, the *Mikasa,* was of British construction. He was well acquainted with developments in the West, and during a visit to England in 1911 he dismissed the idea of a war between the United States and Japan as "mere moonshine."[13] Yet Akiyama Saneyuki, who was on Tōgō's staff and had devised his attack plan at Tsushima, drew up a plan for a possible war with the United States that was officially adopted in 1907. This plan was to influence strategy in the Imperial Navy for many years to come.[14]

Tōgō served as rector of Hirohito's school continuously until it was closed. Afterward he was an éminence grise in naval circles, and from behind the scenes he vigorously opposed those in Japan who wished to accept America's proposals at the 1930 London Naval Conference. At the Ogakumonjo, Tōgō's influence on Hirohito is difficult to ascertain. On the one hand, neither he nor Nogi should be equated with the ultranationalists who dominated the military in the 1930s and 1940s. On the other, they were specifically appointed to these posts to control the climate of instruction at the schools the crown prince attended. Perhaps they did not regulate the content of specific courses, but the civilian teachers and professors were no doubt impressed by the official presence of these two military leaders. Moreover, Tōgō was especially interested in imperial ethics, appears to have approved the appointment of Hirohito's ethics teacher personally, and attended his lectures often.[15] More important, Hirohito learned through these examples to respect the authority of men in uniform.

A range of subjects was studied at the school: ethics, Japanese language and literature *(kokubun),* Chinese-Japanese *(kanbun),* history, geography, physiography, mathematics, physics, natural history, French, calligraphy, art history, law and economics, martial arts *(buka),* gymnastics, horsemanship, and special lectures on military affairs. Except for the special military lectures and horsemanship, these were the same subjects studied in most middle schools at that time. French was chosen for the crown prince instead of English because it was the language of the aristocracy.[16]

Sugiura Shigetake: The Ethics Instructor

The persons selected to instruct the crown prince were important men: a former minister of education, the president of Tokyo Imperial University, and numerous Imperial University professors, all experts in their fields. They were prominent government officials, leaders in education, or had served in the military with distinction—all except the man charged with ethics *(rinri)* instruction, Sugiura Shigetake (Jūgō, 1855–1924). Sugiura was head of Nippon Middle School (Nippon Chū-gakkō kōchō), a prep school for Tokyo Imperial University. He was a well-known educator, had written widely for various newspapers, and had been a bureaucrat in the Ministry of Education.

There was some difficulty in finding an appropriate person to con-duct this course because the professors at the imperial universities were deemed unsuitable for one reason or another. Sugiura was finally rec-ommended by the president of Tokyo Imperial University and took up his duties, officially termed "Imperial Studies" (Teiōgaku), over a month after the school had started.[17] Apparently Hirohito was pleased by his lectures, because he later requested that Sugiura tutor his future wife in private. This instruction continued for several years after the school was disbanded. In fact, during the last ten years of his teaching career one could say that Sugiura had only two students—the future emperor and empress of Japan.[18] The influence of his teaching is a matter of debate, but at least one author has written that "Sugiura's ideas about imperial ethics had an incalculable impact on Hirohito's intellectual development."[19]

Sugiura's Lectures

The content of the ethics lectures was, on the surface, of great variety. The imperial tradition was emphasized for the crown prince in obvi-ous topics like the imperial regalia, Mount Fuji, the military, shrines, rice, and sumo but also in less obvious topics including time, water, George Washington (1732–1799), and Emperor Wilhelm II of Germany (1859–1941). In the introduction to his lectures Sugiura wrote that they were based on three main ideas: the three imperial regalia (san-shu no shingi) as the basis for the Imperial Way *(kōdō)*; the Meiji Charter Oath of 1868 (Gojō no Goseibun) as a standard for the future; and fulfillment of the imperial will expressed in the Imperial Rescript on Education of 1890 (Kyōiku [ni kansuru] Chokugo).[20] Sugiura then explained what he meant by these ideas.

First: The three imperial regalia (sword, jewel, and mirror), together with the rescript promulgated by the Sun Goddess when her grandson descended to earth, are the foundation of the Japanese nation and the source of the "national polity" *(kokutai)*. The three virtues embodied by the three imperial regalia—wisdom, benevolence, and courage—are the guiding principles for leading the nation and ruling the people. Japa-nese emperors have always abided by these principles, thereby mani-festing the virtue and influence of the imperial ancestors throughout history. With these virtues as the basis of the imperial house, it prospers eternally and disseminates its influence to all corners of the world. In the future the prosperity of the imperial house, which rules the country, can be assured only by abiding by this inheritance from the imperial ancestors and by realizing the Imperial Way.[21]

Second: The Meiji Charter Oath, Sugiura explained, was issued when rule was restored to the imperial court in 1868. Since the Kamakura period (1185–1333) political power in Japan had been in the hands of the military houses. The first act of the new imperial government was to formulate a new policy and make an oath to the gods of heaven and earth. This was the Five-Article Meiji Charter Oath. Accordingly, a constitution was promulgated and a parliament established. The ancient dignity of Japan was restored, and all government matters were directed toward accomplishing the intentions of this oath. This was true, not only in the Meiji period, but also in the present Taishō era. Therefore the future emperor, who is to unify and supervise *(suberu)* national policy, must understand this oath well. In accord with the Meiji emperor's broad national plan, the oath should be cultivated by future emperors as the root of their virtue.

Third: The Imperial Rescript on Education, Sugiura continued, was issued in 1890. Since the beginning of the Meiji period a great amount of Western literature has been imported into our country. Everything and everyone is being studied and the people's thinking is confused; they do not understand the ends of morality *(dōtoku no kishu)*. The Meiji emperor became concerned and promulgated an Imperial Rescript on Education. It proclaimed to the people of our country the fundamental principles of morality and became the standard moral teaching for all Japanese subjects *(shinmin)*. (Under the Meiji Constitution, *shinmin* included everyone except the imperial family and the nobility.) The Imperial Rescript on Education was not simply promulgated to all subjects. Indeed, the emperor said: "It is Our wish to take it to heart in all reverence, in common with you Our subjects, that we may all attain to the same virtue."[22] That is, the rescript is a standard of morality to be cultivated by ruler and ruled alike. In unifying and supervising government policy, therefore, future emperors should above all ensure that the public fulfills the intentions of this imperial rescript. At the same time the emperor himself must practice these moral precepts.

Sugiura's first and third guiding ideas were well suited to imparting a nationalistic Japan-centered set of values to the future emperor. The second idea seems to be at odds with this line of indoctrination, but the Meiji Charter Oath was not as progressive as it might seem. Rather than promoting a broad basis of support for the government among the people, Sugiura lent wings to the fantasy that the present regime had already achieved this sort of enlightened rule. In effect Hirohito was taught, illogically, that by following the conservative traditionalist policies of the Meiji oligarchs he was doing the opposite—enhancing moderate politics in Japan.[23]

Sugiura's Milieu

In defense of Sugiura one must emphasize that his three principles of Japanese morals, as well as his interpretation, were in tune with the times. In his impressive study *Japan's Orient: Rendering Pasts into History*, Stefan Tanaka states that Shiratori Kurakichi, who was a colleague of Sugiura's at the crown prince's school, and other Japanese historians were seeking at this time a new basis for their history. Reacting against standard Western treatments of the Orient, meaning Asia, they wished to counter the "concealed ideology behind claims of objectivism" in Western scholarship.[24] They were unhappy because occidental histories implied that Asian countries in general, and Japan in particular, ranked below the nations of the West on their univeralistic scale of national advancement and importance. These Japanese historians were attempting to establish a "prescientific philosophy of history,"[25] one that put Japan on a par, at least, with the West. Sugiura was not a historian, but he does appear to have tried to define a similar "prescientific" frame of reference for Japanese morals.

Sugiura's concerns about public morality and Japanese tradition paralleled those of many other intellectuals of that day—men who had called for something like the Imperial Rescript on Education during the 1870s and 1880s long before it was promulgated. The rescript came after Japan's "moral crisis" of the 1880s. In November 1890, for example, one of Sugiura's like-minded peers, Kuga Katsunan (1857–1907), summarized these feelings:

[Today's] politicians seem to be normal politicians, but today's educators know nothing about education. Looking at the theories *(setsu)* of those who belong to the inner sanctum of the world of education, they appear to want to infer all things theoretically *(gakuriteki ni)*. They seem to want to take the academic theories *(gakusetsu)* of Spencer and apply them even to normal education. Filial piety *(kō)* to one's parents, friendship *(yū)* between siblings, harmony *(wa)* between man and wife, faith *(shin)* among friends, loyalty to the imperial house—these are the ethics characteristic of everyone in Japan, the historical tradition of the Japanese people, the basic elements constituting the fundament of Japanese society. These things cannot be inferred from a theory; they should be confirmed with the passions *(kanjō)*. . . . [That which the educators] regard highly is merely theory—incomplete, cold theory devoid of warm feelings. These people are not educators *(kyōikuka)*; they are learning technicians *(gakujutsuka)*.[26]

Kuga, a political commentator and founder of the newspaper *Nippon*, emphasized the necessity of morality in politics and a strong independent state. He described his eclectic style of nationalism as the "principles of citizenship" *(kokuminshugi)*. Although he himself advocated Confucian values, he opposed those who decried the influence of European ideas on Japanese culture.[27]

Miyake Setsurei (1860–1945), another prominent journalist and colleague of Sugiura's, also emphasized the place of Japan in East Asia and the world. The Japanese, he said, should be self-confident and independent; they should not westernize their culture. His cultural-theoretical approach to nationalism was much different from the Confucianism emphasized by others. Once he tried to define what he called "national essence" *(kokusui):* "National essence (1) has an intangible vitality; (2) is the special quality of one country; (3) is something that cannot be imitated by other countries."[28] A country's national essence was not static, he said, but the unique spirit of a nation, especially Japan's national essence, must be preserved: "Even if the customs of Europe and America are adopted, even if the customs of ancient times are destroyed, the traditional Japanese spirit—this must be preserved, this must be exalted, this must be fostered."

Miyake's writings exemplify one of the dilemmas that plagued many Meiji intellectuals. He insisted that the Japanese should be modern, but they must not westernize their culture. Yet it appears that Miyake, intent on being modern, appropriated Western sophistication for Japanese cultural values and fell into this trap himself—in other words, he unwittingly "westernized" Japan's national essence. As noted in the Introduction, in Japan "gods are gods because their divinity is always bestowed from a beyond reaching to infinity. Therefore, only as *mediums* do gods become gods, and they are mediums to the revelations of infinity, not of an ultimate source."[29] There is no break between the gods and this worldly existence. Unlike Christianity and Islam, Japanese belief posits that holy revelations go back to infinity, not some transcendental being standing above human existence. Miyake's Japanese spirit—which must be preserved and exalted even in the face of a break with infinity "if the customs of ancient times are destroyed"—transcends the realm of Japanese belief. It becomes, perhaps, as sublime as Western objects of spiritual veneration, and this was important for the foundation of Miyake's nationalism, the national essence. But Miyake was blind to the fact that in asserting that Japan's national essence must remain intact in this way, he was transforming it into a non-Japanese transcendental entity. By "elevating" the national essence he westernized it.

Miyake's nationalism was theoretically different from Kuga's. Their ideas, together with those of Sugiura, are examples of the great variety of approaches to defining the Japanese national polity. Despite these differences, their doctrines conformed, finally, with the nationalism found in the Imperial Rescript on Education, which was considered "ordinary morality" by most Japanese in 1890 and thereafter. Moreover, this type of morality was generally accepted in other nations. When the rescript was published in English in 1907, it was praised for its "highest kind of principles, ethical and moral," by the president of the Chicago Board of Education. At the same time, the International Workers of the World termed it "the veriest commonplaces of capitalist morality,"[30] a comment that no doubt would have confused the Confucian-oriented Japanese had they seen it.

If the Japanese read their concerns about national polity and their view of Confucianism into foreign theories, they were not alone in this respect. Many Japanese intellectuals went further—arbitrarily appropriating European concepts to lend a modern coloring to traditional Japanese ethics. During this period Sugiura may be counted among those who were so inclined. Later his former student, the Shōwa emperor, did the same when he claimed that British constitutional monarchy was the model for his reign.

Sugiura's Background

Sugiura's concern for the preservation of Japanese tradition came early in life, but in a rather roundabout manner. He began his academic career and climb to semiprominence as a student of English and the natural sciences.[31] He attended the Daigakunankō, forerunner to Tokyo Imperial University, and eventually specialized in chemistry. Pursuing his education in England from June 1876 to March 1880, he studied under well-known chemists like Sir Henry Roscoe and published in the *Journal of the Chemical Society*. At about the time these publications appeared and his work in chromatic chemistry was being praised (1878), Inoue Kaoru (1836–1915), a prominent politician, special envoy in Europe, and later foreign minister in the first official Japanese parliamentary cabinet, invited him for a talk and encouraged him to continue. Instead of being stimulated and encouraged, Sugiura told Inoue that he was undecided about carrying forward this sort of research and he recommended another student for the honor of continuing his studies with government support.

In fact his interest had already turned toward the English idea of "science for its own sake" and he was intrigued by the philosophy of chemistry, physics, and mathematics.[32] He pursued this line of study and in 1879 first projected what was to become his guiding light in examining Japanese tradition and teaching traditional morality—"scientism" (rigakushū). Sugiura's scientism, a pseudoscientific explanation of the preeminence of the imperial house and Japan's *kokutai*, was a curious blend of theories adapted from the physical sciences and references to the mythical origins of the Japanese state. At first glance it appears to be a simple crank school of thought hardly worthy of attention. This type of logic was nevertheless important to the advancement of learning and defining social roles in early modern Japan. More to the point, it was important to Emperor Hirohito's understanding of Western constitutionalism and his view of himself as a constitutional monarch.

Within the context of Japanese intellectual history, Sugiura has been compared with Ishida Baigan (1685–1744) and Ninomiya Sontoku (1787–1856). Ishida was a "merchant-philosopher" who taught, contrary to official Tokugawa Neo-Confucian ideology, that honest hardworking merchants were comparable in their service to the state to elite samurai officials. Ninomiya, a highly successful agriculturist near Edo, helped others with practical reforms in their work and taught his fellow farmers mutual cooperation and long-term planning. The comparison with Sugiura derives, not from similarities in the content of their thought, but from the manner in which each came to develop his characteristic school of thinking: a vocation and an associated way of living were put forward as a philosophy of life. Just as Ishida's way of the merchant, *shingaku* or "learning of the mind," evolved from the abacus and Ninomiya's way of the peasant, *hōtokukyō* or "Returning Virtue sect," came so to speak from the blade of a hoe, Sugiura's scientism was a by-product of his intensive study of natural science in England.[33]

Sugiura sought to apply the principles of physics to human affairs and analyze the relation between science and social welfare, culture and happiness, and so forth. "Seeds not planted will not grow" was one of his sayings. Another was: "If mature, something is hidden."[34] The meaning behind these sayings, like much of his writing, was rather opaque. Similarly, his application of the principles of physics to human relationships was extremely arbitrary. The rational method and reliance on evidence that one associates with the physical sciences are conspicuously absent from his thought.

Sugiura remained true to his scientism throughout his life. For him the Rigakushū was a combination of love of country—Nippon—and the sciences of physics and chemistry. And this is what interests us. In 1911, three years before beginning his lectures on morality to Crown

Prince Hirohito, Sugiura wrote the following about "Japan's so-called gods":

> When considering the gods of our country, one is not referring to a supreme creator *(zōbutsushu)*. These gods are something like great persons or a sovereign, those entirely above ordinary persons—extraordinary persons who die and afterward are revered to the end of time. These are called gods. Concerning these gods, what I want to explain is their attendant [spiritual] energy *(seiryoku* 精力*)*. The people who have accumulated an abundance of this energy are honored for all time and retain a light *(hikari)* for all time. This happens according to the [law of] the conservation of [physical] energy *(seiryoku* 勢力*)*—the "conservation of force" deduced from physics. This means that the one who conserves the greatest surplus of [physical] energy continues to exist for all time.[35]

Sugiura insists that human affairs cannot be separated from the laws of physical science. He then explains the Japanese *kokutai* by using scientific principles (meaning his scientism):

> The founder of our imperial family and the emperor's ancestors are the ones in this country who have accumulated [physical] energy over the longest period of time. They were revered in the past as gods, and because there is a continuous line of descent that extends down to today, from the point of view of the principle of the conservation of energy one must conclude that in Japan they certainly have the most energy [power]. Regarding the entire world, broadly speaking, no one else has continuously accumulated energy for such a long period of time. To assert that Japan is unsurpassed among nations, then, is no empty theory. It may be inferred from the principles of physics that no other nation has accumulated more energy [power]. ... If this energy continues to be accumulated from now on, one can expect that this energy [power and influence] will increasingly extend throughout the world.[36]

Sugiura unabashedly applied the laws of physical science to spiritual notions based on a similarity in vocabulary ("energy," "force," and the like). No doubt his innovations would have surprised his English mentors in chemistry, but this type of thought was widely accepted among social commentators in Europe at the time of his stay in England. Indeed, Henry Thomas Buckle in his *History of Civilization,* published in 1857, "attempted to prove scientifically and statistically that human affairs are governed by laws as invariable and predictable as those in the physical realm."[37] Herbert Spencer's (1820–1903) theory of evolution and Charles Darwin's (1809–1882) theory of natural selection both tended in this direction. Of special interest are the ideas of Walter Bagehot (1826–1877), whose essay "The English Constitution" so influenced early twentieth-century notions about constitutional monarchy.[38] In an earlier work, "Physics and Politics: Or

Thoughts on the Application of the Principles of 'Natural Selection' and 'Inheritance' to Political Society," published as a series of essays beginning in 1867, Bagehot employed the "Lamarckian use-and-wont theory of the inheritance of acquired characteristics" to explain the development of higher civilizations and advanced states.[39] Thus Bagehot too was inclined to use the laws of the physical sciences to analyze social change. But unlike Buckle he "repudiated any material cause of progress and placed the moral motivation first: 'It is the action of the will that causes the unconscious habit; it is the continual effort of the beginning that creates the hoarded energy of the end; it is the silent toil of the first generation that becomes the transmitted aptitude of the next.' "[40]

Sugiura's scientism—his "conservation of force" and the imperial line's accumulation of energy and power—might be seen, then, as a Japanese elaboration of these European theories. It should be noted, however, that with the exception of certain aberrant pseudoscientific interpreters of Darwin, Spencer, and Nietzsche,[41] such ideas were not taken as literally, nor applied to folk and state, in the manner seen in Sugiura's writings. In the late 1880s and 1890s Sugiura worked hard at disseminating these ideas. He published numerous articles explaining them in journals like *Nipponjin* and the newspaper *Nippon*, which he helped found, and in a national newspaper, the *Yomiuri shimbun*. He also wrote regularly in a comparable vein for another national newspaper, the *Tokyo Asahi shimbun*, from May 1892 until December 1904. In addition, Sugiura was instrumental in forming a number of political societies advocating doctrines close to his own.

In 1891, for example, one of the many associations founded to foster "progressive" nationalism—not to mention abrogation of the unequal treaties forced on Japan in the late 1860s—was the Tōhō Kyōkai (Far Eastern Society). The society was to meet once a month "to discuss trade, military and colonial policy, international relations, history, statistics, and geography in the Far East *(tōhō)*." On the board were the publisher Kuga, the journalist Miyake, the professor of philosophy at Tokyo Imperial University and "house ideologue" of the Meiji oligarchs Inoue Tetsujirō (1856–1944), and Sugiura.[42] Sugiura's activities and his writings show that he consistently interpreted Japanese history and contemporary affairs by deliberately citing modern European authorities and ancient Japanese texts out of context as it suited his patriotic prejudices.[43] And Sugiura brought this scientism to bear in educating the living embodiment of Japanese tradition: the future emperor of Japan.

Teiōgaku: Imperial Studies

At the Ogakumonjo, the crown prince's secondary school, Sugiura's instruction in traditional ethics included a variety of subjects. This variety, however, does not mean that his instruction can be characterized as cosmopolitan. At least thirty topics from foreign countries were addressed, but by far the majority of these were aspects of classical Confucianism from China—a topic dear to the hearts of the Meiji intellectuals concerned about Japanese morals. Closer to home a similar trend toward moralizing can be discerned. It is noteworthy, when considering the nature of Hirohito's later adherence to constitutional monarchy, that moral instruction took precedence over constitutionalism. The imperial edict admonishing the people to be frugal and industrious after the Russo-Japanese war (the *Boshin Shōsho* of 1908) was lectured upon four times, "The Rescript for Soldiers and Sailors" (the *Riku, Kaigun (ni kudashitamaeru) Chokuron* of 1882) five times, the Imperial Rescript on Education eleven times, and the Meiji Constitution of 1889 only once.[44]

This trend toward patriotic moralizing is vividly demonstrated in an early lecture titled "The Imperial Regalia." It begins with an undiluted dose of imperial tradition:

> The founder of the imperial family, Amaterasu Ōmikami, bequeathed the imperial regalia when she had her grandson [Amatsuhikohikoho no] Ninigi no Mikoto descend to Oyashima no Kuni [the earth], and she promulgated an imperial rescript: "My child, when thou lookest upon this mirror, let it be as if thou wert looking on me. Let it be with thee on thy couch and in thy hall, and let it be to thee a holy mirror."[45]
>
> The imperial regalia, that is the mirror, jewel, and sword, were not simply bequeathed as a sign *(mishirushi)* of imperial status. Concerning them, Kitabatake Chikafusa in the distant past, and somewhat later Nakae Tōju, Yamaga Sokō, and Rai Sanyō, have all interpreted the vast sacred teachings which have come down to us similarly: In the last analysis [the mirror, jewel, and sword] stand for the three virtues of wisdom, benevolence, and courage [*chi, jin,* and *yū*].[46]
>
> For example, the mirror should be made clear and bright and should not become clouded. The myriad things are then illuminated, right and wrong, forthrightness and distortion discerned. In terms of the heart *(jin-shin)*, this accordingly is knowledge. Wisdom is similar to when a mirror illuminates something; good and bad, black and white, are discerned. The jewel denotes harmony, nurturing warmth, as with a person of deep compassion *(jihi)* and calmness. This is much the same as benevolence, and benevolence is that which gives rise to humanity. Again, it hardly needs explaining that the sword signifies courageous determination.[47] [See Appendix 4.]

The symbols of imperial power and influence give the incumbent emperor authority because they have been handed down by the supreme goddess of Japanese tradition, Amaterasu Ōmikami. Modern imperial authority derives from ancient myths, and one of the most highly regarded histories of ancient Japan, the *Nihon Shoki,* is quoted to support this assumption.

Sugiura's assertion—"In the last analysis [the mirror, jewel, and sword] stand for the three virtues of wisdom, benevolence, and courage [*chi, jin,* and *yū*]"—appears over and over throughout his lectures and reveals much about the content of Hirohito's instruction. Examining the tradition of thought in which this assertion is embedded not only demonstrates that Sugiura's thinking was quite conservative but shows that the future emperor's education was very patriotic and less broad-minded than later evaluations lead us to believe. "It is misleading," notes Stefan Tanaka, "to cast the issues in terms of a struggle between liberalism and nationalism."[48] After all, it was quite possible for a "liberal constitutional monarch" and his advisers to be nationalists. At the same time, this possibility should not lead us to ignore the significance of nationalism in Hirohito's education for his later activities. One possible source of this trend in Hirohito's thinking is presented here: Sugiura's imperial studies and the scientism on which they were based.

Sugiura's Sources

Japanese thought is much more varied than is generally known outside specialist circles. In fact, a wide variety of schools and philosophers were available to Sugiura. One was a book by the philosopher Inoue Tetsujirō, *Nihon kogakuha no tetsugaku* (Philosophy of the Ancient Learning School in Japan). In a commentary on Yamaga Sokō's "Kokutairon" (On the National Polity), Inoue quotes Yamaga:

> Our Imperial Court *(honchō),* as the descendant of Amaterasu Ōmikami, is the legitimate line from the age of the gods down to today without a single reign being an exception. . . . The three [virtues], wisdom, benevolence, and courage, are the three virtues of a sage *(seijin).* If only one of these virtues is lacking, then it is not the way of a sage. Now, with these three virtues as a sign, our court is by comparison superior to other courts.[49]

Yamaga did not mention the link between the two triads—the mirror, jewel, and sword with wisdom, benevolence, and courage—but the parallel with Sugiura's interpretation is obvious. Whether Sugiura's thinking derived from Inoue's work is impossible to ascertain, however, because this interpretation was not unusual.

During the Tokugawa period (1603–1868), Sugiura's specific line of interpretation was well known among scholars of Chinese learning.

This interpretation can be seen, for example, in the writings of one of the most influential philosophers of the period, an originator of Tokugawa Neo-Confucianism, Hayashi Razan (1583–1657):

> The three regalia are three virtues. The human mind is empty, alert, and transparent; it reflects and apprehends. Is it not truly a mirror? The human mind *(kokoro)* is round and perfect in its virtue, as stainless as jade, the symbol of humanity *(jin)*. It is a jewel, is it not? The mind is brave and resolute, and makes decisions in accord with its sense of duty *(gi)*. This signifies courage, which is represented by the sword, is it not? The three regalia are divine, and the three virtues are those of the human mind, which is the abode of the divine. So they are one in three and three in one, essentially inseparable. The divine is not finite; only in the object does it become manifest. The mind leaves no trace of itself; only through the medium of matter do we observe its reactions. The interrelation of heaven and man is truly wondrous.[50]

Here, preceding the scholars cited by Sugiura, is a Neo-Confucian expression of what he explained more simply in the second paragraph of his lecture.

Other Tokugawa scholars may have based their interpretations on the works of Hayashi. Inoue maintained that they all were inspired by the fifteenth-century statesman and Neo-Confucian scholar Ichijō Kaneyoshi (Kanera; 1402–1481). In his *Nihon Shoki sanso* (Commentary on the *Nihon Shoki*) Ichijō introduced this comparison between the Japanese imperial regalia—mirror, jewel, and sword—and the classical Chinese Confucian virtues—wisdom, benevolence, and courage.[51] Examining Ichijō's text closely, however, shows that his main concern was not the explication of these Confucian and Japanese virtues. He was interested, rather, in demonstrating the oneness of the three main religious traditions in Japan—Shinto, Buddhism, and Confucianism—while maintaining the ultimate superiority of Shinto.[52]

This argument fits well with Sugiura's thinking, but Ichijō's work is a bit obtuse and was not well known during the Meiji period. For these reasons it is doubtful that Sugiura adopted Ichijō's explanation. Likewise he probably did not follow Hayashi as he did not engage in the metaphysics dear to the Tokugawa Neo-Confucians. Instead, one can find similarities between Sugiura and the tenor and argumentation of a still earlier essay from the middle of the fourteenth century by the highly regarded author Kitabatake Chikafusa. He too had a great influence on later thinkers. In fact Ichijō's interpretations can be traced back to Kitabatake's works: they are a mixture of the Neo-Confucian metaphysics and Shinto doctrine found in Kitabatake's writings.[53] Despite the direct correspondence between the triads compared by Ichijō Kaneyoshi and Hayashi Razan, the lectures by Hirohito's ethics teacher are closer to Kitabatake's thought. Some passages he simply copied from Kitabatake's work.

The *Jinnō Shōtōki*

Kitabatake Chikafusa was no doubt selected by Sugiura because of his direct and simple-to-understand description of the legitimacy of the imperial line. In early Japan, the imperial house was respected and allowed to exist for political and religious reasons. Politically it was impotent; religiously it was protected by Japan's highest deity, the Sun Goddess. With Kitabatake's *Jinnō Shōtōki*, completed in 1343, legitimacy theory in Japan shifted from the Sun Goddess' protection of the imperial line to its divine descent. The opening lines of the text clearly reflect this change, and they were adopted *tout à fait* by Sugiura: "Great Japan is the divine land. The heavenly progenitor [Kuni-no-Tokotachi-no-mikoto, "Lord Who Permanently Established the Country"] founded it, and the sun goddess bequeathed it to her descendants to rule eternally. Only in our country is this true; there are no similar examples in other countries. This is why our country is called the divine land."[54]

Kitabatake legitimized the supreme position of the imperial house in terms of a line of true descent. Only the imperial line reached back, unbroken, to the age of the gods. Thus only the head of that lineage could become emperor. This thesis conforms completely with Sugiura's "scientific" explanation of *kokutai* based on the conservation—or in his case the continuous accumulation—of energy. Instead of an unbroken bloodline he based his theory on the uninterrupted accumulation of energy (and power). His adaptation of the science he learned in the West was used to "modernize" the folklore legitimizing the position of the imperial house in Japanese society. This type of thinking, in turn, appears to have been embraced by the future emperor. One need only remember the way Hirohito upheld this teaching after World War II when he renounced his divinity but insisted on his true descent from the gods.[55] He may well have intended to affirm the symbolic importance of the imperial house in Japanese society,[56] not to claim he was literally or biologically a descendant of the Sun Goddess. Yet one cannot disregard his assertion, however symbolic, of the preeminent position of the imperial house in Japanese society immediately after this devastating defeat.

Comparing the two premodern texts, the *Nihon Shoki* and *Jinnō Shōtōki*, with Sugiura's lectures shows how he pieced his prescientific instructional "philosophy" together: he quoted the former and took his interpretation from the latter. The phrase from the *Nihon Shoki* by Sugiura cited earlier also appears near the beginning of the *Jinnō Shō-*

tōki, for example, and his interpretation, though in a slightly different form, is to be found in Kitabatake's text:

> Amaterasu's mandate on the imperial regalia informs us of the proper way for governing the country.
>
> The mirror possesses nothing of its own, but with an unselfish spirit illuminates all things. There is nothing, good or bad, that is not reflected in it, and its virtue is to reveal all forms with perfect fidelity. The mirror is the source of all honesty *(shōjiki).* The virtue of the jewels is gentleness and yielding, and they are the source of compassion. The sword, which is the fount of wisdom, has as its virtue strength and resolution. Unless a ruler possesses the virtues of all three of the regalia, he will find it difficult indeed to govern the country. Amaterasu's mandate is clear: its words are concise, but their import is far-reaching. Should we not feel the greatest gratitude because the spirit of the mandate is embodied in the imperial regalia?[57]

Kitabatake maintained that the mirror, jewel, and sword were the source of honesty, gentleness, and resolute wisdom, respectively. This interpretation is only slightly different from Sugiura, who says the mirror, jewel, and sword are symbols that embody the virtues of wisdom, benevolence, and courage. The difference may be explained by the fact that Kitabatake borrowed his vocabulary from the *Shu Ching* (Book of History),[58] Sugiura from the *Chung Yung* (Doctrine of the Mean). Nonetheless, the logic behind their respective theories is the same: each utilized Chinese moral principles, out of context, to support Japanese ethnocentrism based on the sociospiritual superiority of the imperial house.

While Sugiura consistently borrows phrases from the eighth-century history *(Nihon Shoki),* his interpretive bent is closer to the loyalism of the *Jinnō Shōtōki.* In an interesting turnabout, for example, Sugiura says that these three virtues are Japanese, not Chinese. They are found in the Confucian classic, the Doctrine of the Mean, but there, according to him, they stand above even the Chinese archetypes of ethical conduct acknowledged by most in the Far East: the five Confucian relationships. The superiority of his three traditional "Japanese" virtues is, Sugiura implies, supported by Chinese authority. This idea too may have come from his fourteenth-century source, the *Jinnō Shōtōki.* Kitabatake wrote:

> Sovereigns and ministers alike have received the bright light of divine descent, or they are the descendants of deities who received Amaterasu's mandate. Who does not look with awe upon this fact? The highest purpose of all learning, both Buddhist and Confucian, is to make people aware of this and to prevent them from going against the way upon which it is based. Dissemination of Buddhist and Confucian learning has been the force in propagating this way (Shinto).[59]

Kitabatake, Sugiura, and many others believed that the truths of Shinto were superior to all others. Buddhist and Confucian learning were approved insofar as they propagated these truths. Taking a leaf from this book, one can further extrapolate and conclude that Western learning—science and constitutional theory, for example—is good as well insofar as it contributed to the well-being of the Japanese folk. That was Sugiura's message. Moreover, in this lecture Sugiura compared in a general way the three Japanese virtues with those of Japan's rivals on the world stage, the Western Powers. He does not cite specific examples of virtue in the West. Rather, he asserts the superiority of the mirror, jewel, and sword—wisdom, benevolence, and courage.

Throughout the discussion of the imperial regalia Sugiura relies on Kitabatake's interpretations. Although he cites the *Nihon Shoki*, it is Kitabatake's logic of descent that he emphasizes. Other important texts and scholars are ignored—for example, the *Kojiki* and the noteworthy commentary on it by Motoori Norinaga (1730–1801) are not mentioned. Motoori, the principal advocate of "national learning" *(kokugaku)*, believed that "the sun-goddess attached her very spirit to the mirror, which was thus endowed with all her spiritual attributes."[60] But the Japanese were intent upon impressing the West with their modern, European-style development at this time (1914–1921), and Motoori's mystic interpretation was not suited to this purpose.

The Question of Reliability

Questions of interpretation and veracity aside, Sugiura's citations from these texts do not accurately represent their content. The *Nihon Shoki* does not say the imperial regalia were given to the Sun Goddess' grandson, Ninigi no Mikoto, as Sugiura claimed. They were presented to his father, Oshiho Mimi no Mikoto, to whom the foregoing statement was made. Later she gave him some "things" that may have included the imperial regalia. In other words: Sugiura interpreted his source very loosely in order to support the theory of imperial descent,[61] and his interpretation had little to do with history.

Sugiura obviously did not accept the contention of some Japanese historians that the transmission of the regalia, along with most episodes found in these two histories, are inventions created to legitimize the claim of the imperial house to sovereignty over Japan. But neither can he be counted among those modern historians who are inclined to accept the historicity of these texts. The foremost modern-day scholar of ancient Japanese history, for example, the late Sakamoto Tarō, wrote:

To think that the compilers invented such myths in order to justify the rule of the imperial house over Japan is to impute too much modern consciousness to the people of ancient times. The most effective part in demonstrating this legitimacy would have been the divine vow of the Sun Goddess to protect the imperial line forever, but this is not even entered into the main text; it appears only once in "one book," and eight such "one books" are cited in the text. The main figure who dispatches the Heavenly Grandchild is the deity Takamimusubi, and the Sun Goddess is seen in a secondary position; this is hard to explain by the theory of invention.[62]

Sakamoto proposed that rather than affirming or denying the value of the ancient histories, one must discriminate between what is clearly myth and what may be history. He was known for his ability to read ancient texts at first sight; he could handle vast amounts of materials; and he could see historical connections that others could not. Though a conservative with a positive view of the imperial house, he always put evidence ahead of theory. Thus he was highly critical of Tsuda Sōkichi's analyses of the anachronisms in the *Nihon Shoki* and *Kojiki* but equally critical of the National Scholars in prewar Japan who maintained that the myths in these texts were literally true. Sakamoto has been criticized for his arbitrary decisions about what constituted evidence and what did not, but no one doubts his rationalist approach to history.[63] Sugiura, differently predisposed, utilized myth and history as it suited his purpose—here the indoctrination of the future emperor. This can be seen in his selection and use of authorities to interpret the imperial regalia.

Sugiura adapted ancient history to the exigencies of Japanese nationalism. Medieval Japanese history was similarly used, though it required far less adaptation. According to his rendering, historically and philologically the three virtues were embodied personally by "actual" imperial ancestors. The characters for names of the emperors Tenji, Nintoku, and Jimmu "demonstrate" Sugiura's point:

Tenji 天智　 "heavenly wisdom" (here the classical character for wisdom is used)
Nintoku 仁德 "benevolent virtue"
Jimmu 神武　 "divine military power"

This is not the place to undertake a detailed examination of the historical accuracy of the earliest Japanese histories and the persons described in them. Briefly summarized, the historicity of emperors Tenji and Nintoku is generally accepted, though not all the exploits attributed to them. The traditional dates of Nintoku's reign (313–399) are doubted by most. Jimmu's conquest of the eastern provinces, present-day Osaka and Nara, may vaguely reflect reality, but the details and dates are totally fictitious.[64] Sugiura did not, of course, tell this to Crown Prince Hirohito. Conforming to accepted practice in all schools in Imperial Japan, he maintained that the information was historically true. But he was not concerned with the factual reliability of ancient Japanese history. He was illustrating the virtues he thought Hirohito should embody. Finally, given this context, it is not surprising that Sugiura asserts the founder of the modern Japanese state, Emperor Meiji, Hirohito's grandfather, incorporated all three virtues—wisdom, benevolence, and courage—in his person.

Shiratori Kurakichi: The History Professor

Sugiura's view of history—conservative and centered on Imperial Japan—was not unusual in Japan at this time. The Tokyo Imperial University philosophy professor Inoue Tetsujirō pointed out, for example, the importance of Japanese national history as a basis for national identity. Most historians, who one might assume should know better, were swept up in the search for Japan's unique national identity. Among them is one of particular interest because he taught at the crown prince's secondary school. The man who taught Hirohito history, Shiratori Kurakichi (1865–1942), was concerned with explaining historically Japan's preeminent position and role in the world. The founder of "oriental history" *(tōyōshi)* in Japan, Shiratori was a sophisticated and highly respected academician. He did not agree with Inoue's approach to this problem, but he did concur that the imperial system was central to this endeavor. It was a "spiritual force that both placed [the] Japanese within the history of mankind and made them unique."[65] History was to legitimize the present, not objectify the past.

The science of history, as opposed to premodern Japanese and sinological approaches, was established with the help of a German scholar, Ludwig Riess (1861–1928). But it would be wrong to assume that Riess alone was responsible for what finally developed. Certain aspects of German historiography were selected by the Japanese from a number of possibilities.[66] Certainly Riess, in Japan from 1887 to 1902, fostered an atmosphere at Tokyo Imperial University conducive to a historicist approach to the past. But the historicist aspects of Meiji, Taishō, and early Shōwa Japanese historiography are due not only to Riess' instruction but to a high esteem for Leopold von Ranke (1795–1886), as well, and Riess was not, as many assume, a student of Ranke.[67]

Ranke's reputation among Japanese historians was not due to Riess. Shiratori and others found in Ranke something they were looking for: Ranke's universal spirit specific to time and place was especially useful in making Japan and Asia equivalent to the West while at the same time emphasizing the unique character of the Japanese political system.[68] Shiratori selected Ranke's historical methodology as a model for his own because the German's spiritual historicism provided a "scientific" method for explaining the Japanese *kokutai*. Shiratori's "spiritual force" was adapted from Ranke's "universal spirit." Ranke was used to legitimize the special nature of the Japanese polity and within it the unique imperial line. Which is to say: Shiratori's nationalistic interpretation of the past for the sake of enhancing the present may have been adapted from Ranke and influenced by Reiss, but it was not preordained by Western teachers or sources. Indeed, Shiratori and others selected legitimizing authorities for preconceived nationalistic ends.

Shiratori Kurakichi graduated from the History Seminar of Tokyo Imperial University in 1890. Using methods from linguistics and ethnology he did groundbreaking research on the various peoples of Korea, Manchuria, Mongolia, and Inner Asia. Eventually he held simultaneous appointments at Tokyo Imperial University and Gakushūin University (The Peers School) as professor of Far Eastern history. Moreover, Shiratori taught Japanese as well as world history at the Ogakumonjo and supervised academic instruction. We do not have a formal record of the lectures Shiratori delivered at this school, and he avoided commenting on his impressions of the future emperor. We do, however, have numerous articles and public lectures published during this time, a few of which Shiratori delivered as lectures at the school.

In Imperial Japan, university students and prospective schoolteachers were told that research on Japanese history, especially the history of the origins of the nation, was to be separated from teaching in the national interest.[69] In other words: the results of basic research that might undermine the national polity were not to be used in the classroom. Apparently Shiratori observed this custom when teaching at the Ogakumonjo. If we compare the few presentations to the crown prince later published as articles with Shiratori's academic publications, we find significant differences between what Shiratori taught his royal pupil and what he published professionally. The latter can be described as "scientific" insofar as history can aspire to such; the former, while not jingoistic, were indeed more nationalistic and less objective.

A good example of Shiratori's approach to his teaching at the Ogakumonjo is the lecture he presented on the occasion of Hirohito's formal investiture as crown prince in 1916. Titled "Kokutai to Jukyō" (Our National Polity and Confucianism), it was delivered on the day before the investiture ceremony and published in January 1917 in a commemorative issue of *Kokugakuin zasshi* (Journal of the Japanese Academy of Learning).[70]

Kokutai and Confucianism

After a short formal introduction Shiratori began his lecture with a question: "Properly speaking, why is the structural strength of our country Japan superior to all nations?" His answer was Japan's great age. According to Chinese Confucianism the greater the age of a folk, nation, or dynasty the more authority it wields. In effect, Shiratori sought to use Chinese Confucianism to show that Japan is superior to China:

> The Japanese folk *(minzoku)* came to these islands and established a nation in the ancient, ancient past; one can even say it is hardly possible to acquire knowledge about these origins. This antiquity certainly is one reason for Japan's superiority. . . . Among existing nations none has origins which are as old as those of our country. Which is to say there is an indication that the origins of the imperial house which has been bestowed upon our people lie in the very ancient past. Therefore nothing in the world compares to the divine nature *(shinsei)* of the imperial house and likewise the majesty of our national polity. Here is one great reason [for Japan's superiority].

Shiratori made a deficiency—the lack of documentary evidence in Japan from ancient times—into a virtue: the obscure origins of the Japanese state were declared so old that they were beyond all recollection. He then lists the countries to which Japan is superior: China, the various countries of Asia, and the countries of the West including Great Britain, Germany, France, and Russia. This is followed by a familiar theme: Japan has a long history of receiving things from foreign countries and skillfully adapting them to its own customs. Confucianism from China, Buddhism from India, Western culture—all have been assimilated. But these were not simply copied; rather, they were adapted to Japan's special situation. The national polity, he emphasized, must not be tainted. Import foreign things, but do not be enslaved by them. This is true not only of politics but of all things.

As for Chinese Confucianism, he continues, Japanese records say the *Analects (Lun-yü)* were brought to Japan during the reign of Emperor Ōjin (270–310). According to Chinese records Han culture was transmitted to Kyūshū even earlier. In any case, Shiratori says Chinese thought was first conveyed to Japan at a very early date. And he interpolates:

> Today one can well say that Confucianism has permeated the Japanese people such that it is one element of their blood. When one considers the reason for this, it is because Confucianism has many aspects well suited to our

thought; it is because the Japanese took Confucianism and through it were able to advance continuously their original national character *(kokuminsei)*.

An example of this permeation and advancement is the Imperial Rescript on Education of 1890: "The inherent spirit *(seishin)* of Japan was expressed in the Imperial Rescript on Education using Confucian terminology." In the last analysis, he says, Confucianism coincides in many places with the original national character of Japan. Therefore, one can say the spirit of Japan is greatly enhanced *(kenma,* "polished") by Confucianism and made manifest by it.

Shiratori then laments the decline of Confucianism in Japan with the introduction of Western culture after the Meiji Restoration in 1868. It is a mistake, he admonishes, to look at contemporary developments in China and prejudge the value of Confucianism. All countries rise and fall. A strong country today may have been weak in the past; a nation that is weak at present may well have had a glorious culture in ancient times. Three thousand years ago Chinese culture was very advanced. Today's students should learn to appreciate both Eastern and Western culture. There is still much to be gained from studying Confucianism.[71]

"But this does not mean we should simply swallow Confucius' teachings whole," Shiratori warns. He then relates how some years ago, in 1909, he had been branded an enemy of Confucianism. This was due to his suggestion that the ancient sage-emperors of China, Yao and Shun, and the reputed founder of the legendary Hsia dynasty, Yü, were imaginary and not historical figures. But he did not say this to denigrate Confucianism. On the contrary, he wanted to promote its true value. One must investigate Confucianism using the best scientific methods: "We must maintain an independent view with respect to Confucianism and be critical of it. One must discover thereby that which is of value in it. It is not good to become a slave of Confucianism."[72] With respect to ancient Japanese tradition, though, he was more concerned with national solidarity than maintaining a critical point of view.

Shiratori's concept of "research" *(kenkyū)* and "study" *(manabu)* was similarly influenced by his concern for establishing Japan's national prestige. He advocated doing research on Chinese thought "fairly" and "thoroughly." But his elaboration of this notion reveals a view of research that has little to do with objective investigation. Yao's selflessness in that he did not rule arbitrarily or solely for the sake of his progeny; Shun's filial piety and his sincerity in friendship; Yü's diligent devotion to duty—all are exemplary models *(tehon)* not only for Japan but the entire world. But, he continues, "because Yao, Shun, and Yü are manifestations of the spirit of the Chinese people, this thought also contains points that Japanese should not study." Shiratori singles out especially the fact that Yao, in order to safeguard the throne, set aside his own son and appointed Shun his successor. Such behavior must be regarded as something peculiar to the political situation in China. It has nothing to do with Japan and should not be studied. There are many good things in Confucianism well worth study, Shiratori says repeatedly, but it would be a mistake to adopt everything uncritically.

At this point a brief note about the word *"manabu"* (to study) is necessary. *"Manabu"* can mean to learn in the sense we use it in the West. It can also mean to imitate. This second meaning, which is not clearly divorced from the first in Japan even today, is familiar to those who have "studied" karate, judo, or one of the other martial arts. The same is true of traditional pursuits like flower arranging and calligraphy. One learns by imitating a master. This manner of teaching was true as well of classical learning earlier in both China and Japan. Classical Chinese texts are telegraphic in nature, and their meaning is not self-evident without proper instruction. In the Confucian academies students learned by repeating a text after an instructor and then writing the texts out. Only after years of rote memorization were they taught what the texts meant. Here too students were given standard interpretations to memorize. They were not taught to read and explicate the texts according to the times or their own interpretive powers.[73] In practical terms, the education process was designed to test students who wanted to enter the government bureaucracy; theoretically, models of deportment were provided for the students to observe throughout their lives. Education did not promote analysis and selection.

Shiratori may well have had this in mind when he delivered his lecture to the crown prince. Certainly he himself opposed this sort of rote learning and uncritical scholarship, as his attack on classical Chinese studies in Japan *(kangaku)* demonstrates. Nevertheless, due to his arbitrary manner of designating some events as "historical facts" and excluding others, Shiratori has been called "scientistic" at best.[74] A scholar of modern Japan has gone so far as to term his method an "inductive . . . reading of the past through the contemporary situation."[75] That it certainly was. This lecture—along with many other publications including the one on Yao and Shun—is an example of what he considered to be a modern scientific methodology. He warned his students about unthinking acceptance of the truth of Chinese customs and imitating them as one would a professor of classical learning. At the same time he taught that one should profit from the wisdom of the Chinese sages only insofar as it could be applied in a nationalistic manner to present-day problems in Japan. Later Hirohito would apply this selective method to his interpretation of constitutional monarchy. This approach to constitutional monarchy was essential to its adaptation to the situation in Imperial Japan—especially to maintaining the emperor's prerogatives.

Shiratori then cites ancient and medieval precedents for his views. He underscores the difference between Japanese and Chinese culture. (See Appendix 5.) Even if ideas from foreign countries are imported, he says, the Japanese are not to be subservient to them. That is, Japan is open to new ideas but freely adapts them to its inherent temperament *(seishin)*. When Buddhism came from India, the Japanese did not reject it; they only strove to comprehend it. During one period, for example, Buddhists compared the Sun Goddess Amaterasu Ōmikami to the Vairocana Buddha.[76] But Amaterasu Ōmikami is not Vairocana, of course, nor is Vairocana the Sun Goddess. That was a mistake. But even here one can see that the Japanese attempted to assimilate Buddhism to their own mythology. The same is true for Confucianism and Western thought. In summary, then, one can say the Japanese people have their own distinctive character—and that Chinese Confucianism, which furnishes regulations for the morality of personal relations, made a great contribution to this character. In this age when people tend to look upon one another with contempt, Shiratori argues, one should not reject Confucianism but emphasize it all the more.

Despite his commendable conclusion, comparing Shiratori's treatment of Chinese and Japanese tradition reveals serious inconsistencies. He did not use the same critical methods to investigate texts on the founding of the Japanese nation that he employed in debunking Confucianism. Indeed his interpretations of the *Nihon Shoki* and *Kojiki* were faulty. He maintained—in support of the supreme position of the imperial house and consistent with Kitabatake's interpretation widely accepted since the fourteenth century—that these texts show the imperial line to be directly descended from the highest of the heavenly gods. The ancient texts, however, do not support this interpretation. This is an example of the uncritical manner in which Shiratori viewed his own Japanese traditions while insisting on critical evaluation of imported foreign cultures. Intellectual discernment was called for when regarding foreign imports; intellectual testimonials were sought when examining native Japanese history and tradition.

In China, by contrast, at least one prominent contemporary intellectual, the *chin-wen* theorist and politician K'ang Yu-wei (1858–1927),

provoked considerable controversy because he questioned the historically based traditions of his own country. K'ang "presented Confucius
as a reformer who purposely attributed institutional reforms to antiq-
uity in order to have precedents, even to the extent of imagining great
achievements of sage-emperors Yao and Shun whose historicity is
doubtful. This bold dismissal of the age-old Confucian idols virtually
amounted to a revolution."[77] For a comparable revolution in Japan one
might cite Tsuda Sōkichi's interpretation of the ancient texts—an interpretation that Shiratori vigorously opposed. Shiratori, the foremost historian of the day, advocated using the best scientific methods to investigate another culture, Chinese Confucianism: "We must maintain an
independent view with respect to Confucianism and be critical of it.
. . . It is not good to become a slave of Confucianism." But he saw no
danger in being less than objective with respect to his own culture and
the Japanese "age of the gods"—or, for that matter, in becoming a ser-
vant to those who manipulated the Japanese people using these myths.

The Imperial Regalia: A Japanese Interpretation

Before leaving Shiratori, let us consider one more example of his treatment of Japanese mythology—in particular one element of the imperial regalia, the jewel. The topic first appeared in "The Basic Meaning
of the Enthronement Ceremony Banquet" (Daijōsai no konpongi)—a
lecture Shiratori presented at a joint meeting of the Association of
Japanese History and the Association of Japanese Literature (Kokushi-
gakkai and Kokubungakkai Rengōkai) on 26 September 1915. It was
published in the October 1915 issue of *Kokugakuin zasshi*. In the introduction to the lecture on Confucianism mentioned earlier, Shiratori
reminded his students of the previous lecture on the enthronement
ceremony.[78] Through this reminder, we know that the lecture was also
delivered at Hirohito's school. It is of special interest because Shiratori
interprets the meaning of the imperial regalia in a manner very different
from Sugiura.

Shiratori begins with an exhortation to study the ancient texts: one
should not merely look at them from afar in awe; if one only admires
the texts on the age of the gods one cannot understand their logic.
Unless one studies the ancient histories one cannot understand the
origins of the imperial house, the basic meaning of the imperial regalia, rites *(gishiki)*, ceremonies, and the like or grasp the original nature
of the shrines at which Japanese make offerings. Only by examining
these texts carefully can we understand the thinking of our ancestors,
especially their thoughts on the imperial house and ceremonies like

the enthronement banquet. Shiratori then demonstrates what he means by explaining several passages from the age of the gods in the *Kojiki* and *Nihon Shoki*. One of these explanations has to do with the Sun Goddess Amaterasu Ōmikami and the imperial regalia, in particular the sacred jewel.

Here Shiratori's methods must be carefully examined. One should not confuse a philological examination of these texts with a critical approach to historical materials. Shiratori was a skilled and imaginative philologist; he was not an analytic historian. He studied the ancient texts in order to affirm the position of the imperial house, not to see if they in fact supported the imperial tradition. The preeminent position of the imperial house was a given; the latter issue did not arise. Shiratori did not question. Instead he constructed a theory about the meaning of the sacred jewel, as an important source of legitimacy for the imperial line, based on an involved explanation of Japanese mythology. This led him to a critique of the Confucian interpretation of the imperial regalia that was entertained among others by Sugiura. His thesis may be summarized as follows.

According to pure Japanese tradition Amaterasu Ōmikami was sent to the plain of high heaven as the guardian of cereals *(kokumotsu)*, meaning foodstuffs. This was her great merit—as the god charged with protecting cereals, which exist to sustain human life, she is synonymous with them (Uka no Mitama no Kami). Which is to say: Amaterasu is the guardian of foodstuffs and hence the progenitor of the Japanese people. She must care for their happiness and well-being. She is the spirit of undying benevolence *(jinji)* and therefore causes the grain to prosper. Morality and religion, of whatever type, have to do with realizing human life. For the birth and development of human life, then, cereals, that is, foodstuffs, are necessary. Therefore one of the two original progenitors, Izanagi, decreed to Amaterasu that it was her "virtue" *(toku)* to grow and preserve grain. Grain, as one can readily see, has a shape similar to the jewel of Japanese tradition. Thus the object of attention of the gods and the imperial line was a symbol for grain—the sacred jewel.

After the importation of Chinese culture in ancient times, the sacred jewel of the three imperial regalia was compared to benevolence *(jin)*.[79] "Benevolence," in the sense of universal love, means in the Confucian context to nurture the people morally—to further a sense of humaneness in human relations. In Japan, Shiratori maintains, benevolence had a much more concrete meaning: it is associated with grain, meaning the concrete necessity of providing enough food for people to live.

Because Amaterasu was made responsible for an abundant supply of grain, her virtue is to nurture the people in a practical way that has nothing to do with Confucian morality. (See Appendix 6.)

In this lecture Shiratori was obviously concerned with establishing a pure Japanese theory about the meaning of the imperial regalia. But his analysis is misleading. In the *Kojiki* and *Nihon Shoki* the mirror is more important than the jewel. The jewel *(magatama)*, as a symbol for rice, undoubtedly had to do with sustaining life as Shiratori asserts. But a continuing connection between the imperial house and the sacred jewel, or even the imperial regalia collectively, is tenuous. Contrary to popular assumptions, they are not mentioned, for example, in connection with the succession of the first emperor, Jimmu, to the throne. Moreover the jewel, as we have seen, was not mentioned specifically in the *Nihon Shoki* when Amaterasu presented the regalia to Ninigi no Mikoto, or his father, when the former descended to earth. In these references to the imperial regalia it is the mirror, not the jewel, that takes precedence over the other objects.[80] Here one should remember that critical research was being done on Japan's ancient origins well before Shiratori wrote this lecture. Moreover, he must have been aware of this research as it was being carried out by one of his most talented former students, Tsuda Sōkichi (1873–1961). Tsuda taught at a leading private university, Waseda, and using methods similar to those of his teacher did pioneering research on ancient Japanese history. In 1913 he published his "New Research on the History of the Age of the Gods" *(Jindaishi no atarashii kenkyū)*. Tsuda proposed that the portrayals of the age of the gods in the eighth-century histories the *Kojiki* and *Nihon Shoki* were not true history. They were compiled, he said, to justify the rule of the imperial house.[81]

In the late 1930s Tsuda was strongly criticized by nationalist scholars at Tokyo Imperial University, and in 1940 he and his publisher were indicted for insulting the imperial dignity. Both were convicted on one of nine counts in 1942, but they were set free due to a procedural error.[82] The historical reliability of his interpretation is a matter of debate, even today, but not the thesis behind it concerning the fictitious nature of the beginning of the Japanese imperial dynasty. But if Tsuda's work aroused any doubts about the divine origins of the imperial house in Shiratori's mind, he did not reveal them to Hirohito at this time. Indeed, it appears that he entertained no such doubts. Instead, Shiratori had an abiding concern for the sacred jewel's importance for the imperial tradition and the unique sacred quality of the imperial line.

During the war he again addressed this subject, emphasizing the native Japanese attributes of the jewel, in an article that appeared posthumously after the war. Between December 1947 and September 1948, more than five years after his death, this article appeared in three installments in the distinguished journal *Tōyō gakuhō* (Far East Quarterly). In this work, "Jindaishi no shinkenkyū" (New Research on the History of the Age of the Gods), Shiratori specifically denied the Confucian interpretation of the regalia.[83] The title of the article, one notes, is virtually the same as the one published by Tsuda in 1913. It is a lengthy elaboration of the lecture to the crown prince in 1916 and the subsequent article published in 1917. Originally Shiratori may have intended them to challenge his own student's conclusions: Tsuda had used his teacher's methodology—philology—to demystify the age of the gods and explain the origins of these myths in terms of power politics in ancient times; Shiratori, however, used these methods to elucidate ancient Japanese mythology and support the classical interpretation of the imperial house's place in Japanese history.

In emphasizing the uniquely Japanese nature of these myths Shiratori rejects the Confucian interpretation accepted by many intellectuals: "According to conventional explanations, the jewel stands for benevolence, the sword courage, and the mirror wisdom [or knowledge 智]. But the results of our research show that instead they are to be understood as things with a more concrete, profound meaning."[84] In Japanese belief, according to Shiratori, that which has a concrete, immediate relation to sustaining human life has a more "profound meaning" than a theoretical moral construct. Throughout this last essay he elaborates on this meaning along the lines of the earlier article. The jewel is associated with grain and procreation and symbolizes the virtue and powers of the Sun Goddess. It is also given precedence over the sword and mirror.

In short, Shiratori presented a pseudoscientific explanation of the worldview indicated by Japanese myths, proposing in particular their superiority to Chinese Confucianism. He employed academic terminology in elucidating the concept of Japan's national polity and the divine nature of the imperial house to lend the legitimacy of science to this ideology. His methodology is not unlike the proof of Japan's unique polity proposed by Sugiura based on his version of late nineteenth-century English natural science. Their methods and purposes—scientism in the service of Imperial Japan—were the same but their means to this end were different. Sugiura used specific elements of foreign cultures to lend sophistication and legitimacy to the position of the imperial line in Japanese society. Shiratori reacted against non-Japanese influences and emphasized native Japanese culture over imports from abroad.

This difference of opinion is an important aspect of the reception of foreign cultures in Japan. On the one hand there is adulation of foreign imports; on the other there is an overemphasis on native customs and beliefs; together these two extremes lead to the adaptation of foreign cultures to the "Japanese way of life." This tension between native and foreign cultures has been described by at least one Japanese historian, Ienaga Saburō,[85] as a significant consideration throughout Japanese history. Here, in Hirohito's teachers of Japanese ethics and history, one can see a modern example of this phenomenon.

Education and Influence

There is never a one-to-one relationship between what a person is taught as a child and what one does as an adult. Certainly it would be an exaggeration to say that Emperor Hirohito lived out historical examples presented to him when he was crown prince. But Japanese historical figures were presented in a manner calculated to stimulate respect for "traditional" virtues, and there are certain parallels between Hirohito's positions in the prewar years and the actions of exemplary figures in ancient history. The models cited from ancient history also had a noteworthy aspect in common with modern figures like General Nogi—they were all noblemen or high-ranking military officers who acted decisively in the interests of the imperial house and imperial state.

Shiratori and Sugiura adapted ancient history and ethical teachings to modern ideology. Ancient Chinese culture was presented with the same slant: to highlight the superiority of Japanese history and ethics. As Sugiura indicates in the introduction to his lectures, the unique character of Japanese morality—the sublime nature of the Japanese folk and the supreme position of the imperial house—was to be given special attention.

Crown Prince Hirohito may have found these lectures boring; he may have taken exception to the lessons preached and examples presented. But this seems unlikely. On the contrary, he appears to have taken the lectures by Sugiura and Shiratori very seriously. Otherwise he would not have displayed an interest in history;[86] he would not have had Sugiura tutor his future wife; nor would he have requested that Sugiura continue his lectures for him and his wife at the palace after the school was disbanded. Moreover, it appears that the future emperor adopted the methodology of Sugiura and Shiratori. Both tutors manipulated Western science and ancient Japanese history to legitimize and explain the preeminent position of the imperial house in Japan. The Shōwa emperor later borrowed the notion of English constitutional monarchy similarly to explain with a modern theory his action and inaction as head of the imperial line—disregarding the Meiji Constitution and the decision-making process in prewar Japan of which he was part. His misuse of "constitutional monarchy" is especially obvious in his distortion of his role in prewar military planning. It seems significant, therefore, that the imperial ethics and Japanese history taught to Hirohito were based on a distortion of scientific principles using distortions of historical reality.

6

·

Ancient Institutions and Foreign Cultures:

New Interpretations for Modern Times

Hirohito's teachers of ethics and history, Sugiura Shigetake and Shira-tori Kurakichi, employed pseudoscientific methods in handling ancient Japanese history and Chinese culture. Here Sugiura's lectures are examined once again, this time with special emphasis on his treatment of foreign influences on Japanese culture.

Taika Reforms: Ancient and Modern Implications

Throughout Sugiura's teaching program, emperors were singled out to illustrate moral lessons. Of a total of 154 lectures, however, only one took a member of the imperial house as its main topic. This was the talk on the leader of the Taika Reforms, Crown Prince Nakanoōe no Ōji (626–671), who later became Emperor Tenji. The Taika Reforms of 645 played a singular role in legitimizing the imperial house in Japan. They have been an object of controversy and intensive study for many centuries but remain little known outside that country. This was also true in Sugiura's day. The reforms, which included extensive changes in Japan's administrative apparatus, were modeled after T'ang political institutions. Sugiura began his Taika lecture with an important message for all Japanese leaders ancient and modern: the value of foreign imports. Even the highly esteemed culture of China was of value only after it had been adapted to Japan's unique situation:

From time immemorial our country has had a feudal system *(hōkensei)*, and [with the Taika Reforms] it was transformed into a prefectural system. Various institutions were styled after those of the Chinese T'ang dynasty, but basically the national customs of China and those of our country are different. Therefore, the T'ang system was not simply copied. It was changed and adapted to our national customs. This is the rationale behind the great brilliance manifested in the new Taika government. Since the [Meiji] Restoration our country has been styled after the institutions of Western civilization, but these were adapted to Japan's national conditions and in the future we must also pay attention to this.[1]

Significantly, after this introduction, Sugiura did not review the Taika Reforms as such. He praised them but never told the crown prince what they were. Instead, he was intent upon imparting his message: foreign institutions and ideas must be evaluated and adapted in light of Japan's special situation. Just as Crown Prince Nakanooe adapted Chinese institutions to Japan's needs in the seventh century, Crown Prince Hirohito should do the same with Western systems in the twentieth. When we assess Hirohito and his assertions about being a "constitutional monarch," we should keep this advice in mind.

Precedents for Modern Times

Sugiura's choice of Crown Prince Nakanooe no Ōji as a lecture topic is interesting. The ancient histories have little to say about him during his reign, but a great deal to say about his activities as crown prince.[2] The lecture was given in the fall of 1916 on the occasion of Hirohito's investiture as crown prince.[3] According to Sugiura, Nakanooe is an especially good example of the courage and wisdom expected of a future emperor. National history, as Sugiura saw it, contained numerous examples in ancient times of exemplary crown princes.

The first was Yamato Takeru, who pacified the Kumaso in the west and subdued the Emishi in the east.[4] His military prowess illuminates the pages of Japanese history and has been admired by many in following ages. He died in middle age, however, and never ascended the throne. (Legend says he was thirty-two.) Next comes Shōtoku Taishi (574–622).[5] He was a precocious child who supposedly spoke from the day he was born. As an adult he was known for his great wisdom, and he promoted the importation of Chinese culture and Buddhism. His Seventeen-Article Constitution is one of the outstanding achievements of Japan's history.[6] But he too died in his middle years without becoming emperor. After Shōtoku Taishi, Sugiura introduced Crown Prince Nakanooe, who, with Nakatomi no Kamatari's counsel, accomplished great things. He saved the country from the dangers confronting it, and later he instituted legal codes *(ritsuryō)* and organized government affairs. He is revered in history as the wise leader of a restoration *(chūkō)*. These reforms in 645—the Taika Kaishin—were often cited by Meiji leaders as the model for the Meiji Restoration.

The entire historical section of Sugiura's lecture follows very closely the text of the *Nihon Shoki* (years 642–644).[7] Many precedents are cited for future emperor Hirohito, not the least of which is Nakanoōe's agreement with Kamatari. The importance of reporting this agreement cannot be overemphasized, because Kamatari was the founder of the Fujiwara House. The Fujiwara became the highest-ranking noble house and traditional advisers to the throne, a tradition that reached into modern times.[8] Since this is one of the most important episodes in Japanese history and Crown Prince Nakanoōe was introduced as an exemplary model for Hirohito, a passage from Sugiura's rendition is translated in Appendix 7.

In the mid-seventh century, the danger confronting the country was the imperial ambitions of the Soga family. The Taika Reforms were, in part, an answer to this threat. Crown Prince Nakanoōe and Kamatari planned a course of action together to deal with the upstart Sogas. Nakanoōe is presented as a heroic figure because he and Kamatari saved the nation from a group of usurpers, much as Hirohito would do in February 1936.[9] But here again Sugiura edits events to suit his purposes.

Soga no Iruka hatched a plot to have his candidate, Prince Furubitonoōe, put on the throne, and he sent his henchmen to seize Prince Yamashironoōe, Shōtoku's son. The prince fled to the mountains and was urged by followers to resist. There he decided to sacrifice himself rather than start a civil war and have the accompanying bloodshed on his conscience:

> If we did as thou sayest [Yamashironoōe said to his supporters], we should certainly succeed. In my heart, however, I desire not to impose a burden on the people for ten years. For the sake of one person only, why should I distress our myriad subjects? Moreover, I do not wish it to be said by later generations that for my sake anyone has mourned the loss of a father or mother. *Is it only when one has conquered in battle that he is to be called a hero? Is he not also a hero who has strengthened his country with the sacrifice of his own life?*[10]

These noble sentiments, however, were not included in Sugiura's lecture. And years later Hirohito, despite his assertions about wanting to abdicate and live the quiet life of a scientist, was to follow the path of the combative Crown Prince Nakanoōe, not that of the thoughtful Prince Yamashironoōe.

Shortly after making this statement Yamashironoōe returned to the temple from which he had fled, and there he and his family strangled themselves. They were not exterminated or wiped out *(horobosu)* by someone else as indicated by Sugiura. Here again Sugiura relies mainly on the earlier *Nihon Shoki* text but interpolates from the *Jinnō Shōtōki*, which better suits his purposes. In the eighth-century text the word *"jikei"* can only mean that they strangled themselves, as Aston has translated. Sugiura, however, inserts the verb from the fourteenth-century text, *"horoboshitatematsuru,"* indicating that Iruka "killed" Prince Shōtoku's descendants.[11] Sugiura interprets Japanese history freely to make his case. The enemies of the imperial house seem even more wicked than they were, and he erases what may have been regarded in modern Imperial Japan as a blemish on the imperial tradition: lack of courageous action by Shōtoku's son.

Throughout his lecture, moreover, Sugiura ignores the fact that Confucian norms and administrative reforms "for the good of the nation" gloss over a struggle for power between the foremost families of that day. In the contest between the Sogas and Prince Nakanoōe that brought about the end of Prince Shōtoku's line, Soga no Emishi wanted to place Furubito on the throne because he was the son of Emperor Jomei (r. 629–641) and one of Emishi's daughters. He had succeeded in opening what came to be the time-honored path to power for those outside the imperial house in ancient Japan: placing a daughter at court as an imperial consort who bore the emperor a son—in this case Nakanoōe's elder half-brother, Furubito. Emishi was by rights the grandfather of the heir-apparent to the throne, and his influence would grow accordingly. Nakanoōe's appointment as crown prince obstructed this plan.

Nakanoōe too was Jomei's son, but his mother was Empress Kōgyoku (r. 642–645), the daughter of one of Emperor Jomei's brothers. Nakanoōe was appointed crown prince because both his father and mother were well within the royal household, posing no threat to the dominance of the imperial house. Later he became emperor because, with Kamatari's help, he defeated the Sogas and solidified his family's position at the pinnacle of Japanese society. The chroniclers who composed the *Nihon Shoki* recounted these events with an emphasis on Confucian ethics and statecraft, but family ties and family politics were in fact the deciding factors. In the future, Kamatari's descendants, the Fujiwara, would also seek to enhance their political influence just as the Sogas had done: by placing a daughter at court who bore an imperial son and heir to the throne.

Politics in ancient Japan, as in other times and places, had little to

do with ethical niceties. Sugiura, however, was concerned with extracting moral lessons from ancient politics regardless of the realities. This
meant legitimizing the supreme position of Hirohito's house in Japan.

Nakanoōe and Hirohito

Nakanoōe's accomplishments as crown prince, for the good of the
nation, were more important than "assuming the imperial dignity."
Kōtoku remained on the throne for almost ten years. Upon his death,
Crown Prince Nakanoōe again was in a position to be elevated to
emperor. But again he demurred, and the former Empress Kōgyoku
reascended the throne as Empress Saimei (r. 655–661). Nakanoōe
remained crown prince by his own choice. Sugiura states that he did
so because, together with Nakatomi no Kamatari, he wished to con-
centrate on carrying out the Taika Reforms. Here Sugiura may be putting thoughts into Nakanoōe's head, but at least he is not stretching
his sources as elsewhere. There are many notations in the *Nihon
Shoki* about the difficulties encountered during the reign of Emperor
Kōtoku in carrying out the reforms. The following statement, however, appears to be a typical embellishment.

According to Sugiura, Japan almost became involved in a war at this
time. On the Korean peninsula the kingdom of Silla with the aid of the
T'ang Chinese defeated the kingdom of Paekche. The latter sent
envoys to Japan requesting aid, which was granted. In the First Month,
661, a fleet was dispatched to the west, but it only got as far as Tsuku-
shi, near present-day Hakata, when the empress died and the fleet
turned back. Crown Prince Nakanoōe, according to the lecture, then
countermanded the former empress' decision. Rather than pursue the
course of a warlike state and send an expedition abroad he cut off relations with Korea altogether. Internal and external affairs were regarded
in terms of "root and branch" or "substance and shadow" (*honmatsu*),
and many historians, according to Sugiura, have subsequently praised
this policy of emphasizing domestic affairs.

In fact, the *Nihon Shoki* says envoys arrived from Paekche as stated
above in the Seventh Month, 660, and an imperial ship (not a fleet) put
to sea on the Sixth Day, First Month, 661, which shortly thereafter
turned back. But the empress was still alive and the entire description
of Nakanoōe's cancelation of the expedition is not mentioned.[12] Perhaps this story about Crown Prince Nakanoōe comes from a later
source, but the account is not to be seen in the two well-known histories, the *Jinnō Shōtōki* or the *Dainihonshi*. In view of the ready avail-
ability of the *Nihon Shoki* when Sugiura was writing his lectures, as
well as his numerous references to this work, one is led to believe

that, again, his principal interest was not history. He was bent upon telling a morality-tale. The immediate lesson would seem to be the necessity of enlightened but firm administration at home and avoidance of foreign adventures. It appears this lesson was not lost on Hirohito. At the beginning of his reign in 1928, for example, when the warlord Chang Tso-lin was murdered in Manchuria, Hirohito heeded this advice: he demanded an investigation of the incident and saw the matter consequently to its end.

Nakanoōe was crown prince for twenty-three years. He was forty-three years old (forty-two by Western count) when he became emperor, a fairly advanced age in the seventh century. Known as Emperor Tenji, he died in the fourth (tenth in fact) year of his reign. His greatest achievements, Sugiura reminded Hirohito, were accomplished while he was crown prince. He was a model of courage and decisiveness. His wisdom was like that of a mirror reflecting things as they really are. Particularly important for a Japanese leader of state, he "japanized" *(nihonka)* Chinese institutions *(bunbutsu,* meaning law, learning, the arts, religion, and so forth) with great facility. He well understood the logic of changing times and was full of humility. He recognized talent in other men and appointed Kamatari to responsible positions. He deliberated carefully and made meticulous preparations. Therefore, Sugiura concluded, Crown Prince Nakanoōe has been revered in later times and is known by the posthumous name "Heavenly Wisdom" (Tenji).

Sugiura had a reputation as a masterful teacher, and here he demonstrates this talent. Not only did he impart general knowledge about how ancient institutions including foreign imports should be adapted to conditions in Japan, he also spoke to his students directly. In this case he ended his lecture in a manner calculated to address Hirohito's situation. In 1916 the future emperor was already crown prince, but no one knew how long he might so remain. Emperor Taishō's mental debility could well render him incapable of carrying out the ceremonies and functions of his office without killing him, and Hirohito might be called upon to assume the burdens of a monarch as regent for his father for many years. Hirohito was in fact appointed regent in 1921, five years before his father died. In 1916 Sugiura may have believed it was imperative to prepare the crown prince to assume the de facto duties of emperor.

George Washington, Ōyama Iwao, and the Ethics of the Day

Prior to the turn of the century, Sugiura uncritically incorporated the Japanese insular mentality into his scientism. Prior to World War I, he incorporated it into his lectures to the emperor who would authorize World War II. His reaction to the death of the "elder statesman" *(genkun)* Field Marshal Ōyama Iwao (1842–1916), former lord keeper of the privy seal, supreme commander of Japanese military forces in Manchuria during the Russo-Japanese War, president of the House of Councilors, army minister, and more, is a good example of his peculiar way of thinking: it prompted him to lecture on the similarities between Ōyama and the first president of the United States, George Washington.[13] As these similarities may not be self-evident, this lecture is summarized in detail in Appendix 8. The lecture concluded with a short quote from one of Sugiura's sources of inspiration:

> Respectfully, I would consider the Imperial Rescript on Education: "The teachings bequeathed by Our Imperial Ancestors . . . are infallible for all ages and true in all places."[14]
>
> Even among Westerners like Washington, although there are differences between conditions in countries East and West, it appears that with respect to the beauty of that which is said and done, many persons are mutually in accord with the morality *(dōtoku)* of our country. Confucius evaluated Yü Wang saying, "I can find no flaw in the character of Yü."[15] One can also say this of George Washington: Likewise, I can find no fault in him as a Westerner.[16]

Sugiura's point is that Washington, even though a foreigner, is a fine example of Japanese values.

This sort of teaching agrees with what Japanese moral reformers in the late 1880s were advocating—men like Kuga Katsunan, Miyake Setsurei, and Inoue Tetsujirō.[17] And much earlier, in 1879, the founder of the Japanese Armed Forces and a later prime minister of Japan, Yamagata Aritomo (1838–1922), wrote:

> Since the Restoration we have modeled our legal system on foreign laws, and the people now know that we must have laws to preserve society. But we have failed to realize that society must also be maintained with morals and customs *(dōtoku shūkan)*.[18]

These men were not against adapting models from the West to further Japanese values, but this in no way meant supplanting the latter with the former. Through properly defining the "national essence" *(kokusui)*, ideologues like Kuga and Miyake argued, "this definition of the nation might then become the center of a 'citizenship' *(kokuminshugi)* that would admit Western influence and at the same time preserve Japan's distinctive national character *(kokuminsei)*." That is, they were concerned about developing a "concept of citizenship" *(kokuminteki no kannen)* based on indigenous values, meaning the *kokutai* and imperial house. To this end they had nothing against using foreign models, so long as one did not lose sight of the ultimate goal—a strong nation based on "being Japanese."[19]

Meiji Japanese interest in foreign lands, one must add, was not unique. It paralleled that of their foreign contemporaries. Consistent with the unquestioned concepts of statecraft of that day, European and American statesmen saw the world outside their national borders as a source of raw materials for local industry, as well as cheap exotic goods to bolster the home economy, and expansionist policies brought political power and influence at home and abroad. Japanese ideologues too looked abroad, not for the sake of contributing to the international community, but for the sake of promoting national unity at home and expansion overseas. Opinion makers from "among the people" *(min-kan)*[20] were at the forefront of those calling for war with China in 1894, war against Russia in 1904, and expansion throughout Asia. Just prior to the conflict with China, for example, Kuga published articles in his newspaper with titles like "A Country Which Obstructs Our Nation's *(teikoku)* Korea Policy Is Not a Civilized Country *(bunmei koku)*" and "Our China Policy Requires a War Solution." In 1904 similar articles were forthcoming—for example, "No Opening of Hostilities (Only Watch Russia's Stupidity)."[21] Publications like these had a great influence on the Japanese public.

Sugiura's thinking as revealed in his lectures clearly conformed with the ideas of these intellectual advocates of "cultural nationalism." These men were much more important, perhaps, than Sugiura.[22] But in the end he may have had a more lasting effect on Japanese history through his role in educating the Shōwa emperor. His handling of George Washington illustrates his approach to foreign cultures—as does a further example, his lecture on the emperor of Germany, Wilhelm II. The Japanese adopted and adapted many things from Germany in the late nineteenth century, including much German constitutional theory and Germany's military system.[23] In 1920, however, many Japanese, including Sugiura, were critical of Germany.

Kaiser Wilhelm II: Facts versus Fiction

Kaiser Wilhelm II is one of the more trying figures in recent German history. As one American biographer wrote: "Although never boring, Wilhelm II was not a particularly pleasant person who surrounded himself with other not particularly pleasant people."[24] Just before the turn of the century, one aspect of this unpleasantness, his impulsiveness, was thought by many high officials to be endangering the throne and the state.[25] Nevertheless, during World War I the Kaiser was not a very effective figure, and from the middle to the end of the war he was "little more than a mouthpiece for the military."[26] Sugiura did not know this, nor was he concerned about German history. He wanted Crown Prince Hirohito to learn from Wilhelm's mistakes. In order to do this he misrepresented his source of information.

Sugiura began his lecture on "The Former Emperor of Germany Wilhelm II" with a summary of the immediate concerns confronting those governing Japan as a result of World War I:

> The great world war that took place recently not only completely altered the situation of the various nations; it was also an extraordinary event that gave impetus to great changes in the thinking of the people in each country. For example, the various monarchies of Russia, Germany, Austria, and so forth not only collapsed; the dilemma arose of whether or not the republican governments established after their collapse should be retained. Also, the thinking of various people in various countries was buffeted by the economic problem of the distribution of wealth and the political problems of equality and freedom.[27]

Sugiura's preamble reflects the worries of the ruling elite in Japan: highly respected European monarchies had fallen; people throughout the world were being tempted by dubious social and political theories. This was not, however, an original analysis of the contemporary situation. Sugiura borrowed it from a book by the former foreign minister of Austria-Hungary, Count Ottokar Czernin (1872–1932).[28] There were many complex reasons behind Germany's defeat in World War I, and Sugiura thought Emperor Wilhelm II played a central role in these developments. To depict the sort of a person Wilhelm was, he constructed a critique of his character from the book by Count Czernin.

Sugiura acquired this book from Hozumi Nobushige (1856–1926), a prominent legal scholar, who received it from Miura Yagorō in France. Sugiura and Hozumi probably came to know one another at the forerunner to Tokyo Imperial University, the Daigakunankō, which they attended at the same time. Hozumi was in England and Germany studying law between 1876 and 1881. After returning to Japan he became a professor at Tokyo Imperial University. One of his most important works, "A Theory of the Evolution of Law" (*Hōritsu shinkaron*), contains an extensive comparison of the German and English legal systems. Hozumi appears to have had a good command of German, but Sugiura did not. His lecture differs greatly from the German original. The mistakes or misinterpretations show how Sugiura departed from the information available to him in order to present Hirohito with moral instruction. Reality was, once again, adapted to the exigencies of the day. The following tra:.slation is from Sugiura's lecture to Crown

Prince Hirohito. (The page numbers in brackets refer to the German text.)

I. Every individual is a product of his lineage, education, and experience. When judging Wilhelm II one must first keep in mind that the emperor, from the time he was a child until he became an adult, was always deceived. He was only shown a society that never existed. [p. 70]

II. I do not think there is a ruler, after all, who had better intentions than the emperor of Germany. The emperor lived for the sake of his calling as he saw it. All of his thoughts and desires were focused on Germany. All the emperor's pleasure was greatly, moreover happily, related to only one ideal —the German people. If great things were simply the result of good intentions, the emperor could have accomplished them. [p. 71]

III. The emperor never understood the real effects of his own actions. He truly was misled, not only by those close to him, but by the entire German people. [p. 71]

IV. The emperor lacked training *(kunren)* in the school of real life. Therefore he continually erred in his estimates of human nature *(ninjō)*.[29] [pp. 77–78]

V. So far as I know, there was only one general who regularly spoke frankly with the emperor. This was Alois von Schönburg.[30] [p. 80]

VI. The atmosphere of the emperor's daily life probably would have caused even the healthiest plant to wither and die. The emperor's words and deeds, whether good or bad, immediately received ardent approbation. There were always a dozen people or so near at hand who praised the emperor to the heavens.[31] [p. 83]

VII. If someone had explained the bad effects of his actions to the emperor—that throughout the world mistrust of the emperor is growing, this would have promoted self-reflection on his part. This would have been the case, that is, if instead of having one or two such people there had been many.[32] [p. 90]

VIII. The emperor is thoroughly kind and moreover a good person. Doing good things brought him true happiness. He did not hate even his enemies. [p. 91]

Ottokar Czernin was a career diplomat. He became foreign minister in 1916 and advocated a quick separate peace at Germany's expense. In this way he sought to save the monarchy and aristocracy, which earlier he had staunchly defended. Czernin was obliged to resign in April 1918 due to his involvement in the Sixtus Affair—a separate peace officially initiated by the Austro-Hungarian emperor and strongly supported by the foreign minister. As Czernin knew Wilhelm II personally and was in a position to judge his character, Sugiura chose a good source for his information. But he misrepresented Czernin's work.

Although the chapter cited by Sugiura is titled "Wilhelm II.," throughout the original text there are comparisons with Emperor Karl of Austria-Hungary. Moreover, Czernin often speaks of monarchs in general. No distinction is made throughout the Japanese text, however, and it is introduced as a critique of Wilhelm II. Sugiura did not trouble himself with this difference because it suited his purpose—the construction of a moral lesson—to criticize the last German emperor. Of course, one could argue that he simply did not understand the source he used. But this is unlikely because it implies he did not take his mandate to instruct the future emperor seriously enough to investigate his sources thoroughly. When Sugiura erred, moreover, he erred consistently in the direction of making Wilhelm seem even worse than he was in order to fit his moral instruction.

Hirohito's teacher continued in the same vein in summarizing Czernin's main points—a summary that varies considerably from his source. Kaiser Wilhelm II, according to Sugiura, was a wise planner. He was a good and virtuous person, religious, the model of what an enlightened ruler should be. Nevertheless, due to the bad atmosphere at court he misled his country and himself. Because the Kaiser was always secluded at court, he was unfamiliar with the real world, said Sugiura. This criticism is at once striking and dismaying. Not only has it little to do with what Czernin wrote, but Sugiura criticized the lifestyle of Kaiser Wilhelm II and those around him without seeing that this same lifestyle was being forced on the future Japanese monarch.

Throughout history, East and West, Sugiura continued, this sort of isolation has been a problem. Indeed, an emperor's conscientious advisers have often feared that because of it their sovereign's wisdom would suffer. For this reason, since ancient times, one spoke directly with the ruler and diligently remonstrated with him. Sugiura cites mythical and real Chinese emperors from the distant past who have been acclaimed for accepting this practice and condemned for disregarding it. For example, there was the second emperor of the Ch'in dynasty (221–207 B.C.), who listened only to the flattery of the eunuch Chao Kao (one of the most infamous villains in Chinese history) and brought an early end to his dynasty.[33] Ancient Japanese emperors are cited too: Yūryaku (r. 456–479), whose line was disqualified from imperial succession due to the (fictive) atrocities of a descendant (Buretsu, r. 498–506), and exemplary models like Tenji (r. 662–671), Murakami (r. 946–967), and of course Emperor Meiji.

Almost all emperors were careful to accept the practice of remonstration, Sugiura observed. If a ruler hears himself praised and is proud, he is foolish. Ancient monarchs of this type invited disaster. Similarly,

Wilhelm I (1797–1888, r. 1861–1888) in Germany built up the Reich using men like Otto von Bismarck (1815–1898) and Helmuth Moltke (1800–1891). Bismarck habitually spoke very directly to the emperor. Wilhelm II, on the other hand, had long been displeased with Bismarck and shortly after his enthronement relieved him of office. (In fact Bismarck stayed on for over a year.) Instead of appointing men of great talent as Wilhelm I had done, Wilhelm II relied on limited and biased figures, men like Erich Ludendorff (1865–1937), who decided all things on their own. Sugiura then criticizes Ludendorff from a perspective that would have surprised Czernin. Ludendorff, known for his forthright nature, did not always act in accord with Wilhelm's wishes, and together with Hindenburg was, practically speaking, a military dictator in Germany during the last two years of the war. Perhaps this disturbed Sugiura. But the Austrian foreign minister, Czernin, a strong personality himself, found the same quality laudable.[34] Wilhelm II, said Sugiura, did not welcome good advice and thus invited ruin on himself and his country. This is not the way of a great leader, Sugiura repeated, regardless of how superior he is.

History in various European countries over the last several hundred years, Sugiura concluded, has been the record of the struggle between the right of kings to rule versus people's rights or tyranny versus freedom. When the Romanoff dynasty in Russia fell, not a single noble among many thousands was prepared to risk his life for it. Likewise with the fall of Emperor Wilhelm II. On the one hand this may be the natural flow of history; on the other the emperor and aristocracy brought this calamity upon themselves. The course of history in our country, said Sugiura, is completely different. Certainly the close relation between emperor and ministers is not comparable to that found anywhere else in the world. But contacts with Europe and America have brought their theories rushing in upon us arousing doubts among many—all the more reason for the Japanese to take note of the downfall of the German emperor. And with the collapse of the German monarchy, Sugiura completed a full circle that ended where he began: with the menace of foreign ideologies to naive Japanese. No doubt he believed that the people's rights movement in the middle of the Meiji period and the rice riots shortly before he gave this lecture were due to foreign influences, not shortcomings in Imperial Japan.

Sugiura used, somewhat arbitrarily, Wilhelm II to illustrate two points: empty flattery from sycophants is no substitute for sound advice, and separation from the real world can have disastrous consequences. But judging from Sugiura's own methods, sound advice and one's view of the real world need not be based on that world. The similarities between Hirohito's situation and Wilhelm II's as described by Sugiura seem to have escaped him. Neither he nor the officials charged with administering this school were capable of distancing themselves from their immediate surroundings in order to analyze their own actions as Sugiura had "analyzed" those of Emperor Wilhelm II. The message—the conduct ideally suited to the head of the imperial house —was more important than historical fact or self-critical analysis. Sugiura's imperial ethics were erected on a foundation of sand. Hirohito was taught to be a wise ruler so that he would not endanger the continued existence of the imperial line. But basically Sugiura's method—using scientific and historical information without regard for its original context and meaning—contradicted his intent: to acquire wisdom. In the future this contradiction would have dire consequences for the emperor. As demonstrated by his participation in military planning, he was inconsistent and did not always address contradictions between theory and reality—advocating friendly relations with Britain, for example, while approving surprise attacks on Britain's concessions in the Far East. Such problems display interesting parallels with Sugiura's teaching methods.

The Meiji Charter Oath: A Progressive Proclamation?

Finally, one must consider the manner in which the Meiji Charter Oath of 1868 was introduced to the future emperor. Hirohito was no doubt well acquainted with it because of its hallowed place in the tradition of modern Japan. But the oath was not terribly progressive, and Sugiura's lecture on it was even less so. The Meiji Charter Oath is quoted by Sugiura in full:

> With this oath we set up as our aim the establishment of the national weal on a broad basis and the framing of a constitution and laws.
>
> 1. Deliberative assemblies shall be widely established and all matters decided by public discussion.
> 2. All classes, high and low, shall unite in vigorously carrying out the administration of the affairs of state.
> 3. The common people, no less than the civil and military officials, shall be allowed to pursue their own calling so that there will be no discontent.
> 4. Evil customs of the past shall be broken off and everything based on the just laws of nature.
> 5. Knowledge shall be sought throughout the world in order to strengthen the foundations of imperial rule.[35]
>
> Our country is undergoing an unprecedented change.[36] With I myself [the emperor] leading the people and making this pledge to the deities of

heaven and earth, broadly speaking this sort of nation is to be established. Setting up the way of national integrity *(banmin hōzen)*, the multitudes also should strive together with this basic purpose![37]

Different people produce different readings of the oath. The last lines added by Sugiura, for example, are not included in most standard versions. His lecture to the crown prince was not as progressive as many later interpreters claim early Meiji leaders intended the Charter Oath to be, and including these lines indicates the direction of his thought—the imperial institution was to have an important role in leading the people. Of course, the Meiji emperor was too young and inexperienced when the oath was promulgated to lead the people personally, but Sugiura may have been closer to the intent of the oath's authors than its later interpreters. The claims of the latter enbody a good deal of wishful thinking based more on foreign ideals than historical reality in Japan.

The Meiji Charter Oath was a "backward-looking" proclamation whose seemingly progressive content was in fact deliberate vagueness on the part of its framers. They wanted to maintain a broad alliance among the contending feudal houses in 1867–1868 and attract as many parties as possible to the struggle against the Tokugawa shogun. According to one historian the Charter Oath

> was a public statement of the government's intentions in the emperor's name which promised that public policy would be formulated only after wide consultation, and that the "base customs of former times" would be abolished. The implication was that the old exclusiveness of Bakufu rule was not to be repeated, or a new Bakufu established. This was to reassure those who were suspicious of Satsuma and Chōshū. It was also to provide a basis for reconciliation with the defeated Tokugawa and the trained officials in their service.[38]

In short, the original framers of this document sought to overcome the problems of the past, as perceived at the time of the Charter Oath, through an appeal to foreign ideals such as representative government. This sort of thinking was not unknown to Sugiura.

Immediately preceding his presentation of the Charter Oath Sugiura reviewed the history of imperial rule in Japan—or, correctly speaking, the lack of same. More than seven hundred years ago Minamoto no Yoritomo (1147–1199) seized power and established the shogunate in Kamakura (near present-day Tokyo). Since then one military man *(bujin)* or another had ruled Japan until 1868. Retired Emperor Gotoba attempted to restore imperial rule during the Jōkyū era (1219–1222) and failed.[39] Emperor Godaigo (1288–1339, r. 1318–1339) succeeded in reestablishing imperial rule during the Kemmu era (1334–1336),[40] but it lasted for only two years. A succession of military rulers followed: the Ashikaga, Oda, Toyotomi, and Tokugawa. Finally, with the reign of Emperor Meiji, the Tokugawa shogun returned the administration of the country to the emperor. "This is truly one of the greatest events in our history," Sugiura commented. Following the recitation of the Meiji Charter Oath and his historical commentary on it, Sugiura noted that Emperor Meiji was only seventeen years old (sixteen by our count) when the oath was promulgated. For the next fifty-odd years this oath served as a guiding light for the people and was the foundation of the nation. He then explained the meaning of each of the articles. (This explanation is detailed in Appendix 9.)

The salient features of Sugiura's lecture on the Meiji Charter Oath constitute a good example of how he used foreign "progressive" ideals in the service of the imperial state. His ideas included: the central importance of the imperial house; a class-oriented concept of personal aspiration that contradicted the freedom from arbitrary rule and the parliamentary system promised in the oath; and an oportunistic appreciation of the usefulness of foreign cultures. Despite the oath's progressive vocabulary, the exhortations to abandon old feudalistic customs, pursue one's personal aspirations, search for new knowledge overseas, and implement it in Japan were not intended to benefit people according to their efforts and abilities. Rather, these pursuits were to enhance the glory of the imperial house and build a more powerful Japan.[41]

Sugiura's summary of his lecture on the Charter Oath constitutes an apt précis of his lectures on Japanese ethics, as well, meaning imperial studies, and indicates the nature of their impact on the crown prince. Sugiura propounded a "prescientific Japanese morality," to adapt from Stefan Tanaka, intended as a foundation for building a powerful Imperial Japan. This morality became the basis of Hirohito's renowned scientific predisposition, especially his concept of constitutional monarchy: theories and ideas overshadowed empirical knowledge. Consistent with examples found in Sugiura's lectures, Hirohito developed a tendency to impose his preconceptions on the real world. This did not influence his approach to physical science and marine biology, but it did color his perception of society and politics in prewar Japan. His feelings about English constitutional monarchy blinded him to the differences between political realities in Japan and Great Britain. Just as Germaine Hoston has shown there was Japanese-style liberalism in prewar Japan,[42] so too was there Japanese-style constitutional monarchy. But practically speaking such differences were often overlooked by the future emperor.

Hirohito and Monarchy

Hirohito maintained throughout his reign that he was a constitutional monarch and never wished to be anything else. He was impressed by the royal house in Great Britain during his visit, and this was the model he claimed he wanted to emulate.[43] But other than this short visit to England, whose people he encountered only in broken French or through translators because he knew no English, little else in his early education or experience would seem to have instilled such a set of convictions.

Another possible source for these beliefs was Hirohito's grandfather. Hirohito venerated his grandfather, Emperor Meiji, and his popular image could well have influenced him in the direction of constitutional monarchy. But Meiji was much better informed about a rather different style of constitutional monarchy. Unlike Hirohito, who apparently received only one lecture, in English, on Walter Bagehot and English constitutional monarchy,[44] Meiji was given a number of lectures at court, in Japanese, on the theories of the German constitutional scholar Lorenz von Stein (1815–1890). Prior to these lectures Itō Hirobumi and many others visited Stein in Vienna, where he was a professor, to learn about his ideas. Moreover, Stein prepared special lectures in English for translation into Japanese and presentation to the Japanese emperor—lectures that dealt in particular with the relation between the emperor and the national polity.[45] Clearly Stein's concept of constitutional monarchy was well known and highly appreciated among Meiji leaders, including the emperor.

Stein's vivid description of the organ theory of state exemplifies his influence and methods. Stein was a fanatic for systematizing his ideas using graphic presentations. One such presentation, adapted to the Japanese polity, depicted a human body with Japanese government ministries imposed on it. This conceptualization of government and its association with the *kokutai* was well known in late nineteenth-century Japan, and Stein's use of this metaphor made his theories much easier to grasp.[46] Moreover, his ideas were better suited to Japanese purposes than those of the English. While Stein called for a "social monarchy," in which the sovereign stood above society and was a neutral mediator between conflicting parties within it, he categorically opposed a division of powers: "The head of state, parliament, and administration . . . were a united entity that was embodied by the head of state personally." In particular, all officers of the armed forces stood directly under the emperor's command.[47]

This concept of constitutional monarchy was very different from that of Walter Bagehot, who believed that royalty "is not to be involved directly with the business of government but to be the head of society."[48] Certainly this is what the Shōwa emperor's advisers advocated later. But it was Stein, not Bagehot, who influenced the Meiji concept of constitutionalism. If Hirohito's grandfather influenced him in this respect, it was in the direction of placing all state power and authority in the hands of the sovereign. Thus Hirohito would have learned about the consolidation of power in the emperor's person, not the separation of powers characteristic of the Anglo-Saxon system of government.

Moreover, like his grandson, Emperor Meiji was popular but not a man of the people, at least during the years when Hirohito could have known and observed him. Though Emperor Meiji made many outings, the press complained in 1910: "Only nobles and men of status were permitted in the imperial presence, while 'in a constitutional system the people are supposed to be the bulwark of the throne.' "[49] Similarly, the government was not a government of, by, and for the people. It had been established as "His Majesty the emperor's government."[50]

Later Ideology

Not just constitutional monarchy but also the mythology surrounding the imperial line would become important to Hirohito's feelings about the significance of the imperial house in Japan. This can be seen, for example, in the emperor's announcement of Japan's surrender at the end of World War II and the reasons for this decision. If civilization and the Japanese folk are destroyed, he asked, "how are We to save the millions of Our subjects; or to atone Ourselves before the hallowed spirits of Our Imperial Ancestors?"[51] English constitutional monarchy was forgotten; now he was moved by the ideology of the imperial line. The emperor adhered similarly to the "Japanese" virtues illustrated by the figures from ancient history cited earlier. He stood for the virtues Tenji and Nintoku supposedly embodied, he repeatedly emphasized, and would have us believe that Jimmu was unimportant to him. This, however, was not the case. As we have seen, Hirohito often asserted his prerogatives as head of the imperial line in talks with Japan's military leaders.

Indeed, numerous incidents show this imperial ideology was accepted in the 1930s and 1940s by many. Although the imperial rescript declaring war on the United States and Great Britain contains no reference to the regalia, for example, the imperial ancestors, the descent of the Shōwa emperor from same, and his responsibility to them appear prominently at the beginning and end of the document. In the declaration the war is justified, Japan's grievances against the Western Powers are listed, and Japan's own peaceful intentions are enumerated. It also contains Hirohito's famous disclaimer: "It has been truly unavoidable and to be sure is contrary to Our wishes."[52] In evaluating this document, however, one must distinguish between the meaning of the myths for the notion of national polity and the universalistic interpretations of them offered up later. Moreover, actual grievances and the immediate necessity of absolving the imperial house from responsibility for this decision should be distinguished.

Shortly after this rescript was made public the well-known nationalistic writer Tokutomi Iichirō published a commentary with conspicuous reference to the imperial regalia and the three virtues:

> The virtue of sincerity is represented by the Mirror, the virtue of love is represented by the Jewels, and the virtue of intelligence is represented by the Sword.... The interpretation given by Kitabatake Chikafusa has indeed grasped the true meaning. Then, it is not wrong to liken the Three Sacred Treasures to the three virtues of intelligence, love, and courage by saying that the Mirror represents the intelligence which reflects everything, the Jewels, the love which embraces everything, and the Sword, the courage which judges between justice and injustice, honesty and dishonesty.[53]

Here again abstract concepts are associated with specific Japanese symbols of imperial rule. This was a trend common to persons concerned about elevating the national polity, as the foundation of the Japanese nation, to a position equal at least to the moral foundations of other nations. Sincerity, love, and intelligence (Tokutomi), honesty, compassion, and wisdom (Kitabatake), wisdom, benevolence, and courage (Sugiura) are represented by the mirror, jewel, and sword, respectively. And although their terminology varied, the meaning they attached to the symbols was similar. Thus, for example, Kitabatake's sword of wisdom meant "strength and resolution," which is not very different from Sugiura's "courage" and Tokutomi's "intelligence"— which he associates with the courage to make correct judgments. More to the point, the logic inherent to these associations is the same throughout. All explain the imperial regalia partly in terms of Japanese pseudohistory or mythology and partly in terms of widely accepted ethical concepts. Japan's particularistic imperial tradition is legitimized using general concepts accepted in China and the West. Tokutomi was well versed in this ideology and way of thinking—and familiar, too, with at least one of its sources, the *Jinnō Shōtōki*, also used by Sugiura in his ethics lectures to Crown Prince Hirohito. Later the emperor appears to have acted within the same set of assumptions when he conferred with his military leaders as emperor and head of the imperial line while claiming to be a constitutional monarch.

This way of thinking was simultaneously the basis of the Imperial Way and a justification of the decision to go to war. During the war the Japanese translated Tokutomi's essay into English and presented it to the rest of the world to justify their actions. So deeply ingrained were the tenets of this ideology that apparently it did not occur to them that this "justification" appeared to most non-Japanese more like a confirmation of the wrongness of the war and the irrational character of Japanese politics at that time. As for the emperor personally, even if he did not believe literally in the mythology supporting the position of the imperial house, these generalized moral interpretations were well known to him. Hirohito himself did not author the myriad of imperial rescripts he signed. But in view of his early education and actions up to the end of the war, it is difficult to maintain that the rhetorical conventions found at the beginning and end of every rescript were of absolutely no significance to him. Imperial line mythology did reflect the accepted state ideology, and Hirohito participated in its perpetuation.

The Impact on the Crown Prince

Hirohito appears to have been sympathetic to this selective approach to Japanese history and Western learning even as a youth. An early example of this sort of thinking from the crown prince himself is still extant and serves as an introduction to his perception of modern Western concepts.

On 17 August 1921 Sugiura Shigetake visited the palace and discussed the crown prince's school activities with Imperial Household Minister Makino Nobuaki (1861–1949). On this occasion he gave Makino two short essays, one by Hirohito on the Versaille Peace Treaty and one by the future empress, Nagako, on the founder of Wang Yang Ming Neo-Confucianism in Japan, Nakae Tōju. The essay by Hirohito is translated here. He wrote it in January 1920, about one year before he completed his formal education:

> My Impressions on Reading
> the Imperial Proclamation Establishing Peace
>
> On 28 June 1919 in Versailles a treaty with Germany was signed between the allies, meaning the Allied Nations, and Germany. Then it was first ratified by Germany, followed by Italy on 6 October, England on 8 October, France on 13 October, Japan on 30 October. According to the stipulations in the peace treaty, when the three great powers ratified the treaty it was supposed to go into effect. But because Germany did not quickly sign the non-

compliance protocol of the armistice agreement, piling delay on delay, finally the first ratifications took place on the tenth of this month.

Herewith the relationship between Germany and the Allied Nations returned to peace. Anticipating the establishment of peace between the principal opposing powers, the imperial proclamation on establishing peace was issued.

Arriving at this juncture We *(gojin)* were extremely happy. Reading this imperial proclamation now we relate a few of Our feelings and expectations with regard to it.

In this proclamation it is written, "Now there has been a great turn in the course of events and circumstances are changing more and more." But how has the world changed? The realm of ideas in the world is confused. Radical thought is spreading throughout the world and labor problems are becoming rampant. Looking at the postwar misery of the people, one loves peace and believes all countries should cooperate together. Here one looks to the formation of the League of Nations and the convening of a labor conference. In this way the world has changed. On this occasion, as is said in the imperial proclamation, our people should strenuously practice the way of accommodation at all times *(zuiji junnō)*. In particular the imperial proclamation says the following about the League of Nations.

"I [the emperor] truly found this a happy event, and at the same time also believe that from now on the state's responsibilities will be very great." We [Hirohito] also offer Our congratulations on the formation of the League of Nations. We respect and honor the bylaws of this league, and moreover will promote the spirit of the league. We must bring to a conclusion the great duty of establishing everlasting peace in the world. How should one fulfill this responsibility? Our imperial subjects *(teikokujin)* should demonstrate their magnanimity, think about the welfare of all countries, and manage the country together in an amiable manner. By respecting the official rights *(kōze)* of all countries and in accord with the great teachings *(daikyō)* of the world eternal peace should be realized. The proclamation says, "Each person as an individual should favor dignity and steadfastness; should eschew ostentation and luxury." Now in our country extravagance is fashionable. One should pay special attention to this these days.

An important item in the proclamation says, "By nurturing the nation's strength we should ride the tide of fortune." If military preparations are insufficient, in time of an emergency the country cannot be defended. Also negotiations that are beneficial in foreign affairs are difficult to accomplish. Moreover, if industrial production and transport are not improved and labor efficiency is not raised a prosperous country cannot be developed. If these things are not done, we cannot keep pace with other countries.

Regarding that which is set down above, the people—from the upper to the lower classes, military men, civil officials, also workers and entrepreneurs—if they do not strive together as it says in the imperial proclamation no advances in the national destiny can be made.

Our countrymen should bear in mind the felicitous intentions of the imperial proclamation. At the same time these intentions should also be absorbed by the people of the future.

I, who will be entrusted with the great responsibility of guiding political affairs after many years, will honor these intentions and thereby cause the nation to flourish, establish eternal peace, and thereby requite the virtue of my honorable father.

Composed in January 1920[54]

This essay displays the influence of Hirohito's teachers—Shiratori, Sugiura, and the military men in charge of his education. World peace, international cooperation, military preparedness, and industrialization are to be employed to advance Japan's national destiny. To do this, the four social classes—virtually the same ones that made up the despised Tokugawa "feudal order"—were supposed to "strive together" self-lessly. Just as Sugiura warned at the beginning of his lecture on Wilhelm II, radical thought was unsuitable. Japan, unchanged socially, was to advance into the modern age. And Hirohito was to lead them— to guide political affairs. The crown prince saw no contradiction in this appeal. Selected foreign ideas were adopted in a facile manner without regard for inconsistencies between their social and political implications and the domestic social-political situation. Hirohito strongly advocated peace and praised at great length the League of Nations and its goals while displaying some knowledge of the problems of a modern state. But the possibility that "japanized" Confucian ethics ("eschew ostentation and luxury") and the Tokugawa social order might not be appropriate for promoting everlasting world peace and building an industrialized society did not occur to him.

With the exception of radical thought, the crown prince did not recognize the incompatibility of foreign ideals for Japan's domestic society. Indeed, Hirohito's reception of foreign ideas and his perception of prewar Japanese society remind one of the concept of *amae*, introduced to the West many years ago by Takeo Doi.[55] *Amae* refers to self-indulgent behavior in which a person presumes upon a special relationship. The relationship is one of emotional dependency—the parent-child relation, for example. Doi defines a variety of terms to describe the dimensions of this emotional give-and-take, and he notes that this phenomenon is not confined to interpersonal relations. He cites, for example, the manner in which the Japanese react to foreign cultures. First the Japanese seek to "win favor with" *(toriiru)* a respected overseas authority and later to "take it over for their own purposes" *(torikomu).*[56]

Modern Japanese history from the Meiji Restoration to the end of the Greater East Asia War is a typical example of this tendency: "The Japanese are sensitive to trends outside their own world and seek at once to identify with or take over whatever seems in any way superior to themselves." But Doi also refers in the same discussion to a statement by a renowned scholar of Buddhism, Nakamura Hajime: "Generally speaking, in adopting foreign religions, the Japanese have already had some practical ethical framework which they regard as absolute, and have taken over and adopted only insofar as the newcomer would not damage, or would actually encourage and develop, what already existed." The same may be said for political philosophies. This can be seen in the methods and teachings of Sugiura and Shiratori, who "took over" Western notions to reinforce the established ethical and historical framework in Japan. And this way of thinking is clearly present in the essay by Hirohito. On the one hand, the League of Nations, world peace, and modern statecraft are all praised with the assumption that they complement the established Japanese social-ethical framework. Radical thought, on the other hand, would have damaged this framework and was denounced.

Another term introduced by Doi aptly describes Hirohito's relations with his own people: *enryo*.[57] *Enryo* refers to self-restraint and consideration for others. It is related to the Japanese sense of "inner" and "outer" human relationships and the corresponding possibility of imposing self-indulgently on someone *(amaeru)*, depending on the relation. Inner relationships are those of family and immediate relatives. Outer relationships are graded in accord with their emotional proximity to this inner circle. The absence of *enryo*—the necessity of exercising self-restraint and showing consideration for others—within the family is regarded as ideal. One may *"amaeru"* as he pleases. And by definition, relations with people beyond the outermost circle of one's personal acquaintances, complete strangers *(tanin)*, are also characterized by a lack of *enryo*. Consideration for others unknown to one is simply not necessary, because *amaeru* is impossible. In Doi's words: "It is significant that both a high degree of *amae* and its total absence should give rise to the same lack of concern for others." While the latter situation may also lead to self-indulgent conduct, it has a completely different connotation: since there is an utter lack of *amae*, or empathy, with the persons imposed upon they cannot react favorably to it. *Amae* as self-indulgence becomes a brutal lack of concern for others.

Hirohito's unreflecting assumption that the Japanese people were satisfied with their lot shows exactly this lack of consideration. The question arises, however, whether this is because they were part of his family, so to speak, in the "family state" Imperial Japan or because they were so distant from him socially that it was not necessary to show consideration for them. One might answer from the Western point of view that both answers are correct. In the international context, the Japanese people were part of his family state and hence he need not have consideration for them. In the domestic context, they were total outsiders and likewise beyond his consideration. But in the context of *amae* this is impossible. Either a relationship is one of *amae* or it is not. It cannot be both. This tension between what was and what ought to be may help to account for Hirohito's ambivalent behavior vis-à-vis his subjects in prewar Japan.

Moreover, *amae* may have been instrumental in arousing the emperor's admiration of constitutional monarchy. He may have unconsciously sought to "win favor" with his former English hosts and later wished to "take over" this superior style of monarchy for his own purposes. His purposes, however, were not those of the English. Instead of promoting democratic government, Hirohito was intent on furthering the imperial line. A key factor here was the emperor's education.[58] Placed in the emotional context of *amae*, it made him acutely aware of his responsibilities as head of state *and* head of the imperial line— and "taking over" constitutional monarchy was one way of satisfying both constituencies. The imperial line was given the sophistication of a modern Western theory legitimizing monarchy; the state was adorned similarly with a theory of rule that was highly respected in the international community.

Reflections on Hirohito's Education

Sugiura, Hirohito's ethics teacher, deplored the decadence and repression of the feudal age but was blind to the detrimental effects of imperial repression at home or abroad during his own time. He was unable to transcend the Japanese milieu of his immediate existence. Such problems were hardly an exclusive preserve of the Japanese,[59] of course, but reverence for the imperial tradition blinded him to the essential ideals of Western learning—especially respect for dispassionate observation and objective analysis of sociopolitical developments. Within Japan's borders it never occurred to Sugiura and his contemporaries to doubt the primacy of Japan in the world, the status of the imperial house in Japan, or the superiority of the aristocratic houses over those of lesser "commoners." The Japanese penchant for thinking in hierarchical terms put the imperial house at the top of Japanese society and Japan at the pinnacle of the world order. Any other order was unthinkable.

Sugiura's attitudes were not unusual. He was not only a leader of sorts and an opinion maker but a mirror of his age. It would have been natural, then, for Hirohito to adopt his mentor's values. Moreover, the lectures by Hirohito's history teacher reinforced what Sugiura taught: science was put to work for Japanese nationalism as Shiratori elucidated the supposed origins of the Japanese state. During his secondary school years Hirohito may have been attracted to history as well as biology.[60] If this is true, one can only wonder about the depth of his reported pro-Western inclinations given the conservatism of his teachers.

Stefan Tanaka maintains that Shiratori was interested in oriental and Chinese history as a means of creating a "true Japanese history" and establishing Japan's national identity. This identity meant a presence in Asia and the world that was superior to Japan's Far Eastern neighbors and equal, at least, to the nations of the West. Tanaka observes: "Like Leopold von Ranke's and Hegel's ideas on the combination of spirit and history this Japanese variation [the imperial system as a universalistic spiritual force] allowed them to explain themselves as well as their connection to both China and the West."[61] Or in Shiratori's words:

> When asked what is our religion, it is rooted in the imperial household. . . . Our Japaneseness *(yamato damashi)* and our national spirit *(kokumin-teki seishin)* are nurtured through this [belief]. . . . Thus the foundation of the Japanese national spirit is immovable. Because it is immutable, when Confucianism entered from China, we accepted Chinese thought and systems *(seido)* to the extent suitable to this fundamental spirit. And when Buddhism came from India, we accepted only the complementary parts of those teachings. For this reason, the spiritual world of our country has become rich *(hōfu)*, for the fundamental spirit of the Japanese people has not been lost due to the introduction of foreign ideas and systems. This unique belief stands as the central pillar.[62]

The "unique belief" refers, of course, to the imperial house. Elsewhere Tanaka maintains that in Shiratori's hands history demonstrated Japan was a "unique and superior politico-cultural entity" and this was a scientific finding, not historicism.[63] If Hirohito was attracted to Japanese history, his interest was no doubt consistent with the Japanese adaptation of foreign cultures throughout history: the crown prince was enamored by what was offered—confirmation of his position and that of his house in Japanese society, likewise the position of Japan in the world.

Others carried the prostitution of history and social science in the interests of the empire to even greater extremes. Hirohito's supporters insist he was little influenced by this trend. They claim that he acted contrary to the tenor of the times. For example, he is said to have approved of the "organ theory of state" proposed by the prominent legal scholar Minobe Tatsukichi, a thesis that was attacked ferociously by right-wing radicals in the 1930s.[64] But one might view this approval in another light. Not only did the theory pose no danger to the position of the imperial house as head of state in Japan, but it lent modern "scientific" support to this tradition. In praising Minobe's theory, therefore, Hirohito approved of a new sophisticated sanction for the established social order. According to Minobe's theory, the emperor was not simply an organ of the state—he was the highest organ. Thus modern legal theory qualified vaguely the emperor's powers and simultaneously served ancient tradition. It reaffirmed the emperor as the unquestioned head of the sociopolitical order. Hirohito in supporting this theory in no way supported changing that order.

This was exactly what Hirohito had been taught in school. Employ science to interpret and legitimize in a modern manner officially sanctioned traditions—this was what Shiratori and Sugiura had taught when lecturing to Crown Prince Hirohito on history and ethics. It should not surprise us if Hirohito later looked on science and other Western institutions similarly when he was emperor. It would be surprising if he had not. Constitutional monarchy eventually had the same import for the emperor as science had for Sugiura and Shiratori. Each utilized—or in the context of *amae* "took over"—the authority of a Western ideal to legitimize a traditional interpretation of Japan's national destiny,[65] even though these ideals were the basis in the West of a political and social order they were ill prepared to understand, accept, or endorse.

But the European order itself was not homogeneous, of course, and Japanese perceptions of value were not always the same. Between the Meiji and Shōwa eras, there was a break in political ideology—Vienna was succeeded by London, Lorenz von Stein by the followers of Walter Bagehot. In both eras reality was divorced from ideals, and few took note of this divergence. With time both the real world and the Japanese ideals changed, but the change was incomplete and Hirohito was brought up in the breach. This helps to explain the anomalies in the education he received and the policies he later pursued.

Misunderstandings about the nature and import of Hirohito's early training with regard to his prewar activities are not confined to his formal education. His early advisers too are in need of reexamination. Many who maintain that Hirohito was an enlightened exception to traditionalist trends in Japan point to the atmosphere at court—to advisers like Makino and Saionji. But were these men so enlightened? At least one, Count Makino Nobuaki, appears much less so on close examination. The problem of progressive constitutional monarchy in prewar Japan as represented by Makino, one of Hirohito's key advisers between 1921 and 1935, will be taken up next.

7

·

Hirohito's First Adviser:
Count Makino Nobuaki

Makino Nobuaki (1861–1949), along with Saionji Kimmochi (1849–1940) and Kido Kōichi (1889–1977), is generally acknowledged as one of Emperor Hirohito's most important prewar advisers. In terms of Japanese domestic politics the first two have been called "liberal constitutional monarchists."[1] They sustained and sometimes pushed the young sovereign to support progressive politics. Makino and Kido were in a position to do this because of their proximity to the crown prince and emperor officially; Saionji had an unofficial but no less important position in the body politic.

Makino was imperial household minister (1921–1925) and lord keeper of the privy seal, that is, the emperor's political adviser (1925–1935). Saionji, the last "elder statesman" (genrō), was counselor of the emperor from the mid-1920s to the late 1930s. Kido, in contrast to the other two, has been called a "traditionalist" by at least one prominent historian;[2] he was lord keeper of the privy seal from 1940 to 1945. All except Kido spent a great deal of time overseas before attaining their respective positions of influence. The journal written by Saionji's secretary, Kido's diary, and the record of his testimony before the Tokyo war crimes trials have been studied extensively.[3] For this reason Makino will be examined here, using his diaries and other contemporary accounts, to show the character of his political convictions and his influence on Hirohito.

Makino and Japanese Liberalism

Ambassador Joseph Grew called Makino a "moderate" in contrast to the militarists in the 1930s.[4] More recently, at least one modern Japanese scholar, Nakamura Masanori,[5] has called him a "liberal." It seems appropriate, then, to comment here on his reputation in the light of early modern Japanese liberalism. Liberal thought in Imperial Japan, especially as applied to the imperial institution, was rather different from the tradition bearing the same name in the West.[6] Makino was a man of Meiji at home in the high circles of society. Germaine Hoston's description of liberal Meiji elites fits him well:

> [They] held firmly to distinctions among classes and had limited faith in the ability of commoners to rule themselves. In addition, the appeal of the emperor as a symbol of the body politic standing in a special paternal relationship with his people constrained the views of Meiji liberals on the proper constitution of the Japanese polity.[7]

Like others of similar standing and background, Hoston continues, Makino "departed from the tenets with which we have identified political liberalism in two major respects." Not only did loyalty to the throne crimp his "commitment to the contractualist notion of a polity based on popular sovereignty," but many also had difficulty in applying the principles of liberalism "to the liberation of nations from foreign [Japanese] rule." The latter aspect was less pronounced in Makino's case, but it colored his feelings about Japan's position among the nations of the world. Moreover, though regarded a liberal by many of his contemporaries, he was not as liberal as certain Taishō critics of the political system. These liberals, together with the Marxists, "aspired to the fulfillment of the promise of a bourgeois-democratic revolution contained in the Meiji Restoration." Advocates of liberalism as a political philosophy, they stood for "academic freedom, universal suffrage, and liberalization of restraints on education imposed by the *kokutai* orthodoxy."[8]

Makino's thought and actions differed sharply from this purist liberalism. As we shall see, these departures and the constraints noted earlier shaped his political convictions and his influence on Hirohito. In effect Makino's loyalism coincided nicely with the tenets of the history and ethics taught to the crown prince at his school, and it contributed greatly to Hirohito's conception of his role as emperor in prewar military decision making.

Background, Career, and Political Persuasion

Makino Nobuaki (Shinken) was the second son of Ōkubo Toshimichi (1832–1878). His original name was Ōkubo Shinyū (Nobukuma). His was a leading *bushi* (samurai) house in the fief of Satsuma (present-day Kagoshima), and his father Toshimichi played a leading role in the Meiji Restoration of 1868. At an early age Nobuaki was designated heir to the ruling house *(daimyō)* Makino of Mikawa (present-day Aichi). The connection between the two houses was from the time of his great-grandfather, whose daughter married into the Makino family. Nobuaki was brought up in the Ōkubo house, however, not in Mikawa, and he accompanied his father to Tokyo in 1871 shortly after the restoration. Later he went overseas with him on the Iwakura Mission to Europe and America (1871–1873). He remained in America to attend school and returned to Japan in the fall of 1874. At about this time he assumed the name Makino Koretoshi, and three years later he changed his given name to Nobuaki.

Makino attended the newly founded Tokyo Imperial University, but he left before completing his studies and entered the Foreign Ministry. In 1880 he was sent to serve in the Japanese Legation in London. There he may have met the framer of the Meiji Constitution, Itō Hirobumi, when Itō was visiting Europe to study constitutional systems. In 1882 Makino returned to Japan. Thereafter he served in a number of official posts at home and abroad. In 1896 he was appointed envoy extraordinary and minister plenipotentiary and sent to Italy. In 1899 he was sent to Austria and appointed to serve simultaneously in Switzerland. He returned to Japan in 1902. In 1906 he was appointed minister of education in the first Saionji cabinet; in 1911 he became minister of agriculture and commerce in the second Saionji cabinet; in 1913 he was appointed foreign minister in the Yamamoto Gombei cabinet. In 1918–1919 he attended the Paris Peace Conference with Saionji.

Count Makino, though twelve years younger than Saionji, came to his position of influence vis-à-vis Hirohito before the venerable prince. He was appointed imperial household minister in February 1921, and Crown Prince Hirohito was made regent for his mentally ill father, Emperor Taishō, in November of the same year. In 1925 Makino became lord keeper of the privy seal. Thus, including his time as imperial household minister, he was actively engaged in guiding the young crown prince and emperor (r. 1926–1989) in his duties as head of state for fourteen years. There are no exhaustive studies of Makino. What follows, therefore, is a long overdue examination of his influence and reputation—both of which were important to Hirohito's view of himself as head of state and commander in chief of the armed forces.

Western scholars agree that Makino was a guiding force early in Hirohito's career as regent and emperor and that Makino was, "like Saionji, a liberal constitutional monarchist who believed that friendly ties must be maintained with Great Britain and the United States."[9] Because of these convictions, Makino was on the hit list of many radical reformers and assassins in the 1930s.[10] Even so, his reputation as a moderate needs to be qualified.

Makino's memoirs indicate that he was an elitist and a nationalist. He recalls, for example, his respect for Saionji, who worked to abolish the fiefs and establish prefectures *(haihan-chiken)* early on to promote a strong national government. In late nineteenth-century Japan this was considered progressive in comparison with Tokugawa "feudalism," and Makino describes Saionji as a "progressive thinker" ahead of his time. He himself was a product of his time, however, and a moderate only in comparison with the militarists of the 1930s. His admiration of Saionji was explicitly defined within the context of "imperial restoration" *(ōsei fukko).*[11] He saw Saionji as a champion of imperial rule and emphasized the roles played in the restoration by court nobles *(kugyō),* not common people. Others singled out for praise were also of aristocratic birth: Iwakura Tomomi (1825–1883) and Sanjō Sanetomi (1837–1891). Iwakura was a high-born aristocrat closely associated with Makino's father, and Makino says no one else could have guided the restoration with such noble intentions and great acumen.

The conservative tenor of Makino's thought is demonstrated by numerous statements in his memoirs.[12] A further example is a notation from 1877. In it Makino says the new government officials, having served in comparable capacities in the old feudal system, were not without experience. But without the skilled supervision of Iwakura and Sanjō, he says, an effective government could not have been established.[13] In the future his own supervision of the crown prince and new emperor would be embossed with similar elitist preconceptions about the importance of guidance by the oligarchs.

The achievements of men like Iwakura, Sanjō, Itō Hirobumi, Saionji, and Makino himself are not to be denied. But this does not mean that what they accomplished would not have come about without them. There were a great number of talented men in Japan at this time, some with truly populist ideas, who lost out in the political struggle with the oligarchs. Those who worked for "freedom and people's rights" *(jiyūminken undō),* for example, could have guided the restoration, albeit in a very different direction.[14] Makino certainly knew this. But he had a paternalistic streak that led him to assume a few well-born and well-placed men knew what was best for Japan. Despite these haughty prejudices, and given the extreme nationalism of the 1930s, he subsequently came to be known as one of Japan's leading moderate statesmen. Nevertheless, one should not forget that Makino and his aristocratic colleagues assumed that what was best for themselves was best for Japan. And perhaps more to the point, Hirohito learned from Makino, his tutor in his duties as regent and emperor.

The Politician

Before he came to tutor and advise Hirohito, Makino held a number of political offices. He was associated with the court clique surrounding Saionji, and one can see that his political convictions were well established prior to meeting the future emperor. These ideals are illustrated clearly by his activities as minister of education in the first Saionji cabinet. The cabinet came into office in 1906, shortly after Japan's victory in the Russo-Japanese War (1904–1905). Makino has little to say about the war. Instead, his memoirs are full of praise for Itō Hirobumi's support of the introduction of political parties in Japan despite the opposition of many of his friends in the House of Peers. Proudly he says that the first Saionji cabinet was the first partylike government— an important step in realizing Itō's intentions—and he describes developments within the Seiyūkai political party in some detail.[15]

Upon assuming his duties as minister of education Makino was convinced of the need for a new postwar education policy. His first problem was with personnel and the old-boy network entrenched in the bureaucracy. Generally speaking, Makino had a low opinion of Japan's civil servants *(kanri* and *yakunin)*. But because he had served for four years in this ministry he knew many of the people and this helped him, he says, to select and retain the experts he wanted in education. A number of policy problems confronted Makino, and he needed good people to help him deal with them: increasing the various types of schools, establishing guiding principles for culture *(bunka)*, regulating student activities in the postwar era, fostering knowledge of international developments *(kokusai chishiki)*, and above all extending the period of compulsory education.

Makino was well aware of how the Japanese education system had come into being in the early 1870s—through a series of emergency measures brought about by a combination of the need to catch up with the West quickly and a total lack of trained teachers or education materials. He was well aware, too, of the significance of education for Japan as a nation and the people's general acknowledgment of its importance:

"There were people who maintained with respect to the [Russo-Japanese] war that the distinguished service of our primary school teachers decided the issue of victory or defeat."[16]

This says a great deal about the value Japanese ascribe to education. Education is for the advancement of the Japanese folk; self-help and self-betterment are of secondary importance at best. Makino, for example, did not want to extend compulsory education in order to improve the lives of his countrymen. He was concerned about the state. With the Japanese empire in mind, Makino saw that the period of compulsory education was eight or nine years overseas while in Japan it was only half that. Japan's achievements had been acknowledged throughout the world; but to compete effectively with the West, Japan must improve its basic education. Makino proposed to extend the period of required education from four to six years and to make the higher school curriculum *(kōdōka)* two or three years long.

This meant that Japan's educational facilities had to be expanded significantly. Reflecting Makino's concern about a lack of teachers to carry out this program, women were given equal status with men as schoolteachers after one or two years of additional training. Here one must be wary of foreign evaluations of Japanese actions. Giving women equal status with men as schoolteachers was a progressive step matching many European countries' standards of equal rights in 1906. But Makino's proposal was not based on modern principles. It was based on conservative nationalistic concerns: women were necessary to supply sufficient numbers of teachers to build a powerful nation.

Schooling above the primary level was considered a matter entirely separate from compulsory education. It was to be expanded only slightly because too many people wanting too much education was bad for the country. A surfeit of advanced education was a waste of money. Education was not for the individual's good but to benefit the nation, and a surplus of highly educated persons would not be employable in useful nation-building pursuits.

The importance of the state can be seen, as well, in Makino's thoughts about a national art exhibition initiated during his term of office. At the opening ceremony in March 1907 he made a speech to the judges in which he emphasized the necessity of freeing artists from the paternalistic system of "schools" *(ryū* and *ha)* and the house traditions *(kaden)* of the Tokugawa period. With the entry of foreign influences after the Meiji Restoration in 1868, such institutions had become unpopular. "Pure" devotion to art *(senshin geijutsu)* was propagated but not in fact promoted:

We ask you gentlemen [the exhibition judges] also to bear this responsibility in accord with the wishes of the state. . . . We expect the exhibition to occupy the place of highest judgment *(shinpanjo)* in the art world in our country, comparable to the Court of Cassation (Daishin'in). In the future, standard examples of art will also come from this organization, giving a signal within and without, properly guiding colleagues in the same fields.[17]

Makino aimed at freeing artists from oppressive feudal traditions, a laudable undertaking, but putting art under the jurisdiction of the imperial government seems a dubious cure for the illnesses of feudalism. Makino simply could not imagine that the measures proposed by the government to rid Japan of the feudal vestiges of Tokugawa rule could be anything but liberating. He saw no contradiction in proposing that artists should take cues from the authorities at the national art center, much as they had from their respective house or school masters up to that time. He did not see the problem inherent in his policy—that it could lead to a centralization of the old dictatorial practices with fewer dictators and even less freedom of expression than before.

Either the notion of freedom of expression was unimportant to Makino, or he simply did not understand it. The wishes of the state—using art to further Japan's prestige in the world in this case—were his paramount concern. His view of art was similar to Shiratori Kurakichi's approach to history. Both looked on these pursuits in terms of "nation building" and establishing Japan as an advanced country internationally. And Hirohito's future view of the military and military discipline was similar.

Finally, Makino commented extensively on the problems with foreign language instruction. The specific issues were much the same as those still the subject of impassioned debate in Japan ninety years later: poor teachers; poor teaching methods; and, despite the expenditure of a great amount of time and effort, poor results. Again, he was concerned about the lack of success because of the consequences for the empire.

The Moralist

Makino's memories of his experiences as minister of education end with his discussion of foreign language study. With his extensive overseas experience he was certainly in a position to comment on this subject. But none of these issues were as important or controversial as the one problem about which he is silent—the burning issue of that day and his contribution to it, the question of national morals.

In June 1906 Education Minister Makino issued a "morals directive" *(fūki kunrei)*. A prominent authority on Meiji ideology, Carol Gluck, says this directive

> set the tone for the promotion of wholesome thought *(kenzen naru shisō)*. It sought to combat spiritual "despondence," moral "decadence," and licentious "self-indulgence" on the one hand, and socialism and the "poison" of radical ideas on the other. Both were linked to "the recent publications that have increasingly tempted young men and women with dangerous opinions, world-weary attitudes, and depictions of the baser sides of life." To prevent the erosion of school and family authority and the disruption of the "foundations of the state" and of the "social order," Makino instructed educators to "scrutinize the contents of books read by students and pupils. Those that are deemed beneficial should be encouraged, while those likely to arouse unwholesome results *(furyō no kekka)* should be strictly prohibited both in and out of school."[18]

Strangely, Makino does not mention this controversy or his directive in his memoirs. His reasons can only be speculated upon. It is extremely unlikely that he forgot about this issue, but he may have been embarrassed by it later. In 1906 it aroused more debate than his proposal to lengthen compulsory education.[19] Moreover, it illustrates Makino's basic position: the affairs of state and arranging the new social order in Japan were not to be left to "free thinkers." Direction was needed from high government leaders who were by definition well informed and well intentioned. He, as a responsible member of this elite group, was not one to shirk his responsibilities.

Elitism and Its Consequences

Makino's activities prior to becoming an adviser to the future Shōwa emperor show that he was well educated and had wide experience overseas as well as in Japan. One could say he was a "moderate," in the context of his time and place, in that he did not oppose representative government and the freedom of individuals to act or express themselves. But he did try to channel the thinking and action of the Japanese people in a distinctly nationalistic direction. Whether he realized it or not, this approach to governing subverted the foundations of free government and was little different in method, as opposed to content, from what the militarists promoted and practiced in the 1930s and 1940s.

Alexis de Tocqueville (1805–1859) formulated what have come to be regarded as two of the basic prerequisites of democratic government: "democracy requires an apprenticeship in freedom," and people have to learn to govern themselves.[20] In Japan nearly a hundred years later Makino may have seen himself as a tutor of the emperor and his people, but freedom and democracy were not his highest educational priorities. Moreover, de Tocqueville, his like-minded English contemporary John Stuart Mill (1806–1873), and many others who later addressed the problems of democratic government were profoundly concerned about the danger to individual freedom from society itself. But, like the militarists, Makino and his colleagues did not see this as a problem. Indeed, manipulating public opinion for "higher purposes" was valued over freedom and open responsible expression of opinions about government policy. The Japanese were taught, by civil as well as military leaders, not to govern themselves but to follow the dictates of a small minority of self-ordained spokesmen who defined the national polity and defined, as well, what a good Japanese should be. Unlike the ultranationalists of the 1930s Makino was urbane and cosmopolitan; but, very much like them, he was committed unquestioningly to the idea of Imperial Japan as a world power. This meant giving highest priority to furthering both aspects of this concept—"imperial" solidarity at home and "world power" abroad. If society restrained individual freedom in the process, that was not necessarily a bad thing. Civil rights, liberties, and responsibilities were clearly of little importance to Makino. Public discipline and obedience were.

Later, Hirohito looked naturally to the authority and influence of the imperial house as an ideal instrument of rule. He did not question Makino's basic elitist assumptions about how to govern. Moreover, one can see definite parallels between this orientation and the history lessons and imperial ethics learned at the Ogakumonjo. Makino's elitism agreed well with the suppositions about the imperial house taught there. The position of the emperor and his advisers in modern Japan was sanctioned by traditional ethics and ancient history. And as we have seen, Hirohito's later actions as a "constitutional monarch" were shaped by this convergence of early teaching and later advice.

Politics and the Imperial House

To his role as tutor in state affairs to Crown Prince–Regent Hirohito, Makino brought the principles of a constitutional monarchist and the convictions of an elite Japanese steeped in the myths of the imperial tradition and the sacrosanct position of the imperial house. Makino became imperial household minister when he was sixty years old. Shortly thereafter Hirohito was made regent at the age of twenty. Makino was old enough to be the new regent's grandfather, and some of the advice he gave Hirohito appears very much in this vein. In June 1924, for example, he told his young protégé:

Harmonizing old and new and proceeding systematically is the proper way of reasoning. Be aware that respecting history, and progressing in the new era with mutual relations in a manner that promotes harmony, is the way of wisdom. Embrace all elements within the country—differing opinions in the intellectual world, various social classes, the situation of the minds and hearts of young and old.[21]

Such statements indicate that Makino entertained some very liberal convictions and imparted them in his advice to Hirohito.

At the same time these convictions were aligned in support of the emperor as head of state—a political function—and, more, a godlike guardian of the established order. Both sets of ideals—liberalism and traditional reverence for the imperial line—contributed to Makino's advocating that the emperor's position (as well as that of the oligarchs) was not to be compromised by direct participation in politics. And Makino carried this conviction to an extreme. He wrote, for example, that the third cabinet of Katsura Tarō (1847–1913) lasted for such a short time, 21 December 1912 to 19 February 1913, because Katsura violated this principle by mixing court affairs and public politics. The logic behind Makino's conclusion may be summarized as follows.

Some months prior to being asked to form a cabinet, Katsura was appointed lord keeper of the privy seal. While serving the new Taishō emperor in this capacity by "giving the emperor advice in matters pertaining to the affairs of state" *(hohitsu)*, he received the mandate to form a new cabinet. But it appeared that as adviser to the throne Katsura had figured prominently in his own appointment as prime minister—a suspicion that disturbed not only political circles and the parliament but the people in general. Katsura attempted to explain the matter, and Saionji, who had just resigned as prime minister, sought as well to quiet the uproar. Neither was successful. Saionji then resigned as head of the Seiyūkai political party, and Katsura dissolved his cabinet. The message according to Makino was obvious: the separation of court and state affairs *(kyūchū fuchū no betsu)* could not be violated.[22] He even refused an appointment as imperial household minister in the next cabinet because he and the future prime minister, Yamamoto Gombei (1852–1933), were both from Satsuma, and this might imply collusion between court and cabinet.[23] But this was not the only issue in this dispute, and Makino's interpretation of the Katsura affair reveals his court-centered view of politics.

The short life of the Katsura cabinet can be traced to a number of causes. More important than his relation to the court were Katsura's problems with the military and the members of the Diet. He was caught between competing demands by the army and navy for more divisions and warships, the need to reduce the budget due to the expenditures caused by the Russo-Japanese War, and demands in the Diet for tax reductions and increases in public works. Although he found ways to appease the military, he ran afoul of the politicians when he tried to set up his own political party to deal with the Diet. Ultimately Katsura had to resign after having the Diet suspended three times by imperial order to avoid no-confidence votes.[24] Thus it was the common politics of taxes and competition between the military services in a time of budget cuts that brought the Katsura government down. Makino's doubts about the correctness of Katsura's appointment as prime minister while he was lord keeper of the privy seal were of little import.

Makino's reservations about close ties between the court and the elected government were due to his desire to separate the emperor completely from any direct participation in politics, which unavoidably involve controversy. The emperor was to be a transcendental authority —the foundation of traditional Japanese morals, which included reverence for state-sponsored imperial folklore. Makino was of the same opinion as Shiratori and Itō Hirobumi, who "saw in the imperial house a native Japanese emotional equivalent to Western religion." In 1888 Itō argued:

> In Europe, not only have the people become proficient in constitutional government since it first took seed; there was also religion, and this constituted the axis, deeply infusing the popular mind. In this the people's hearts found unity. . . . In our country there is only the Imperial House that can become such an axis.[25]

The emperor was a religious figure with a political role. His role was to infuse the minds and hearts of the people such that they would unquestioningly follow government leadership. Although he was not to be an active part of this leadership, the connection between his role as a transcendental authority and building a powerful state cannot be overlooked. Makino was faithful to this dictum throughout his life: "Because where there is religion, a military power can easily be built up, but military power without religion, this can only be realized with difficulty."[26] Makino may not have been acquainted with the author of these lines, Niccolò Machiavelli (1467–1527), but he was clearly aware of this line of thought.

Makino, the Court, and Constitutional Monarchy

In principle the court was not to interfere in politics, but the same cannot be said for the politicians' handling of the court. When it suited their purposes they quite readily took court matters into their own hands. Makino was no exception. This can be seen in his description of two problems that immediately confronted him upon becoming imperial household minister in 1921: the possible color blindness of Hirohito's proposed bride and the crown prince's appointment as regent for his father, the Taishō emperor.[27] The color blindness issue will be addressed first. It is important because it illustrates how the oligarchs and civil officials meddled in court affairs and shows that Hirohito did persevere and prevail on occasion.

Prior to Hirohito's return from Europe on 3 September 1921, Makino held a number of conferences with various people about this problem, especially with Yamagata Aritomo (1838–1922). The conservative elder statesmen, led by Yamagata, had dominated the court during the first ten years of the Taishō era. Makino's appointment as a prominent politician and associate of Saionji to be imperial household minister seemed to usher in a new epoch—that of the "constitutional monarchists."[28] Nevertheless, the uproar caused by Yamagata's opposition to the proposed marriage between Hirohito and Princess Nagako demonstrated the continuing influence of the old guard. (In response Nagako's father threatened to kill her and then commit suicide if the marriage was called off.) The reasons behind Yamagata's objection were essentially ones of traditional clan rivalry—residual animosities, from the time of the restoration, between the principal activists from Satsuma and Chōshū. Yamagata was from Chōshū; Nagako's mother was from a prominent Satsuma family. This rivalry still was of consequence in the 1920s and would continue to agitate court, political, and military circles for some time. Some say Yamagata was forced to withdraw his opposition because of the heat it had drawn to him and his "cohorts" from Chōshū. This may be true. Makino recorded that the old man did not change his mind but merely said he would not meddle further in the controversy.[29] The affair did not, however, come to a swift end. The debate continued after Hirohito was appointed regent and was not resolved until the crown prince insisted on wedding Princess Nagako.

With respect to Hirohito's appointment as regent, his father's increasing inability to remember persons, places, and past events, not to mention his unpredictable conduct at state ceremonies, concerned everyone at court as well as leaders in the higher echelons of government. Prime Minister Hara Takashi and the elder statesman Matsukata Masayoshi (1835–1924) took the initiative with this project. The following account is from the perspective of Makino's diary. Here one can see that Makino took himself and his duties quite seriously and, occasionally, overemphasized his own importance. There was no doubt in Makino's mind about the necessity of appointing the crown prince regent, and he pursued the matter in a forthright yet diplomatic manner. He consulted extensively with the members of the imperial household and underlined the importance of receiving their approval. But this deference was due simply to his personal feelings about the imperial family. Though the Meiji Constitution and Imperial Household Law stipulated otherwise, they had no effective voice in the matter.[30] In fact, it was after obtaining Genrō Yamagata's agreement that Makino acted. Elder statesmen *(genrō)* were appointed advisers to the throne by imperial proclamation, but they had no legal status according to the Meiji Constitution. In 1921 Makino was concerned about obtaining the influential Yamagata's approval, not that of high government officials or imperial household leaders. He does not mention the prime minister, for example, even though he was actively involved in the matter. When Makino asked what should be done, Yamagata told him it was the imperial household minister's responsibility. Makino's diary indicates that he then took the initiative and began supervising preparations for the regency.[31] In Makino's own words, he took steps to emasculate the official head of state and the imperial house—the emperor—only after obtaining the approval of a powerful, but unofficial, functionary.

Makino's attitude illustrates another major failing of prewar government in Japan that ensued from practices established during the Meiji period. Though he himself was a government official, he handled government matters in a privatized manner. During the Meiji, Taishō, and Shōwa eras, civil officials and military officers were accustomed to formulating government policies not as public activities but as agreements between acquaintances in high places—a practice that had serious consequences for the government in Tokyo in the 1930s and 1940s.[32] It also led to a misunderstanding about Hirohito that extends even into the present.

Hirohito's appointment as regent was privately organized for public consumption. The proceedings have not been thoroughly investigated, however, and this has helped perpetuate certain misconceptions about the emperor. Today it is all but unknown, for example, that certain highly placed persons near the crown prince, who questioned the appointment, were very critical of Hirohito's intellectual proclivities. The criticism, recorded in the fall of 1921, is notable in that it had nothing to do with the celebrated drinking party he organized shortly after his return from Europe. Moreover, it differs sharply from the glowing portraits of Hirohito still accepted even by critics of the emperor system.

Chinda Sutemi (1857–1929), chief attendant *(gubuchō)* from the Foreign Ministry (former ambassador to Germany, Great Britain, and the United States and later grand chamberlain), who traveled with Hirohito to Europe, gave Makino a detailed account of the crown prince's activities during the trip. He concluded by saying that generally he should be monitored continuously: "By temperament he [Hirohito] lacks composure *(o-ochitsuki no tarazaru),* and he lacks an inquiring mind *(go-kenkyūshin no usuki)*—there are shortcomings like these."[33] This is a surprising statement, but it should not be dismissed. Chinda was an experienced, well-traveled diplomat, a man accustomed to dealing with the slights and discrimination Japanese suffered in the West without becoming upset. Nor was he particularly enamored with Western civilization. During his career, for example, Chinda attempted to help Japanese in California in 1913 with a dispute over their right to own land. Although ultimately he was unsuccessful, he earned the respect of officials in Washington and also the diplomatic corps.[34] Chinda reveals an unstable aspect in Hirohito's personality seldom recorded and seldom considered in evaluations of his activities as emperor. Indeed, he is almost universally given high marks for his composure and intellectual acumen—an assessment that must be revised.

Moreover, another personal inclination that later affected public policy—an inclination that is often misinterpreted—surfaced during this period. At about this time Hirohito clearly expressed the principle of separating public and private functions, a dictum that supposedly became a strict rule during the Shōwa emperor's reign: "If public and private affairs *(kōshi)* are differentiated and managed [separately] there can be no trouble."[35] This principle is generally acknowledged by historians—David Titus used the concept as a basis for analyzing "palace and politics in prewar Japan"—but the meaning of separating public and private affairs at court is nevertheless controversial. Certainly it makes Hirohito's personal power and influence hard to discern, for publicly he never disagreed with the ruling government. His supporters claim this policy prevented him from interceding in policymaking in general and against the war in particular; his detractors say it was only a smoke screen behind which he manipulated policy decisions. But as we have seen, Hirohito did not always follow his own advice and differentiate clearly between his public image and private self. Because he was indecisive about being decisive, his actions were contradictory at times. Although it was not an issue at the time, Chinda sensed this character trait early on.

In 1921, then, Makino consulted extensively with the members of the imperial house, imperial uncles as well as the empress. During these consultations several interesting questions arose. Less than two months before the official appointment, the empress, Hirohito's mother, a beautiful, intelligent, formidable woman, raised the following points on 11 October: first, she was against the guidance (called for by Chief Attendant Chinda) because she "feared power would naturally accrue to the guiding members of the imperial family *(kōzoku)*"; second, the Aoyama Palace was unsuitable as a residence and the crown prince did not like it either; third, she urged continuing consultations between government leaders and the emperor because he enjoyed them and she wondered what would become of him if he had nothing to do.[36] The extent of the empress' influence behind the throne is unknown, but obviously she was trying to maintain whatever power she had. Later, just before the appointment, she requested Makino's assistance in guiding the crown prince in his new duties. Clearly Makino's "assistance" at court was another way of assuring her voice would be heard. Indeed, the empress is said to have compared Makino to Motoda Eifu (1818–1891), the famous Confucian scholar who assisted Emperor Meiji and greatly influenced the writing of the Imperial Rescript on Education. Such a comparison must have been very flattering to Makino.

Makino's self-esteem can be seen in his account of how he fulfilled his responsibilities. In the process one also sees his basic convictions about the position of the imperial house in the body politic. On 25 October Prince Asaka (Yasuhiko, b. 1906), the eighth son of Imperial Prince Kuni who was the father of the future empress, Nagako, visited Makino together with Prince Kitashirakawa. Despite his youth (he was just fifteen) Prince Asaka asked Makino what would happen if the emperor did not agree with the plan to appoint Hirohito regent. Makino answered:

> This affair will be decided entirely on the initiative of the members of the imperial family *(kōzokukata)*, not according to the wishes of the emperor. However, even though the emperor must not be informed and even if this process is correct legally speaking, with respect to my duty as a "retainer" *(shinshi)*, proceeding without [giving the emperor] prior notice would be unbearable. I intend to report [the regency] to the emperor beforehand.[37]

Although the emperor was to be informed formally of the action to be taken, his opinion, for or against, was legally speaking superfluous. Makino consulted with the emperor out of personal feelings, not out of official necessity. On 28 October Makino repeated his point of view —that it was legally correct to appoint a regent for the emperor without consulting him—to Prince Asaka's father, Imperial Prince Kuni. Later, on 21 November, he said the same thing to Prince Fushimi.[38]

In fact, Makino had not been entirely candid with the members of the imperial family. Concerned about conducting the affair smoothly, he sought their approval; but officially and politically he acted as if he did not need it. For the good of the state he sought to avoid the danger anticipated by the empress—the growth of the influence of lesser members of the imperial house—and therefore turned to the oligarchs, especially Yamagata. So far as Makino was concerned, the emperor served at the discretion of the leading politicians and bureaucrats regardless of what he or his family thought. It was they who decided government matters and determined whether the leading member of the imperial house was fit to carry out his duties as emperor.

Behind Makino's actions in 1921 and his later advice were his convictions about the supremacy of the oligarchs and similar right-minded politicians and bureaucrats. Makino took it upon himself to advise Hirohito in his new duties with this in mind. The emperor was to lend splendor and authority to the actions of these men. They in turn supported the ideology of the imperial tradition and the supremacy of the imperial house in Japanese society. Consistent with this tradition, social supremacy did not mean sovereignty as a real ruler. The real rulers were the oligarchs. The government was led by the nation's political leaders, the oligarchs, in the name of the emperor. This was constitutional monarchy in Japan.

Repercussions

His father's fate may have been an object lesson for Hirohito early in life, a lesson that was reinforced by Makino's "advice." The emperor's insecurity about his own position in the 1930s and 1940s—his fear of being replaced or subjected to a regency himself—may have originated here. Makino was not a militarist, and certainly he did not stimulate the young emperor's fears, but his sentiments about the relation between the oligarchs and the emperor paralleled the assumptions of Japan's military leaders about their relation to the emperor: both saw the emperor as a figurehead who was supposed to legitimize their policies unquestioningly. After the war Hirohito often said that had he opposed the militarists he might well have been declared insane and replaced by someone—his own son as a minority emperor with Prince Higashikuni as regent, for example. As Higashikuni was known to favor the militarists' ideas,[39] this turn of events could have resulted in an even greater catastrophe. However true this may be, it is not the whole story.

First, the position of the Taishō emperor was precarious indeed, but this did not mean he was merely a marionette. Hirohito's father, unlike Hirohito himself, was clearly mentally ill, and Makino, following Hara's policy (which he does not mention), went to great pains to document this condition medically. Second, Hirohito often referred to constitutional monarchy, but it would be naive to assume he was motivated solely by this concern as for almost twenty years he alternately offered carefully calculated resistance to, and approval of, the imperialistic plans of Japan's military leaders. Hirohito was raised and educated to be concerned about his ancestors, his offspring, and the position of his house in Japanese society. The prominence of the imperial house and the surrounding tradition were of paramount importance to him. Although his advisers counseled him to refrain from "meddling" in political affairs, Hirohito did not consistently follow this advice. Instead he sought to use his influence adroitly behind the scenes to shore up the position of his family at the pinnacle of society and opposed anyone who would weaken or usurp this position. Thus, for example, he did not oppose war in principle, but he was against the arbitrary actions of the army. After the war he especially emphasized the fear that during the war years he would have been declared incompetent or insane—shades of his father's fate—had he not gone along with military leaders. But here we enter a gray zone. Were these merely postwar claims made to facilitate his survival and that of his house, actual fears before and during the war, or a combination of both?

Hara's Assassination

As preparations for appointing Hirohito regent were nearing their conclusion, disaster struck. On 4 November 1921 Prime Minister Hara was assassinated. The gravity of this incident, its impact on Makino, and his steadfast pursuit of his plan to establish the regency show that he was absolutely determined to carry out this policy and make Hirohito regent come what may:

> Before eight o'clock an urgent message came from Takahashi [Mitsuzō, the prime minister's] chief secretary. He was in receipt of a sad report about a disaster *(sōnan no hion)* at Tokyo Station. [The assassination] was truly shocking, but one should not be consumed by heartrending introspection.
>
> On a day like today one must appear internally and externally *(naigai)* to be essentially in control of the situation. It may be safely said that this rash youthful outrage perpetrated by a nineteen-year-old child has damaged public order. Boundless remorse. I went directly to the palace, and afterward took a car to the prime minister's residence. There I conferred with the lord keeper of the privy seal and discussed an order of merit [for Hara] and the dissolution of the cabinet. Reversing my steps I returned to the palace. Unbearable anxiety about the future.[40]

This reflection is followed by further discussions about whether or not the cabinet should resign. (It did.) Although there was great concern about preserving public order, Makino did not allow this to deter him from his plan to appoint Hirohito regent. In fact, he appears to have approached the two concurrent crises—Emperor Taishō's mental derangement and Hara's assassination—along parallel lines as if there were no connection between them. When Prince Fushimi attempted to link them by referring to the problems that might ensue from Hirohito's inexperience if an imperial decision *(shinsai)* were required shortly after his appointment, Makino waved him off. The appointment could not be postponed until the political situation was calm and predictable. After all, one never knew when an emergency might arise.[41] On 25 November 1921 Crown Prince Hirohito was officially designated regent.

Ladies-in-Waiting and Modernization

Shortly after Hirohito became regent, he announced his famous ban on palace concubines and a drastic reduction in the ladies-in-waiting at court. Supporters as well as critics have attributed this ban to his prudish ways and extreme devotion to his wife.[42] Makino's description of the affair, though, emphasizes a rather different consideration. Hirohito wanted to abolish the custom that women employed in the imperial palace should live there. They should work there during the day, he contended, and leave. He was especially concerned because

> the present high-ranking court women were brought up in the interior of the palace and know absolutely nothing of the everyday world. They are really foolish. Actually, the other day I heard a discussion in which it was not known if Numazu or Hayama was further from Tokyo. That is because the circumstances of their daily lives are impossible. After a lifetime of public service, a person only becomes stupid *(gudon)*. Besides, concerning the empress, in the future she must have considerable knowledge of the things of the world, but surrounded by court women of this sort her development is well-nigh hopeless. Also, when children come I do not agree with what has been done up to now—entrusting them to someone outside [the palace]. I think it is proper to raise them at a place in the palace, and with respect to this it is absolutely impossible to delegate this responsibility to the present court women. Moreover, in the interest of family harmony something should be said when I or someone makes a mistake, but if this is rumored about all the time it would be very undesirable.[43]

Hirohito went on to emphasize that since it was necessary to accommodate with the times, Makino should carry out this task discreetly but decisively and bring about these changes soon. Hirohito was concerned with solidifying his family and harmonizing with the times, which meant in both instances assuring the education of his wife and children. His teachers—Meiji and Taishō government officials and military leaders—all assumed that high-quality education was indispensable to Japan's advancement as a nation. Hirohito had been educated by these men, continued to be tutored by a select few of them, and sought, in a like manner, through advanced education, to confirm his family's position in Japanese society.

Hirohito was very correct, straitlaced even, and always strove to do what he thought proper. But that was not the issue. Hirohito proposed to change the system of ladies-in-waiting, not for reasons of propriety, but because he thought it detrimental to his family. He wanted to strengthen his family and assure its place in the traditional hierarchy. To do this would require their formal education in the ways of the world, and reducing the influence of these "stupid" women in the palace was part of this project. Modern education was to serve traditional ends: the supremacy of the imperial house in Japanese society.[44] The parallels between this line of thought and state policy are striking. Modern education, modern industry, and a modern military were to further Japan's position in the world, seen in terms of a heady East-West combination—Japanese status consciousness blended with traditional nineteenth-century European imperialism.

Makino's Control Over His Regent

Makino appears to have monitored the young regent's public and private activities rather closely. It is difficult to ascertain, however, the exact nature of this "control" because our sources are vague at best. Shortly after Hirohito became regent, for example, Makino had him informed regularly of military and political matters. The first military report *(fukumei)* recorded by Makino took place on 16 March 1922. It was conducted by the minister of the navy, Katō Tomosaburō (1861–1923), who gave a general report on the authority of the sovereign *(zenken)* that lasted about one hour.[45] Unfortunately Makino's diary does not go into detail concerning the content of these reports although he was often present.

Makino, in other words, tells us a considerable amount about private problems, like the ongoing debate over Hirohito's proposed marriage, but not political or military matters. A further example: on 13 September 1922 he notes that the regent summoned him to discuss the resignation of the lord keeper of the privy seal, which was to take place the following day. "Therefore I went for an audience," wrote Makino. "I related the details of the coming events in private to the regent and explained how he should react to what the privy seal will say."[46] We can see that Makino was a source of information for Hirohito, as well as a tutor who advised him about protocol with regard to the affairs of state. What exactly was said, however, is in many cases not recorded in Makino's diary and thus the nature of his information and instructions is often impossible to ascertain. It is clear, however, that as regent Hirohito did little without Makino's approval. At least this is the impression one receives from reading Makino's diary. And there is little reason to doubt that both he and Prince Saionji tightly supervised Hirohito's appointments and early activities.

Yet another example of the prevailing situation are Makino's consultations with Hirohito shortly after the Great Kanto Earthquake. On 1 September 1923 a powerful quake rocked the Tokyo area (magnitude 7.9 on the Japanese scale), and the ensuing fires destroyed much of Tokyo, Yokohama, and the surrounding suburbs and villages. Over 90,000 people died, more than 13,000 were missing, and well over half the homes in the Tokyo-Yokohama metropolitan area were destroyed. On 16 September Makino had an audience with Hirohito. The regent reported seeing extensive devastation and suffering and had been deeply moved. Under the circumstances, he said, he found it impossible to continue with the plans for his marriage in the fall and requested that the ceremony be postponed. Three days earlier the mayor of Tokyo had made exactly the same request, but Makino had rejected it. The earthquake was a local matter affecting only the capital and surrounding environs, he said, whereas the coming marriage of the crown prince was an affair for the entire nation. One could not allow local matters, even one so grievous as this, to interfere with state affairs. Makino maintained the same attitude with Hirohito. He praised him for his concern but said there were various opinions on the matter. Makino had already spoken with government leaders and members of the imperial family, and they were in favor of continuing the preparations. Even the common people would be encouraged by Hirohito's going on with the event. In the end, however, Hirohito prevailed and the wedding was postponed. Makino acquiesced graciously. Shortly thereafter he noted approvingly the regent's attitude and predicted that later on he would certainly carry out state affairs well.[47]

Here again Makino's priorities are clear: the state took precedence over everything, even the course of nature. Key members of the government and aristocracy decided the best procedures for the state, and the people should be heartened by their resolute actions. If Makino ever had second thoughts about the inevitable harmony between the opinions of high government leaders and those of most people, he did not express them. His diary does not mention that Hirohito pursued his initial line of thought—that it would be inappropriate to hold a sumptuous wedding ceremony for the peerage at a time of great distress for the common people—nor did he note that the wedding was finally delayed. His reasons for giving in to the crown prince are unclear. As Hirohito was extremely sensitive about controlling matters related to his household, perhaps Makino retreated in the face of the crown prince's insistence.

Makino's high-handed attitude with regard to state affairs extended to his handling of Hirohito. The consultations with the new regent are noteworthy for their concern with ceremonial formalities and lack of political import. Makino was intent upon confining the regent and head of state to a purely ceremonial role. Hirohito was consulted with respect to the revised message about the wedding sent to the emperor and empress in Nikko, and he was properly informed of the appointment ceremony for the new foreign minister (19 September).[48] The new foreign minister, Ijūin Hikokichi, and Makino later decided that the regent should visit the construction site of the American Red Cross Hospital, soon to be completed, without consulting him (9 October). After consulting with the prime minister, Makino informed the regent that the prime minister would petition the throne about the distribution of imperial proclamations; this took place and Hirohito "approved" (10 November). Makino consulted with him about selecting new women to serve at court, but Hirohito indicated he had no particular opinion on the matter (14 November). Hirohito attended the graduation ceremonies at the Imperial Army Academy (29 November). Makino also notes that Hirohito for the first time authorized the Festival of New Rice (Kaname-no-matsuri) (23 November).[49]

Disaster relief measures following the Tokyo earthquake, including pacifying the souls of the dead, were another matter. Makino was quite worried about this problem—especially the question of placating the souls of the dead born during the Meiji era. Something needed to be done so the Meiji emperor's soul would be reassured (18 September). Makino was not alone in his concern. The mayor of Tokyo called on him in the same regard (11 October), and he later discussed it with the empress, Hirohito's mother (23 October). If the crown prince–regent was consulted, Makino did not deem it important enough to note in his diary. At this time, moreover, the director of the No. 15 Bank brought up the danger of repercussions for the aristocracy, whose members often dealt with this bank, should it be attacked politically along with the Satsuma faction. No doubt this issue had to do with the dispute between the Satsuma and Chōshū factions in the government over the pending marriage between Hirohito and a woman with connections to Satsuma. This is not elaborated on in the text. Apparently members of the aristocracy from Satsuma figured prominently in its affairs. Destabilizing the bank would be another way of attacking them. If Makino brought the regent into these discussions, he did not note it.

One might argue, of course, that as imperial household minister Makino was not supposed to advise the regent about political affairs. That was the responsibility of the privy seal. Makino's duties were confined to the imperial household itself. Despite this division of responsibilities, Makino's diary reveals that he participated actively in the political affairs of the day. Perhaps in deference to his official role, Makino did not discuss political policies with the crown prince—or, if he did, he did not always note it in his diary for the same reason. He appears to have thought that Hirohito was very young and inexperienced. In any case, he no doubt believed that the acting head of the imperial house should be excluded from exposure to controversial political matters.

Makino's Controls and His Convictions

Makino's guidance of Hirohito was based on his feelings about the importance of the national polity *(kokutai)*. These sentiments were expressed clearly in his diary on 27 December 1923. On that day Crown Prince and Regent Hirohito was to proclaim the opening of the next session of the National Diet. Shortly before the ceremony disaster nearly struck again. Afterward Makino noted that he

> could not bear to record the day's events. Nothing but simple dread; recent changes in thinking are increasingly extreme. It is a fact that one segment of the people even has gone so far as to yearn for dismaying changes in the ideas concerning the national polity. Of course it goes without saying that this is something limited to a very small minority. But actually it is impossible to conceive that there are people who would attempt to do something like this.[50]

This was the day of the Toranomon Incident. Nanba Daisuke, son of a member of the House of Representatives, attempted but failed to assassinate Crown Prince Hirohito on his way to the Diet for the ceremony. During his trial Nanba insisted he had acted out of his communist convictions.

If Hirohito was affected by the attack he did not show it, and this made a deep impression on Makino. Hirohito's comments, recorded in the imperial household minister's diary, were extremely succinct: "I thought it was a blank shot. . . . In situations like this a police escort is useless." He went straight to the ceremony as planned. When the chief adjutant asked if he wanted something to drink, he replied that he did not need anything. Shortly thereafter Makino noted that Hirohito was more excited than usual, but the crown prince read the imperial proclamation in a "splendid manner."[51]

Many other politicians and bureaucrats entertained Makino's sympathies—that respect for the national polity and imperial house was on the wane—and this assassination attempt was a key event leading to the passage of the 1925 Peace Preservation Law that conservatives had been unable to enact in 1922. It also reinforced those favoring the expansion of the "special higher police force" (Tokubetsu Kōtō Keisatsu, known and feared by its sobriquet "Tokkō") and the supression of the communist movement in Japan.[52]

The next notation about Hirohito is from 14 January 1924. On that day Professor Mikami Sanji of Tokyo Imperial University lectured to the crown prince on the invasion of Korea advocated in 1873 by Saigō Takamori (1827–1877). The talk lasted an hour and a half and Makino was present. In the lecture, as described by Makino, Professor Mikami outlined the arguments of high court and government leaders without judging them. The government's vaccilation and the emperor's solicitude were described in an impartial manner. Then came the auspicious imperial decision and the country returned to its proper course. This was the most critical situation of the early years of the Meiji era. In 1873, while most government leaders were out of the country with the Iwakura Mission, Saigō persuaded his followers and the young Meiji emperor to allow him to lead a diplomatic mission to Korea. They were to demand that the Koreans reverse their new anti-Japanese policy. Saigō himself expected to be killed, bringing on a war between Korea and Japan.[53] After the Iwakura Mission returned to Japan, however, other government leaders opposed this policy, especially Ōkubo Toshimichi, Makino's father. In October of the same year the imperial decision to send an envoy—Saigō—to Korea was rescinded. Saigō resigned all his posts, except that of army general, and left Tokyo. This marked the end of his government career and the beginning of his rise in history as a "failed hero." Later in 1877 he led a rebellion in Satsuma against his former government colleagues, another campaign that miscarried. Saigō was wounded and committed seppuku.[54] In 1924 Makino concluded that it was good for the crown prince to hear Professor Mikami's version of these events—about the emperor's deep anxiety and the ministers' devotion to national affairs—and urged that such lectures should be held again in the future.[55]

Makino's understanding of his role vis-à-vis the new regent and future sovereign of Japan is clear. He was to tutor Hirohito in his

duties—not only what they were but how they were to be performed—
and, equally important, the place of the imperial house in the Japanese
body politic. Until his pupil had absorbed these lessons and adopted
the correct attitudes, Makino regarded it as proper to "shield" him from
undue pressures, that is, from having to take stands or make decisions
for which he was not prepared. Makino was afraid that the young
regent, and later the young emperor, would compromise the transcendental position of the imperial house in Japanese society if he impru-
dently became involved in politics. The Chang Tso-lin Affair is a good
illustration of what he meant.

Controls Loosen: The Chang Tso-lin Affair

After Hirohito became emperor his attitude about his own position
and competence changed dramatically: he began to assert his authority in a very consequent manner. Emperor Taishō died on 25 December 1926. Hirohito immediately became emperor, although the official
enthronement ceremony was not held until 1928. In 1927, before Hirohito had been on the throne for a calendar year, Makino became concerned about his penchant for mixing in politics—a tendency that
could be detrimental to the imperial house. In particular, Makino and
Saionji were worried about the young emperor's consternation over
Prime Minister Tanaka's handling of the assassination of Chang Tso-lin
in June 1928 by officers in the Kwantung Army.

After the murder of Chinese warlord Chang Tso-lin in Manchuria
on 4 June 1928, Prime Minister Tanaka Giichi (1863–1929), a baron
and general, promised the emperor that the Kwantung Army's role in
the incident would be thoroughly investigated. He indicated that the
Imperial Army appeared to be involved. In May 1929, however, under
pressure from the army and the conservative Seiyūkai political party,
Tanaka told the emperor it was unclear who was responsible (although
everyone knew that members of the Kwantung Army had planned and
carried out the action). Hirohito was incensed by this obvious attempt
to cover for army radicals, and Tanaka resigned. After his resignation,
Tanaka's supporters spread rumors to the effect that the cabinet had
been toppled by a group of plotters among the elder statesmen (*jūshin*)
and court officials. This rumor greatly disturbed Hirohito, who had a
greater role in Tanaka's resignation than was assumed for many years.
With the publication in 1990 of his 1946 "monologue," it became
clear that in 1929 he did not just refuse to see Tanaka again. He asked
for Tanaka's resignation point blank.[56] And the emperor apparently felt
responsible for the commotion that followed.

This incident and Hirohito's ensuing regrets—because he had gone beyond the role of a "constitutional monarch"—are well known. Less well known is the fact that from about the time of the formation of the Tanaka cabinet (20 April 1927) Hirohito began to take an active interest in the prime minister's handling of state affairs, just as he said he would in his essay from 1920 (see Chapter 6). Less than three months later Makino sought out Prince Saionji to discuss this issue. At Saionji's residence on 3 July 1927 Makino brought up the problem of the questions addressed by the emperor during imperial audiences with political officials. He proposed that Saionji act as an intermediary between emperor and prime minister to avoid direct discussions of this kind. Saionji was reticent about this proposal, due to the additional time state decisions would take, but in the end he agreed. Afterward Makino noted that the foremost consideration was to avoid a direct line of responsibility to the emperor. Saionji, he said, agreed completely.[57]

Here Japanese tradition—the emperor reigns but does not rule—coincided with the exigencies of modern statecraft and constitutional monarchy. Political activity inevitably results in successes and failures. Those involved in politics sometimes inspire admiration, at other times hate and envy. A constitutional monarch is removed from this danger because he cannot participate actively in politics. This policy agreed well with the traditional role of the emperor—obviously the man who embodies the institution revered as the symbol of the unity and sublime destiny of the Japanese people must stand above mundane affairs. He must not be tainted by appearing to be the source of some policy that becomes the object of partisan bickering, proves to be ill conceived, or fails. Makino, Saionji, and later Kido Kōichi all understood this very well. And they used this situation to enhance their own powers as representatives of the imperial will in public. Hirohito came to understand this dimension of his office later—which is no doubt one reason for his inclination to constitutional monarchy. But on certain occasions he found it difficult personally to act out this role: the embodiment of Imperial Japan's national destiny as designated in the political ideology and cosmology propagated by government leaders. Hirohito was well aware that the emperor stood for something higher than civil government or the military. But sometimes his role as the spiritual embodiment of the Japanese folk was overshadowed by his concern about the power of the imperial family. He consistently reacted strongly when he thought its position was being impaired. This difficulty manifested itself for the first time clearly with the ouster of Prime Minister Tanaka.

From Chang Tso-lin's assassination to Tanaka's resignation, little more than a year elapsed. During that time Makino records a number of deliberations about how the Chang Tso-lin Affair should be handled by various leaders of the day. On 27 March 1929, for example, he records that Saionji's secretary, Harada Kumao, told him about a meeting reported to him by General Ugaki Kazunari (1868–1956) between the general, Prime Minister Tanaka, and Chinda Sutemi. In this meeting Tanaka retreated from his announced intention to investigate the matter thoroughly and punish those responsible. Harada commented that the matter would not be easily resolved. Makino then went directly to the palace.[58] On the same day in a discussion with Makino and Grand Chamberlain Suzuki Kantarō (1868–1948), Harada repeated what he had said earlier. Moreover, it came out that Army Minister Shirakawa Yoshinori (1869–1932) had made a private report to the throne earlier that day. In view of the latest information from Harada, both Makino and the grand chamberlain were concerned there might be inconsistencies between what had been reported to the emperor previously and this new report from Shirakawa. The next day the grand chamberlain took the opportunity afforded by an audience with the emperor to ask if this had been the case. The emperor replied that this time there had been no particular problem. Both Suzuki and Makino were greatly relieved.

Obviously some months before the crucial meeting between Hirohito and his prime minister the emperor's two closest advisers were well aware that Tanaka and his army minister had quite different opinions about how the assassination should be handled. Their principal concerns, however, were not correctness, discipline, or justice.[59] They were worried about the formal management of the affair and the image of the army, the nation, and the emperor. Makino and his colleagues insisted the emperor's position should not be compromised publicly by inconsistent reports. Hirohito himself was not thinking of justice and human rights; he was worried about his authority and the image of the army—the emperor's army. At home and overseas, both should be restored by a thorough investigation and a military tribunal if necessary. Later the emperor noted a discrepancy between Tanaka's first and final reports. The former indicated that the army appeared to be behind the assassination; the latter absolved the Imperial Army of responsibility for the incident. This difference is recorded as the reason for the emperor's displeasure and Tanaka's resignation. There is no hint of the extent of Hirohito's dissatisfaction, let alone any indication he asked for Tanaka's resignation. Makino wrote that Tanaka himself presented his resignation in a private audience. If he knew of Hirohito's forthright demand for it, one gets only a bare hint of this: Makino says the emperor looked on tolerantly as the handling of this very serious affair was bungled.[60]

A general account also appears in the record of Prince Saionji's activities kept by his secretary Harada.[61] Like Makino, Saionji conveys a version of this event—Tanaka resigned in remorse due to his loss of imperial confidence—that had been accepted as conventional wisdom until the revelations of the Hirohito Monologue were published in 1990. In fact, the emperor sought to preserve his own authority. He acted as head of the nation *and* the imperial house in accord with the importance attached to the latter institution by his instructors of history and ethics. Apparently the significance of constitutional monarchy for his future well-being had not yet been fully absorbed. His advisers vaguely perceived this. They were concerned about Hirohito's participation in state affairs, but seem not to know how far it had gone.

In the summer of 1929, despite imperial displeasure and unofficial but solid information to the contrary, the first Manchurian Incident was handled as if the Imperial Army had had little to do with it: the assassination had simply occurred in an area under the jurisdiction of one of its units, the Kwantung Army. On 1 July the commander of the Kwantung Army, acknowledging his "responsibility" for the incident, was replaced. On the following day Prime Minister Tanaka officially presented the resignation of his cabinet. That was the end of the affair for the army. Not so, however, for the emperor and his political adviser, Makino.

Curbing the Emperor

Shortly after Tanaka's resignation, on the day prior to selecting his successor, Makino enacted his plan for removing the emperor from direct participation in political policy discussions. At this time it was not a question of Hirohito's youth or inexperience. The issue now was lines of responsibility. The imperial house must be clearly separated from the political decision-making process. For the sake of constitutional monarchy—and, more important, the preservation of the imperial house—the emperor must not appear to be responsible for political policy. He must be entirely dissociated from government actions and any personal liability for them. Makino brought up this pressing issue with the emperor. He suggested that Hirohito ask Saionji for his opinion, knowing full well that Saionji agreed with him. Imperial thoughts could be transmitted by telephone, Makino suggested, or perhaps the grand chamberlain could be dispatched to transmit imperial inquiries. Saionji said the grand chamberlain should be sent to present imperial questions "courteously." The emperor thought this a very welcome solution, Makino noted.[62] This procedure, as it turned out, was to have an ominous effect. Makino could prevent direct communication between the emperor and Japan's civil leaders, but he could not do the same with the military.

Military leaders were guaranteed the right of direct access to the throne. This practice was not part of the Meiji Constitution—which stipulated that all ministers were to "give their advice to the Emperor, and be responsible for it" (Article 55)—but was based on a loose interpretation of a ministerial regulation that preceded the promulgation of the constitution in 1889. The regulation allowed the army and navy chiefs of staff to report directly to the throne. Following the audience the two service ministers and the prime minister were to be informed of the content of the reports.[63] The part of this regulation indicating that the service ministers and prime minister were to be informed about these proceedings was ignored for the most part, and later this "custom" was perpetuated in the regulations for cabinet organization (*naikaku kansei*) drawn up in 1889. According to these regulations, military secrets could be reported directly to the emperor. This information too "was to be reported to the service ministers and prime minister, with the exception of those matters transmitted directly to the cabinet by the emperor."[64] Again, it was never intended that the military should establish a separate existence beyond the control of the cabinet or act independently in the name of the emperor. But that was how military leaders in effect conducted their affairs from the middle of the Meiji period until the end of the Pacific War. The law professor Minobe Tatsukichi (1873–1948) analyzed the situation very clearly in the early 1920s. He acknowledged the independent political status of the military but denied it had any grounds in the Meiji Constitution.[65]

During the audiences with military leaders the emperor's political adviser, the lord privy seal, was not in attendance unless invited on specific occasions. Military matters were to be kept free of political influence. In practice this meant the prime minister and other civil leaders could not question policies decided by the army and navy. Military men were responsible only to the emperor. They needed only to report their decisions to the prime minister and other civil officials after they had been made and approved by the emperor. Communication between the two groups did occur at unofficial meetings (*renraku kaigi*). But practically speaking, up until the first Manchurian Incident in 1928, the emperor was the only conduit of influence between civil and military leaders.

In 1928 Makino and Saionji worked to prevent the emperor from participating directly in the political decision-making process by having the grand chamberlain present imperial questions to civil leaders. This had an unforeseen side effect: it not only removed the emperor from direct participation in political policymaking but also constricted contact between the military and civil branches of government—furthering, in the end, the independence of the military.

The emperor was to be protected from involvement in the daily affairs of government that might lower him, a "living god," in the eyes of the Japanese people. Likewise such involvement would undermine his claims to being a constitutional monarch and make him responsible for these affairs. Not to be overlooked is the fact that this policy also increased the power of the court officials surrounding the emperor, including Makino. These bureaucrats maintained that they enunciated the "imperial will." But because Makino and his colleagues at court could not prevent the emperor from actively discussing military affairs, high military officers claimed in a like manner to represent the "imperial will." In effect two groups of unelected officials who were responsible only to their inbred peers—court and military officials respectively—presumed to represent the imperial will, the highest determinant of Japanese government policy. Political decision making became a contest between two groups of bureaucrats. A third group—parliamentary leaders led officially by the prime minister, whose access to the throne was limited by the foregoing measure—was often reduced to kibitzing from the sidelines.

For many years after the war, the lines of influence and responsibility between Japan's prewar leaders and the emperor remained obscure. Therefore one could say Makino was successful: he restrained the emperor from being, or appearing to be, responsible for specific political policies. But the cost was high. Decision making was increasingly privatized, and behind the scenes the military, relieved of civilian pressure through the emperor, was able to expand its power. As the military gained the upper hand it was deemed necessary to make career officers prime ministers in order to bridge the gap created between civil and military officials. Shielding the emperor from political responsibility, as suggested by Saionji and implemented by Makino, was partly responsible, then, for the rise of the military in prewar Japan. Certainly this was not their intention. But by restricting Hirohito's access to civilian leaders, they inadvertently contributed to this development.

National Destiny

Makino was a liberal politician and bureaucrat. This meant in the Japanese context that he was progressive in comparison to his feudalistic

Tokugawa predecessors and moderate in comparison to his chauvinistic military contemporaries—but no less concerned about his own power and influence and no less nationalistic. In 1924 Makino made a brief notation about the place and meaning of the imperial house in Japanese society:

> Today the relationship between the imperial household and the people is a direct one. If matters concerning the imperial household are all to be known and discussed in general, they must be considered with great circumspection. Especially today, when the national destiny *(koku'un)* is being buffeted about and not a few hidden crises lie in wait, one must forestall and resist by all means that which distresses human feelings. Due to the supreme virtue and majesty of the imperial household, unity is preserved. Within the imperial household that which impairs ethics and morality must by all means be avoided. With respect to the national destiny, government authorities must of course pay careful attention to it and make appropriate efforts.[66]

Here his underlying beliefs about the central position of the imperial line in Japan are readily apparent: the imperial household was directly related to the national destiny and central to the unity of the Japanese people. For this reason the public image of the imperial house, its ethical and moral condition, must at all times be protected. This belief obviously colored his reportedly moderate views, and it must be accounted for when considering his activities as the emperor's closest political adviser. Moreover, this belief conforms with the crown prince's education. Makino provided the link between Hirohito's early instruction and his subsequent view of his role in sustaining the national polity, including his participation behind the scenes in military planning.

The emperor was an integral part of a milieu imbued with patriotic sentiments. Makino and many others thought the imperial house was indispensable to the continued existence of the Japanese state, folk, and religion in prewar Japan.[67] Hirohito, as we have seen, was well educated in the central place of the imperial house in Japanese history and ethics, and it appears he agreed with this interpretation of the symbolic meaning of his house in Japanese culture. But as illustrated by his participation in military planning, neither this belief nor his advocacy of constitutional monarchy precluded his participation in state affairs. The Manchurian Incident of 1931 set the stage for these later developments.

The Second Manchurian Incident: 1931

In 1931–1932 the Kwantung Army took over Manchuria by force, a takeover known as the "Manchurian Incident." Hirohito's postwar supporters say the emperor, devoted to peace, was adamantly opposed to the takeover.[68] There is solid evidence to support this view, but a close examination of the records shows that his opposition was inconsistent. At different times he supported different policies.

The Manchurian Incident did not happen all of a sudden without prior notice. Rumors about unrest in Manchuria were first heard in the summer of 1931, but Makino, among others, did not think them important.[69] The situation had changed by September, however, and Prince Saionji's secretary, Harada, noted that one week before the incident the emperor warned the army minister about unauthorized troop movements in Manchuria and Mongolia. This warning was passed to the commander of the Kwantung Army, Honjō Shigeru, on 14 September, but Honjō may not have seen this message before the outbreak of the incident.[70] The same source says that after the attack was reported, the prime minister was very concerned that Chinese troops may not, as telegraphed, have initiated the hostilities. The possibility that it was another illegal army action was immediately apparent to leaders in Tokyo.

But the prime minister, among others, seems to have been unsure what was going on or what to do about it. On the morning after the incident, Prime Minister Wakatsuki asked Army Minister Minami directly if indeed the Kwantung Army was acting in self-defense against an attack by the Chinese army. Minami answered, "That is precisely the situation."[71] Of course, no one would expect the army minister to have answered otherwise. But after the army minister reported to the emperor, the prime minister told Hirohito that the army's report was correct. That evening the prime minister began to question his own assurances. He called Harada to his office and in a long monologue expressed concern about the events in Manchuria. He compared it with the Tanaka Incident in 1928 and worried about the issue of troop movements without imperial consent (*gosaika nashi ni*). Later there was a meeting at the palace with Makino, the grand chamberlain, and Kido Kōichi at which the same fears were discussed.[72] Two days after the incident was reported in Japan, 21 September 1931, Makino noted that the emperor told the ministers of the army and navy, the chief of staff, prime minister, and his court advisers that the incident should not be allowed to expand.[73] But even at this early date, the army minister's vagueness in adhering to this policy stimulated criticism in cabinet meetings. The finance minister was unhappy about the lack of coordination between military actions and government policy. Foreign Minister Shidehara reported rumors in Manchuria to the effect that the whole thing was an army plot and complained about the resulting complications for international relations.

These matters were all reported to Makino. One might assume, though it is not specifically noted, that Makino passed on this information to Hirohito. Reporting and interpreting political developments to the emperor was after all Makino's principal duty as lord privy seal. The records kept by Makino, Kido Kōichi, and Prince Saionji's secretary all indicate the same thing—that the Kwantung Army was beyond their control. Therefore, it must have been clear to all high government officials, bureaucrats and politicians, and the sovereign that practically speaking it was going to be very difficult to restrain the army. On 25 September, for example, an army official told Kido it would take a long time to clear up the situation in Manchuria and a new policy was needed. The head of the Manchurian Railway Agency supported this view.[74] Makino himself was aware, too, that the chief of staff had begun acting in a high-handed manner. The latter informed the prime minister that the army would not interfere in what he called "the Manchurian independence movement"; troop withdrawals would be made in short order; and in the future the government should not meddle in supreme command affairs. Makino notes that the prime minister reported these and other peremptory statements by the chief of staff to Saionji to give him a clear picture of the situation.[75]

Here was a clear challenge to Hirohito's authority as commander in chief of the armed forces. Leading officials in Tokyo were not sure what was going on in Manchuria because the army was not reporting in a candid manner on the activities and intentions of its field officers. The discrepancies, suspicions, and confusion indicated, or should have indicated, that strong statements backed up by resolute action were called for. In Tokyo, however, resolute leadership was conspicuously absent.

Leaders in Tokyo were in disarray. They were not without influence, but they were unsure how to use it. Before the incident Honjō Shigeru, commander of the Kwantung Army, apparently was reluctant to go along with the plans of his junior officers because he knew that initiating troop movements overseas without the emperor's approval was a violation of imperial prerogative. Moreover, he needed the approval of the chief of staff, which he did not have. Honjō reportedly took his time in deciding to support his subordinates, therefore, deliberating until three in the morning under a great deal of pressure from them.[76] Honjō was hesitant due to the authority of those in Tokyo, but he nevertheless went ahead. No adverse consequences were forthcoming; indecision and inaction abetted further insubordination. Honjō met the next day with the leading officers under his command, among others the architect of the plot, Lt. Col. Ishiwara Kanji. They discussed how they should respond to the situation, including troop dispositions, with no mention of anyone in Tokyo—neither the army high command, the civilian government, or the emperor.[77] Finally, support was requested from Japanese troops in Korea and they were mobilized.

Then, in a clear demonstration that the tail was indeed wagging the dog, support for the military actions on the mainland was mobilized in Tokyo. Four officers on the general staff were assigned to write a paper showing why the independent mobilization of troops was not a violation of imperial prerogative and why there should be an ex post facto imperial sanction for moving the troops.[78] And on the very same day (21 September) that the emperor told the army and navy ministers, the chief of staff, and others that the incident should be contained, Honjō received a telegram from the army minister that shows he must not have been listening to his supreme commander in the imperial palace. Minami affirmed the conviction in central army headquarters that the disrespectful attitude of the Chinese, officials and people alike, must be dealt with and all areas in Manchuria pacified. This disrespect, he said, was the reason for the attack. He himself was engaged in talks with the Tokyo government regarding this matter. Everyone in Manchuria and Mongolia, he said, should live happily together under Japanese rule. On the previous day, the army chief of staff had said something similar to Harada.[79] Thereafter, soldiers continued to be moved and advances were made on the mainland in an apparent violation of Hirohito's expressed "will," if not his orders.

By 21 September Honjō already had his troops advancing northward and had again requested aid from Korea. The commander in Korea then sent about three thousand men over the border, into Manchuria, without imperial sanction. On 22 September, Honjō answered Minami's telegram by saying that it was rather unlikely that in the near future everyone would live peacefully under Japanese rule in Manchuria. On 5 November the general staff, responding to pressure in Tokyo, ordered Honjō to limit operations in the north. Disregarding the emperor's instructions of 21 September, he sent a telegram to Chief of Staff Kanaya asking if this was not a violation of the "prerogative of supreme command."[80] Although Makino may not have known all the details of these developments, both he and the emperor must have been aware that matters were out of hand. What were the emperor and his advisers doing?

The Emperor's Actions and Their Significance

An indispensable source of information about the emperor and the Manchurian Incident is Chief Aide-de-Camp General Nara Takeji.[81] One of the first things one notes in his record of the incident is that shortly before its outbreak in 1931 the emperor issued not one but a number of warnings to military leaders about preserving discipline. On 8 September he admonished both the army and navy ministers about this matter. On the tenth he again addressed the navy minister in a similar manner, and on the eleventh came the warning cited earlier.[82] In 1930, by contrast, during the talks about limiting the size of the Imperial Navy at the London Naval Conference, only one such warning, to the army, is recorded in Nara's diary.[83]

In other words: although he was not privy to the diaries and records kept by the figures cited here, the emperor had sufficient information to expect trouble. This is why he issued these warnings. Whether they came because he personally was concerned about preserving peace, because he was concerned about the formal prerogatives of the imperial house, the right of supreme command, constitutional monarchy, or a combination of all these issues cannot be definitively ascertained. Makino, who was totally surprised by this turn of events, has nothing to say on the matter. He records the concern of everyone in the government, but if he gave the emperor any advice he is markedly silent about it.[84] As for the emperor's actions, Makino may have restrained him from getting directly involved. Certainly memory of the Tanaka Incident may have made Hirohito hesitant, but he appears to have done his best to maintain the authority of the Meiji Constitution and the imperial house.[85] Nothing in the emperor's previous training, however, would indicate Hirohito might have been worried exclusively about preventing war. Indeed, much of that training concerned the place of the imperial house in Japanese history and society and the importance of preserving it. Clearly the imperial tradition was an important factor in the emperor's deliberations. Nor should we ignore the possibility that as advocates of constitutional monarchy and international peace Hirohito and Makino were also advancing the position of the imperial house and court within Japan.

Hirohito's concerns at this time, however, were never consistently defined. The "Shōwa Emperor's Eight-Hour Monologue" does not even discuss the Manchurian Incident.[86] Given the gravity of the situation, one can only wonder why. One modern scholar, Yamada Akira, indicates that the emperor may have misjudged the seriousness of these events and sought to take advantage of them to further Imperial

Japan's influence overseas. Yamada bases his assertion on a statement by the emperor to Chief Aide-de-Camp Nara Takeji: "If Chang Hsueh-liang's troops should regroup in the area of Jehol, might this inevitably lead to an expansion of the incident? If necessary, it is possible that I would agree to an expansion of the incident." This statement was immediately transmitted to the assistant chief of staff with the comment that if Chang Hseuh-liang rebuilt his forces and challenged the Japanese, this would amount to an expansion of hostilities. Yamada concludes: "[The emperor] assumed the following position: while avoiding friction with the major powers England, America, and others, if in Manchuria Japan's interests *(ken'eki)* can be expanded, or if by using military force national prestige can be promoted, [he] had nothing against it."[87] Stephen Large, by contrast, says the emperor was "incensed" by these developments and "feared that eventually he would be obliged to authorize expansion of hostilities against Chang in Jehol."[88] It appears the emperor's stance in 1931 was not entirely clear, and one can well imagine that Hirohito may have purposely omitted mention of Manchuria in 1946 because, after Japan's defeat, he steadfastly maintained that before and during the war he only wanted to protect peace and the constitution.

In any case, Yamada's conclusion needs qualification. The documents may be interpreted in various ways, and they do not support one-sided conclusions. Despite the contradiction between Hirohito's statements on 21 September and 9 October, Nara, Harada, Kido, and Makino show that the government, including the army high command and emperor, was attempting to control events during the Manchurian Incident—as indeed is the proper role of the central government. As for the emperor personally, he was placed between containment and equivocation. And at this point Makino appears to have been of little help. He did not pursue the issue of the military's insubordination, noting only that Hirohito was concerned about maintaining military discipline.[89] Nara, the emperor's military adviser, presents a similar picture. Hirohito asked him if ordering troops to cross the border between Korea and Manchuria required imperial sanction—or did the war plans presented by Army Minister Minami, previously sanctioned, cover this eventuality? If they did not, did this constitute a violation of the imperial prerogative of command *(taiken kampan)?* Nara answered that although an imperial sanction was necessary, calling this a violation of imperial prerogative would not be appropriate.[90]

To claim that these events indicate the emperor and Makino were for constitutionalism and peace is possible, but perhaps misleading. After all, one cannot overlook Hirohito's statement to Nara about opposing Chang Hsueh-liang. It shows the emperor was undecided at one point in time at least. As these events unfolded, Makino along with the emperor and the men close to him were no doubt "dismayed" by them as Large, among others, has written.[91] But their own action, or lack of action, was equally "dismaying." They were upset because of the deterioration of respect for the central government, meaning themselves. Yet when Makino took it upon himself to tell Army Minister Minami on 14 September 1931 that the army should take the opinions of the emperor more seriously,[92] and commented on the broad political and foreign policy implications of the military's actions, he did not propose direct countermeasures. He was addressing the issue of the power of the civilian arm of the government, of which he was an important part. Defying the emperor's authority meant defying the authority of those who advised him. This was not in the emperor's interests, or those of his established advisers.

Indecision led to inaction. The emperor and Makino (and Saionji) failed to control the military in Manchuria. It was a failure for constitutional monarchy, for international peace, and for Makino and his allies in Japanese politics. It was also a personal setback for the emperor. He and his advisers had been presented with a fait accompli, and in the future Hirohito attempted to avoid a repeat performance by consulting with his military leaders extensively behind the scenes. Hirohito's inclination to act behind the scenes and his education in imperial morality and national history contributed to this development. In 1931–1932, intent on maintaining the authority and dignity of his house, he dealt with the situation as best he could. When the League of Nations condemned Japan for violating peace and persons in Manchuria, Kido Kōichi said: "Japan had to withdraw [from the league] as a matter of national honor."[93] Japanese national interests were put before peace. The emperor too proposed not peace but concessions around Jehol to improve international opinion and make it unnecessary to leave the league. But in the opinion of Makino things had gone too far. There was no turning back now. "The question of who must bear responsibility for these developments is not an easy one. This must be left to future historians to decide,"[94] Makino said. The same may be said of the Shōwa emperor himself.

Makino and Saionji: Complementary Roles

Makino and Saionji were both called "liberal" and "moderate" in prewar Japan. But as we have seen, these terms meant something other than what is connoted in the West. Ambassador Grew's observations with respect to Makino's moderate politics, like Kido's well-known assertion that the emperor was a pacifist,[95] must be put in context to be properly understood. Moreover, one must take into account the complexity of the personalities who influenced Hirohito when evaluating his role in prewar policymaking. A brief comparison of Count Makino with Prince Saionji makes this clear.

Whereas one might call Makino a liberal bureaucrat, Saionji was a liberal aristocrat. Makino was born a high samurai. His influence was based on his advantageous family origins, a network of personal contacts in business and government, and his active pursuit of a career as a high-ranking official. One reason Makino, for example, was on the hit-list of the radical officers was due to personal opposition to them. In 1926 he had Kita Ikki and Nishida Mitsugi jailed because they publicly criticized his sale of imperial land in Hokkaido to a private party. Makino did this not only due to the criticism, but because he was an "ally" of Ōkawa Shūmei, who had recently fallen out with Kita.[96] This indicates that Makino was more deeply involved in right-wing political factionalism than is usually acknowledged, and he was indeed involved with moneyed interests as the "young officers" later charged. Saionji appears to have been above such activities. His political influence was more impressive and almost exclusively dependent on his high birth and aristocratic demeanor. Saionji appears, in contrast to Makino, to have been little interested in personal political power and influence.[97] Both men "had limited faith in the ability of commoners to rule themselves."[98] And for both "the appeal of the emperor as a symbol of the body politic standing in a special paternal relationship with his people" was important. Makino's activities were colored by his drive to promote Japan's national interests, which he often equated with his own; Saionji, self-assured as a leading aristocrat, appears more sovereign in his concern about Japan's position in the world. At the time of the dispute in Japan over the ratification of the London Naval Treaty he told his secretary Harada:

> The reason that Japan maintains her world power status is that she holds the baton of command with England and America. If Japan loses her grip like France and Italy, how will she develop as a world power?[99]

He opposed Japan's withdrawal from the League of Nations for the same reason:

> What advantages can we obtain by withdrawing from the League? . . . It is imperative that we stand with England and America in our capacity as a member of the League and work for the advantage of Japan by bolstering her position whilst extending the greatest cooperation.[100]

Makino, even more than Saionji, supported Japan's entry into the League of Nations for pragmatic reasons of national self-interest.[101] Later he opposed with Saionji the military and chauvinists who wanted Japan to withdraw from the league after the Kwantung Army's coup on the mainland.[102] But in the end, when the league published its report on the Manchurian Incident (15 February 1933), both gave up the fight. In Saionji's estimation, using the throne to back a losing cause would only undermine the authority of the imperial house.[103] Makino agreed and the emperor went along.

Japan's entry into the League of Nations and its exit are an example of the priorities of these leading statesmen: Saionji and Makino were concerned about internationalism and constitutional monarchy; but, quite naturally, this meant they were concerned about Japan's standing as a world power and their own influence at home. Their internationalism, therefore, might be dismissed as a means to a Japanese end, not something worthwhile in itself in terms of peace and world cooperation. But this imposes a standard on the Japanese to which the Western powers could not measure up either.

Saionji's liberal credentials were not, however, questioned by his contemporaries. Even foreign members of the diplomatic corps were impressed by them. At the time of the Paris Peace Conference, the British Foreign Office noted that Saionji was indeed an idealist:

> Eighteenth century French liberalism had made a lasting impact on Saionji's thought. His commitment to a successful outcome to the conference and the League was not only pragmatic but was a natural consequence of an ideological internationalist outlook learned in France a half century earlier.[104]

On the one hand, Saionji was a liberal idealist; on the other, this idealism was tempered by Japanese nationalism. This amalgam is reflected in the policies Saionji advocated. Makino's nationalism, by contrast, was more pronounced at home and abroad.

At the conclusion of the only study in a Western language of Prince Saionji, Lesley Connors writes:

> "Liberal," as applied to the Saionji group [of which Makino was a prominent member], implied first and most importantly a commitment to constitutional monarchy; that is to a monarch who reigned but did not rule and whose powers were limited by the provisions of the Constitution, the exercise of which powers was subject to the scrutiny of popularly elected representatives of the people in their capacity as law makers.[105]

But Connors immediately qualifies this definition by noting that Saionji was "an elitist liberal." Indeed he was elitist. This can be seen, for example, as he endeavored to enunciate the imperial will from behind the scenes in the late 1920s and early 1930s. The emperor's exercise of power was to be scrutinized, not by "popularly elected representatives of the people," but by unelected elites like Saionji and Makino who assumed they knew what was best for the people.

Saionji and Makino equated their political policies with the imperial will. In so doing, however, the self-proclaimed constitutional monarchists opened the Pandora's box of arbitrary sanction using the "imperial will": ultranationalists and various army officers came to assume the same for their policies—that they reflected the imperial will. Military and civilian officials then competed for control over the public imperial will, and the emperor himself sought from behind the scenes to impose his personal will on the process.

Saionji and Makino appropriated the imperial will in order to limit the emperor's role in politics and remove the imperial house from any responsibility for state policy. This they did, in the name of constitutional monarchy, for the sake of preserving the imperial line. Makino, different from Saionji, actively associated himself with both principles to further his political career. But each in his own way regarded Japanese history and modern English political theory as twin pillars for the preservation of the imperial house. A constitutional monarch, according to English precedent, reigns but does not rule. Japanese emperors, for centuries, wielded no actual power. This is one of the main reasons for the continued existence of the imperial line. In the prewar years, the Japanese imperial tradition was given an aura of modernity, new life and authority, as it was associated with the English system.

Hirohito shared this interest in constitutional monarchy and the preservation of his house. For him the former was a means to the latter. In this respect he was similar to Saionji; but, like Makino, he was also interested in politics as a means of promoting his own interests. If one assumes for a moment that these two elderly statesmen were not only advisers but also role models for Hirohito—looking at what they did instead of what they said—Saionji was the model Hirohito was supposed to follow and the one he personally advocated. Like the prince the emperor was to stand above the political fray and symbolize national unity. Behind the scenes, however, he emulated Makino. Which is to say, like his political adviser, the emperor tended to participate actively in politics "in chambers." This participation extended to military as well as political affairs.

Both men greatly influenced the emperor. Saionji, the enlightened aristocrat and the last genro, had more authority and was more impressive than Makino; but Makino stood in closer proximity to the emperor day in and day out. Both, in advising and supporting the emperor, attempted to promote civilian rule, restrain the militarists, and protect and preserve the imperial line in the name of constitutional monarchy. They achieved only mixed success, at least in military matters.

8

·

Conclusion

The relation between the emperor of Japan's personal convictions and his participation in prewar decision making is a perplexing question. Many separate Emperor Hirohito from the emperor system, exonerate the former, and condemn the latter. Others convict and condemn both —based on systems of ideology (communism, socialism, capitalism) or Western legal concepts that had little to do with the realities of his personal or official existence. Much has been said about English constitutional monarchy; but Hirohito was the emperor of Japan, not the king of England. Although his authority and limitations were defined in the Meiji Constitution (based on Prussian precedents), his power and influence rested on the conventions of Japanese history and tradition.

We are considering a man who lived a long and complicated life, moreover, a man who interpreted his position in Japanese history and government differently at different times. Many studies of the Shōwa emperor and the emperor system slight the national polity, its apparent demise, and the changes in thinking a normal person experiences as he grows older. This, however, is a mistake. All men change, and it is unrealistic to assume that Hirohito did not. The crown prince of 1916 was not the new emperor of 1926. Nor was he the head of the imperial house whose position and authority were challenged in 1936 or the newly secularized head of a defeated state in 1946. Those who argue that Hirohito was merely a figurehead emperor can point with justification to his activities during his regency and at the beginning of his reign as emperor. But one should differentiate between a newly appointed regent in his early twenties and a reigning emperor in his mid-thirties and early forties who had been on the throne over ten years—as was the case with Hirohito when war broke out first with China and later with the United States and its allies. Consider, too, the differences between the 1940s and the 1980s just before Hirohito died. Only shallow paradigms—the Shōwa Emperor as an enlightened monarch above the fray or Hirohito as an Asiatic Machiavelli—support the thesis that Emperor Hirohito consistently conducted himself as a westernized constitutional monarch or a scheming nationalistic warlord.

To maintain that the emperor, during the prewar years, "was absolutely consistent in using his personal influence to induce caution and to moderate, and even to obstruct, the accumulating, snowballing impetus toward war," as the American historians Stephen Large and Charles Sheldon would have it,[1] is to make the emperor into a god, which almost everyone agrees he was not. Large himself says elsewhere that the emperor was a mediocre man.[2] Yet it is equally tenuous to make him into a "Fighting Generalissimo" and assert, as the historian Herbert Bix does, that "it was the emperor, more than anyone else, who delayed Japan's surrender."[3] The present study offers an alternative point of view. Distinguished from a "head of state" in the Western sense of the term, Hirohito is presented here as the emperor of Japan and head of the imperial house. He was educated in this belief and was both empowered and obliged by Japanese tradition to serve not only his country but also his house as best he could. Often the latter took precedence over the former. Depending on the constellation of forces around him, he sought peace or made war, referring always to the constitution but preoccupied mainly with assuring the position and continued existence of the imperial house in Japan.

Schooled in the traditions of the Japanese imperial house, educated to be a modern head of state, Hirohito was influenced by both: ancient imperial-line tradition and modern education reinforced one another as he approached the problems of state. Many tend to assume there is a tension between tradition and modernity in a person's character—a source, ultimately, of inner dissonance. One should not make this assumption with the Japanese emperor. In Hirohito these strains were complementary. The imperial tradition was the source of his position, power, and well-being. Modern Western learning, especially constitutional theory, the natural sciences, and military strategy, was a means to preserve and enhance this position—the supremacy of the imperial house in Japanese society—and likewise Japan's position in the world. This complementary relation between modern Western learning and the imperial tradition is an important aspect of Hirohito's long advocacy of constitutional monarchy, not to mention the politics of his mentors Makino and Saionji. The meaning of the Meiji Constitution to the emperor must also be considered in this light.

Imperial Rule and Modern Monarchy

Throughout Japanese history—witness Gotoba and his sons in the first half of the thirteenth century and Godaigo in the fourteenth—emperors have enjoyed little political power, virtually no military might, and have been summarily deposed when they ran afoul of those who did. Hirohito was urged not to take part in political and military affairs in order to avoid appearing responsible for the outcomes and endangering his position and that of the imperial house. Those were the lessons of Japanese history, recently reinforced by examples from overseas: Russia, Germany, and, most ominously, China. Emperors reign and do not rule in Japan. This is the main reason for the long "unbroken" line of the imperial house. In this context, references to constitutionalism had a dimension that is often ignored: the special status of the imperial line in the Meiji Constitution.

The Meiji Constitution, on paper at least, vastly improved the emperor's situation. His status as a living god was reaffirmed. He was made head of state and the armed forces. Rules of succession were stipulated in the Imperial House Laws. The imperial house was to govern its affairs independent of politics and even the constitution.[4] Constitutional monarchy under the Meiji Constitution had positive implications for the emperor because it made arbitrary meddling in imperial house affairs difficult. But like other issues in Imperial Japan involving interpretations of the constitution, the provisions concerning the emperor in fact had a vague meaning. After the war Hirohito often repeated his reasons for not opposing more vigorously the militarists in prewar times: he was only a constitutional monarch and feared being deposed if he did not go along with the militarists. This simple statement contains, however, some complex considerations. Hirohito's fears, his claims that he was in danger, derived from Japanese historical experience and contemporary threats. Therefore he turned to support from abroad. He sought a quid pro quo with the army and navy based on the Japanese constitution, the precedents of Japanese history, and his conception of English constitutional monarchy. All precluded his being deposed by force so long as he refrained from participating in politics openly.

As contemporary participants in prewar affairs and later students of them—Prince Saionji and Stephen Large, for example—have pointed out, "one can find a considerable number of examples [throughout Japanese history] where, urged on by hangers-on, a younger brother [Imperial Prince] has killed an older brother to ascend the throne."[5] In a note in the margin Saionji comments that such actions are wrong—but that was not enough to ease his fears or those of the emperor. Additional support was sought, moral and emotional, and references to British constitutional monarchy gave the Meiji Constitution and the emperor's position in the body politic a ring of modernity and authority. At the same time they removed the emperor from direct involvement in political and military decision making. In effect, Britain's concept of constitutional monarchy may be seen as a theoretical support for the continued preeminence of the imperial house in Japan: it attenuated fears of the emperor, and certain oligarchs, about the precarious position of the Japanese emperor and the imperial line in Japanese history and contemporary society.

Emperors and the Military

Emperors have been confined, impoverished, ignored, exiled, perhaps even killed, but not one emperor or crown prince has ever committed seppuku in the style of a samurai. For the reasons just described, emperors normally did not get involved in military affairs. Earlier in history court aristocrats, including those from the imperial house, traditionally engaged in cultural activities, or pretended to, and regarded the samurai and their overlords as uncouth boors. Leading armies and such was beneath their dignity.[6] This all changed with the Meiji emperor beginning in 1868.

Hirohito's grandfather purposely cultivated the image of himself as military leader. He decreed that all male members of the imperial house were to receive military training and, with the exception of the crown prince, serve in the army or navy. Emperor Meiji's brothers, as well as Hirohito's father and his brothers, were brought up in this manner as were Hirohito and his brothers. (The Taishō emperor, Hirohito's father, discontinued his training due to his infirmity, but he continued to appear in public wearing military uniforms.) Fujiwara Akira has pointed out that Hirohito was brought up in the newly established military tradition of the imperial house and received an education that enabled him to comprehend military matters in a way that far exceeded the grasp of ordinary politicians of the prewar era.[7] This conservative military training was reinforced by the steady inculcation of traditional patriotism.

Imperial Ethics

This study has shown that Hirohito's education, leaving aside its specific military content, was steeped in traditional teachings about the sublime quality of Japanese culture and the imperial house. His teacher of imperial ethics (teiōgaku), Sugiura Shigetake, was not a Shinto jingoist as Edward Behr and other critics have described him.[8] But his approach to "knowledge in the broadest possible sense" was severely slanted. Here Stephen Large is poorly served by his informant, Yamamoto Shichihei.[9] Sugiura certainly did lecture on a wide variety of subjects, as Yamamoto says, but his interpretations are anything but broad-minded. The beginning of the lecture he delivered to the future emperor on "The Imperial Regalia" illustrates this point: "The founder of the imperial family, Amaterasu Ōmikami, bequeathed the imperial regalia when she had her grandson descend to the earth." The young crown prince was not taught that the source of the emperor's authority was the constitution or the people. Rather, the emperor of Japan received his authority from the ancestress who founded his family, his dynasty, and the empire of Japan—the supreme goddess in heaven.

Sugiura's fixation on the imperial house and Japan also manifested itself in lectures on topics where the connection might seem farfetched—for example, George Washington. Moreover, Sugiura qualified "modern" sources to make them fit his imperial ethics mold. In his lecture on the Meiji Charter Oath, for example, the promise that "each shall be allowed to pursue his own calling" was interpreted to mean: "In accord with one's status, each is to receive the opportunity to pursue his aspirations." (See Appendix 9.) Sugiura inculcated nationalist thought in his students in a manner calculated to strengthen the crown prince's commitment to the established order in Imperial Japan.

More seriously, perhaps, science was misused to serve the primitive ideology of Japan's unique national polity. Sugiura, who introduced Hirohito to native and foreign cultures, believed that Japan was unsurpassed among nations due to the length of its imperial dynasty. This he inferred from his understanding of a so-called principle of physics— the "law" of the accumulation of energy. This pseudoscientific approach to what we now call social science apparently appealed to the future emperor. Not only did he ask Sugiura to similarly instruct his future wife, but Sugiura was one of the few teachers at the school who regularly visited and lectured to the crown prince after the Ogaku-monjo was disbanded.

Hirohito, later known for being quite out of touch with the every-day lives of his subjects, was indoctrinated with "imperial ethics" that had little in common with the "modern" sociopolitical norms he later advocated in public. Among other things he was taught that the op-pressive policies of the Meiji oligarchs in Imperial Japan constituted an enlightened constitutional monarchy. To be sure, he appears to have been unaware of these basic contradictions and the social consequences of the political policies Japan pursued. After all, with respect to social and political developments, he was not taught to base his thinking on verifiable evidence. Rather, his mentors used the authority of Western science to validate predetermined Japanese ends.

History and the National Polity

Similar problems are to be found with Hirohito's highly respected teacher of history, Shiratori Kurakichi. Although Shiratori forbade dis-tribution of the lectures he gave Hirohito, several examples subsequent-ly printed in academic journals arouse serious doubts about the scien-tific nature of his teaching materials at the Ogakumonjo. Some of his talks verged on polemics. In a lecture to the crown prince on Chinese Confucianism and the Japanese national polity *(kokutai)* he even main-tained that the national polity should not be sullied by foreign im-ports. Import foreign things but do not be subservient to them, Shira-tori emphasized. At the same time he presented the mythology of the imperial house uncritically, unconcerned about becoming a slave to those who manipulated it. This is not to say he actively supported the ultranationalists of the 1930s; rather, at best, he did not recognize the danger that lurked in these right-wing quarters.

Many years later Hirohito was no less ingenuous. He finally re-nounced his claim to divinity in 1946 but held fast to the symbolism of imperial succession from the gods.[10] In sum, then, the emperor's teachers, Sugiura and Shiratori, employed Western science to lend legit-imacy to Japan's national polity and the divine nature of the imperial house.[11] Later, Hirohito himself similarly advocated constitutional monarchy, as seen in Great Britain, to buttress the traditional suprem-acy of his house in Japanese society.

Historicism and the Imperial Line

It is well to remember that Japanese history, the imperial line, and its role in Japan's political as well as literary culture have not always been interpreted as they were after the Meiji Restoration in 1868. Meiji leaders actively "reconstructed" the imperial tradition in order to provide a spiritual core for their modernizing efforts.

As others have pointed out, to solidify these truths the academic discipline of history was established during the Meiji period as a "legitimizing science."[12] German historicism and a critical approach to primary source materials agreed well with the Japanese tradition of compiling historical documents. The historicism was brought to bear on the documents to provide the desired foundation for the modern state the Meiji politicians were building. This foundation was to have a role similar to that played by Christianity in the countries they visited in the West. Other intellectuals, of course, participated as well in this effort. But the history and ethics taught to Hirohito, Tōjō, and their contemporaries—the facts and fantasies surrounding the imperial line —were not mere constructs for them. This was the Truth, just as God and Country were ultimate truths for the men and women on the other side of the Pacific with whom the Japanese eventually fought a war.

Hirohito's Version of Constitutional Monarchy

The influence of Sugiura and Shiratori on Hirohito cannot of course be "proved." It has been shown, nevertheless, that both the content of their lectures and the way they employed Japanese history and Western learning to explain and legitimize the social order in Imperial Japan paralleled the emperor's later approach to constitutional monarchy. Hirohito advocated British constitutional norms not only as a model for governing but, more important, to preserve, protect, and legitimize in modern terms the imperial line and the supreme position of his house in Japanese society.

This sort of thinking played a significant role in Emperor Hirohito's participation in prewar military policymaking and, later, his claims about nonparticipation. It allowed him do both in good conscience. He participated in consensus decisions as a traditional leader in Japan often does: as an important member of a group of prewar power brokers who made political and military decisions. But at the same time the decision-making process precluded him from unilaterally determining policies as a president or dictator in the West would do. Therefore Hirohito could simultaneously explain himself and justify his actions, or lack of action, in terms of Western constitutional monarchy. And this, one must repeat, he did in good conscience. He was not consciously engaged in duplicity or deception, at least not to any greater extent than is normal for a head of state. A fortuitous convergence of circumstances, only partially of his making, permitted him to actively fill his traditional role as emperor of Japan and concurrently, in the interests of modernity, aspire to be a British-style constitutional monarch. His first adviser, Imperial Household Minister and later Lord Keeper of the Privy Seal Makino, was instrumental in promoting this development.

Makino and Constitutional Monarchy

Makino Nobuaki has a reputation for being one of the moderate liberals at court who strongly supported the idea of constitutional monarchy.[13] At the same time, throughout his career Makino advocated and enacted policies designed to enhance the power of the imperial government. Despite his liberal reputation, some of his policies were almost fascist in import—such as his concept of a centralized national art institute and a controversial morals directive to censure pupils' reading materials both in and out of school. These measures were all designed to strengthen *kokutai* solidarity at home and promote Japan as a world power abroad. Later, constitutional monarchy from Makino's perspective was good for the Japanese polity because it placed the imperial institution above everyday politics—and at the same time made it easier for court officials like Makino to assume the mantle of imperial authority for their policies.

Prince Saionji, by contrast, was more idealistic but no less concerned about Japan's image overseas. An aristocrat by birth and demeanor, he was influenced by eighteenth-century French liberalism, which led him to become a strong proponent of liberal constitutional monarchy. But Saionji's brand of constitutional monarchy included giving preference to the well-born above the common people, whom he did not trust. Similarly, his advocacy of Japan's association with England and America was based not only on their systems of government but on their status as world leaders as well. Saionji's high-flown liberalism, in short, agreed nicely with his elitism.

Hirohito was advised and tutored almost daily by Makino from the time he became regent whereas Saionji served as an éminence grise in the background. At first Hirohito could do little without his adviser's "advice," and he no doubt learned much from Makino. His handling of the Manchurian Incident in 1931 demonstrates what he had learned. From behind the scenes he interrogated his military aides and officials and urged them to contain the incident. This was not only a breach of international peace; army leaders had not received imperial approval for this action, meaning they had acted in an insubordinate manner. But the emperor did not confront anyone publicly or issue orders that might not be obeyed. A good leader does not issue orders that have a high probability of being disobeyed, because this subverts his own authority. After all, the tradition of emperor as supreme commander was a relatively new one. Military men were not in the habit of taking orders from an emperor, and the Meiji Constitution did not clearly delinate the emperor's right of supreme command.

In the second Manchurian Incident one can also see the practical nature of the Japanese commitment to liberal ideals. Makino, Saionji, and the emperor were "liberal" constitutional monarchists. But these ideals—for example, "the liberation of nations from foreign rule"— were not to be allowed to endanger the position of Japan in the world or the imperial house at home. International ideals were to be kept within bounds that were defined by national interests. Liberalism and constitutional monarchy were a means to an end. And that end, quite naturally, was the welfare of the imperial institution and Imperial Japan.

The nature of constitutional monarchy in Japan was even more clearly demonstrated in two contentious incidents early in Hirohito's reign: Prime Minister Tanaka's resignation in 1929 and Hirohito's reaction to the officers' revolt in February 1936. Hirohito indicated repeatedly that he regretted his role in the Tanaka Affair and professed to be concerned, too, because he had violated the principles of constitutional monarchy during both incidents. In the end, though, both constitutional monarchy and the authority of the imperial house were preserved. Like his teachers, Sugiura and Shiratori, Hirohito availed himself of modern science (Western legal concepts) to support ancient Japanese tradition. But obviously the continued existence of the center of that tradition, the imperial house, was more important than these abstract foreign principles.

Decision Making in Prewar Japan: The February 26 Incident

The army officers' revolt of 26 February 1936 has been discussed extensively by Western as well as Japanese scholars. All agree that Hirohito did not equivocate in the least when he heard of its outbreak.[14] On that morning about fourteen hundred members of the First Division of the Imperial Army mounted an insurrection. Their officers called for a "Shōwa Restoration." The power of the politicians and finance barons was to be "restored" to the emperor—meaning the army would rule in his name. Government leaders like Makino (retired), his successsor Saitō Makoto, Saionji, the prime minister, the finance minister, and army personnel from the Control faction (Tōseiha) who opposed the ultranationalist Imperial Way faction (Kōdōha) were to be eliminated.[15] The rebels assassinated Saitō, Finance Minister Takahashi Korekiyo, and Inspector General of Military Education General Watanabe Jōtarō of the Control faction and narrowly missed killing Grand Chamberlain Suzuki Kantarō, (prime minister at the end of the war), Makino, and Prime Minister Okada Keisuke. Occupying the center of Tokyo, the officers called for the cabinet's resignation and the formation of a new government under General Mazaki Jinzaburō. They assumed the emperor sympathized with their aims at home and abroad. Once his treacherous advisers were removed, they surmised, he would gladly proclaim the Shōwa Restoration. They erred grievously. Obviously they knew nothing about what sort of man Hirohito was.

When Chief Aide-de-Camp General Honjō Shigeru (commander in chief of the Kwantung Army in 1931) informed the emperor of the revolt, Hirohito immediately ordered that it be put down and referred to the officers as "rebels" *(bōto)*. Honjō, greatly disturbed, asked him not to use this word. The emperor's answer reveals his feelings about who the emperor of Japan was: "Without Our *(Chin)* orders Our troops have been willfully moved. Whatever they are called, they are not Our troops."[16] Hirohito did not refer to the rebels as Imperial Army troops, First Division troops, or Japanese troops. He used a pronoun *(Chin)* that can only be used by the reigning emperor of Japan, the royal "Our." The veil of constitutional monarchy was dropped. Hirohito was deeply angered because "His" troops had been mobilized without his command. It was a highly unconstitutional act, and more: the emperor's choice of words and conduct indicate that he perceived the revolt as a personal affront—to the emperor of Japan.

Shortly thereafter Hirohito ordered Army Minister Kawashima Yoshiyuki to "suppress the rebels within one hour," and he demanded reports from the chief aide-de-camp every thirty minutes. The next day, when told by Honjō that little progress was being made by the high command in quashing the rebels, Hirohito told him: "I Myself will lead the Konoe Division and subdue them."[17] This he did not do, but he did demand regular progress reports as on the previous day. The rebels surrendered several days later on 29 February. Clearly the emperor's opposition to them was a key factor in their ultimate failure. And this opposition assumed a very personal dimension. Contrary to the protestations of Hirohito's postwar supporters, it was not just an abstract constitutional monarch who brought his troops back into line; it was the emperor of Japan personally. Harada's source for Hirohito's statement about "His troops" is unknown, but it does not seem far-fetched. Recall, for example, the difficulty Makino and Saionji had in restraining the emperor from participating directly in political affairs.

Then in 1936, as with the Tanaka Incident of 1929, Hirohito repeated his regrets about exceeding the boundaries of constitutional monarchy. But more than the constitution would have been compromised had the rebels succeeded. The position of the imperial house as well would have been endangered. The military's extraconstitutional position would have expanded from independent control of military affairs to control of all state functions. Even the emperor would have been subjected to their dictates.

Some interpreters of this incident, citing Hirohito's protestations about constitutional monarchy, have raised arguments about his ability to affect the course of events in prewar Japan. Due to the tension between his devotion to constitutional monarchy, they say, as opposed to his responsibility for restraining the military, problems arose.[18] These arguments are misleading because they are irrelevant. They focus not on how decisions were made in prewar Japan but on how the victors in the Pacific War, along with many journalists and scholars on both sides of the Pacific, have insisted decisions should have been made. They totally ignore the manner in which Hirohito acted behind the scenes to press his interests. The emperor of Japan was never supposed to make decisions alone—partly because he was a constitutional monarch but mainly because historically this authority was not his to exercise. In this instance Hirohito took a firm stand. He did not act as a constitutional monarch and wait for the government to react, a course of action that would have been irresponsible under the circumstances. But he did not act as an "oriental despot," either, by simply issuing a mandate, retiring, and expecting it to be carried out. Despite his position, the emperor did not act independently. He and those around him ordered, argued, prodded, and persuaded. They built a consensus. In the end Prince Chichibu, known to be sympathetic to the rebels, urged them to surrender and the Control factions of the army and navy moved to oppose them with force.

The efficacy of Hirohito's intervention, as Sheldon and Large point out, "lay in its timing, when no decision had been worked out yet by military and government authorities." But to assume that he did this "in order to defend constitutional government"—and that "as in the aftermath of Tanaka's dismissal, he remained highly conscious of the constitutional limits of his powers"—is somewhat of a distortion.[19] It overemphasizes the limits of the emperor's authority at the expense of his persuasive powers. As Ernst Lokowandt has noted, according to the Meiji Constitution "the Tennō was the absolute ruler, and the government and leaders of the military reported accordingly to him on a regular basis. Even if the emperor did not want to make use of his constitutional possibilities, the way was always open to discreetly make his wishes known when he received reports."[20] Of course, the report of a rebellion by elite units of the army was a unique threat to the government and Hirohito's position. The emperor's reaction was, appropriately, not at all discreet. Despite the extreme character of this incident, however, it is a good example of how decisions were made and put into effect in prewar Japan. Precisely this sort of prodding and persuading, to form a consensus, is the essence of what decision making in Japan is all about.[21]

Perhaps Hirohito exceeded his own boundaries as emperor at this time. After taking such a hard line, had he not been successful it would have been difficult not to "take responsibility" and abdicate if the victorious rebels had been so inclined. This illustrates another important point, well summarized by Lokowandt, about constitutional monarchy in prewar Japan:

> One is presented with a confusing picture. On the one hand the Tennō was the divine, legitimate, absolute ruler, the possessor of all governmental powers, and not bound by anything—not even the constitution. On the other hand the constitution was, of course, also binding on the emperor. A third aspect is the fact that the emperor in no way possessed the authority which was granted him by the constitution—limited or not. Insofar as this was true, the constitution was, after all, not binding. The closer it was related to the constitution, the weaker the factual competence of the Tennō became.[22]

Which is to say: the emperor's power and influence were not, practically speaking, clearly established. They depended on the personalities involved in an issue and the importance of the groups they represented. In the end, in February 1936, as with many other important issues in prewar Japanese politics, the emperor had his say. And this time he got his way. Constitutional monarchy was emphasized (after the fact) because the emperor did not want to relinquish this modern form of theoretical legitimacy and protection. No doubt this was one of the great attractions of this ideology for his "liberal" aristocratic supporters also.

Beginning and Ending the War: Parallels

The same type of struggle can be seen in the adroitly orchestrated end to the war when the emperor was carefully presented with a constellation of balanced forces in the government. The issue was different, as were the people involved, but the decision-making mechanism was the same. A decision had to be made. But contrary to what is often asserted, the emperor did not make it alone. His advisers had prepared the way in advance and indicated what the decision should be—for the good of the nation and, more important, the imperial house. On 25 July 1945, for example, Kido informed the undecided emperor that the army's plans for a decisive battle on the main islands were eyewash. Enemy airborne troops could isolate the emperor wherever he went. He could well be captured and the 2,600-year imperial dynasty terminated.[23] This argument, as well as the atomic bombs of August, influenced "his" decision less than a month later. Four years earlier, when the war began, the imperial line was in no immediate danger and Hirohito was not called upon to enunciate a decision. But, in the manner of a traditional Japanese leader, he did participate in the policymaking process—exerting influence behind the scenes before decisions were made on, among other things, the military policies that led up to and included the decision to attack Pearl Harbor. At the same time he adhered to the principles of modern constitutional monarchy by sanctioning these decisions publicly when they were presented to him officially.

Hirohito and the Military

The emperor was presented with such a mountain of reports to sign that he could not review, critique, or remember them all. Nevertheless it seems safe to say he paid special attention to the annual operations plans presented to him by the army and navy. From well before the time Hirohito became emperor, the Imperial Army (1906) and Imperial Navy (1914) began drafting annual operations plans and presenting them to the emperor for approval. In certain periods, particularly during the Taishō emperor's reign, receiving imperial sanctions for these plans was purely a formal exercise. In the latter half of the 1930s, however, Hirohito used this process on a number of occasions to influence the plans—as documented in Imperial Army and Navy records from that time. These records also show the disagreements between the army and navy in minute detail. Not only were there disputes over the allocation of funds and raw materials, but leading generals and admirals were sharply divided on strategic issues as well. The emperor was well informed about these quarrels. He also knew that basic policy decisions were being delayed because there was no consensus. He did not take advantage of such stalemates and consistently intervene to prevent war. But he did consistently protect the interests of the imperial house and assert the emperor's right to be heard behind the scenes on these matters. Later, he was equally consistent in referring to his position as constitutional monarch to justify his public inaction and safeguard the position of his house. Finally, what he said and did in the late 1930s shows that Hirohito too was undecided about the proper course to take. This indecision is demonstrated by the contradictory policies he supported for over three years prior to the start of the Pacific War.

At the beginning of 1938, as we have seen, the annual operations plan could not be completed because of a dispute between the army and navy over the advisability of war with a third country before the war in China was won. Yet the emperor did not intervene. True, neither party had asked the emperor for a decision. But no one had asked him for his opinion on numerous other occasions when he freely voiced his mind and lobbied for specific measures. As emperor he did not have to wait to be asked. In 1939 he blocked temporarily the alliance with Nazi Germany; he required military planners to change plans that would have violated the neutrality of Thailand; he greatly influenced the selection of two prime ministers, Abe and Yonai. These moves improved the position of those opposed to an alliance with Germany and against war. But this was not the whole story. Hirohito usually acted very differently when dealing with military as opposed to political matters.

In the context of prewar consensus policymaking the emperor was not without influence, but he seems to have been concerned about something other than peace and constitutionalism. The gist of the oral reports presented to the throne by navy leaders in 1938 and 1939 show they would have welcomed some moderating influence from the emperor. This, however, was not readily forthcoming. The dispute between army and navy leaders over basic military strategy was the very type of impasse that the postwar Hirohito insisted had not existed before the war: a pat situation that would have allowed him to intervene on the side of peace. He allegedly blocked the alliance with Germany due to disunity in the government. Disunity in the high command, however, did not stimulate the emperor to act where it counted most—in military as opposed to political matters.

There seems to have been a significant discrepancy between Hirohito's perceptions of military and political policy-making at this time. The emperor vigorously opposed his foreign minister's plan (strongly supported by the army) for an alliance with Germany. But in 1938, when confronted with the possibility of war with England, America, and the Soviet Union, in addition to China, a dismaying prospect for any peace-loving man, he did nothing. Moreover, it is well to note that in 1938 the heart of the dispute between the army and navy—the navy's reluctance to fight a war with the United States versus the army's eagerness to do just that—was the same as the policy differences that precipitated the crisis between Prime Minister Konoe and Army Minister Tōjō in 1941. At that time the army for reasons of pride and prejudice insisted on pursuing a war against the United States. The navy, after looking at estimates of the economic and material aspects of prosecuting a modern war, was again less enthusiastic. On both occasions, in 1938 and 1941, the emperor acted not at all or indecisively. The reasons for this equivocation are difficult to ascertain, but the constitutional monarchy argument alone seems weak. After losing the war, of course, the emperor was against it. Before the fact he appears to have been undecided.

Following the debate and indecision in 1938–1939 the navy's operations became more ambitious with respect to fighting a war with the United States. Hirohito may have welcomed the increasing decisiveness. By 1941 he may have been mentally prepared to go to war after so many years of being readied for it by the general staffs. The oil embargo gave those favoring war a compelling argument. These developments, however, only brought out the ambivalent nature of the war issue. Hirohito appears to have been stimulated by the prospects of a greater, stronger empire—and, simultaneously, hesitant out of fear of losing a war. No doubt there also were thoughts about the possibility of a military putsch if the plans were not approved. A putsch would not only have endangered constitutional monarchy; it could also have had grave consequences for Hirohito and the imperial house. As he himself said, no doubt a regent or emperor more amenable to the desires of the army would have been selected. Then in the event of defeat, it would be even more difficult for the imperial house to avoid responsibility for the war, greatly jeopardizing its existence.

Tōjō and Hirohito

Another figure central to these events—the beginning of the Pacific War, its prosecution, and the survival of the emperor and his house—was Tōjō Hideki. Tōjō is not one of the more popular figures in Japanese history, modern or otherwise. He is known as an uncompromising Imperial Army general and the prime minister who led Japan for the greater part of the Pacific War. Many writers, particularly supporters of Hirohito, lament the demise of advisers like Saionji and all but ignore the relationship between Tōjō and the emperor.[24] Tōjō deserves a better press.

Despite the conquering exploits of Jimmu, the first emperor of Japanese mythology, throughout history emperors have not enjoyed much loyalty from their military underlings. Tōjō was acutely aware of this situation and strove in his own way to be otherwise. This is not to say

Tōjō had more conviction than his fellow officers. In the 1930s in Japan there was no lack of conviction, especially among young army officers. Tōjō, however, appears not only to have believed deeply in the Japanese national polity; he also had sufficient humility to honor Emperor Hirohito's representation of the *kokutai* above his own interpretation of it. This does not mean he unquestioningly carried out orders from the emperor, however strange that may sound. He too was aware of the pluralistic nature of Japanese leadership—and, equally important, the "traditional position," beginning in the Meiji era, of the emperor in that body politic.

Emperors did not give orders; they guided the consensus-forming process. Therefore, although he had previously opposed it in the Konoe cabinet, Tōjō carried out the review mandated by the emperor when he was appointed prime minister: the review of the course set for war. When the group that conducted the review reached a conclusion he knew might be contrary to the emperor's feelings, he presented that conclusion in all sincerity to him. The outcome of this review made war in the Pacific, barring unexpected concessions from the United States, unavoidable from the Japanese point of view. No doubt Hirohito was moved to accept this conclusion not just by the threat to his position from army radicals, among whom Tōjō did not count himself, but also because of Tōjō's formal correctness and sincerity. Tōjō kept the emperor apprised of the proceedings. Not only did he send his cabinet ministers to him, but he reported to Hirohito himself as prime minister and army minister. The emperor was given ample opportunity to influence those making the review, therefore, and could not have been surprised by its outcome. This was constitutional monarchy, Japanese style, in action. The emperor was part of the process, not the victim of a plot, and was not presented with a fait accompli.

There are sufficient grounds for concluding that events at the end of October and beginning of November 1941 occurred in this way, for these reasons, and that the emperor was a party to the decision for war. The review itself has been described in detail by contemporary observers, corroborating the fact that Tōjō sent his ministers repeatedly to report to the emperor. Chief of the General Affairs Section of the Prime Minister's Office Inada Shūichi, Tōjō's private secretary Akamatsu Sadao, and Lord Keeper of the Privy Seal Kido Kōichi, Hirohito's political adviser, all attest to this. Moreover, the content of the review was known to Hirohito then and is known to us now. For everyone involved, including the emperor, peace was not the primary topic of concern. The entire reexamination revolved around the question of whether the war could be won and under what conditions it would be prosecuted. Without thinking through the implications of his statement, Hirohito said in 1946 that the focal point of the discussions was oil.[25] Unwittingly the emperor repeated the the arguments used by the military and right-wing leaders before and just after the beginning of the Pacific War. A lack of oil was the issue that led navy leaders to oppose war; acquiring oil and other strategic materials was the reason the army and others favored war; and the oil embargo was cited to shift the blame for starting the war away from Japan onto the United States.

The emperor's trust in Tōjō's handling of this and other affairs is confirmed by his support of him during the war and his statements about him immediately after. Had he not been convinced of his former prime minister's correctness and sincerity, he certainly would have blamed him for the calamity that overtook the emperor and the nation in the course of the war. He was extremely critical of a number of former government leaders. His foreign minister in the late 1930s, Matsuoka Yōsuke (1880–1946), was in particular an object of imperial wrath because he lobbied so strongly for the alliance with Germany. The alliance with Germany was anathema to Hirohito,[26] but he never discussed his own missed opportunities vis-á-vis military planning at the same time. Indeed, he never admitted his role in it. Perhaps this circumstance was one reason for his strong criticism of Matsuoka and those who acted with him. Hirohito sought to deflect attention from his mistakes in the late 1930s using Matsuoka, just as he charged the imperial army with laying a smoke screen by referring to the United States and Great Britain as the real enemies when things went bad in China.

Tōjō and Kido were among the few who were spared the emperor's criticism. Hirohito had known Kido from childhood. Tōjō was known for his unusual loyalty. Tōjō's convictions are demonstated by the inordinate number of visits he made to Shinto shrines during his term of office, his own statements in private to his secretaries, and his conduct after the war when on trial for his life. Most interesting in this respect is his veneration of the medieval samurai Kusunoki Masashige.

In the summer of 1944 when Tōjō made his remarks about the significance of Kusunoki and his self-sacrifice for Emperor Godaigo in the fourteenth century, he may have sensed what lay in store for him. Practically speaking the war was lost. He was in a position to know this, and he may have been seeking emotional support for the coming hardships. Even if that was the case, Tōjō held onto his professed convictions and carried out with extraordinary tenacity his self-appointed mission of protecting the Shōwa emperor. Kusunoki, as an ideal supporter of the imperial house, was central to this resolve.

The affiliation between Prime Minister Tōjō Hideki and the Shōwa emperor was based on their common convictions. That which bred the former's loyalty infused the latter's priorities. Insofar as a man can be absolutely consistent throughout his life, especially one so long as Hirohito's, the emperor was consistent in only one respect: he constantly protected the interests of the Japanese imperial house. That was what he was taught to do, advised to do, forced to do by reason of birth. As a result he valued men like Tōjō. And one can see from his appreciation of Tōjō, as well as a number of the emperor's prewar positions, that his ways and means of achieving his goals were not always compatible with one another. While advocating peace, he declared war; while praising British constitutional monarchy, he carried out his obligations as the traditional leader of the Japanese polity. He was commander in chief of the nation's armed forces and the high priest of the national religion, but he wanted to be a scientist. In Imperial Japan prior to the advent of the Pacific War, two of the emperor's acts have attracted attention and stimulated acclaim and censure: his forthright stand in February 1936 and his unwillingness to reverse the decision to go to war in the fall of 1941. Hirohito, Tōjō, and the emperor's supporters subsequently maintained with respect to these two very different events and his seemingly contradictory actions that the Shōwa emperor was in reality doing the same thing: upholding constitutional monarchy. This he did and more.

These events were not isolated islands of activity or inactivity on the part of the emperor. Before, after, and in between he assiduously participated in military and political decision making behind the scenes with the other elites involved in formulating government policy. In so doing there was one overriding consideration common to his activities, a concern that also marks these two eye-catching events: at all times the Shōwa emperor worked resolutely for the sake of preserving the imperial house. Tōjō Hideki was an integral part of this effort.

The Emperor and the National Polity

Hirohito's personal convictions and his participation in prewar military decisions are intimately related with classical Japanese tradition, history, the memory of past emperors, and what future memories there might be—meaning the fate of the imperial line. Questions about his role in arriving at these decisions, his war responsibility, are an enigma that tantalizes historians, jurists, and moralists alike. Indeed, many answers from various quarters have been offered. One of the few things consistent about these hypotheses, is that virtually all of them ignore the role of Japanese tradition in the emperor's thinking. This is a glaring oversight. We have seen the emphasis on the imperial line in Hirohito's education and the importance of the imperial tradition for the national polity and men like Tōjō Hideki: the emperor's very reason for existence in prewar Japan was the inviolability of the imperial line, an axiom grounded in Japanese history, religion, and morality.

The position of the emperor of Japan was stipulated in the Meiji Constitution, and Hirohito made much about being a constitutional monarch after the English model. But the imperial house owed its existence to Japanese tradition and history, not to a Prussian-style constitution or the English-style ideals of the reigning emperor. It was the Japanese imperial-line tradition that attracted Tōjō's idealism and loyalty, not some foreign ideology. And while the emperor may have acted like a Western constitutional monarch as he consulted, encouraged, and warned his ministers behind the scenes, he did this in the unique context of Imperial Japan. The events immediately before and after Tōjō's appointment to head a new government illustrate this.

Based on his traditional position as "Tennō," Hirohito appointed a leading army officer prime minister. The reason for his selection was that he was supposed to be able to control the army, much as a shogun was appointed due to his ability to exercise authority over the contending warlords of his day. At the time of the appointment, the emperor ordered his new prime minister to review a decision that had been ratified by an extraconstitutional body, an imperial conference, which supposedly was irrevocable. Then he accepted unofficial reports about the progress of this review, commented upon them, and sanctioned again, however reluctantly, the same decision to go to war. He did this, not in regular official conferences as the constitutional head of state, but as a godlike individuum in the inner sanctum of the imperial palace where Tōjō, and his cabinet colleagues, were no doubt impressed by the aura of the emperor of Japan.

The Postwar Emperor as Symbol of State

Looking beyond this time frame, at the end of the war the emperor acted decisively for the same reasons. He brought an end to the war because

> should We continue to fight, it would not only result in an ultimate collapse and disappearance of the Japanese nation, but it would also lead to the total destruction of civilization. Such being the case, how are We to save

the millions of Our subjects; or to atone Ourselves before the hallowed spirits of Our Imperial Ancestors?[27]

Hirohito's priorities are clear. In ascending order of importance he acted to save "human civilization" and the Japanese folk, to be sure, but above all to protect the legacy of his imperial ancestors by preventing the destruction of the imperial house. Since the Sun Goddess was responsible for the well-being of the people (according to, among others, Hirohito's history teacher Shiratori), Hirohito as the head of the imperial line was responsible for them too. Both the people and the emperor were part of the national polity. One could not exist without the other. This did not, however, negate the hierarchical relation between them or nullify the greater importance of the emperor's survival compared to the others who were part of this polity. Thus Hirohito was concerned about the continued existence of the Japanese people as a whole, and especially the imperial line, when he accepted the Allies' surrender ultimatum. Later, the same priorities would color the way in which the imperial institution was adapted to American-sponsored democracy after the war.

Democracy and business became the coin of the day in postwar Japan. But it would be wrong to assume that "the new [postwar] constitution created what the Japanese have called the 'symbol emperor' *(shōchō tennō)*, or 'symbol emperor system,' . . . meaning an emperor deprived of all political authority and removed from government."[28] This clearly is what the American victors planned for the imperial institution and put into effect after the war.[29] The Japanese, however, had their own tradition which on the surface appears very similar but in fact stems from very different sources than those of the Allied Nations. Prominent prewar scholars and postwar dignitaries were well aware of this, though today it is often overlooked in Japan and abroad.[30]

At most the new constitution revived an old tradition that had been forgotten by nearly everyone. The "symbol emperor" had been created much earlier. It is the essence of what the emperor system has been since early in Japanese history. Kitabatake Chikafusa codified this tradition in the middle ages. The source of this ideology is his essay, the *Jinnō Shōtōki*, which may be translated into English as "The Chronicle of the Direct Descent of Sovereigns." It was written at a time, the Northern and Southern Courts period, when an opposing faction at court led by Nijō Yoshimoto (1320–1388) supported the new shogun Ashikaga Takauji's claim that the emperor should be chosen for his personal virtue regardless of his line of descent.[31] (This is the same Ashikaga who defeated Kusunoki Masashige and thwarted Emperor

Godaigo's restoration.) Kitabatake and his supporters succeeded in blocking the Ashikaga claim by emphasizing that the emperor was a symbol of the unique Japanese folk. The symbol was the imperial line, not the emperor personally. Its continuity was made an object of veneration.

Many centuries later, in 1945, for the same reason—the survival of the imperial line—Emperor Hirohito discarded his army uniform and appeared ever after in "salaryman" suits. Costumes changed, the commander in chief became a father figure, but ultimately he was still doing the same thing: whatever was necessary to preserve the "line of emperors unbroken for ages eternal." Notwithstanding these efforts, the question of Hirohito's war responsibility has not been resolved.

Pearl Harbor and the Decision for War

In addressing the question of the emperor's war responsibility, one must distinguish between legalistic assumptions in the postwar West and the emperor's responsibilities in prewar Japan. The question asked so frequently after the Pacific War—whether Emperor Hirohito was for or against it—often disregards the prewar context. Before the conflict, war was one aspect, albeit an important one, of policymaking and the struggle for power in Japan. Emperor Hirohito as head of the imperial family had a right to participate in these affairs. But this right, as he himself was fond of pointing out, was not that of a dictator. At the same time it was not the right of a Western monarch, constitutional or otherwise.

Arguments both for and against the emperor's constitutional powers can be made. But this line of discussion is confusing because many forget that Hirohito's stand for constitutional monarchy complemented —"modernized"—rather than contradicted his role as the head of the imperial house and emperor of Japan. Many tend to forget, as well, that the emperor's actual influence, and the restraints placed on his power, were defined in Japan, not in Western Europe. This was even more true of the obligations that accrued to the "office." As can be seen in Japanese history in general, the moral education of Hirohito in particular, and the advice of Makino and his other advisers, the emperor's primary responsibility was neither political nor military: it was the preservation and advancement of the imperial house itself.

Hirohito's postwar supporters and critics alike have assumed the perspective dictated by the atmosphere surrounding the war crimes trials. They focus on whether Hirohito was a militarist or a constitutionalist: was he personally accountable for the war?[32] But peace and Western constitutionalism were not the main concerns of the emperor in Imperial Japan. They were important as ends in themselves, perhaps, but more important as a means to a greater end—the preservation of the imperial house.

Constitutional government was not the ultimate end for Chiang Kai-shek, Roosevelt, Churchill, or any of Hirohito's contemporaries. It has not been the ultimate goal of any statesman in history, East or West. Achieving power and keeping it is the principal goal of a statesman. Hirohito had to work within the confines of a Japanese tradition that limited *and* protected his powers, and he had the overriding obligation to preserve his house at all costs. One might argue, of course, that the royal houses of other nations are no less concerned with their own preservation. But one only need look at the fate of Wilhelm II and his house in Germany after World War I, or Pu-yi and his house after the revolution of 1911 in China, to see that uncritical comparisons are deceiving. The contours of the imperial house's role in Japanese history, religion, ethics, and politics are different from those of other royal houses. Though less involved in the overt wielding of political power, it pervaded various aspects of society and culture more deeply. In Japan the head of the imperial house had a more subtle, but no less important, influence on political and military decisions. This must be taken into account.

Taking into account the influence of the imperial house on decision making in prewar Japan means examining what the emperor stood for and what he did. During the crucial time immediately before the outbreak of war, he stood for the imperial line—and that meant asserting his right to participate in the decision-making process. Army and navy records clearly indicate this, as can be seen in the events leading up to the decision to go to war. In particular, consonant with his role as the emperor of Japan, Hirohito was told well in advance exactly how the attack on Pearl Harbor was to be carried out. This was done in a private audience on 3 November 1941. If Hirohito had any objections—as he had expressed unmistakably in similar private audiences previously—they were either not voiced or were made but not recorded later by the two military leaders present.

Prior to this audience the emperor ordered a review of the decision made in the 6 September imperial conference. Once again war was decided upon by Imperial Japan's pluralistic leadership. The disclaimers by Prime Minister Tōjō and the emperor about this decision not being the latter's will are well known. One Japanese authority has written: "The words of the emperor were not the words of the emperor." Stephen Large, expanding on these sentiments, says of the imperial conference of 1 December 1941 sanctioning war: "Tōjō and everyone else present that day knew perfectly well that the imperial will for war was not the Emperor's personal will and that the government, not the Emperor, had decided upon war."[33] Both scholars adopt an idealized view of constitutional monarchy and overlook the emperor's long-standing participation, along with other leaders, in forming military and political policy behind the scenes before formal ratification. The emperor was not the government. But despite postwar protestations to the contrary, the emperor was a participating member of the government. If he was so adamantly opposed to the war, why did he not speak out one month earlier in audience with his military leaders, as he had done many times before? Hirohito was an integral part of the leadership that led Japan into war. Like any member of a collective group of leaders, he was not always able to prevail. But this does not mean he was not a party to the decisions, and responsible for them.

Could Hirohito Have Vetoed the Decision?

Because the emperor did not wish to risk destruction of the social and political order he headed, the question of vetoing the war never arose. Large's reading of Hirohito's postwar statement—"In retrospect, he said, 'I probably would have tried to "veto" the decision for war, if at the time I had foreseen the future' "—is incorrect.[34] Hirohito did not say this at all. Large has left out part of the sentence and changed the meaning. The text says: "Because Japan's future prospects were such at the time of the opening of the war, if I had 'vetoed' the decision to open the war, within the country there surely would have been a great rebellion."[35] The phrase beginning "such . . ." *(kaki no gotoki ari-sama)* is deleted by Large. It refers to the military and industrial collapse and resulting coup d'état that would have ensued, according to Hirohito, due to the oil embargo and consequent economic ruin. In other words: after reviewing the options, the emperor adopted the military's point of view—a choice between war or economic ruin. Other alternatives, such as international negotiations that would have entailed compromises and concessions, were rejected. Internally an agreement with the army had already been reached.

In introducing the dark consequences for the nation that seemed to make war inevitible, Hirohito also said: "In retrospect, my first thinking was correct." This meant his decision not to intervene and oppose the war was correct. Blocking the decision would have resulted in considerable domestic turmoil, not to mention danger to the imperial house. What he did not say, however, was that an important reason for this turmoil and danger was the fact that "vetoing" the war would have involved reversing himself, since a consensus concerning the military's proposals had previously been achieved in a private audience. This fact militates against the often repeated defense that the emperor, according to his principle of constitutional monarchy, could not intervene. Likewise, the assumption that Hirohito acted as he did due to the tension between constitutional monarchy and authoritarian rule inherent in the Meiji Constitution does not explain his actions. Hirohito did not refrain from acting. Nor was he torn between roles. The emperor participated behind the "chrysanthemum curtain" in the prewar pluralistic, consensus-oriented decision-making process and then sanctioned the result in public. Vetoing a decision after it had been made would not only have violated the mutual trust necessary to forming a consensus, it would have destroyed the decision-making process itself. And this, quite possibly, would have brought on the chaos Hirohito feared. Being held responsible for the disintegration of the national polity was, to be sure, a more odious prospect than being responsible for a war.

This does not mean simply that the emperor was responsible for the war. He was responsible for preserving the national polity, insisted on participating in the decision-making process, and in so doing shared in responsibility for the Pacific War. Hirohito was responsible for the *kokutai* and its center, the imperial line. In the prewar era, a Japanese national polity without the imperial line was unthinkable. The emperor was obliged to ensure that he, his house, and the tradition they represented survived come what may. If as a consequence a war ensued, that was extremely unfortunate but unavoidable. Constitutional monarchy and Hirohito's participation in prewar military planning must be evaluated in this context. Hirohito was not interested in constitutional monarchy or the military as such. The imperial line was not to be an instrument of military policy. Nor was it thought of as a vehicle for introducing an enlightened system of rule into Japan. Rather, constitutional monarchy, science, industry, and the military were the horses that were to draw the imperial institution into the modern age. When considering Hirohito's prewar priorities one can in his case put the cart, that is, the imperial carriage, before the horses.

Appendixes

Appendix · I

Division of Duties Between Military Ministries
and General Staffs in Imperial Japan
(June 1913 Revision)

| Duties | Division of Duties[a] | | | | |
	1	2	3	4	5
Peacetime organization					
Military services, military schools, government officials[b]	C	M	M+C	—	—
Administrative officials, schools[c]	M	C	C+M	—	M
Service schools[d]	I	M+C	M+I	—	—
General wartime organization	C	M	C	—	M
Revision of organizational regulations for arms, ordnance, etc.	M	C	M	—	M
Wartime organization: general	C	M	C	—	M
Wartime organization: accounting, medical corps, supply	M	C	M	—	M
War planning and directives	C	M	C	C	—
Mobilization: planning orders and executive directives	C	M	C	—	M
Annual mobilization: planning orders and executive directives	C	M	C	—	M
Mobilization and demobilization orders	C	M	C	—	M
Missions and operations of mobilized units	C	M	C	C	—
Overseas deployment: units, missions, operations	C	M	C	C	—

a. 1 = planning; 2 = reporting; 3 = recipient of imperial sanction; 4 = execution; 5 = administration; C = army/navy chiefs of staff; M = army/navy cabinet ministers; I = inspector general for military education.

b. Schools under the chiefs of staff: the military academies; officials under same: Land Survey Office.

c. Schools under army/navy ministries: those not under chiefs of staff or inspector general.

d. Schools under inspector general: special service schools, supplementary training for field-grade officers.

Source: Fujiwara Akira, *Tennōsei to guntai* (The emperor system and the military) (Tokyo: Aoki Shoten, 1978), pp. 117–118. (Revisions effective until the end of the war.)

Appendix · 2

Japanese, American, and British Naval and Air Forces in the Far East in 1938

Forces	Japan	United States	England
Ships			
Battleships	6	15	0
High-speed battleships	4	0	—
Aircraft carriers	5	6	1
Heavy cruisers	14	18	4
Light cruisers	21	18	2
Modern destroyers	73	61	12
Dated destroyers	41	175	—
Modern submarines	39	23	15
Dated submarines	14	69	—
Totals (excluding dated vessels)	162	141	34
Aircraft			
Fighters	226	106	12
Attack planes	176	72	—
Bombers	177	108	0
Torpedo planes	—	—	54
Recon.	0	198	12
Water recon.	351	182	—
Flying boats	40	213	12
Land attack	132	200	—
Fighter recon.	—	—	8
Totals	1,102	973	98

Sources: This summary is based on two separate sources: *Nichibei heiryoku hikaku (Shōwa jū-san nendo sue)* (Comparison of Japanese and American military forces [end of 1938]) in Bōeichō Bōeikenkūjo Senshibu (NIDS), ed., *Kaigun nendo sakusen keikaku* (Navy annual operations plans) (Tokyo: Asagumo Shimbunsha, 1986), pp. 156–157; and a table accompanying the same volume, *Eikoku Kyokutō sakusen yōsō heiryoku* (Estimated military forces for England's Far Eastern operations). The two estimates appear to have been made independently; a dash indicates that this item does not appear in the estimate. Both estimates for the United States and England are of "peacetime" forces. The estimate of US forces is dated January 1939. Some of the estimates—for example, the number of US battleships in the Far East—are mistaken.

Appendix · 3

Tōjō and Nakano: Two Sources Compared

At the meeting about Nakano, Tōjō, Interior Minister Andō Kisaburō, Minister of Justice Iwamura Michiyo, Attorney General Matsuzaka Hiromasa, a police director and a police inspector, the head of the legal department, a leading police detective and the head of the Tokyo Kempeitai, Colonel Shikata, and several others all gathered in answer to a call from the chief cabinet secretary. (Ōtani says they came at Tōjō's behest to discuss what to do about Nakano.)[1]

Tōjō maintained that something should be done about the Nakano faction because of the coming special session of parliament. The interior minister said an investigation had been going on for two months, but there was not enough condemning evidence for administrative detention. However, he did not see the individuals involved, Nakano and his assistant Mitamura, as an important problem. The issue of interfering with the war effort was of much greater concern. In this respect he completely agreed with Tōjō and had no compunction about detaining Nakano. The minister of justice was of the same opinion. (Ōtani, who is consistently critical of Tōjō, does not mention this support for the prime minister. He has him acting alone in an autocratic manner.) But Attorney General Matsuzaka objected. He said detaining a representative during a session of the Diet was contrary to the spirit of the constitution. So far the police investigation was not sufficient for an indictment of a member of the Diet. Then a heated argument ensued between the interior minister and Attorney General Matsuzaka. (Ōtani says the discussion was between Tōjō and Matsuzaka.) Nevertheless Tōjō wanted to prevent Nakano from participating in the coming parliamentary session. The state minister and leading politician in the Imperial Rule Assistance Association (Yokusan Seijikai), Ōasa Tadao, agreed with the attorney general that legally an arrest of Nakano was on shaky grounds. But his main reason for opposing the move was that it could well turn the Diet against the Tōjō cabinet. So far most Diet members had not supported Nakano, but this might cause them to sympathize with him, if only out of fear of the same thing happening to them. Prime Minister Tōjō was insistent, but he did say it should be done according to the law.

According to the Tōjō Agenda, the meeting ended without reaching a conclusion at 11:30 P.M. On the following day Tōjō met with Ōasa and Hoshino again to discuss the affair. A separate note *(besshi)* says the Kempeitai prepared materials till noon, and Nakano was brought to admit his transgressions ("Nakano Seigō wo jinin su"). Nakano promised not to go to the parliament. The Kempeitai gave the police authorities the materials they had prepared at about six in the evening. Mitamura was released; Nakano faced detention for investigation. The paperwork and other formalities for this process lasted until 1 A.M. on the morning of 26 October. Later the same morning, 5 A.M., Colonel Shikata and several police officials came to Tōjō. State Minister Ōasa, the interior minister, and the others were called in, and by 8 A.M. they decided to release Nakano as well as Mitamura. Later the same day, at 7 P.M., Nakano's suicide is noted.

Ōtani says that in the two days following the first meeting Tōjō intervened again in the investigation. On the afternoon of 25 October he told State Minister Ōasa, Cabinet Secretary Hoshino, Director Saka from police headquarters, and Colonel Shikata that he would resign if no indictment of Nakano was forthcoming. According to Colonel Ōtani, Tōjō only said this to raise the pressure on the officials conducting the investigation. It had the desired effect.

Appendix · 4

Sugiura on the Imperial Regalia

If one looks at this in terms of the literary and military arts *(bunbu)*, the mirror is the literary and the sword the military.[1] Having thought this far, it should be increasingly clear that the imperial regalia are the endowment in solid form of the three virtues of wisdom, benevolence, and courage handed down for our edification. Looking at them in China, it is written in the Doctrine of the Mean *(Chung Yung):* "Wisdom, benevolence, and courage, these three things are universally regarded as mature virtue."[2] There is the way of the five cardinal Confucian relationships, but without the three virtues these cannot be completely realized. In other words, the cardinal relations between ruler and minister, father and son, husband and wife, elder and younger brother, and friends are first to be realized through the three virtues of wisdom, benevolence, and courage. The scholars of China already understood this: wisdom is to know the way; benevolence is to embody this way; courage is to follow the way.

Also, one sees these virtues in the theories of the Western World: the three virtues of wisdom, sincerity, and will *(chi, sei, i)* are customarily said to explain the operation of human nature. Wisdom is to apprehend things. Sincerity is unaffected human nature—sorrow, happiness, love, hate, all are included. When pure these natural feelings become benevolence. Will is the desire through which things are carried out. Even in the face of difficulty one does not give in or slacken his efforts. Decisive action is exalted. This is courage. The person with fully mature wisdom, sincerity, and will, this is a complete person. Put in another way, the person with a superior character has mature wisdom, sincerity, and will.

As related above, this tenet was formulated in China and the West similarly. In short, the very cultivation of the three virtues of wisdom, benevolence, and courage is an end in itself. Others explain this theoretically; in our case the difference is simply that the great ancestral goddess indicated her meaning using real objects.

Considering the emperors in our past history, although of course there were many illustrious ones, it is as if Emperor Tenji [626–671, r. 662–671] represented wisdom, Emperor Nintoku [r. 313–399] benevolence, and Emperor Jimmu [r. 660–585 B.C.] courage.

Emperor Tenji perceived the necessity of a complete change in the nation's politics. Consulting with Nakatomi no Kamatari [614–669],[3] the merits of the Chinese system were skillfully taken, harmonized with our national customs, and a prefectural organization was established. Besides this, the various systems were all given in an opportune manner a suitable institutional form. This truly is to be admired as exemplary of wisdom.

Emperor Nintoku was of deep compassionate benevolence. The august phrase that he uttered, "the people's prosperity is none other than Our prosperity,"[4] demonstrates this and must be said to be exceptional.

Again, considering the exploits of Emperor Jimmu, he first decided on the plan for the eastern expedition after the three generations accustomed themselves to living on earth. They departed from Kyūshū. The bold advance into the middle provinces [along the Inland Sea] was an extremely resolute action. Thereby many hardships were experienced; Nagasunehiko [in Yamato] and other violent rebels were subdued.[5] One must say the establishment of the Great Empire of Japan (Dai Nippon Teikoku) was a superior military exploit, a great achievement. The root of this achievement certainly was courage. In deciding the posthumous names of emperors in later times, the logic behind the two characters "Jimmu" [divine courage] served as a precedent.

Even though the emperors of the three reigns described here were historical figures, certainly it is as if they represent wisdom, benevolence, and courage. Of course, it was not a case of courage only and no wisdom. Also one cannot speak of having only wisdom and no benevolence. These episodes are related solely for the purpose of illustrating these remarkable things. As with the Emperor Meiji [r. 1868–1912] who died three years ago, the essence of the three virtues was gathered in him, and one assumes he was endowed equally with all three virtues. His imperial majesty demonstrated this.

Appendix · 5

Shiratori on the Worldview of the Japanese and Chinese

The worldview of the Chinese, Shiratori begins, as judged from texts like the *Book of History (Shu Ching)*, *Analects (Lun Yü)*, and *Mencius (Meng Tzu)* is horizontal, not vertical as in Japan.[1] According to Chinese tradition man stands between heaven and earth, and one could assume this is a vertical cosmos. But the spirit of Chinese culture, especially Confucianism, is centered in human existence, which was born from and received its vitality *(seiki)* from heaven and earth. Comparing this cosmology with Western or other Asian lands, including the peoples of Mongolia and Manchuria as well as the Ainu in Japan, reveals the great emphasis placed on present-day existence by the Chinese. This is one of the outstanding and unique characteristics of Chinese culture.

Naturally this context does not admit of a god who stands above human-kind and rules the world. In China's most ancient classic, the *Book of History*, heaven is described in various ways, but never personified as a god. There are gods, spirits, and the like but they do not stand above and control human activities. The entities most venerated by the Chinese—Yao, Shun, and Yü—were human beings. They are respected as sages *(seijin)*, and they are not thought of as superhuman gods. In another culture these figures would be revered as gods. Not in China. They remain strictly human beings, and it is important to remember that humans are revered in China in the same manner that gods are venerated in other lands.

This, Shiratori continues, has consequences for morality in China. Virtue is the hallmark of a sage, and anyone can accumulate it. Morality is something that can be learned by emulating the sages. One is not dependent on a god or the power of a god. It is a matter of mutual human relations. This can be seen above all in the Confucian *Analects*, which has no parallel in the world as a treatise on human relationships. This is the great masterpiece of Han civilization and the most important contribution of Confucianism to world culture.

Shiratori praises filial piety, loyalty, trustworthiness, and the five Confucian relations as universal values that all people should bear in mind and that further humankind. He reminds his listeners that it is neither disgraceful nor wrong that the Japanese revere Confucianism, which comes from the Chinese. "Indeed our special quality is that we Japanese take the strong points of others and improve our shortcomings," he says. Today we should maintain this attitude and study Confucianism as well as Western culture.

But, Shiratori complains, when one considers the situation in China today it is clear that this wonderful morality *(dōtoku)* regrettably is not being practiced in the land of its origin. Rites *(li)*—that which makes interpersonal relations elegant—are born from the natural human situation. For this reason they are described in such detail in Confucianism.[2] But *li* entails rites that one should observe because one feels they are right, not out of a sense of duty. The latter impulse is a subversion of the natural human order, and unfortunately this is the case in China now. "Today in China the exquisite spirit of Confucianism does not exist; there are only appearances."

The reason for this deterioration is that in China emphasis is placed on "man" *(ningen)*. The strength of Confucian morality, Shiratori believes, is also its great weakness. The Chinese developed the idea of controlling human conduct through human power *(chikara)* by applying sanctions *(seisai)*. Other peoples look to the power of gods outside human affairs, and the rules for human conduct are legitimized by suprahuman authorities. In China there are no such gods, and all problems are aspects of interpersonal relations. There are rites that prescribe reciprocal relations, and if one subverts these rites one subverts basic human relationships. Therefore one is supposed to preserve the rites set down by the ancient sages. But the human situation differs according to time and place, whereas the rites are constant and unchanging. For this reason rites and natural human relations diverge from one another. Preserving the rites is obstructed by everyday life, and society is upset as formal rites are emphasized superficially.

The conservatism of the Chinese may be explained by the need to preserve the rites of the ancient sages in the face of changing times, Shiratori maintains. Also, over the centuries the people who came to China—Koreans, Manchurians, Turks, Tibetans, various barbarian tribes from the south—were all culturally inferior to the Chinese. The Chinese then came to emphasize the superiority of their culture over all others. Viewing various other countries that had been subjugated, the Chinese feared their national character would be dismissed and ignored if they did not rigidly preserve their own customs. In response to this situation they did not make changes in the morality that came down to them, and this is one reason for the decline in Chinese morals. In short, the original ethical teachings of the Chinese people were very wonderful, but due to unsound basic ideals (the unchanging nature of this morality) they deteriorated. This is the weak point of Confucianism, Shiratori says, and this should not be studied. This does not mean there are not many wonderful aspects of Confucianism worthy of study. Our forefathers adopted these customs in ancient times with good reason.[3]

If one compares our country with China, Shiratori continues, one can see that the Japanese social order is similar in various ways to theirs. We both honor and respect loyalty *(chū)* and filial piety *(kō)*, and we both revere our ancestors. But there are dissimilarities also, especially our respective world-views. The Japanese worldview is not horizontal like that of the Chinese. Since ancient times we have had a three-level vertical worldview: the plain of high heaven *(takamagahara)* above; the land of the dead *(yominoguni)* below; and the present world *(arawashiguni)*. Our ancestors were at least able to conceive of this three-level world. This means (in contrast with China) they acknowledged gods above the human world, and we revere the Sun Goddess Amaterasu Ōmikami within this context. Amaterasu is the heavenly goddess of the plain of high heaven. Her grandson descended to earth and founded our imperial house. "This is the source *(engan)* of our national polity, and this sort of thought is not found in Confucianism." Central to our concept of the majesty of Japan's national polity and the divine nature of the imperial house is the conviction that the imperial line descends from a goddess. Not only is the emperor revered in the existing world as a human being; he is also revered as a god—as the descendant of a heavenly goddess. Therefore the position of emperor is termed "celestial successor" *(amatsuhitsugi)*. (This means the emperor succeeded to his post due to a command from a sun goddess.)[4]

Commentary: The idea explained here is not to be found in Chinese Confucianism, as Shiratori says, but it is not to be seen in the ancient histories of Japan either. The emphasis on divine descent comes from Kitabatake Chikafusa in the fourteenth century, but Shiratori does not mention this. He maintains that in Japan the heavenly gods are the ancestors of mankind *(ningen)* and the imperial house descended directly from the highest of the heavenly gods. This idea is to be found in the Japanese texts he cites but is not emphasized in this way. Nevertheless, as Shiratori maintains, here is a basic difference with Chinese thought—that is, the Chinese emperor was not, supposedly, a direct descendant of the highest god in heaven. Moreover, in the hallowed texts *Kojiki* and *Nihon Shoki* the parts dealing with ancient times appear explicitly as the age of the gods. Thus, according to Shiratori, one can readily see the Japanese people are not satisfied with a worldview that emphasizes mundane existence. They believe in a higher world. The Japanese people have a deep sense of reverence for the gods, and due to this feeling they honor the imperial house as they would a god. "Which is to say," Shiratori concludes, "reverence for the gods and veneration of our ancestors define our national character."

Appendix · 6

Shiratori on the Sacred Jewel

After Ninigi no Mikoto first received the imperial regalia from the Sun Goddess, Shiratori begins, only one, the sacred jewel, was never separated from the imperial house.[1] The sword was enshrined at Atsuta and eventually lost; the mirror was enshrined at Ise. Only the jewel never left side of the emperor. Izanagi decreed to Amaterasu, and she to later gods and the imperial line, that in the manner of guardian deities they should never forget this virtue. Which is to say: imperial possession of the sacred jewel means the emperor (or empress) is to provide for the growth and prosperity of the people in all respects.

Following this, the high point of the lecture, Shiratori continues with his philology of Japanese mythology—noting, for example, that the gods leading up to Jimmu Tennō all had names derived from grains. He concludes with a summary of the meaning of the imperial regalia. The sword he introduces with a brief discussion of its origins. The great dragon with eight heads and eight tails, killed by Susano-wo, the Sun Goddess' stormy and unpredictable brother, was a god of the mountains. Slaying the dragon and finding the sword in the tail symbolizes digging in the mountain, finding metal, and making a sword from it. The sword represents the virtue of a retainer (shinka). In tumultuous times it is used to subdue evildoers. The jewel represents the emperor's virtue—it symbolizes complete benevolence (enman jinji). The world is ruled through the cooperation of these two entities. The sacred mirror is a manifestation of the Japanese imperial ancestors (tensō, which can also mean the Sun Goddess Amaterasu). Its august nature is self-evident. Which is to say: the imperial regalia have significance for the spirit inherent in the founding of Japan and for the national polity.

Appendix · 7

Sugiura on Crown Prince Nakanoōe

The following is an excerpt from Sugiura's lecture to Crown Prince Hirohito on Crown Prince Nakanoōe. It depicts how an exemplary leader should conduct himself.[1]

When Emperor Jomei (r. 629–641) died the Crown Prince was sixteen years old. The reign of Empress Kōgyoku followed (r. 642–645). (The two were Nakanoōe's father and mother, respectively.) At about the age of twenty he came to know Nakatomi no Kamatari. At that time the father and son, Soga no Emishi and Iruka (both d. 645), became extremely arbitrary. Emishi had his own ancestral mausoleum built at Katsuragi (old classical form = Kazuraki) Takamiya, and he ordered the people around as he pleased. Moreover, he stipulated that tombs for himself and Iruka were to be built at this place, and the former was to be called the Great Imperial Mausoleum (Misasagi, old classical form = Misazaki) and the latter the Lesser Imperial Mausoleum. At that time Prince Shōtoku's daughter Oyoirahime no Miko said indignantly, "Minister Soga arbitrarily manipulates national policy and commits many improprieties. It is said, there are not two suns in heaven, nor are there two rulers in a country." She harbored this resentment, and it came about that misfortune befell the family of [the late] Crown Prince Shōtoku. Which is to say: Iruka dispatched soldiers who attacked Prince Yamashironoōe (Shōtoku's son) at the Ikaruka (or Ikaruga) Palace. Later the entire family was wiped out (in 643). In this way the Soga clan's self-indulgence knew no bounds. The father and son built mansions at Amakashi no Oka. Emishi's house was called the "Palace Gate" (Uetsu Mikado) and Iruka's the "Royal Gate in the Valley" (Hazana no Mikado). They called their children prince [and princess].

Due to the actions of the Sogas the relation between sovereign and subject (*taigi meibun*) was subverted. Both the country and the imperial house were endangered. Observing this situation, Nakatomi no Kamatari was the first to recognize that a great reform was necessary.

Kamatari was also known as Kamako. He was a descendant of [the god] Amenokoyane no Mikoto. Koyane no Mikoto together with Amenotomi no Mikoto assisted

Emperor Jimmu and was of great merit. The lineage was involved in establishing our country. Along the way it was oppressed by various families such as the Katsuragi, Heguri, and Soga, and the position of the family *(kamon)* declined. Coming to the emergence of Kamatari, witnessing the high-handedness of the Soga family he recognized that for the sake of the country it was necessary to eliminate this [oppression] and thereby thoroughly cleanse our politics. To accomplish this, a capable member of the imperial house must be won over who would join in and promote the plan. Kamatari finally attached his hopes to Prince Nakanoōe. But the prince and Kamatari were not closely associated with one another up to this time, and regrettably Kamatari could not reveal and discuss his intentions [openly]. . . .

In a section deleted here, Sugiura deals with how Kamatari contrived to meet Nakanoōe: "By chance the crown prince was in a group that gathered at Hōkōji for 'football.' " Sugiura shows the extreme politeness with which the crown prince dealt with Kamatari from the very beginning. Sugiwara continues:

In the Sixth Month, Fourth Year, of Empress Kōgyoku's reign (645), three Korean kingdoms were to present tribute. The crown prince planned to carry out the great undertaking on this day and made various preparations. Accordingly, Kurayamada Maro was to read the memorials [of the three Korean kingdoms]. Komaro and Amida were to advance directly and cut down Iruka. The crown prince took a long spear and hid it at one side of the [audience] hall. Kamatari would lend support with a bow and arrows.

On the appointed day, Kurayamada Maro actually read the memorial. Just as Komaro and the others were to advance, overcome by fear they could not proceed. "With water they tried to down their rice, but due to their fear it came back up." The crown prince, afraid that if the reading of the memorials ended beforehand a good opportunity would be lost, came out at once, advanced, and brandishing his sword cut open Iruka's head and shoulder. Komaro and Amida subsequently came forward and each of them slashed Iruka. Iruka tumbled forward before the throne, bowed his head, and said,

"Your subject is conscious of no crime. I ask that this be investigated."

The empress was very surprised and addressed the crown prince,

"I do not understand what has been done. What is the meaning of this?"

The crown prince prostrated himself on the ground and said,

"Kuratsukuri [Iruka] plans to destroy the heavenly order and subvert the solar dignity. Is Kuratsukuri to take the place of the descendants of heaven?"

The empress immediately stood up and retired within. Then Komaro, Amida, and the others all slashed Iruka and killed him. Soldiers were sent to attack Emishi; he too was killed, and great damage to the state was avoided. At the time the crown prince was twenty [nineteen by our count].[2]

Commentary: Sugiwara's account follows the *Nihon Shoki* text very closely, including the metaphor describing the fear in Nakanoōe's followers and his taking the initiative in the attack on Iruka. The attack on Emishi is much abbreviated, and Sugiura leaves out a point important to historians: just before he and his family were "executed," they burned the History of the Emperors, the History of the Country, and other objects of value. Only one text was saved. The destruction of these materials by the Sogas is one of the main reasons why so little is known about early Japanese history.

Nakatomi no Kamatari and Crown Prince Nakanoōe came to know each other at the beginning of 644. Soga no Emishi had the two houses "Palace Gate" and "Royal Gate in the Valley" built and took to styling their children princes and princesses in the Eleventh Month of 644. The provocations of the Sogas occurred over a two-year period, and the planning between Kamatari and Nakanoōe took place in the second year. During this time far more space is taken up in the *Nihon Shoki* with diplomatic relations between Japan and the kingdoms in Korea than with these events. (Interestingly, the *Nihon Shoki* has Prince Furubitonoōe blaming Koreans for Iruka's death.)

Finally, both the authors of the *Nihon Shoki* and Sugiura were careful to have Crown Prince Nakanoōe work in concert with the family descendant from one of the gods who aided Emperor Jimmu in his conquest of the east and with the man who established the house of the highest advisers to the throne, the Fujiwara. The prince did not act in an autocratic manner or alone. But when he did act, he acted decisively.

Sugiura goes on to say that the elimination of the Sogas was a prerequisite to making fundamental reforms in the nation's politics. Of course, the wit and intelligence of both Crown Prince Nakanoōe and Nakatomi no Kamatari were indispensable to accomplishing this. The decisive factor, though, according to Sugiura, was the crown prince's courage and determination displayed when, seeing others falter, he personally sprang forward to slash Iruka.

Empress Kōgyoku abdicated, the lecture continues, in the same year when the Sogas were killed, and she promulgated an imperial rescript naming Naka-noōe emperor. In consultation with Kamatari, however, he declined in favor of the empress' younger brother. This was Emperor Kōtoku (r. 645–654). Sugiura cites the prince's need to reflect on possible shortcomings, and in this way he and Kamatari were able to resolutely carry through one of the greatest reforms in Japan's history—the Taika Kaishin. But the *Nihon Shoki* that says Empress Kōgyoku took this action the day after Soga no Emishi was killed. Nakanoōe declined because Prince Furubitonoōe was his older brother. In conformity with Confucian morality, it would have been improper for him to become emperor while his older brother was still alive.[3]

Appendix · 8

Sugiura on George Washington and Ōyama Iwao

Sugiura begins with praise for Ōyama.[1] In this eulogy he notes that Ōyama was known for his "kindness and consideration, unalloyed sense of honor, intellect, and fine sense of responsibility." Washington died 117 years earlier on 14 December 1799. This was the day of the demise of a true gentleman *(gishi-tōnyū)*, though the Western solar calendar, unlike the Japanese lunar calendar, does not note the auspicious or inauspicious character of a particular day. Washington's funeral was on 18 December, the day on which Sugiura was speaking, one day different from that of Field Marshal Ōyama. This is as it should be, Sugiura notes, because they were very similar men and one could well use the preceding words describing Ōyama to characterize Washington.

He then illustrates Washington's upright manner through several stories from his youth, including the apocryphal tale about his chopping down his father's cherry tree and admitting to the deed when questioned. (The famous phrase that appeared in many primary school texts in the United States until recently, "I cannot tell a lie," is not quoted by Sugiura.) Hirohito's mentor concludes that Washington maintained this respect for the truth throughout his life. Similarly "the unique way of Japan unadulterated by human will, the divine will which has been transmitted from the age of the gods *(kamunagara no michi)*, typifies the essence of the morality *(dōgi)* explained here; Washington was a Westerner and put this into practice very well." Sugiura proceeds to Washington's school years, where he says Washington was devoted to learning. Moreover, he prominently displayed three main virtues: diligence *(kinben)*, neatness *(seiketsu)*, and courage *(yūki)*. Following the description of Washington's education is a sketch of his military and political career.

Appendix · 9

Sugiura on the Meiji Charter Oath

Here Sugiura's explanation of the Meiji Charter Oath to Hirohito is paraphrased.[1] Though he strongly criticizes Tokugawa feudalism, Sugiura propa-
gates social thought characteristic of the feudal order—especially in his paragraph 3. [For reference the text is repeated:]

> With this oath we set up as our aim the establishment of the national weal on a
> broad basis and the framing of a constitution and laws.
>
> 1. Deliberative assemblies shall be widely established and all matters decided by
> public discussion.
>
> 2. All classes, high and low, shall unite in vigorously carrying out the administra-
> tion of the affairs of state.
>
> 3. The common people, no less than the civil and military officials, shall be
> allowed to pursue their own calling so that there will be no discontent.
>
> 4. Evil customs of the past shall be broken off and everything based on the just
> laws of nature.
>
> 5. Knowledge shall be sought throughout the world in order to strengthen the
> foundations of imperial rule.
>
> Our country is undergoing an unprecedented change. With I myself [the emperor]
> leading the people and making this pledge to the deities of heaven and earth,
> broadly speaking this sort of nation is to be established. Setting up the way of
> national integrity (banmin hōzen), the multitudes also should strive together
> with this basic purpose!

1. Arbitrary rule by pedigreed houses (monbatsu) is rejected, and public
(tenka) policy is to be decided through public discussion. To determine public
opinion carefully, assemblies are to be established throughout the land. Now
such assemblies exist in the villages, districts, and prefectures, and there is an

Imperial Parliament for deciding national policy. All policies are to be deliberated by these assemblies, and in this way this imperial idea will be put into effect.

2. From the nobles, princes, and lords above down to the common people, everyone is to strive together in developing our imperial nation. In the feudal age, because the gap between high and low was very great, even if there was some movement between the classes, there was considerable mutual alienation and estrangement. In case of a war, for example, the *bushi* alone were responsible for victory or defeat. It was as though the peasants, artisans, and merchants had nothing to do with the hostilities. This was not good for the advancement of the country. The nation *(kokka)* does not belong solely to the nobility or the military; it belongs to all citizens. Everyone should unite in promoting the country.

3. The imperial opinion expressed here is that among the court nobles, samurai, and even the people, each person can pursue his own aspirations *(kokorozashi)*. When people bowed and submitted, when it was not good to further one's aspirations, everyone suffered a loss of vitality; everyone was weary and gloomy. In order to stimulate the people they must be given the opportunity to further their ambitions. During the feudal age, for example, the nobles were oppressed for the sake of the samurai and only allowed to hold meaningless posts. The common people too were suppressed by the samurai and always had to bow and scrape before them. Thus during the Tokugawa period (1603–1868) the nobles above and the people below were both unable to realize their aspirations. It is the policy of the Meiji Restoration to destroy this evil custom. *"In accord with one's status* (mibun sōō ni), *each is to receive the opportunity to pursue his aspirations."* [Emphasis added.]

Judging from the actual state of affairs today, many nobles *(kugyō)* have become peers *(kazoku)*, and the good treatment they receive from the state is no different from that received by the ancient nobility. Moreover, the common people receive a high-quality education and become civil and military officials, or as members of parliament consider *(gi suru)* national policy. A comparison with the old *bushi* shows no appreciable differences. In other words, the rights *(kenri)* of the four classes are almost the same. This is none other than the realization of the imperial intent informing the third article.

4. The fourth article indicates that the evil customs of the old feudal regime are to be destroyed, and administrative policy based on universal justice is to be established. What were these evil customs? There were many. A few examples are listed here. The Tokugawa Bakufu during the time of the third shogun Iemitsu (1623–1651), aiming at the eradication of Christianity, closed all ports and forbade overseas travel. For this reason our people were not only unable to avail themselves of the stimulus derived from foreign contacts; our seagoing sons were also forced to stay at home in the mountains living out their lives in regret. . . . In the Tokugawa period if one was not born a samurai one could not become one; if not born a noble or daimyo one could not become one. Even if born a prince or feudal lord, if not from an "inner house" *(fudai)*, one could not participate in bakufu politics. And one had to be born into an inner house. Therefore, destroying evil customs like this opened the door to advancing men of talent. This was one of the great reforms of the Meiji government. . . . These are examples of the old evil customs that have

been destroyed. Now our countrymen can again travel overseas, and the way to advancement according to one's talents is open.

5. The fifth article emphasizes the importance of gathering knowledge throughout the world to ensure the strength and independence of the Japanese empire. "Adopt that which is superior to supplement that which is weak" *(shuchō hotan)* has long been a forte of our country. Pure scientific *(rikaga-kuteki)* knowledge as found in the West is lacking in Japan. Therefore, we should adopt this superior knowledge from those countries, compensate for our weaknesses, and firm up the foundations of our empire.

Referring to the present situation, this means warships, weapons, ammunition, and the like. These things are all the result of applying the physical sciences, but they are not the only benefits of science. There are also railroads, the telephone and telegraph, mining, metallurgy, and medicine. In all these areas great progress has been made due to advances in Western learning. In these matters we should adopt Western strengths and make up for our shortcomings, which is to say strengthen our country. This does not mean we should devote ourselves to the West. Just as the famous patron of Chinese culture Sugawara no Michizane (845–903) favored "Japanese spirit and Chinese learning" *(wakon-kansai)*, one should uphold the spirit of the Japanese people and in specific areas adopt the strengths of Western civilization.

Sugiura then repeats the last line of the oath: "With I myself [the emperor] leading the people and making this pledge to the deities of heaven and earth, broadly speaking this sort of nation is to be established. Setting up the way of national integrity *(banmin hōzen)*, the multitudes also should strive together with this basic purpose!" He reiterates that for fifty years since its promulgation adhering to this oath has brought great advances in politics, law, military matters, and various fields of learning. Japan's great achievements up to the present are based on the principles of this oath, and in the future the nation's policies should be based on these same ideals.

Notes

Chapter 1: Introduction

1. Stephen S. Large, *Emperor Hirohito and Shōwa Japan: A Political Biography* (London: Routledge, 1992), pp. 130–311.

2. Inoue Kiyoshi, *Tennō no sensōsekinin* (The emperor's war responsibility) (Tokyo: Gendai Hyōronsha, 1975), "Hashigaki," p. 1 (without numbering) and passim.

3. Daikichi Irokawa, *The Age of Hirohito: In Search of Modern Japan*, trans. Mikiso Hane and John K. Urda (New York: Free Press, 1995), p. 84; see also pp. 71–107.

4. See, for example, ibid., pp. 12–13.

5. Carol Gluck, "The Idea of Showa," in Carol Gluck and Stephen R. Graubard, eds., *Showa: The Japan of Hirohito* (New York: Norton, 1992), p. 16.

6. Masataka Kosaka, "The Showa Era (1926–1989)," in Gluck and Graubard, *Showa*, p. 28. Further examples of this trend can be seen in the articles by Chalmers Johnson and Michio Muramatsu in the same volume.

7. Kinoshita Michio, *Sokkin nisshi* (Shorthand diary) (Tokyo: Bungei Shunjūsha, 1990), pp. 89–90. See also Herbert P. Bix, "The Showa Emperor's 'Monologue' and the Problem of War Responsibility," *Journal of Japanese Studies* 18(2) (Summer 1992): 320–321; here I use Bix' translation.

8. Some maintain that Hirohito was "defending the idea that the emperor is a descendant of the gods only in a symbolic cultural sense." See Emiko Ohnuki-Tierney, "The Emperor of Japan as Deity (Kami)," *Ethnology* 30(3) (1991): 199–215.

9. Hara Shirō, *Taisenryaku naki kaisen* (Beginning a war with no great strategy) (Tokyo: Hara Shobō, 1987); Nakahara Shigetoshi, *Kokuryoku naki sensōshidō* (Directing a war without national resources) (Tokyo: Hara Shobō, 1989).

10. Ernst Lokowandt, "Der Staat als Selbstzweck—Staatszwecke und -ziele in Japan" (Tokyo: OAG, 1994), OAG aktuell No. 61. pp. 7–8. Unless noted otherwise, all translations are the author's.

11. David Anson Titus, *Palace and Politics in Prewar Japan* (New York: Columbia University Press, 1974), pp. 34–35. For extended treatments of the legitimacy of the imperial line before and after World War II see Titus' Chapter II and the works by Titus cited below. The difference between Japanese and unreformed Middle Eastern religion is especially noteworthy. From a popular pamphlet distributed in Germany: "Islam is valid for the entire universe, for all time, one's entire life. . . . This religion extends throughout the world, and is as such the only religion and [world] order, which spans all generations and all ages, reaches into the present and satisfies the needs of everyone." See Cemaleddin Hocaoğlu (Kaplan), "Die islamische Verfassung" (Cologne: Veröffentlichung des Khalifatsstaates, 1993), p. 29.

12. For the relation between Shinto ceremonies, popular loyalty, and imperial authority according to Sakamaki Yoshio, an Imperial Household Ministry official from 1918 to 1936, see Titus, *Palace and Politics*, p. 34.

13. David A. Titus, trans., "The Idea of Revering the Emperor and Its Heritage" (unpublished manuscript), pp. 9–12. This is an abridged and condensed translation of Watsuji Tetsurō, *Sonnō shisō to sono dentō* (Tokyo: Iwanami Shoten, 1943), chaps. 1–3. Professor Titus kindly sent me this and several offprints of his articles together with a detailed and helpful critique of an earlier version of this work. I am greatly indebted to him for his suggestions.

14. Ibid., pp. 15–16.

15. Ibid., p. 20.

16. *Kodansha Encyclopedia of Japan* (Tokyo: Kodansha, 1983), vol. 2, pp. 7–8.

17. Titus, *Palace and Politics*, p. 37.

18. Ibid., p. 40.

19. Ibid., p. 81.

20. David A. Titus, "The Making of the 'Symbol Emperor System' in Postwar Japan," *Modern Asian Studies* 14(4) (1980): 543 and 546. See also David A. Titus, "Accessing the World: Palace and Foreign Policy in Post-Occupation Japan," in Gerald L. Curtis, ed., *Japan's Foreign Policy* (Armonk, N.Y.: M. E. Sharpe, 1993), pp. 68–69.

21. Titus, "Symbol Emperor System," p. 540.

22. Bōeichō Bōeikenkyūjo Senshibu (NIDS), ed., *Kaigun nendo sakusen keikaku* (Navy annual operations plans) (Tokyo: Asagumo Shimbunsha, 1986).

23. "Daihon'ei Rikugunbu: Sanmitsu Dai 438-go Dai 1" (Imperial Headquarters Army Dept.: Secret Proceedings No. 438–1) (8 November 1941), in *Shōwa jū-roku nen jōsō kankei shoruisetsu*, kan ichi; Shōwa jū-roku nen kugatsu—jū-ni-gatsu (Materials relating to imperial audiences in 1941, vol. 1, September 1941–December 1941).

24. This conclusion is drawn from the preceding two sources and others. See Chapters 2 and 3.

25. Titus, "Revering the Emperor," pp. 11–12. This is a theoretical comparison. One cannot say whether the emperor was acquainted with Watsuji's works.

26. Within the Japanese context, if things did not go well, "taking responsibility" might mean anything from making a formal apology to resigning office

or even suicide. In Emperor Hirohito's case, abdication in favor of a son and regent was the obvious option.

27. See Robert J. C. Butow, *Tojo and the Coming of the War* (Stanford: Stanford University Press, 1961).

28. Hara, *Taisenryaku naki kaisen*, p. 255. Hara asserts that Kido Kōichi and Konoe Fumimaro, privy seal and prime minister respectively, must have known about Tōjō's intense loyalty. By extension one might reasonably assume the emperor was accordingly informed.

29. Titus, *Palace and Politics*, passim.

30. Carol Gluck, *Japan's Modern Myths: Ideology in the Late Meiji Period* (Princeton: Princeton University Press, 1985).

31. Bernd Martin, "Verhängnisvolle Wahlverwandtschaft: Deutsche Einflüsse auf die Entstehung des modernen Japans," in Jost Düffler et al., eds., *Deutschland in Europa: Kontinuität und Bruch: Gedenkschrift für Andreas Hillgruber* (Berlin: Ulstein Verlag, 1990), p. 101. See also Bernd Martin, "Zur Tauglichkeit eines übergreifenden Faschismusbegriffes: Ein Vergleich zwischen Japan, Italien und Deutschland," in *Vierteljahrshefte für Zeitgeschichte* (Munich) 1 (1981): 48–73. For a collection of essays in English see Bernd Martin, *Japan and Germany in the Modern World* (Providence: Berghahn Books, 1995).

32. See Germaine A. Hoston, "The State, Modernity, and the Fate of Liberalism in Prewar Japan," *Journal of Asian Studies* 51 (1992): 287–316; Lesley Connors, *The Emperor's Advisor: Saionji Kinmochi and Prewar Japanese Politics* (London: Croom Helm, 1987).

33. Harro von Senger, "Die japanische Initiative zur völkerrechtlichen Verankerung des Grundsatzes der Rassengleichheit vom Jahre 1919," *Frankfurter Allgemeine Zeitung*, 25 April 1994, p. 13. My thanks to the author for sending me a copy of the article.

34. From a lengthy critique of an earlier version of this study by Harro von Senger of the University of Freiburg.

35. "Shōwa tennō no dokuhaku hachi-jikan" (The Shōwa emperor's eight-hour monologue), *Bungei shunjū*, December 1990, p. 100; cited in James W. Morley, ed., *Japan's Road to the Pacific War: The Final Confrontation: Japan's Negotiations with the United States, 1941*, trans. David A. Titus (New York: Columbia University Press, 1994), p. xxxv.

36. Ibid.

Chapter 2: Imperial Navy Planning and the Emperor

1. The phrase "emperor system" *(tennōsei)* first came into use as a leftist term in 1932. When the Japanese Communist Party formulated its program, it stated that the first task of the revolution was the destruction of the emperor system.

2. See Inoue Kiyoshi, *Tennō no sensōsekinin* (The emperor's war responsibility) (Tokyo: Gendai Hyōronsha, 1975), "Hashigaki," p. 1. See also his *Tennōsei* (The emperor system) (Tokyo: Tokyo Daigaku Shuppankai, 1958), which set the tone for postwar criticism of the emperor and emperor system. Given the information available when Inoue wrote these books, they are sound history. There still is much room for interpretation, however, and many Japanese authors do not share Inoue's opinions. Inoue maintains that Hirohito was personally responsible for the decision.

3. See, for example, Yamamoto Shichihei, *Shōwa tennō no kenkyū: sono jitsuzō o saguru* (Research on the Shōwa emperor: In search of his real image) (Tokyo: Shōdensha, 1989). Yamamoto is an independent essayist who first attracted attention in 1970 with his book *Nihonjin to Yudayajin* (The Japanese and the Jews). Although he is not an academic, he is a good example of what many people read and believe. The volume of secondary material in Japanese on the emperor and emperor system is staggering. See Akasaka Norio et al., *Tennōsei nyūmon* (Introduction to the imperial system) (Tokyo: JICC Shuppankyoku, 1989), a bibliographic work with two thousand titles on the Japanese emperor. For a critical appraisal of recently published primary and secondary literature see Gerhard Krebs, "Das Ende des Shōwa-Tennō oder der Shōwa-Tennō und kein Ende: Die Diskussion in Politik und Literatur," in *Japanstudien: Jahrbuch des Deutschen Instituts für Japanstudien der Philipp-Franz-von-Siebold Stiftung* (Munich: Judicium, 1993), vol. 5, pp. 35–88. For an overview of the important bibliographies on the war see James W. Morley, ed., *Japan's Road to the Pacific War: The Final Confrontation: Japan's Negotiations with the United States, 1941*, trans. David A. Titus (New York: Columbia University Press, 1994), p. 373.

4. See, for example, Harada Kumao, *Saionjikō to seikyoku* (Prince Saionji and the political developments) (Tokyo: Iwanami Shoten, 1950–1956), vol. 2, p. 248; Lesley Connors, *The Emperor's Advisor: Saionji Kinmochi and Prewar Japanese Politics* (London: Croom Helm, 1987), pp. 212–213. See also the discussion between Harada and Finance Minister Fujii Masanobu (1885–1935) on 31 October 1934. Fujii withheld bad news from the emperor, and Harada says Saionji disapproves of exactly this practice. The emperor has a great responsibility as sovereign, and there should be a close relation between the emperor and his ministers so he is well informed about everything. See Harada, *Saionjikō to seikyoku*, vol. 4, p. 109. For the February 26 officers' revolt see Chapter 8.

5. See also Robert J. C. Butow, *Tojo and the Coming of the War* (Stanford: Stanford University Press, 1961), pp. 370–371 and n. 13. John Whitney Hall, "A Monarch for Modern Japan," in Robert E. Ward, ed., *Political Development in Modern Japan* (Princeton: Princeton University Press, 1968), p. 47, observes: "By 1871 the first stage in the transformation of the Japanese monarchy was essentially complete. . . . The emperor continued as a transcendental and passive sovereign with authority which was theoretically absolute but which was actually exercised by ministers who governed in his name." See also Toshiaki Kawahara, *Hirohito and His Times* (Tokyo: Kodansha, 1990), pp. 110–114; for critiques see Peter Crome, *Der Tenno: Japan hinter dem Chrysanthemenvorhang* (Cologne: Kiepenheuer & Witsch, 1988), pp. 262–266, and Edward Behr, *Hirohito: Behind the Myth* (New York: Villard, 1989), pp. 253–254. For Allied planning prior to the occupation see Robert E. Ward, "Presurrender Planning: Treatment of the Emperor and Constitutional Changes," in Robert E. Ward and Yoshikazu Sakamoto, eds., *Democratizing Japan: The Allied Occupation* (Honolulu: University of Hawai'i Press, 1987), pp. 1–41.

6. Fujita Hisanori, *Jijūchō no kaisō* (The grand chamberlain's recollections) (Tokyo: Chūōkōronsha, 1987), pp. 205–206. The same citation appears in Yamamoto as "proof" of Hirohito's lack of involvement in the imperial government's important political and military decisions; see Yamamoto, *Shōwa*

tennō no kenkyū, pp. 13–14. Fujita Hisanori (1880–1970), a navy admiral who retired in 1937, became grand chamberlain in August 1944 and served until May 1946. His is a sympathetic insider's view of Emperor Hirohito.

7. "Shōwa tennō no dokuhaku hachi-jikan" (The Shōwa emperor's eight-hour monologue), *Bungei shunjū*, December 1990, pp. 94–145; cited hereafter as Hirohito Monologue. The monologues were held on the following days: 18 March 1946 (Monday), 10:15 A.M.–12:45 P.M.; 20 March 1946 (Wednesday), 3 P.M.–5:15 P.M.; 22 March 1946 (Friday), 2:20 P.M.–3:30 P.M.; 8 April 1946 (Monday), 4:30 P.M.–6 P.M. and 8 P.M.–9 P.M. For the most part, Inada recorded the sessions and Kinoshita later added clarifications where necessary (p. 98). For a short biographical note on Inada see Chapter 3, note 63. At the time of the monologue Matsudaira was director of the Imperial House General Affairs Office (Shuchitsuryō sōsai). This record has been evaluated by Japanese and Western scholars beginning with "Showa tennō dokuhakuroku—watashi-tachi no shōgeki" (The Shōwa emperor's monologue—our shock), *Bungei shunjū*, January 1991, pp. 94–147. The preceding monologue and the evaluations appeared later in book form. (See the Bibliography.) An anonymous critic of an earlier version of this book suggested that Hirohito's "defense" was inept and could have been used against him. This may be true, but obviously Hirohito and his advisers were unaware of their own shortcomings at the time.

8. Ellis M. Zacharias, *Secret Missions: The Story of an Intelligence Officer* (New York: Putnam's, 1946), pp. 199–200; cited in Krebs, "Das Ende."

9. Krebs, "Das Ende," pp. 44–45; see also nn. 12 and 13 on p. 45. In n. 12 Krebs says the telegram is not to be found in the "Magic Summaries" and "Magic Diplomatic Summaries" available on microfilm. In n. 13 he relates that Terasaki's assertions about this activity are rejected by many Japanese scholars. Nevertheless, the assertion with substantiating citations has been published in Japan: Asai Nobuo, "Nichibei kaisen zenya ni okeru Terasaki Hidenari no Yakuwari" (Terasaki Hidenari's role just before the outbreak of war between Japan and the U.S.), *Kōbe Gaidai ronsō* 39(7) (1988): 15–34; see Krebs, "Das Ende," p. 45. For an article on the same subject in English see Gerhard Krebs, "The Spy Activities of Diplomat Terasaki Hidenari in the USA and His Role in Japanese-American Relations," in Ian Neary, ed., *Leaders and Leadership in Japan* (Surrey: Curzon Press, 1996), pp. 190–205.

10. Awaya Kentarō, "Tokyo saiban to tennō 'dokuhakuroku' " (The Tokyo war crimes trials and the emperor's 'monologue'), in Fujiwara Akira, Awaya Kentarō, Yoshida Yutaka, and Yamada Akira, *Tettei kenshō, Shōwa tennō "dokuhakuroku"* (A thorough examination of the Shōwa emperor's "monologue") (Tokyo: Daigetsu Shoten, 1991), pp. 131–132. My thanks to Dr. Krebs for calling my attention to this information.

11. Krebs, "Das Ende," p. 44, n. 11; Butow, *Tojo and the Coming of the War*, pp. 379–384. The departing member referred to by Butow (p. 380) was Terasaki.

12. See note 7.

13. Hirohito Monologue, pp. 100 and 145.

14. See Chapter 7.

15. Headquarters, U.S. Strategic Bombing Survey (Pacific), Interrogation No. 507, Tokyo, 28 November 1945, pp. 2–3.

16. Ibid., Interrogation USSBS No. 379 (NAV No. 76), Tokyo, 17 November 1945, pp. 3–4.

17. Ibid., Interrogation No. 373, Tokyo, 9 November 1945, pp. 2, 13, 17. Admiral Takagi Sokichi was of the same opinion; see Interrogation No. 487, Tokyo, 23 November 1945, pp. 7–8.

18. Ibid., Interrogation No. 487, pp. 18–19, 23.

19. Ibid., Interrogation No. 531, Tokyo, 26 December 1945, p. 11.

20. Bōeichō Bōeikenkyūjo Senshibu (National Institute for Defense Studies), ed., *Kaigun nendo sakusen keikaku* (Navy annual operations plans) (Tokyo: Asagumo Shimbunsha, 1986), pp. 1–11; hereafter cited as Navy Operations Plans. The documents from this volume are all photocopies of the handwritten originals. Terms and translations:

"National Defense Policy" = *Kokubō hōshin*

"Meiji 39 (1906) Imperial Japanese Army Operations Plan Outline" = *Meiji sanjū-kyū nendo Nippon Teikoku Rikugun sakusen keikaku yōryō*

"Annual Operations Plan" = *Nendo sakusen keikaku*

21. See Sanematsu Yuruzui, *Jōhō sensō* (Information war) (Tokyo: Tosho Shuppansha, 1972), pp. 14–20, for copies of all four policies. ("Basic Tactics Outlines" = *Yōhei kōryō*.)

22. Navy Operations Plans, p. 4.

23. Because the navy was primarily concerned with the possibility of a war with the United States and its allies, I examined documents from the Imperial Navy in this part of this study. See Toyama Saburō, *Taiheiyō kaisenshi, 1* (History of the beginning of the Pacific War I) (Tokyo: Kyōiku Shuppan Center, 1985), p. 92. The army was principally concerned with planning operations against China and the Soviet Union. In a document dated 27 July 1940, "Sekai jōsei no suii ni tomonau jikyokushori yōkō" (Outline for managing circumstances in accord with the change in world affairs), the army first recognized that war with England (on the Asian mainland) or the United States inevitably would lead to war with both. In April 1941 the army began coordinating operations plans against the Americans in the Philippines and the English on the Malay Peninsula. These plans were officially mandated in a general plan presented to the throne on 5 November 1941, "Teikoku Rikugun zenpan sakusen keikaku" (Imperial Army general operations plan), ibid., pp. 93–100. The Imperial Army's plan for a war against America, England, and Holland, "Tai Bei, Ei, Ran sensō ni tomonau Teikoku Rikugun keikaku," no longer exists, except possibly for copies in the Imperial Household Agency archives, and has been reconstructed from records of the army chief of staff's reports to the throne and other remaining records. See Bōeichō Bōeikenshūjo Senshishitsu (NIDS), *Daihon'ei Rikugunbu (2)* (Imperial Headquarters, Army), in *Senshi sōsho*, vol. 20, pp. 588–594.

24. Navy Operations Plans, p. 1; "Office of the Police Commissioner" = Keishi Sōkan; "Cabinet Archives" = Naikaku Bunko. This version follows the editors of this volume. For the views of another author see note 62.

25. Nobutaka Ike, *Japan's Decision for War* (Stanford: Stanford University Press, 1967), p. xiv. Ike makes no mention of Navy Operations Plans.

26. See Navy Operations Plans, pp. 2–11, for this and the following discus-

sion. The plan for 1941 is not the final draft presented to the emperor. The documents consulted and English translations are as follows:

"Imperial Navy Operations Plan for the War Against America, Great Britain, and the Netherlands" = *Tai Bei, Ei, Ran sensō Teikoku Kaigun sakusen keikaku*

"Second Stage of Operations for the Greater East Asia War, Imperial Navy Operations Plan" = *Daitōa Sensō dai ni-dan sakusen Teikoku Kaigun sakusen keikaku*

Arthur J. Marder, *Old Friends, New Enemies: The Royal Navy and the Imperial Japanese Navy: Strategic Illusions, 1936–1941* (Oxford: Clarendon Press, 1981), pp. 324–333, used Bōeichō Bōeikenshūjo Senshishitsu (NIDS), *Daihon'ei Kaigunbu, Rengōkantai (1) kaisen made* (Imperial Headquarters, Navy, Combined Fleet (1) to the beginning of the war), in *Senshi sōsho*, vol. 91, and other NIDS materials to outline the "Grand Strategy" of the Imperial Navy in the prewar years. As his focus is naval history, our sources and interpretations vary somewhat.

27. See Bōeichō Bōeikenshūjo Senshishitsu (NIDS), *Nansei hōmen kaigun sakusen: Dai nidan sakusen iryō* (Navy operations for the push to the southwest: Second-stage operations and thereafter), in *Senshi sōsho*, vol. 54, pp. 2–4, for the April 1942 document and pp. 152–157 for the March 1943 document. Both originals are in the NIDS Library. For an English translation of the latter see Zainichi Beirikugun Senshika (U.S. Army in Japan, War History Section), trans., *Daikaishi Eiyaku 1–2*, vol. 1, "Imperial General Headquarters Navy Directives," 5 November 1941–12 September 1945, 540 directives and 3 supplements, also in the NIDS Library. This includes deployments just before the war and directives to commanders after surrender. It was for internal Imperial Navy use, not for presentation to the throne. The April 1942 report to the throne is not included in these directives.

28. "Shōwa jū-ichi nendo Teikoku Kaigun Sakusen Keikaku" (1936 Imperial Navy Operations Plan), secs. 1 and 2–1, paras. 16–22, in Navy Operations Plans, pp. 22–24.

29. "Shōwa jū-ni nendo Teikoku Kaigun sakusen keikaku" (1937 Imperial Navy Operations Plan), sec. 5, ibid., p. 61. Marder, *Old Friends, New Enemies*, p. 325, is not clear here. He has Great Britain added to the 1936 plan, but since this addition was made in 1936 it could not have appeared before the 1937 plan. He also notes that when the emperor questioned the reason for the addition of Great Britain to the list of possible adversaries, Prince Kan'in, chief of the Army General Staff, answered: "We must be prepared for a possible emergency in view of the acceleration of defense preparations at Hong Kong and Singapore and the instability of the international situation."

30. "Shōwa jū-san nendo Teikoku Kaigun sakusen keikaku oyobi dōsenji hensei ni kan shi sōjōan" (Report to the throne with respect to the 1938 Imperial Navy Operations Plan and changes in the same wartime situation); Navy Operations Plans, pp. 76–78.

31. "Shōwa jū-san nendo Teikoku Kaigun sakusen keikaku sakutei ni kan suru rikugun to no kōshō jōkyō kono ta ni kan suru ken" (State of the negotiations with the army concerning the 1938 Imperial Navy Operations Plan

policy and other relevant items), 3 March 1938; ibid., pp. 94–108. See "Kaigun iken," secs. 3–4 (pp. 100–102).

32. "Jū-san nendo sakusen keikaku ritsuan ni kan suru dai ikkai uchiawase" (First meeting on the draft of the 1938 operations plan); ibid., pp. 91–93. The preceding description comes from this document.

33. Shōwa jū-san nendo Teikoku Kaigun sakusen keikaku sakutei ni kan suru ken: Gosai" (Pertaining to the draft of the 1938 Imperial Navy Operations Plan: Imperial sanction), 23 June 1938; ibid., pp. 111–113.

34. Shōwa jū-san nendo Teikoku Kaigun sakusen keikaku" (1938 Imperial Navy Operations Plan); ibid., pp. 276–291. The delay was due to bureaucratic formalities. The plan was completed on 13 August; the chief of the Navy General Staff, Imperial Prince Fushimi, approved it on 27 August; the staff prepared it for official presentation and it was presented for formal consultations to the chief of the Army General Staff, Imperial Prince Kan'in, on 30 August. He gave his assent on 3 September and on that day or the next it was presented to Navy Minister Yonai. After he examined it, Imperial Prince Fushimi presented it to the throne; ibid., p. 114.

35. "Nichibei heiryoku hikaku (Shōwa jū-san nendo sue)" (Comparative Japan-U.S. military strength: End of 1938); ibid., pp. 156–185, particularly pp. 156–157. See Appendix 2.

36. "Tai Shi sakusenchū Rokoku to kaisen suru baai no sakusen" (Operations in case war begins with Russia while the war in China is still in progress); ibid., pp. 186–206. See also "Eikoku Kyokutō sakusen yōso heiryoku" (Estimate of English military operational capabilities in the Far East); ibid., pp. 228–242. This estimate was also drawn up in tabular form. See Appendix 2.

37. "Tai Bei, Ro, Ei, Shi sakusen" (Operations against the United States, Russia, England, and China); ibid., pp. 243–267.

38. "Shōwa jū-san nendo Teikoku Kaigun sakusen keikaku oyobi dōsenji hensei ni kansuru gosetsumei" (Explanation to the throne with respect to the 1938 Imperial Navy Operations Plan and changes in the same wartime situation); ibid., pp. 268–274.

39. "Shōwa jū-san nendo Teikoku Kaigun sakusen keikaku" (1938 Imperial Navy Operations Plan), sec. 2–1, paras. 18–21; ibid., pp. 279–280. At the beginning of sec. 2–2 the responsibilities of each fleet *(kantai)* are enumerated.

40. Klaus-Jürgen Müller, "Deutsche Militär-Elite in der Vorgeschichte des Zweiten Weltkrieges," in Martin Broszat and Klaus Schwabe, eds., *Die deutschen Eliten und der Weg in den Zweiten Weltkrieg* (Munich: C. H. Beck, 1989), pp. 228–235. The Japanese Imperial Army was also confronted with these problems in the 1920s but chose not to deal with them effectively. See Leonard A. Humphreys, *The Way of the Heavenly Sword: The Japanese Army in the 1920s* (Stanford: Stanford University Press, 1995), pp. 79–86.

41. According to one postwar author, at the beginning of the Pacific War in 1941 the balance of naval power had shifted in favor of the Japanese: "The Imperial navy had an overwhelming superiority over the combined British Commonwealth, American, and Dutch, and Free French naval forces stationed in the Far East when war broke out, and a rough equality if we include the US Pacific Fleet in the comparison"; Marder, *Old Friends, New Enemies*, p. 303. Marder's sources for this statement are from the postwar era. These

sources, as well as the prewar Japanese studies, appear to have purposely over-estimated the enemy's strength. The Japanese, for example, put all fifteen U.S. battleships in the Far East. Moreover, the great increase in Japanese strength between 1938 and 1941 is due largely to a classification in the postwar statistics for 1941—"Others," 156 vessels of indeterminate type—not included in the prewar statistics for 1938. Compare Marder's tables on the same page with those in Appendix 2. Marder had a very high opinion of the Imperial Japanese Navy's quality.

42. "Shōwa jū-yon nendo Teikoku Kaigun sakusen keikaku; Kaigun daijin ni nairan no ken: Gosai" (1939 Imperial Navy Operations Plan; concerning a review prior to an imperial audience by the navy minister: Imperial sanction), 22 February 1939, in Navy Operations Plans, pp. 465–466.

43. "Shōwa jū-yon nendo Teikoku Rikugun sakusen keikaku narabi dōkun-rei ni kan suru sanbōsōchō gosetsumeian" (Explanation to the throne by the chief of the general staff about the 1939 Imperial Army Operations Plan and related directives); ibid., pp. 486–524; see sec. 4–4 (pp. 507–512).

44. "Shōwa jū-yon nendo Teikoku Kaigun sakusen keikaku oyobi dōsenji hensei ni kan suru gosetsumei" (Explanation to the throne with respect to the 1939 Imperial Navy Operations Plan and changes in the same wartime situation); ibid., pp. 531–536; see sec. 4 (pp. 532–533). The occupation of Songkhla is noted but not the violation of Thai neutrality; dated 24 February 1939.

45. "Shōwa jū-yon nendo Teikoku Riku- Kaigun sakusen keikaku ni kan suru sōjōan" (Report to the throne concerning the 1939 Imperial Army and Navy Operations Plan); ibid., p. 474. Only one page is duplicated. It is dated 24 February 1939 and has a note added (different handwriting) after the audience. Here the literally translated "difficult to approve" *(mitome-gataki)* obviously means "impossible to approve."

46. "Shōwa jū-yon nendo Teikoku Kaigun sakusen keikakuanchū ichibu shūsei no ken: Gosai" (1939 Imperial Navy operations draft plan concerning the amendment of one part while in planning: Imperial sanction); ibid., pp. 480–484.

47. "Shōwa jū-yon nendo Teikoku Riku- Kaigun sakusen keikaku ni kan suru sōjō shūseian" (Amended proposal to the throne concerning the 1939 Imperial Army and Navy Operations Plan); ibid., p. 477. The revised commentary is recorded in full and dated 27 February.

48. "Ni-gatsu nijūshichi-nichi, Shōwa jū-yon nendo sakusen keikakuan shūsei ni kan suru ryō sōchō sōjō no sai" (27 February: On the imperial audience for both chiefs of staff concerning an amendment to the 1939 operations plan); ibid., p. 485.

49. "Shōwa jū-yon nendo Teikoku Kaigun sakusen keikaku" (1939 Imperial Navy Operations Plan); ibid., p. 551; the added phrase has been italicized here.

50. Stephen S. Large, *Emperor Hirohito and Shōwa Japan: A Political Biography* (London: Routledge, 1992), p. 83.

51. In March and April 1939 the emperor set the limits for a compromise with Germany. In July, however, in a temperamental outburst he said to a key supporter of the alliance, Army Minister Itagaki Seishirō (1885–1948), "No one is as stupid as you!" and blocked the alliance. See Harada, *Saionjikō*, vol. 7, pp. 325–326, vol. 8, pp. 13–15; Inoue, *Tennō no sensōsekinin*, pp. 105–106; Gerhard Krebs, *Japans Deutschlandpolitik 1935–1941* (Hamburg: Mitteilung

der Gesellschaft für Natur- und Völkerkunde Ostasiens, 1984), vol. 1, pp. 248 and 286.

52. Harada, *Saionjikō*, vol. 8, pp. 61–64; Hirohito Monologue, pp. 108–109.

53. Hirohito Monologue, p. 110.

54. Matsudaira Yasumasa, private secretary to the lord privy seal, spoke to Harada about Hirohito's actions at this time in an obviously critical tone, and the latter appears to agree with his evaluation. Inoue, *Tennō no sensōsekinin*, pp. 106–107, believes that the emperor did not go far enough and failed to inform others in the government of his feelings. Fujiwara Akira, *Tennōsei to guntai* (The emperor system and the military) (Tokyo: Aoki Shoten, 1978), pp. 163–164, notes this as an example of the emperor's political influence. See Kawahara, *Hirohito and His Times*, pp. 98–100, for a postwar critique.

55. Hirohito Monologue, pp. 106–108. The disagreement with Imperial Prince Chichibu is one of the few previously unknown incidents revealed by this interview. Hirohito's interpretation of the motives behind the maneuvering for the pact with Germany and Italy is new as well.

56. It is difficult to ascertain to what extent paper plans were matched with military hardware. Reading through these documents leaves one with the impression that the wholesale creation of a number of "fleets" on paper in just two or three years could not possibly be matched by their actual production, manning, and outfitting—unless they were very small fleets.

57. "Teikoku Kaigun senji hensei narabi ni nendo sakusen keikaku ni kan suru sōjō" (Imperial audience on wartime changes concerning the Imperial Navy and the annual operations plan); in Navy Operations Plans, p. 648. For an Imperial Navy General Staff comparison of the 1939 plan and the revision see the same source, p. 629.

58. "Shōwa jū ~~yon~~ -go nendo Teikoku Kaigun sakusen keikaku" (~~1939~~ 1940 Imperial Navy Operations Plan); ibid., pp. 654 and 656.

59. Untitled document; ibid., pp. 697–698.

60. "Shōwa jū-go nendo Teikoku Kaigun sakusen keikaku" (1940 Imperial Navy Operations Plan); ibid., pp. 738–763. The plan was presented to the emperor on 14 December 1939 and sanctioned the same day. See sec. 2–2, para. 25, "Tai Shi sakusenchū Beikoku to kaisen suru baai no sakusen" (Operations in the event war breaks out with America while operations against China are in progress), p. 743.

61. Bōeichō Bōeikenshūjo Senshishitsu (NIDS), *Hawai sakusen* (Hawai'i attack), in *Senshi sōsho*, vol. 10, p. 7.

62. See Nomura Minoru, *Tennō, Fushimi-Miya to Nippon kaigun* (The emperor, Imperial Prince Fushimi, and the Japanese navy) (Tokyo: Kōjinsha, 1988), p. 227. The documents were purposely put in the safe for preservation and then forgotten after the building was destroyed in an air raid. Later they were found and turned over to the prime minister's office. The 1941 annual operations plan, however, was mysteriously lost while the documents were stored there. Nomura believes that Prime Minister Yoshida may have been involved in this timely loss. The presentation to the throne is noted in the diary of naval aide-de-camp Capt. Shiro Eiichirō, cited in Navy Operations Plans, p. 785. Nearly all the documents cited in this study have been made accessible by the National Institute for Defense Studies. The archives of the imperial

house, controlled by the Imperial Household Agency, are open only to selected persons.

63. See the notes to "Shōwa jū-go nendo Teikoku Kaigun sakusen keikaku" (1940 Imperial Navy Operations Plan), in Navy Operations Plans, pp. 738–763. For Germany, Italy, and Holland see pp. 740–741, nn. 3–6 (p. 763). Additional notes on the Philippines are to be found throughout the plan; see, for example, p. 743, n. 9. Note 10 on the same page proposes a surprise attack on Wake Island.

64. "Tai Bei, Ei, Ran sensō Teikoku Kaigun sakusen keikaku" (War against the United States, England, and Holland, Imperial Navy Operations Plan); ibid., p. 802.

65. Ibid., p. 786. Compare with "Shōwa jū-go nendo Teikoku Kaigun sakusen keikaku" (1940 Imperial Navy Operations Plan), sec. 5–1, paras. 79–85 (sec. 6–1, paras. 95–101, of revisions for 1941); ibid., pp. 757–760.

66. "Tai Bei, Ei, Ran sensō Teikoku Kaigun sakusen keikaku" (War against the United States, England, and Holland, Imperial Navy Operations Plan), paras. 5 and 13–14; ibid., pp. 805 and 808.

67. "Tai Bei, Ei, Ran sensō Kaigun sakusen keikaku ni kan suru gosetsume-ian" (Explanation to the throne concerning the war against the United States, England, and Holland, Imperial Navy Operations Plan); ibid., pp. 795–801.

68. For this and the following discussion see "Tai Bei, Ei, Ran sensō Teikoku Kaigun sakusen keikaku" (War against the United States, England, and Holland Imperial Navy Operations Plan); ibid., pp. 801–815. For the oral explanation to the throne see ibid., pp. 795–801, untitled document. See *Senshi sōsho*, vol. 20, pp. 588–594, for the army's plan. See Sanbohonbu (General Staff), eds., *Sugiyama Memo* (Tokyo: Hara Shobō, 1967), vol. 1, pp. 386–388, for the private audience with the emperor on 3 November. See Chapter 3 for the navy chief of staff's report to the emperor on the Pearl Harbor operation.

69. Hirohito Monologue, pp. 118–120. These assertions were often repeated by Hirohito and his supporters after the war and came to be widely accepted.

70. Hayashi Kentarō, "Jikobengo de wa nai" (Not a self-defense), in "Shōwa tennō dokuhakuroku—watashitachi no shōgeki" (The Shōwa emperor's monologue—our shock), *Bungei shunjū* (January 1991): 121. Although Professor Hayashi is commenting specifically on Hirohito's handling of the murder of Chang Tso-lin in 1928, his observations have wider application.

71. Large, *Hirohito and Shōwa Japan*, p. 80. Large makes a good case for this line of reasoning, and his comments about Hirohito's personality are very much to the point (pp. 80–85).

72. Ibid., p. 79.

73. In the spring of 1946 a poet, Miyoshi Tatsuji, published in the popular magazine *Shinchō* a long discourse calling on the emperor to abdicate for exactly this reason. See Herbert P. Bix, "The Showa Emperor's 'Monologue' and the Problem of War Responsibility," *Journal of Japanese Studies* 18(2) (Summer 1992): 314.

74. Ibid., pp. 346–347.

Chapter 3: Pearl Harbor and Decision Making

1. For a detailed description of the documents concerning military operations presented to the emperor from 1941 to 1944 see Yamada Akira, *Shōwa*

tennō no sensōshidō (The Shōwa emperor's war leadership) (Tokyo: Shōwa Shuppan, 1990), pp. 10–42.

2. For a later version of this history see Hattori Takushirō, *Daitōa sensō zenshi* (Complete history of the Greater East Asia War) (Tokyo: Hara Shobō, 1965).

3. Sanbōhonbu (General Staff), eds., *Sugiyama Memo* (Tokyo: Hara Shobō, 1967), vol. 1, pp. 2–3.

4. Nobutaka Ike, *Japan's Decision for War* (Stanford: Stanford University Press, 1967); Tsunoda Jun and Fukuda Shigeo, *Nichibei kaisen* (Beginning of the war between Japan and the United States), in Tsunoda Jun, ed., *Taiheiyō sensō e no michi* (The road to the Pacific War) (Tokyo: Asahi Shimbunsha, 1962–1963), vol. 7. The chapters by Tsunoda have been translated into English: James William Morley, ed., *Japan's Road to the Pacific War: The Final Confrontation: Japan's Negotiations with the United States, 1941*, trans. David A. Titus (New York: Columbia University Press, 1994). This is a superb translation with an excellent introduction by the translator, who also has supplied many references to original sources.

5. Bōeichō Bōeikenshūjo Senshibu (NIDS), ed., *Daihon'ei Rikugunbu Daitōa Sensō kaisenkeii* (Imperial Headquarters, Army, particulars on the beginning of the Greater East Asia War), in *Senshi sōsho* (War history series), vols. 65, 68–70, 76 (Tokyo, 1973–1974). (Hereafter vol. 76 in the series is referred to as *Kaisenkeii.*)

6. Hara Shirō, *Taisenryaku naki kaisen* (Beginning a war with no great strategy) (Tokyo: Hara Shobō, 1987).

7. Hara Shirō, ed., "Daihon'ei senshi: Daitōa Sensō kaisen gaishi: Kaisen ni itaru seisenryaku shidō" (Imperial Headquarters war history: General history of beginning hostilities in the Greater East Asia War: Leadership and political strategy with respect to the beginning of hostilities), 3 vols., pp. 4617–5837; from the editor's introduction to each volume (unnumbered page). These are the first galley proofs (*wabun taipu*, perforated and bound with a string) for the last volume (*Senshi sōsho*, vol. 76) of Hara's five-volume work.

8. Fujita Michitaka, "Kaisetsu" (Commentary), in Hara, *Taisenryaku*, p. 337. "Daihon'ei Riku- Kaigunbu Daitōa Sensō kaisenkeii" = "Imperial Headquarters, Army and Navy Departments, Particulars on the Beginning of the Greater East Asia War."

9. Bōeichō Bōeikenshūjo Senshibu (NIDS), ed., *Daihon'ei Kaigunbu Daitōa Sensō kaisenkeii* (Imperial Headquarters, Navy, particulars on the beginning of the Greater East Asia War), in *Senshi sōsho*, vols. 100–101.

10. *Kaisenkeii*, pp. 336–337. "Battle of Okehazama": a battle between Oda Nobunaga and Imagawa Yoshimoto in the Fifth Month (Go-gatsu), 1560. Nobunaga defeated Imagawa's numerically superior forces through a strong offensive course of action. This was a small but important engagement: had Imagawa won, he might have been able to establish himself in Kyoto. See George Sansom, *A History of Japan, 1334–1615* (Stanford: Stanford University Press, 1961), pp. 276–277.

11. Peter Crome, *Der Tenno: Japan hinter dem Chrysanthemenvorhang* (Cologne: Kiepenheuer & Witsch, 1988), p. 312.

12. "Joseph Keenan Meets the Press," *American Mercury*, 70 (316) (April

1950); cited in Robert J. C. Butow, *Tojo and the Coming of the War* (Stanford: Stanford University Press, 1961), p. 370, n. 13.

13. "Daihon'ei Rikugunbu: Sanmitsu Dai 438-go Dai 1" (Imperial Headquarters, Army Dept.: Secret proceedings no. 438–1):

Date: 8 November 1941

To: Emperor's Chief Aide-de-Camp

From: Army Chief of Staff, Navy Chief of Staff

Subject: "Heigi ni yoru sakusen keikaku gosetsumei ni kan suru ken" (Explanation to the emperor of the attack plans with reference to war games)

In *Shōwa jū-roku nen jōsō kankei shoruisetsu* (Materials relating to imperial audiences in 1941, vol. 1, September–December 1941). Despite its distracting title, the content and vocabulary of this document, identical with that cited in note 10, indicate this is the oral report to the throne cited in the text.

14. Hara, *Daihon'ei senshi*, MS, vol. 2, pp. 5272–5273.

15. *Sugiyama Memo*, vol. 1, pp. 386–388.

16. Extreme secrecy surrounded the Hawai'i attack plan. In the army only Colonel Hattori, chief of the Second Section of the General Staff, had been informed. Officially the army was left uninformed of the navy's intentions until after the attack. See *Kaisenkeii*, pp. 340 and 389, n. 429. For Kido see Awaya Kentarō et al., eds., *Kido Kōichi jinmon chōsho* (Protocol of the interrogation of Kido Kōichi) (Tokyo: Daigetsu Shoten, 1987), pp. 372 and 392. This is a Japanese translation of the interrogation of Kido prior to the Tokyo war crimes trial, IPS Records, RG 331, "Numerical Case Files," Entry 319, Case No. 50, some 800 typewritten pages. It is an excellent translation.

17. *Kaisenkeii*, pp. 329–332. The text is dated 7 January 1941. In parentheses preceding the text Yamamoto wrote that it was for the minister alone; it should be shown to no one and burned after reading. After the attack he showed a copy to Capt. Miwa Yoshitake on the Combined Fleet Staff, saying only the minister had seen it and it would clarify why he felt the attack was necessary. Capt. Fujii Shigeru, on the same staff from December 1941 to August 1943, found a copy of this statement in Yamamoto's effects after he was killed (18 April 1943). He preserved it until after the war, and it came to be stored with Yamamoto's other papers at the NIDS after Fujii's death in 1956. See also *Naval War College Review* 31(2) (Fall 1978): 83–88; Hiroyuki Agawa, *The Reluctant Admiral: Yamamoto and the Imperial Navy*, trans. John Bester (Tokyo: Kodansha International, 1979), pp. 193–194.

18. John J. Stephan, *Hawaii Under the Rising Sun* (Honolulu: University of Hawai'i Press, 1984), p. 81.

19. William H. Honan, *Visions of Infamy* (New York: St. Martin's Press, 1991), especially pp. 167–186. Bywater's book caused quite a commotion in Japan. It was serialized in the the newspaper *Kokumin* and translated three times in book form. Yamamoto probably read it in English, however, acquiring it while he was a naval attaché in the Japanese embassy in Washington.

20. "Tai Bei, Ei, Ran sensō Teikoku Kaigun sakusen keikaku" (War against the United States, England, and Holland, Imperial Navy Operations Plan). See

Chapter 2, note 68, and *Kaisenkeii*, pp. 317–327, especially paras. 5 (pp. 318–319), 13, and 14 (p. 322).

21. For this and the following paragraph see *Kaisenkeii*, pp. 50–52 and 298–299.

22. For Nagano's approval see Bōeichō Bōeikenshūjo Senshishitsu (NIDS), *Hawai sakusen* (Hawai'i attack), in *Senshi sōsho*, vol. 10, p. 114.

23. *Kaisenkeii*, p. 50. See Gordon W. Prange, with Donald M. Goldstein and Katherine V. Dillon, *Pearl Harbor: The Verdict of History* (New York: McGraw-Hill, 1986), p. 534. See also Stephan, *Hawaii Under the Rising Sun*, p. 88; Arthur J. Marder, *Old Friends, New Enemies: The Royal Navy and the Imperial Japanese Navy: Strategic Illusions, 1936–1941* (Oxford: Clarendon Press, 1981), p. 332, n. 46. For a summary of these events see Bōeichō Bōeikenshūjo Senshishitsu (NIDS), *Daihon'ei Kaigunbu, Rengōkantai (1) kaisen made* (Imperial Headquarters, Navy, Combined Fleet (1) to the beginning of the war), in *Senshi sōsho*, vol. 91, pp. 552–553. Yamamoto's extremely strong desire *(tsuyoi yōbō)* to carry out the plan is mentioned, but not a threat to resign.

24. *Sugiyama Memo*, vol. 2, p. 6.

25. *Sugiyama Memo*, vol. 1, pp. 417–431; see Ike, *Japan's Decision for War*, pp. 208–239, for a translation of a transcript of the conference. See also *Kaisenkeii*, pp. 339–340.

26. "Shōwa tennō no dokuhaku hachi-jikan" (The Shōwa emperor's eighthour monologue), *Bungei shunjū*, December 1990, p. 110; cited hereafter as Hirohito Monologue.

27. Stephen S. Large, *Emperor Hirohito and Shōwa Japan: A Political Biography* (London: Routledge, 1992), p. 78. See pp. 87–88 for Saionji's misgivings about the emperor's ability to influence what he sanctioned in these conferences.

28. Herbert P. Bix, "The Showa Emperor's 'Monologue' and the Problem of War Responsibility," *Journal of Japanese Studies* 18(2) (Summer 1992): 346; for a statement from Kido Kōichi showing that Hirohito influenced prewar politics see pp. 346–347.

29. Bix, "The Showa Emperor's 'Monologue,' " p. 346; see Large, *Hirohito and Shōwa Japan*, p. 87, for one example among many.

30. Fujiwara Akira, *Shōwa tennō no jū-go nen sensō* (The Shōwa emperor's fifteen-year war) (Tokyo: Aoki Shoten, 1991), pp. 120–121.

31. Ibid., p. 122.

32. Kido Kōichi, *Kido Kōichi nikki* (Kido Kōichi diary; cited hereafter as Kido Diary) (Tokyo: Tokyo Daigaku Shuppankai, 1966), vol. 2, p. 917; Satō Kenryō, *Daitōa Sensō kaikoroku* (Greater East Asia War memoirs) (Tokyo: Tokuma Shoten, 1966), pp. 184–185. For a record of the 6 September imperial conference see Kido Diary, vol. 2, pp. 905–906; *Sugiyama Memo*, vol. 1, pp. 311–331; and Nobutaka Ike, *Japan's Decision for War* (Stanford: Stanford University Press, 1967), pp. 133–163. See Ike, pp. 154–155, for an explanation of this deadline.

33. Here again it appears that the emperor did not take advantage of a chance to avert war. He was informed at the end of July about the navy's reluctance to go to war (see Chapter 2). This disunity between army and navy coincides with his postwar criterion for acting—disunity in government circles.

34. Higashikuni Naruhiko, *Higashikuni nikki* (The Higashikuni diary)

(Tokyo: Tokuma Shoten, 1968), p. 91; statement made to Higashikuni by Prime Minister Konoe on 15 October 1941. See also Konoe's entry in his own diary, the *Konoe shuki*, from 14 October in *Kaisenkeii*, p. 152.

35. Ibid.

36. For Kido's testimony in 1946 see Awaya et al., *Kido Kōichi jinmon chōsho*, p. 509; Kido Diary, vol. 1, pp. 234 and 470. See Chapter 7, note 39, for secondary accounts. Tsunoda Jun counts Higashikuni among those against the war; see Tsunoda and Fukuda, *Nichibei kaisen*, p. 302. See also Morley, *The Final Confrontation*, p. xxiv. Higashikuni may have been against the war at this time, but according to Kido he was predisposed to the military and the army might well have been able to convince him to go along with their plans.

37. Tsunoda and Fukuda, *Nichibei kaisen*, p. 295. See Morley, *The Final Confrontation*, pp. 230–244, for this discussion.

38. Tsunoda and Fukuda, *Nichibei kaisen*, p. 476, nn. 15–16 and 25. See also *Kyokutō Kokusai Gunjisaiban, Shoshō 1148-gō* (Far East International Military Tribunal, Documentary Evidence No. 1148).

39. Peter Herde, *Pearl Harbor: 7. Dezember 1941* (Darmstadt: Wissenschaftliche Buchgesellschaft, 1980), pp. 168–169. Herde cites Konoe's memoirs and the Kido Diary as they appear in IMTFE Proc. 10266ff, 10276ff, etc.; see p. 503, Nos. 571 and 572. Tsunoda makes the same point but describes Kido's role in the proceedings differently. See Tsunoda and Fukuda, *Nichibei kaisen*, p. 296; Morley, *The Final Confrontation*, p. 234.

40. Kido Diary, vol. 2, pp. 915–916, 16 October (Thursday) 1945; Awaya et al., Kido Interrogation No. 29, 14 March 1946, pp. 499–511, 506–511.

41. Ibid.

42. *Kaisenkeii*, p. 155. From the IMTFE stenographic record of Suzuki's testimony during the war crimes trial (*Sensō Saiban sokkiroku*, No. 333, p. 10).

43. Awaya et al., Kido Interrogation No. 29, 14 March 1946, pp. 506–511.

44. Konoe Fumimaro, *Heiwa e no doryoku* (Efforts for peace) (Tokyo: Nihon Denshin Tsūshinsha, 1946), pp. 97–98. This was written by Konoe's private secretary, Ushiba Tomohiko. See also *Konoe shuki* in *Kaisenkeii*, p. 154. See the same sources for Konoe's interpretation of this statement immediately below in the text.

45. Higashikuni, *Higashikuni nikki*, p. 92 (15 October 1941 entry).

46. Konoe, *Heiwa e no doryoku*, pp. 93–94.

47. See Hirohito Monologue, pp. 116–117, for this and the following. The names of those in the imperial house *(kōzoku)* favoring war are not given.

48. Ike, *Japan's Decision for War*, pp. 138–140.

49. Hirohito Monologue, p. 118.

50. Tsunoda and Fukuda, *Nichibei kaisen*, p. 306.

51. Imai Seiichi, "Cabinet, Emperor, and Senior Statesmen," in Dorothy Borg and Shumpei Okamoto, eds., *Pearl Harbor as History: Japanese-American Relations 1931–1942* (New York: Columbia University Press, 1973), pp. 77–78. Interestingly, Imai refers to Tsunoda and Fukuda, *Nichibei kaisen*, pp. 293–305.

52. Tsunoda and Fukuda, *Nichibei kaisen*, p. 294; *Suzuki Teiichi: Sensei kōkyōsho* (Suzuki Teiichi: Sworn deposition).

53. Kido Diary, vol. 2, pp. 913–914. For a discussion of Konoe's letter of resignation see Inoue Kiyoshi, *Tennō no sensōsekinin* (The emperor's war respon-

sibility) (Tokyo: Gendai Hyōronsha, 1975), p. 139. For previous consultations and a commentary on Kido's audience with the emperor on 13 October see *Kaisenkeii*, pp. 138–139. "Chief Cabinet Secretary" = Naikaku Shokikanchō.

54. Kido Diary, vol. 2, p. 918, 20 October (Monday) 1941. Kawahara includes this citation in his book but fails to discuss its significance; see Toshiaki Kawahara, *Hirohito and His Times* (Tokyo: Kodansha, 1990), pp. 109–111.

55. See the Introduction, note 28.

56. Tsunoda and Fukuda, *Nichibei kaisen*, p. 309; *Hōmushō Shiryō* (Ministry of Justice Historical Records). "Chief of the Military Affairs Bureau" = Gunmukachō; "Chief of the Naval Affairs Bureau" = Gunmukyokuchō.

57. Hirozaki Sadamitsu, "Hishokan Memo" (A cabinet secretary's memoranda), in Jōhō Yoshio, ed., *Tōjō Hideki* (Tokyo: Fuyō Shobō, 1974), pp. 81–82. Hirozaki quotes Tōjō on the occasion of his appointment as prime minister.

58. *Kaisenkeii*, pp. 183–184; "The Record of Supreme Command–Government Liaison Conference Decisions" *(Daihon'ei-seifu renrakukaigi ketteisetsu)* is quoted. See also Tsunoda and Fukuda, *Nichibei kaisen*, pp. 307–308. For a slightly different translation see Morley, *The Final Confrontation*, pp. 248–249. For a partial English translation of the deliberations that ensued see Ike, *Japan's Decision for War*, pp. 187–207. The document translated here is the "paper . . . [that] had been prepared to serve as a basis for discussion" mentioned by Ike, p. 187, n. 19. For the 2 October note see Ike, pp. 179–181.

59. *Kaisenkeii*, p. 184.

60. Ibid., p. 188; Tsunoda and Fukuda, *Nichibei kaisen*, p. 308. Here the superiority of the *Kaisenkeii* is well illustrated. Hara cites the diary of Gen. Tanaka Ryūkichi, *Tanaka nikki*—a useful piece of information because Tanaka is not always a reliable informant. Tsunoda tells us only that this is a War History Office source, *Senshishitsu shiryō*.

61. Morley, *The Final Confrontation*, p. 243.

62. *Kaisenkeii*, p. 185; Satō, *Daitōa sensō*, p. 185, is similar. Compare with Tsunoda and Fukuda, *Nichibei kaisen*, p. 309.

63. Akamatsu Sadao, *Tōjō hishokan kimitsu nikki* (Secret diary of Tōjō's secretary) (Tokyo: Bungei Shunjūsha, 1985), pp. 33–34; cited hereafter as Akamatsu Diary. For Akamatsu Sadao see Chapter 4, note 15. This passage refers to the way Prime Minister Tōjō conducted affairs generally. No specific reference is made to this review, and it is possible, though unlikely, that Hirohito was not informed of the progress of this particular review. Inada Shūichi (1902–1973), son of a legal scholar, graduated from the Law Faculty of Tokyo Imperial University in 1925 and entered the civil service immediately. He was transferred to the Prime Minister's Office in 1931. He became chief of the General Affairs Section (Sōmukachō) in November 1937 and served in this capacity until being made governor of Shiga prefecture in 1945.

64. For several versions of the "polished consensus theory" see Butow, *Japan's Decision*, pp. 324–325, 370–371; David A. Titus, *Palace and Politics in Prewar Japan* (New York: Columbia University Press, 1974), pp. 327–328; Kawahara, *Hirohito and His Times*, passim; Gerhard Krebs, *Japans Deutschlandpolitik 1935–1941* (Hamburg: Mitteilung der Gesellschaft für Natur- und Völkerkunde Ostasiens, 1984), vol. 2, p. 20, n. 84. For the emperor's position see Hirohito Monologue, pp. 144–145.

65. Fujiwara, *Tennōsei to guntai*, pp. 161–181. Fujiwara quotes (pp. 162–163) *Konoe shuki*, pp. 102–103.

66. See Hara, *Taisenryaku*, pp. 254–255, for this and the following.

67. Kido Diary, vol. 2, pp. 919–920.

68. For the following see "Jōsōan: nanpō sakusen zempan ni kan suru ken" (Memorial to the throne: Matters relating to all operations to the south), in *Shōwa jū-roku nen jōsō kankei shoruisetsu.*

69. For the following two paragraphs see "Hōtō shiryō, Tai Bei, Ei, Ran sensō ni okeru sakusenteki mitōshi" (Materials in reply to the throne: The operational outlook in a war with America, England, and Holland), in *Shōwa jū-roku nen jōsō kankei shoruisetsu.*

70. The foregoing is a summary of the document cited in note 69. The document is handwritten with no page numbers.

71. "Tai Bei, Ei, Ran sensō shidō yōkō," in *Kaisenkeii*, pp. 340–343. The plan available to us is a postwar reconstruction by Colonel Ishii, which he assured the author of this work, Hara, was quite close to the original. For the presentation to the throne on 3 November see *Sugiyama Memo*, vol. 1, pp. 386–388. Compare both with the Imperial Navy plan mentioned in Chapter 2, note 68: "Tai Bei, Ei, Ran sensō Teikoku Kaigun sakusen keikaku" (War against the United States, England, and Holland: Imperial Navy Operations Plan).

72. These are only two of many reports prepared by the Imperial Army for imperial audiences. They contain many revisions, sections are stricken and reworded, but their general line of thought is consistent with the two examples, and the internal joint directive, introduced here. See *Shōwa jū-roku nen jōsō kankei shoruisetsu.*

73. Titus, *Palace and Politics*, p. 300. Titus cites the Kido Diary, vol. 2, p. 895.

74. Hara, *Taisenryaku*, pp. 258–259. Unfortunately Hara does not provide footnotes in this volume and I could not find the source in his other work on the same events, *Kaisenkeii.*

75. Ibid., p. 258.

76. Hirohito Monologue, p. 118.

77. Tsunoda and Fukuda, *Nichibei kaisen*, p. 310. Also, as mentioned earlier, Hirohito feared a coup d'état.

78. Akamatsu Diary, pp. 47–48.

79. John R. Pritchard and Sonia Magbanna Zaide, eds., *The Tokyo War Crimes Trial* (Complete transcripts of the proceedings of the International Military Tribunal for the Far East) (New York: Garland, 1981–), vol. 15, pp. 36779–36781; Richard H. Minear, *Victor's Justice* (Tokyo: Tuttle, 1972), pp. 114–115, n. 83.

80. "Hoshino Naoki shuki" (Notes of Hoshino Naoki), in Jōhō, *Tōjō Hideki*, p. 670. See Col. Sakakibara Kazue, "Tōjō Hideki Taishō Ōmori kōchishonai ni okeru kangae" (General Tōjō Hideki's thoughts while in Ōmori prison), December 1945, ibid., pp. 746–754, for a similar statement by Tōjō. This is an interview with Tōjō in November 1945. See the original in the NIDS Library.

81. Kido Diary, vol. 2, p. 945. Other evidence of his war interest: on 13 October he asked Kido and the prime minister for help in drafting a declara-

tion of war; ibid., vol. 2, p. 914. See also *Sugiyama Memo*, vol. 1, pp. 284, 310–311, and 386–388; Kido Diary, vol. 2, p. 933, 8 December (Monday) 1941, and p. 946, 16 February (Monday) 1942, the day after the fall of Singapore. Large, *Hirohito and Shōwa Japan*, p. 116, quotes this statement from Kido, as well, but with a completely different purpose. He uses it to show that the emperor, even when enthusiastic about Japan's first victories, was still looking for peace. But Large omits the second half of the statement beginning "This of course will also be a problem for our adversaries . . ."

82. This active participation in decisions in specific theaters of the war can be documented even as late as the defense of Okinawa. See Fujiwara Akira, *Jūgo nen sensō to tennō* (The fifteen-year war and the emperor) (Tokyo: Azumino Forum, 1988), pp. 31–32.

83. Daikichi Irokawa, *The Age of Hirohito: In Search of Modern Japan*, trans. Mikiso Hane and John K. Urda (New York: Free Press, 1995), pp. 82–83.

Chapter 4: Tōjō and the Emperor

1. Tōjō was also army minister from July 1940 to October 1941, from October 1941 to July 1944, and temporarily filled a number of ministerial posts in his cabinet. See Miwa Kai and Philip B. Yampolsky, *Political Chronology of Japan 1885–1957* (New York: East Asian Institute of Columbia University, 1957), pp. 22–24.

2. In Chapter 3 see Inada Shūichi for a contemporary observation and Irokawa Daikichi for a postwar commentary.

3. Bernd Martin, "Verhängnisvolle Wahlverwandtschaft: Deutsche Einflüsse auf die Entstehung des modernen Japans," in Jost Düffler et al., eds., *Deutschland in Europa: Kontinuität und Bruch: Gedenkschrift für Andreas Hillgruber* (Berlin: Ulstein Verlag, 1990), p. 101.

4. Ibid., p. 110. For the meaning of *"kokutai"* in Japanese culture see Klaus Antoni, "Kokutai—Das 'Nationalwesen' als japanische Utopie," *Saeculum* 37 (2–3) (1987): 266–282; reprinted in Klaus Antoni, *Der Himmlische Herrscher und Sein Staat* (Munich: Judicium, 1991).

5. One *koku* was about 180 liters or 4.96 bushels of rice—supposedly enough to feed an adult male for one year. Thus 160 *koku* was a fairly good stipend, especially for a Nō actor. In the Tokugawa period, samurai family stipends ranged from over 10,000 to 1 or 2 *koku* per year. The average income, calculating all *bushi* (samurai) families together, was only about 35 *koku*. Middle-ranking samurai had on the average an income of about 100 *koku*. See Otto Ladstätter and Sepp Linhart, *China und Japan: Die Kulturen Ostasiens* (Vienna: Carl Ueberreuter Verlag, 1983), p. 354.

6. Hosaka Masayasu, *Tōjō Hideki to tennō no jidai* (Tōjō Hideki and the era of the emperor) (Tokyo: Gendai Jānarisumu, 1979), vol. 1, pp. 14–15.

7. Ibid., p. 16.

8. Georg Kerst, *Jacob Meckel, sein Leben, und sein Wirken in Deutschland und Japan* (Göttingen: Musterschmidt, 1970).

9. Marius B. Jansen, "The Manchurian Incident, 1931, Introduction," in James W. Morley, ed., *Japan Erupts: The London Naval Conference and the Manchurian Incident, 1928–1932* (New York: Columbia University Press, 1984), p. 132. For the relative importance of military spirit see Leonard A. Humphreys, *The Way of the Heavenly Sword: The Japanese Army in the*

1920's (Stanford: Stanford University Press, 1995), especially pp. 99–107; see p. 206, n. 24, for factions. See also Chapter 8, note 15, for factionalism.

10. Seki Hiroharu, "The Manchurian Incident, 1931," in Morley, *Japan Erupts*, pp. 146–147. The first group, the Futabakai, was composed of graduates from the fifteenth to eighteenth classes of the Army Academy. The second, the Kokusaku Kenkyūkai, was made up of graduates of the twenty-first to twenty-fifth classes. The new society, the Issekikai, was made up of graduates from the Army Academy, fifteenth to twenty-fifth classes, excepting the ninteenth class. See Humphreys, *Way of the Heavenly Sword*, pp. 110–116.

11. Jansen, "Manchurian Incident," p. 132; Seki, "Manchurian Incident," p. 147.

12. Humphreys, *Way of the Heavenly Sword*, p. 106; same page for the citation immediately below.

13. Shimada Toshihiko, "The Extension of Hostilities, 1931–1932," in Morley, *Japan Erupts*, p. 256.

14. The phrase "with respect to local administration" was added to the beginning of the sentence; ibid. There were long-standing differences of opinion about the competence and authority of the Army Ministry and general staff.

15. Akamatsu Diary, p. 163. For the same text with slight variations see Jōhō Yoshio, *Tōjō Hideki* (Tokyo: Fuyō Shobō, 1974), p. 420. Akamatsu's text is used here and below. Akamatsu Sadao, born Komatsu (1900–1982), was a career officer who attained the rank of colonel at the end of his career. He served as Tōjō's personal secretary from the time of his appointment as army minister in 1940. The diary was constructed from Akamatsu's earlier notes, the "Tōjō Memo." The original can be seen in the Bōeichō Bōeikenkūjo Senshishitsu, National Institute for Defense Studies (NIDS), Tokyo.

16. Sakamoto Tarō, Ienaga Saburō, Inoue Mitsusada, and Ōno Susumu, eds., *Nihon Shoki*, in *Nihon Koten Bungaku Taikei (NKBT)* (Tokyo: Iwanami Shoten, 1967), vol. 67, pp. 269–271; W. G. Aston, trans., *Nihongi* (London: Allen & Unwin, 1956), vol. 1, p. 176; Karl Florenz, *Die historischen Quellen der Shinto-Religion* (Göttingen: Vandenhoeck & Ruprecht, 1919), pp. 258–260.

17. All dates and events before the middle of the sixth century in Japan must be regarded critically. These early so-called historical events and their dates were "recorded" for political and social reasons in the eighth century and reflect actual happenings only vaguely if at all. According to another text, the *Kojiki* from the year 712, for example, Ise Shrine was established in 97 B.C. (Sujin 1). This too is pure fiction. See Kurano Kenji and Takeda Yūkichi, eds., *Kojiki; Norito*, in *NKBT*, vol. 1, p. 179; Florenz, *Quellen*, p. 96; Donald Philippi, trans., *Kojiki* (Princeton and Tokyo: Princeton and Tokyo University Presses, 1969), p. 199. For a discussion of the problems of dating in ancient Japanese history see Chapter 5, note 45.

18. See Clarence Holtom, *The Japanese Enthronement Ceremonies with an Account of the Imperial Regalia* (Tokyo: Sophia University Press, 1972).

19. Sakamoto et al., *NKBT*, vol. 67, pp. 213 and 580, n. 18; Aston, *Nihongi*, vol. 1, p. 132; Florenz, *Quellen*, pp. 239–240.

20. As a student in Japan I witnessed these protests and was teargassed in the process in downtown Tokyo.

21. Seiitai Shōgun ("Barbarian-Conquering Great General"): only three

others had been granted this title: Sakanoue Tamuramaro in 797, Fujiwara Tadabumi in 940, and Minamoto (Kiso) Yoshinaka in 1184. This title is to be distinguished from Chinjufu Shōgun ("Ezo-Pacifying General"), of which there were seventy, who "pacified" barbarians in the north. See Minoru Shinoda, *The Founding of the Kamakura Shogunate, 1180–1185* (New York: Columbia University Press, 1957), pp. 244–245. None before Yoritomo had established an independent government apparatus.

22. Jien (1155–1225), *Gukanshō*, in Okami Masao and Akamatsu Toshihide, eds., *NKBT*, vol. 86, pp. 275–276. See Delmer M. Brown and Ichirō Ishida, *The Future and the Past: A Translation and Study of the Gukanshō, an Interpretive History of Japan Written in 1219* (Berkeley: University of California Press, 1979), pp. 153–155, 407–408. For the development of the retired emperor *(insei)* institution see G. Cameron Hurst III, *Insei: Abdicated Sovereigns in the Politics of Late Heian Japan, 1086–1185* (New York: Columbia University Press, 1976). Some emperors wanted not only to reign but to actually rule. They were thwarted by the nobles, especially the Fujiwara, and also by their numerous ceremonial duties. To circumvent these hindrances a few abdicated, placed a minority-aged son or grandson on the throne, and sought to manipulate political developments from behind the throne.

23. *Gukanshō*, p. 282, and the editors' explanation on p. 513, n. 25. See Brown and Ishida, *Gukanshō*, pp. 160 and 334, n. 82.

24. *Gukanshō*, pp. 125–126. See Brown and Ishida, *Gukanshō*, p. 346. For a contemporary source describing this "war" see *Shōkyūki* (Tokyo: Hakubunkan, 1912–1915) *(Kokubun sōsho*, vol. 15). For a translation see William McCullough, trans., "Shōkyūki: An Account of the Shōkyū War," *Monumenta Nipponica* 19 (1964):163–215 and 21 (1966):420–453; and his "The Azuma Kagami Account of the Shōkyū War," *Monumenta Nipponica* 23 (1968): 102–155.

25. Akamatsu Diary, p. 163.

26. See Itō Takashi, Hirohashi Tadamitsu, and Katashima Norio, eds., *Tōjō naikaku sōridaijin kimitsu kiroku* (The prime minister's secret agenda during the Tōjō cabinet) (Tokyo: Tokyo Daigaku Shuppankai, 1990), passim, for the visits to shrines; cited hereafter as Tōjō Agenda.

27. Akamatsu Diary, p. 33.

28. Iwanami Yūjirō, ed., *Taiheiki*, in *NKBT*, vols. 34–36. The text was put together sometime in the fourteenth century; the author is unknown. Even during the middle ages these two insurrections—the "Shōkyū no ran" at the beginning of the thirteenth and the "Kemmu Shinsei" at the beginning of the fourteenth century—were compared. See Helen Craig McCullough, trans., *Taiheiki: A Chronicle of Medieval Japan* (New York: Columbia University Press, 1959), pp. 3–6.

29. *Taiheiki*, *NKBT*, vol. 34, pp. 216–224; McCullough, *Taiheiki*, pp. 181–188.

30. Mieno Makoto and Nakamura Atsuko, "Kusunoki Masashige shiseki" (Kusunoki Masashige's historical legacy), in Sato Kazuhiko, ed., *Kusunoki Masashige no subete* (All about Kusunoki Masashige) (Tokyo: Shinjinbutsu Ōraisha, 1989), pp. 229–240, especially pp. 232–233. The Sakurai Station is in Osaka: Osaka-fu, Mishima-gun, Shimamoto-chō, Sakurai itchōme. See Ivan

Morris, *The Nobility of Failure: Tragic Heroes in the History of Japan* (New York: Secker & Warburg, 1975), pp. 106–142.

31. H. Paul Varley, *Imperial Restoration in Medieval Japan* (New York: Columbia University Press, 1971), pp. 142–144.

32. Morris, *Nobility of Failure*, pp. 384–385, n. 6.83. See Jiro Numata, "Shigeno Yasutsugu and the Modern Tokyo Tradition of Historical Writing," in W. G. Beasley and E. G. Pulleyblank, eds., *Historians of China and Japan* (London: Oxford University Press, 1961), pp. 264–287.

33. See Kume Kunitake, "Shintō wa saiten no kozoku" (Shinto is an outmoded custom of worshiping heaven), *Shigakkai zasshi* (1891). Kume resigned in 1892 and moved to Tokyo Semmon Gakkō, later Waseda University, where another historian unpopular with imperial authorities also taught, Tsuda Sōkichi. Shigeno left one year later. For a discussion of Kume see Stefan Tanaka, *Japan's Orient: Rendering Pasts into History* (Berkeley: University of California Press, 1993), pp. 71–75.

34. Personal communication from Professor Nagae Tarō, National Institute for Defense Studies, 20 January 1994.

35. Kaizu Ichirō, "Kusunoki Masashige to Nihonjin: Kyōkasho ni miru Masashige-zō no hensen" (Kusunoki Masashige and the Japanese: The changing image of Masashige as seen in school textbooks), in Satō, *Kusunoki Masashige*, pp. 175–204. See also Carol Gluck, *Japan's Modern Myths: Ideology in the Late Meiji Period* (Princeton: Princeton University Press, 1985), p. 225, for a comment about Kusunoki's popularity.

36. From 1903 schoolbooks were officially regulated in the following subjects: ethics, history, Japanese language, and geography; Gluck, *Japan's Modern Myths*, p. 147. Kusunoki appears ever more frequently in these books, and he is also to be found in songbooks and calligraphy texts; Kaizu, "Kusunoki Masashige," p. 179.

37. Gluck, *Japan's Modern Myths*, pp. 149–150.

38. Akamatsu Diary, pp. 163–164, citing Tōjō. Kusunoki was made a prince posthumously because of his loyalty and service to the throne.

39. *Kodansha Encyclopedia of Japan* (Tokyo: Kodansha, 1983), vol. 2, p. 7.

40. Robert J. C. Butow, *Tojo and the Coming of the War* (Stanford: Stanford University Press, 1961), pp. 73–74.

41. Hosaka, *Tōjō Hideki*, vol. 1, p. 97.

42. Tōjō, as is well known, attempted to commit suicide before he was arrested but failed. Tōjō apparently felt, as did many others, that he should remain alive to take the blame for the war and shield the emperor. His reasons for attempting to do otherwise seem related to his sense of honor. He did not want to be tried by the victors. See Butow, *Tōjō*, pp. 449–469.

43. Butow, *Tojo*, pp. 42 and 307.

44. Hara Shirō, *Taisenryaku naki kaisen* (Beginning a war with no great strategy) (Tokyo: Hara Shobō, 1987), p. 253.

45. Yatsugi Kazuo, "Shōwa memo," in *Bunshun* 7 (1956); cited in Ōtani Keijirō, *Shōwa Kempeishi* (History of the Shōwa Kempeitai) (Tokyo: Misuzu Shobō, 1987), p. 442. Yatsugi was a confidant of Gen. Mutō Akira and was often in the Army Ministry. Therefore Ōtani regarded him as a reliable source. Ōtani Keijirō (1897–1976) was a career officer and member of the Kempeitai.

Shortly before the end of the war he was commander of the Kempeitai in Tokyo and later all of eastern Japan. The Kempeitai were a type of military police especially concerned with questions of loyalty to the emperor, as prescribed in the Meiji Constitution.

46. Hirozaki Sadamitsu, "Hishokan memo" (A cabinet secretary's memoranda), in Jōhō, *Tōjō Hideki*, p. 81. Meiji-Jingū we have already discussed. Tōgō-Jinja commemorates the naval hero from the Russo-Japanese war, Tōgō Heihachirō, who defeated the Russian fleet in 1905. Yasukuni-Jinja was, until the end of 1945, the official state shrine commemorating Japan's war dead.

47. Yatsugi, "Shōwa memo," pp. 442–443.

48. Ibid., pp. 453–454; quoted by Yatsugi.

49. Ibid.

50. Butow, *Tojo*, pp. 492–494. In fact, the trustworthiness of Tanaka's testimony during the war crimes trials was seriously questioned.

51. Tōjō Agenda, pp. 54–55.

52. Yatsugi, "Showā memo," pp. 442–443. The author gives no full names, and Katō's I could not find.

53. See Leslie Russell Oates, *Populist Nationalism in Prewar Japan: A Biography of Nakano Seigō* (Sydney: Allen & Unwin, 1985).

54. Jōhō, *Tōjō Hideki*, pp. 603–604. See Oates, *Populist Nationalism*, p. 104, for a short description of the article; see pp. 102–103 for a speech with similar content that Nakano made previously at Waseda University. Nakano had criticized the government earlier on many occasions without suffering any consequences.

55. Tōjō Agenda, pp. 276–281; Ōtani, *Shōwa Kempeishi*, p. 455. See also Oates, *Populist Nationalism*, pp. 111–113, for a short version. The other protesters associated with Nakano were Mitamura Takeo, Nakano's parliamentary assistant, and Amano Tatsuo, a lawyer and right-wing radical.

56. Ōtani, *Shōwa Kempeishi*, pp. 456–457.

57. Ibid., pp. 457–458.

58. Although distinctions between the emperor personally and the emperor system are emphasized in postwar defenses of Hirohito, most people in prewar Japan did not differentiate between the two. See Chapter 2, note 1.

59. Akamatsu Diary, p. 33.

60. Army Minister Tōjō Hideki, *Guntai naimuryō* (Army internal ordinances), 11 August 1943 (reprint, Tokyo: Ikeda Shoten, 1970).

61. Erik Erikson, *Kindheit und Gesellschaft*, trans. Marianne Eckhardt-Jaffé (Stuttgart: Klett-Cotta Verlag, 1971), p. 320.

62. John R. Pritchard and Sonia Magbanna Zaide, eds., *The Tokyo War Crimes Trial* (Complete transcripts of the proceedings of the International Military Tribunal for the Far East) (New York: Garland, 1981–), vol. 15, pp. 36779–36781. See Richard H. Minear, *Victor's Justice* (Tokyo: Tuttle, 1972), pp. 114–115, n. 83.

63. Minear, *Victor's Justice*, pp. 110–117.

64. Nezu Masashi, *Tennō to Shōwashi* (The emperor and Shōwa history) (Tokyo: Sanichi Shobō, 1976), vol. 2, p. 303. The supposition that U.S. government policy was greatly influenced by fear of the spread of communism in the Far East at this early date is usually presented in connection with justifying the A-bomb attacks at the end of the war. See Richard Rhodes, *The Making of*

the Atomic Bomb (New York: Simon & Schuster, 1986), pp. 621–644. The connection between the fear of communism and the generous treatment of the emperor after the war can be deduced from the situation then: General MacArthur demanded one million troops to quell social unrest should the emperor be put on trial. The communists could have used the uprisings for their own purposes. See Minear, *Victor's Justice*, pp. 111–112; Butow, *Tojo*, p. 503; Stephan E. Ambrose, *Rise to Globalism: American Foreign Policy Since 1938* (New York: Penguin Books, 1985), 4th rev. ed., pp. 70–72.

65. "Hoshino Naoki shuki," in Jōhō, *Tōjō Hideki*, p. 670. See also Col. Sakakibara Kazue, "Tōjō Hideki Taishō Ōmori kōchishonai ni okeru kangae," December 1945, ibid., pp. 746–754, for a similar statement by Tōjō. This is an interview with Tōjō from November 1945. The original manuscript can be seen in the NIDS Library, Tokyo.

66. See David A. Titus, "Introduction," in James W. Morley, ed., *Japan's Road to the Pacific War: The Final Confrontation: Japan's Negotiations with the United States, 1941*, trans. David A. Titus (New York: Columbia University Press, 1994), p. xxx.

67. Ōe Shinobu, *Tōsuiken* (The authority of supreme command) (Tokyo: Nihon Hyōronsha, 1983), p. 171. The phrase in Japanese is "Tatakai wa sōzō no chichi, bunka no haha de aru."

68. Morley, *The Final Confrontation*, p. v. Although a German authority assured me that the citation is from Clausewitz, I was not able to find it in the original. But *Vom Kriege* was translated into Japanese and widely read by military officers even before the Russo-Japanese War (1904–1905). See Werner Hahlweg, "Vorrede," in Carl von Clausewitz, *Vom Kriege*, 19th ed. (Bonn: Dümmlers Verlag, 1980), pp. 124–125.

Chapter 5: Scientism, History, and Confucianism

1. For typical narratives see Ōkita Saburō, Ōgiya Shōzō, and Kusayanagi Taizō, eds., *Tennō Hirohito* (Emperor Hirohito) (Tokyo: Kōdansha, 1986), p. 17. See also Nezu Masashi, *Tennō to Shōwashi* (The emperor and Shōwa history) (Tokyo: Sanichi Shobō, 1976), vol. 1, p. 13. These two secondary sources are completely different in persuasion. Ōkita and his colleagues have produced a picture-book "history" of the Shōwa emperor's reign. It is uncritical, contains some factual errors, and is typical of laudatory works about the imperial house. Nezu is an independent author specializing in Japanese history. His account is critical but contains unsubstantiated rumors and is slanted against the imperial house as an institution.

2. Ōkita et al., *Tennō Hirohito*, pp. 24–27. Nationalism refers throughout this study to a predisposition favoring one's place of birth or childhood, one's mother tongue, and the customs and folkways of one's country. It is a combination of primitive feelings and convictions that manifest themselves in many as a tendency to denigrate others who do not conform with this predisposition. See Hans Fenske, Dieter Mertens, Wolfgang Reinhard, and Klaus Rosen, *Geschichte der politischen Ideen: Von Homer bis zur Gegenwart* (Frankfurt: Fischer Taschenbuch Verlag, 1987), pp. 473–482. Obviously education in other countries was nationalistic too. The following account is intended, not as a comparison with other nations, but as a correction of the widely held belief that Hirohito's education was largely free of such elements.

3. Stephen S. Large, *Emperor Hirohito and Shōwa Japan: A Political Biography* (London: Routledge, 1992), p. 17.

4. Ōtake Shūichi, *Tennō no gakkō* (The emperor's school) (Tokyo: Bungei Shunjūsha, 1986), p. 10.

5. S. N. Eisenstadt, "Education and Political Development," in Don C. Piper and Taylor Cole, eds., *Post-Primary Education and Political and Economic Development* (Durham: Duke University Press, 1964), p. 27.

6. Carol Gluck, *Japan's Modern Myths: Ideology in the Late Meiji Period* (Princeton: Princeton University Press, 1985), especially chap. 5, "Civil Morality," and chap. 6, "Social Foundations," pp. 102–212. Among the numerous studies focusing on Japanese education the classic example is Ronald P. Dore, *Education in Tokugawa Japan* (Berkeley: University of California Press, 1965). For two noteworthy studies of postwar education see Benjamin C. Duke, *The Japanese School: Lessons for Industrial America* (New York: Praeger, 1986), and Thomas Rohlen, *Japan's High Schools* (Berkeley: University of California Press, 1983). For studies of prewar education see Ivan P. Hall, *Mori Arinori* (Cambridge, Mass.: Harvard University Press, 1973); Harold J. Wray, "Changes and Continuity in Japanese Images of the Kokutai and Roles toward the Outside World: A Content Analysis of Japanese Textbooks, 1903–1945," Ph.D. dissertation, University of Hawai'i, 1971; Wilbur M. Freidell, "Government Ethics Textbooks in Late Meiji Japan," *Journal of Asian Studies* 29 (1970): 823–834; and Donald T. Roden, *Schooldays in Imperial Japan: A Study of the Culture of a Student Elite* (Berkeley: University of California Press, 1980).

7. See Charles D. Sheldon, "Japanese Aggression and the Emperor, 1931–1941, from Contemporary Diaries," *Modern Asian Studies* 10(1) (1976): 1–40.

8. Stefan Tanaka, *Japan's Orient: Rendering Pasts into History* (Berkeley: University of California Press, 1993), p. 16. Tanaka is referring here to the entire generation, not just Hirohito's educators.

9. See Ōtake, *Tennō no gakkō*, for the most detailed description of this school. I follow his terminology and use the short form "Ogakumonjo" instead of the formal designation "Tōgū Gogakumonjo" in the following.

10. Telegram quoted in Ōtake, *Tennō no gakkō*, p. 59.

11. Gluck, *Japan's Modern Myths*, pp. 221–225. Gluck quotes a discussion in *Taiyō*—according to Gluck the most widely read and influential opinion magazine at that time—from November 1912: "Nothing has so stirred up the sentiments of the nation since the vendetta of the forty-seven *rōnin* in 1703" (p. 221).

12. Related in May 1941 at a hotel in Matsue-shi, Shimane-ken; cited in Ōkita et al., *Tennō Hirohito*, p. 20.

13. William H. Honan, *Visions of Infamy* (New York: St. Martin's Press, 1991), p. 37.

14. Bōeichō Bōeikenshūjo Senshishitsu, *Daihon'ei Kaigunbu, Rengōkantai (1) kaisen made* (Imperial Headquarters, Navy, Combined Fleet [1] to the beginning of the war), in *Senshi sōsho*, vol. 91, pp. 115, 124, 189, 214. See also Honan, *Visions of Infamy*, pp. 73–77.

15. Satō Kunio, *Tōgō Heihachirō: Gensui no bannen* (Tōgō Heihachirō: The fleet admiral's last years) (Tokyo: Asahi Shimbunsha, 1990), p. 50.

16. Ōtake, *Tennō no gakkō*, p. 10. Ōtake cites the content of this education to show the opposite of my thesis: he maintains it enabled the emperor to pre-

serve his liberal, constitutionalist posture in the face of much controversy. See p. 12.

17. Ōkita et al., *Tennō Hirohito*, pp. 19–21; Nezu, *Tennō to Shōwashi*, p. 14.

18. Ōtake, *Tennō no gakkō*, p. 14.

19. Citation from Toshiaki Kawahara, *Hirohito and His Times* (Tokyo: Kodansha, 1990), p. 25. Large, *Hirohito and Shōwa Japan*, p. 18, has summed up Sugiura's influence as "ethically conservative and politically nationalistic ... but ... very open to what the world could offer both to a future monarch and to Japan's continuing national quest for wealth and power generally."

20. Sugiura Shigetake, *Rinri goshinkō sōan* (Draft of the ethics lectures to the crown prince) (Tokyo: Yamato Bunkō, 1984), vol. 1, p. 1.

21. Ibid., pp. 1–3, for this and the following two paragraphs.

22. This is the last line of the rescript. For the official English translation published by the Japanese government in 1907 see Ryusaku Tsunoda et al., *Sources of Japanese Tradition* (New York: Columbia University Press, 1958), pp. 646–647.

23. Of course Meiji government leaders were "moderate" in comparison to their Tokugawa predecessors. Their policies were not extremist in comparison to the militarists of the 1930s, either, but they were carried out in a conservative manner that required sacrifices from many and restricted participation in government to a chosen few.

24. Tanaka, *Japan's Orient*, pp. 18–19.

25. Ibid., p. 18, referring to Jürgen Habermas.

26. Kuga Katsunan, "Shidōron" (Concerning leadership), originally published in the newspaper *Nippon* (3 November 1890), in Nishida Taketoshi and Uete Michinari, eds., *Kuga Katsunan zenshū* (Collected writings of Kuga Katsunan) (Tokyo: Misuzu Shobō, 1968–1975), vol. 2, pp. 749–750.

27. Gluck, *Japan's Modern Myths*, pp. 112–113. Gluck translates *"kokuminshugi"* as "nationalism"; the standard reference work *Kōjien* says to see *"kokkashugi,"* also usually translated as "nationalism." David Titus in a critique of an earlier version of this book suggested "principles of citizenship," and in this context I agree with him.

28. Miyake Setsurei, "Yohai kokusuishugi o shōdō suru, ani! gūzen naranya" (Advocating our policy of national essence, ah! not by chance.), (18 May 1889, in Motoyama Yukihiko, ed., *Miyake Setsureishū* (Collection of Miyake Setsurei's writings), *Kindai Nihon shisō taikei* (Great works on modern Japanese thought) (Tokyo: Chikuma Shobō, 1975), pp. 251–253, for this and the following. *"Kokusuishugi"* is normally translated as "nationalism."

29. See page 4 and note 13 in the Introduction.

30. Gluck, *Japan's Modern Myths*, p. 154; *Industrial Union Bulletin*, International Workers of the World, 2 November 1907, as cited in Gluck, n. 230, pp. 353–354.

31. Ōmachi Keigetsu and Ikari Shisan, *Sugiura Shigetake sensei* (Teacher Sugiura Shigetake) (Kyoto: Shibunkaku Shuppan, 1986), pp. 91–93. This is a classic example of a laudatory publication about a distinguished scholar presented to him on an important birthday late in life. This volume, presented to Sugiura on his seventieth birthday, is a flattering biography with many excerpts from his writings.

32. Ibid., pp. 133–141.

33. Ibid., p. 161.

34. Ibid. The first saying: "Makanu tani wa uenu"; the second saying: "Mitsureba, kakuru."

35. Ibid., p. 165. From "Shintō Seen from the Point of View of Science," in *Shōkō jukuhō*, 1911. The word translated as "[spiritual] energy" refers to human vitality and spiritual force. The word translated as "[physical] energy" refers to power in the physical and political sense of the term. "Conservation of force" is written in "Japanese-English" using *katakana* phonetic symbols.

36. Ibid., pp. 165–166.

37. Harry R. Sullivan, *Walter Bagehot* (Boston: G. K. Hall, 1975), pp. 111–112.

38. Ibid., pp. 138–140, for a summary and references.

39. Ibid., pp. 112–125. It is well to remember that Gregor Mendel's discovery of the laws of genetics was still unknown; for lack of a better one, Jean Lamarck's (1744–1829) theory was accepted by many.

40. Ibid., p. 113.

41. Joachim C. Fest, *Hitler*, trans. Richard and Clara Winston (London: Weidenfeld & Nicolson, 1974), pp. 54–56.

42. *Nippon*, no. 778, 22 July 1891, p. 2. See *Kuga Katsunan zenshū geppō* (Monthly report, collected writings of Kuga Katsunan), no. 3, September 1969, p. 12. See also Gluck, *Japan's Modern Myths*, p. 131. She translates "Tōhō Kyōkai" as "Oriental Society." Here I follow a suggestion by Titus. For Inoue see Klaus Antoni, *Der Himmlische Herrscher und Sein Staat: Essays zur Stellung des Tennō im modernen Japan* (Munich: Judicium, 1991), pp. 76–99, "Inoue Tetsujirō (1855–1944) und die Entwicklung der Staatsideologie in der zweiten Hälfte der Meiji-Zeit."

43. Ōmachi and Ikari, *Sugiura Sensei*, pp. 221–270, 293–308.

44. Nezu, *Tennō to Shōwashi*, p. 15; Sugiura, *Rinri goshinkō sōan*, passim. Eleven lectures were held on the Imperial Rescript on Education between October 1914 and March 1915. See Sugiura, vol. 3, pp. 1101–1176. These lectures are of interest but not important for the present theme. Here I wish to show that Sugiura slanted his presentation in a nationalistic, imperial house–centered direction. Since the Imperial Rescript on Education needs no adaptation for this purpose, Sugiura's interpretation is not considered here.

45. This is a direct quote from the *Nihon Shoki* (720). See Sakamoto Tarō, Ienaga Saburō, Inoue Mitsusada, and Ōno Susumu, eds., *Nihon Shoki, NKBT*, vols. 67, pp. 152–153; W. G. Aston, trans., *Nihongi* (London: Allen & Unwin, 1956), vol. 1, p. 83; here I have used Aston's translation. Though a subject of debate among Japanese experts, the two titles *"Nihon Shoki"* and *"Nihongi"* are used interchangeably. The dates cited from the *Nihon Shoki* are to facilitate placing events in traditional time and are for general reference only. This is in no way an affirmation of the historical reliability of these dates. Generally, the earlier a date the less reliable it is. A similar passage appears in the *Kojiki* (712) and is said to be the high point of that part of the book. See Kurano Kenji and Takeda Yūkichi, eds., *Kojiki; Norito, NKBT*, vol. 1, pp. 126–127; Donald Philippi, trans., *Kojiki* (Princeton and Tokyo: Princeton and Tokyo University Presses, 1969), p. 140. " 'This mirror—have (it with you) as my spirit, and worship it just as you would worship in my presence' "; Philippi's translation. For a discussion of the problems of dating in ancient Japanese his-

tory see André Wedemeyer, *Japanische Frühgeschichte* (Tokyo: MOAG, 1930), suppl. II, and Sakamoto et al., *Nihon Shoki,* vol. 67, pp. 561–562, n. 10, and p. 347, n. 39; mythological dates have been repeated faithfully in many modern history books despite their lack of factual foundation. They are given here for orientation only.

46. Kitabatake Chikafusa (1292–1354), author of the *Jinnō Shōtōki;* Nakae Tōju (1608–1648), founder of the Wang-yang Ming (Yōmeigaku) school of Neo-Confucianism in Japan; Yamaga Sokō (1622–1685), founder of Classical Learning (Kogaku); Rai Sanyō (1780–1832), Neo-Confucian historian and author of *Nihon gaishi.*

47. Sugiura, *Rinri goshinkō sōan,* vol. 1, pp. 1–4.

48. Tanaka, *Japan's Orient,* p. 45.

49. Inoue Tetsujirō, *Nihon kogakuha no tetsugaku* (Philosophy of the ancient learning school in Japan) (Tokyo: Fusanbō, 1931), pp. 81–82.

50. Hayashi Razan, "Jimmu tennō-ron" (On Emperor Jimmu), in *Hayashi Razan bunshū* (Collected writings of Hayashi Razan) (Tokyo: Pelikansha, 1979), p. 281. See Ryusaku Tsunoda et al., *Sources of Japanese Tradition,* pp. 359–360; here I have used Tsunoda's translation.

51. Inoue Tetsujirō, *Kokumin dōtoku gairon* (Outline of our national ethics), rev. ed. (Tokyo: Sanseidō, 1922), pp. 144–145.

52. One must remember that Japanese in the fifteenth century thought of all three traditions as "religious" though we now may classify Confucianism as a philosophical system or ethical teaching. See Ichijō Kaneyoshi, *Nihon Shoki sanso* (Commentary on the *Nihon Shoki*), in Tenri Toshokan Zenhonsō-sho, *Nihon Shoki sanso, Nihon Shokishō* (Tokyo: Yagi Shoten, 1977), vol. 27. See p. 133 for the mirror and wisdom and p. 100 for the sword and will *(iyoku);* the jewel is mentioned in a few places, but I was unable to find this specific interpretation. For a study of Ichijō see Klaus-Albrecht Pretzell, "Das Bunmei-ittō-ki und das Shōdan-chiyō: Zwei Lehrschriften des Ichijō Kanera" (dissertation, Hamburg University, 1966), especially pp. 84–86 and 94.

53. For a comparison of Kitabatake and Ichijō see Wajima Yoshio, *Chūsei no Jugaku* (Medieval Confucianism) (Tokyo: Yoshikawa Kōbunkan, 1965), especially pp. 159–162.

54. Kitabatake Chikafusa, *Jinnō Shōtōki,* in Iwasa Tadashi et al., eds., *Jinnō Shōtōki; Masukagami, NKBT,* vol. 87, p. 41; H. Paul Varley, trans., *A Chronicle of Gods and Sovereigns* (New York: Columbia University Press, 1980), p. 49. For an interpretation that emphasizes the nationalistic content of Shinto and matching character of the Japanese people see Inoue, *Kokumin dōtoku gairon,* "Shintō to Kokutai," pp. 86–103; summarized in Antoni, *Himmlische Herrscher,* pp. 94–95. The interpretation, in line with the *Jinnō Shōtōki,* that "legitimacy theory in Japan shifts from the Sun Goddess' protection of the imperial line to its divine descent," is supported by the Japanese editor of the text, Iwasa, its American translator, Varley, Ishida Ichirō, and others. This transition seems to have been ignored by the National Learning school (Kokugaku) of the Tokugawa period; Antoni, "Der 'göttliche Untertan,' " ibid., pp. 65–66. For this reason, perhaps, it was later forgotten or ignored. This is not to deny that descent was a part of early mythology. (See the Introduction and Appendix 8.) It is to emphasize protection rather than descent as the basis of the authority of the imperial house up until the late fourteenth century.

55. Kinoshita Michio, *Sokkin nisshi* (Shorthand diary) (Tokyo: Bungei Shunjūsha, 1990), pp. 89–90. See Herbert P. Bix, "The Showa Emperor's 'Monologue' and the Problem of War Responsibility," *Journal of Japanese Studies* 18 (2) (Summer 1992): 320–321.

56. Emiko Ohnuki-Tierney, "The Emperor of Japan as Diety (Kami)," *Ethnology* 30(3) (1991): 199–215.

57. *Jinnō Shōtōki, NKBT,* vol. 87, p. 61; Varley, *Chronicle,* p. 77.

58. James Legge, *The Chinese Classics* (Hong Kong: Hong Kong University Press, 1970), vol. III, "Shoo-King," p. 333. "The three virtues: The first is correctness and straightforwardness; the second, strong rule; and the third, mild rule"; see Tsunoda et al., *Sources of Japanese Tradition,* p. 281, n. 8.

59. *Jinnō Shōtōki, NKBT,* vol. 87, p. 61; Varley, *Chronicle,* p. 78.

60. *Kojiki-den* II, p. 800; Philippi, *Kojiki,* p. 140, n. 9. See Shigeru Matsumoto, *Motoori Norinaga, 1730–1801* (Cambridge, Mass.: Harvard University Press, 1970), pp. 92–93.

61. Philippi, *Kojiki,* indicates in a note that it was the grandson who received the imperial regalia, but the text is in fact not clear. For the texts and translations see note 45 above.

62. Tarō Sakamoto, *The Six National Histories* ("Rikkokushi"), trans. John S. Brownlee (Vancouver: University of British Columbia Press; Tokyo: University of Tokyo Press, 1991), pp. 55–56. Sakamoto seeks to preserve the authenticity of these ancient texts and protect their value as historical sources. Since he relegates the Sun Goddess to a "secondary position," he discredits the association (made by Kitabatake, Sugiura, and Meiji leaders) of the Sun Goddess with the first person to descend to earth to establish the imperial house and the great country Imperial Japan. Thereby doubts arise about the uniqueness and significance of the "true line of descent" and the transmission of the imperial regalia in general and the mirror in particular to the imperial house.

63. John S. Brownlee, "Translator's Introduction," in Sakamoto, *Six National Histories,* pp. xxvi–xxviii.

64. In Japan the historical reliability of all events and their dates before the mid-sixth century must be evaluated very carefully. For a discussion of this problem see note 45 above.

65. Tanaka, *Japan's Orient,* p. 21.

66. See Bernd Martin, "Deutsche Geschichtswissenschaft als Instrument nationaler Selbstfindung in Japan," in Gangolf Hübinger et al., eds., *Universalgeschichte und Nationalgeschichten* (Freiburg: Rombach Verlag, 1994), p. 214.

67. From 1883 Riess worked as a copyist for Ranke but probably met him only two or three times. Properly speaking he was a student of Hans Delbrück, his "Doktorvater." He was also influenced, according to Riess himself, by the medievalist Harry Bresslau and the Prussian historian Johann Gustav Droysen; Martin, "Deutsche Geschichtswissenschaft," pp. 215–217. For an example of the assumption that Reiss was a student of Ranke, see Tanaka, *Japan's Orient,* pp. 25–26.

68. Tanaka, *Japan's Orient,* p. 65.

69. Brownlee, "Translator's Introduction," pp. xxiii–xxiv.

70. See Shiratori Kurakichi, "Kokutai to Jukyō" (National polity and Confucianism), in Shiratori Kiyoshi, ed., *Shiratori Kurakichi zenshū* (Collected

works of Shiratori Kurakichi) (Tokyo: Iwanami Shoten, 1969–1971), vol. 10, pp. 276–289, for this and the following summary of Shiratori's lecture to Hirohito on Confucianism and Japanese culture.

71. This is a paraphrase. For a translation of this section of the essay see Tanaka, *Japan's Orient*, p. 130.

72. Compare with Tanaka, *Japan's Orient*, pp. 117–122.

73. For the situation in early Japan see Peter Wetzler, "Yoshishige no Yasutane: Lineage, Learning, Office, and Amida's Pure Land" (Ph.D. dissertation, University of California, Berkeley, 1977), pp. 8–59.

74. Tanaka, *Japan's Orient*, p. 119.

75. Ibid., p. 122.

76. "Birushanabutsu" in Japanese. Although the Sanskrit term ("Vairocana") originally referred to the sun, it came to refer to the infinite knowledge of the Buddha and is the main object of veneration in Kegon Buddhism, one of the six schools first introduced to Japan. For a brief synopsis of the teachings see Masaharu Anesaki, *History of Japanese Religion* (Tokyo: Tuttle, 1963), pp. 93–94.

77. Wing-Tsit Chan, *A Source Book in Chinese Philosophy* (Princeton: Princeton University Press, 1963), p. 724. See Tanaka, *Japan's Orient*, p. 127 and n. 35, for a summary of the debate in China.

78. See *Shiratori zenshū*, vol. 10, p. 276, for the reminder; see vol. 10, pp. 249–260, for this lecture.

79. Here Shiratori uses the generally acknowledged Chinese character 仁, usually translated as "benevolence"; see *Analects*, passim. The combination *jinji* 仁慈 is standard Japanese (found in the *Kōjien*); it appears that Shiratori used it to express a contrast with the classical Chinese; it is a combination of the Confucian character and a character used more often in Buddhist works. The character 慈 is the translation of the Pali *mettā* (Sanskrit *maitra*), meaning love and affection for all living beings producing a profound sense of happiness.

80. *NKBT*, vol. 67, pp. 570–571, n. 19; Jean Herbert, *Shintō: The Fountainhead of Japan* (New York: Stein & Day, 1967), pp. 153–154, 294–296.

81. Brownlee, "Translators Preface," p. xxiv. For an English-language example of Tsuda's writings see Sōkichi Tsuda, "On the Stages of the Formation of Japan as a Nation and the Origin of the Belief in the Perpetuity of the Imperial Family," in Japanese National Commission for UNESCO, comp., *Philosophical Studies of Japan* (Tokyo: Japan Society for the Promotion of Science, 1963), vol. 4, pp. 49–78.

82. See Yun-tai Tam, "Rationalism vs. Nationalism: Tsuda Sōkichi," in John S. Brownlee, ed., *History in the Service of the Japanese Nation* (Toronto: Joint Centre on Modern East Asia, 1983), pp. 165–188.

83. *Shiratori zenshū*, vol. 1, pp. 418–512. Here the selection is entitled "Kōtenhara to tensonkōrin no shō" (Chapter on the plain of high heaven and the descent of the heavenly grandson).

84. Ibid., p. 441.

85. Ienaga Saburō, *Nihon bunkashi* (Cultural history of Japan), 2nd ed. (Tokyo: Iwanami Shoten, 1982), passim. See also the introduction to the German translation, Karl Friedrich Zahl, "Einleitung des Übersetzers," in Ienaga Saburō, *Kulturgeschichte Japans* (Munich: Judicium, 1990), pp. 8–20, especially

pp. 11–14. "Ienaga setzt die Mittel der individualisierenden Geschichtsschreibung bewusst ein, um das Spannungsverhältnis zwischen der Kontinuität ererbter Strukturen und ihrer Herausforderung durch exogene Kräfte zu kennzeichnen" (p. 13).

86. The true extent of this interest is not clear. See Chapter 6, note 60.

Chapter 6: Ancient Institutions and Foreign Cultures

1. Sugiura Shigetake, *Rinri goshinkō sōan* (Draft of the ethics lectures to the crown prince) (Tokyo: Yamato Bunkō, 1984), vol. 2, pp. 453–454.

2. See *Nihon Shoki*, 720, NKBT, vols. 67–68; Empress Kōgyoku, Emperor Kotoku, Empress Saimei, and Emperor Tenji, vol. 68, pp. 236–381; Aston, *Nihongi*, vol. 2, pp. 171–300. Tarō Sakamoto, *The Six National Histories* ("Rikkokushi"), trans. John S. Brownlee (Vancouver: University of British Columbia Press; Tokyo: University of Tokyo Press, 1991), p. 47, shares this evaluation.

3. Officially he became successor to the throne after Emperor Meiji's death when his father automatically became emperor in 1912, but the investiture ceremony was held later on 3 November 1916.

4. See Sugiura, *Rinri goshinkō sōan*, vol. 2, pp. 448–455, for the preceding introduction and the following. Yamato Takeru, a mythological figure, was crown prince during the mythological reign of Emperor Keikō (r. 71–130).

5. Crown Prince Shōtoku actually lived when indicated, but he could not have accomplished all that has been attributed to him.

6. For the Seventeen-Article Constitution: *Nihon Shoki*, 604, Fourth Month, Third Day; NKBT, vol. 68, pp. 180–186; Aston, *Nihongi*, vol. 2, pp. 128–133.

7. See *Nihon Shoki*, 642–643; NKBT, vol. 68, pp. 243–254; Aston, *Nihongi*, vol. 2, pp. 178–185. Other texts that Sugiura might have consulted, such as the *Jinnō Shōtōki* and the *Dainihonshi* (Great history of Japan) from the end of the seventeenth century, give only abbreviated accounts of this episode. See Kitabatake Chikafusa, *Jinnō Shōtōki*, in Iwasa Tadashi et al., eds., *Jinnō Shōtōki; Masukagami*, NKBT, vol. 87, pp. 96–97; Varley, *Chronicle*, pp. 130–131; Tokugawa Mitsukuni (1628–1700) et al., *Dainihonshi* (Great history of Japan), ed. Gikō Seitan Sambyakunen Kinenkai (Tokyo: Dainihon Yūbenkai, 1928–1929), pp. 109 and 123–124; Yamaji Yakichi, Yamaji Aizan, and Nishida Keishi, *Yakubun Dainihonshi* (Translation [into modern Japanese] of the Great history of Japan) (Tokyo: Kōraku Shoin, 1912), pp. 112 and 127–128.

8. Prince Konoe Fumimaro (1891–1945), prime minister and imperial confidant in the 1930s and 1940s, was the head of this extended family in prewar Japan. One reason for his selection as prime minister and his access to Hirohito was this long-standing precedent.

9. This and other events during Hirohito's reign are dealt with in more detail in preceding chapters and in the Conclusion.

10. *Nihon Shoki*, 643, Eleventh Month; NKBT, vol. 68, pp. 250–251; Aston, *Nihongi*, vol. 2, p. 182. Translation edited and emphasis added.

11. *Nihon Shoki*, 643, Eleventh Month; NKBT, vol. 68, p. 252; Aston, *Nihongi*, vol. 2, p. 183; *Jinnō Shōtōki*, NKBT, vol. 87, p. 97; Varley, *Chronicle*, p. 130.

12. *Nihon Shoki*, 660, Seventh Month, and 661, First Month, NKBT, vol. 68, pp. 336–337 and 348–349; Aston, *Nihongi*, vol. 2, pp. 258–259 and 270.

13. See Sugiura, *Rinri goshinkō sōan*, vol. 2, pp. 478–487, for the following.

14. "Imperial Rescript on Education," in Ryusaku Tsunoda et al., *Sources of Japanese Tradition* (New York: Columbia University Press, 1958), p. 647.

15. *Analects*, bk. 8, chap. 21; James Legge, trans., *Confucius: Confucian Analects, The Great Learning, and The Doctrine of the Mean* (New York: Dover, 1971), p. 215. King Yü was the mythical founder of the Hsia dynasty, 2205 B.C., in China.

16. Sugiura, *Rinri goshinkō sōan*, vol. 2, p. 487.

17. For Kuga, Miyake, and Inoue see Chapter 5.

18. "Kokkai kaisetsu ni kansuru kengi" (Proposal on the establishment of a national assembly), in Ōyama Azusa, ed., *Yamagata Aritomo ikensho* (Yamagata Aritomo opinion papers) (Tokyo: Hara Shobō, 1966), p. 85; translated in Carol Gluck, *Japan's Modern Myths: Ideology in the Late Meiji Period* (Princeton: Princeton University Press, 1985), p. 119. For a slightly different translation see Robert F. Hackett, *Yamagata Aritomo in the Rise of Modern Japan, 1838–1922* (Cambridge, Mass.: Harvard University Press, 1971), p. 93.

19. See also Gluck, *Japan's Modern Myths*, pp. 112–114.

20. Ibid., pp. 9–10.

21. For China: *Nippon* (29 July and 2 August 1894) in *Kuga Katsunan zenshū* (Collected writings of Kuga Katsunan), ed. Nishida Taketoshi and Uete Michinari (Tokyo: Misuzu Shobō, 1968–1975), vol. 4, pp. 563–564 and 567–568. For Russia: *Nippon* (13 January 1904), ibid., vol. 8, pp. 229–230. See also Gluck, *Japan's Modern Myths*, p. 114.

22. Ōtake Shūichi, *Tennō no gakkō* (The emperor's school) (Tokyo: Bungei Shunjūsha, 1986), p. 16.

23. For a recent sudy see Bernd Martin, "Verhängnisvolle Wahlverwandschaft: Deutsche Einflüsse auf die Entstehung des modernen Japans," in Jost Düffler et al., eds., *Deutschland in Europa: Kontinuität und Bruch: Gedenkschrift für Andreas Hillgruber* (Berlin: Ulstein Verlag, 1990), pp. 97–116.

24. Thomas A. Kohut, *Wilhelm II and the Germans: A Study in Leadership* (New York: Oxford University Press, 1991), p. vii.

25. Wolfgang J. Mommsen, *Bürgerstolz und Weltmachtstreben: Deutschland unter Wilhelm II: 1890 bis 1918* (Berlin: Propyläen Verlag, 1995), p. 291.

26. Thomas Nipperdey, *Deutsche Geschichte 1866–1918*, vol. 2: *Machtstaat vor der Demokratie* (Munich: C. H. Beck, 1992), p. 826. Imperialism at this time was that of the Germans, not the Kaiser (pp. 885–888).

27. See Sugiura, *Rinri goshinkō sōan*, vol. 3, pp. 1055–1061, for this and the following on Wilhelm II.

28. Ottokar Czernin, *Im Weltkriege* (Berlin: Ulstein, 1919), p. 70: "Der verlorene Krieg hat die Monarchen hinweggefegt, aber die Republik wird sich ihrerseits nur halten, wenn sie den Völkern die Überzeugung beibringt, dass es ihr besser gelingt, die Massen zufriedenzustellen, als es den Monarchien gelungen ist, ein Beweis, den—wie mir scheint—die deutsch-österreichische Republik bisher noch schuldig geblieben ist."

29. Ibid., pp. 77–78: "Den Monarchen fehlt diese Lebensschule, und sie taxieren die Psyche der Welt daher gewöhnlich falsch." The Japanese word used here for the German emperor, *"teiō,"* might refer to Wilhelm II in particular or to emperors in general; here the German obviously means the latter. Moreover, with respect to points III and IV, at least one prominent German histo-

rian believes that Wilhelm was a mirror image of the German folk at that time: he was neither deceived by them nor terribly different from them; Nipperdey, *Machtstaat*, pp. 802–905.

30. Alois von Schönburg (1858–1944), commander of the Sixth Army on the Piave in the Austro-Hungarian Armed Forces, was vice president of the House of Schönburg-Hartenstein (1898–1918). Here Czernin is writing about Schönburg's manner with Emperor Karl of Austria-Hungary. Sugiura obviously errs in assuming the comment was about Wilhelm II.

31. Czernin, *Im Weltkriege*, p. 83, has "dutzendweise" (dozens of people).

32. Czernin (p. 90) is writing about the emperor's activities prior to the war and his possible responsibility for starting World War I. It is not, as Sugiura led his listeners to believe, a general statement about Wilhelm II and his advisers.

33. See Burton Watson, *Records of the Grand Historian of China: Translated from the "Shih chi" of Ssu-Ma Ch'ien* (New York: Columbia University Press, 1961), vol. 1, pp. 14, 47–48.

34. Czernin, *Im Weltkriege*, p. 79, describes Ludendorff very positively: he was natural and self-confident in the presence of Wilhelm II and not servile in manner.

35. Tsunoda et al., *Sources*, p. 644; translation adapted by the author. For the original see *Kokushi daijiten* (Great dictionary of national history) (Tokyo: Yoshikawa Kōbunkan, 1979–1993), vol. 5, p. 582. The translation in *Kodansha Encyclopedia of Japan* (Tokyo: Kodansha, 1983), vol. 1, p. 267, is flawed.

36. Gluck, *Japan's Modern Myths*, p. 74, n. 6, remarks that this line, though in the original, is not included in the Tsunoda translation. It is not in the version cited in the *Kokushi daijiten* either. According to Sugiura this and the following lines should also be included.

37. Sugiura, *Rinri goshinkō sōan*, vol. 2, pp. 564–565. Sugiura does not include the introductory paragraph of the oath reproduced here; it is not always cited with the body of the text.

38. W. G. Beasley, *The Modern History of Japan* (New York: Praeger, 1963), p. 101. Satsuma and Chōshū, present-day Kagoshima and Yamaguchi prefectures, were leaders of the restoration.

39. Gotoba (1180–1239) reigned from 1193 to 1198. Thereafter he attempted to influence politics from behind the throne as a "retired emperor" *(insei)*. For the significance of this practice see G. Cameron Hurst III, *Insei: Abdicated Sovereigns in the Politics of Late Heian Japan 1086–1185* (New York: Columbia University Press, 1976).

40. For the Kemmu Restoration see H. Paul Varley, *Imperial Restoration in Medieval Japan* (New York: Columbia University Press, 1971), pp. 66–94.

41. The extent to which liberal ideals about individual rights and equality before the law were realized in countries like France, Great Britain, and the United States might also be questioned. One must remember, however, that these ideals were cited in Japan mainly for the sake of building a strong centralized state whereas they were proposed in the West to advocate personal freedom.

42. Germaine A. Hoston, "The State, Modernity, and the Fate of Liberalism in Prewar Japan," *Journal of Asian Studies* 51 (1992): 287–316.

43. Stephen S. Large, *Emperor Hirohito and Shōwa Japan: A Political Biography* (London: Routledge, 1992), p. 22. Large's references to postwar English

scholars on constitutional monarchy seem misleading. Obviously the postwar scholars could not know what King George said to Hirohito.

44. Ibid., pp. 21–22. Elsewhere Large says that Sugiura "encouraged him [Hirohito] to respect the principles of constitutional monarchy in emulation of Meiji" (p. 212). But Sugiura never lectured on this topic and, given the content of his other lectures, it is doubtful that this was a matter of great importance to him. See Sugiura, *Rinri goshinkō sōan,* passim.

45. Reinhard Zöllner, "Lorenz von Stein und *kokutai,*" in *Oriens Extremus* 33(1): 65–76. The lectures were prepared in English, instead of German, so the Japanese could understand and translate them into Japanese. For additional authoritarian influences see Noriko Kokubun, *Die Bedeutung der deutschen för die japanische Staatsletre unter der Meiji-Verfassung* (Frankfurt: Peter Lang, 1993). Itō Hirobumi (1841–1909), framer of the Meiji Constitution, was a prime minister and one of Japan's leading politicians during the Meiji period.

46. Zöllner, "Lorenz von Stein," pp. 70–72. For example: "Itō Hirobumi sprach darin vom Souverän als Gehirn des Staatskörpers und von den Extremitäten und Knochen. Er hob ausdrücklich den Zusammenhang zwischen 'modernen' Staatslehren, womit er Lorenz von Stein meinte, und dem Aufbau des japanischen Staates, dem *kokutai* Japans, hervor"; ibid., p. 71. This is not to say the idea was new with Stein. It can be found in Greek and Roman writings about government, and Zöllner traces it back in Indo-European culture to the *Rg-Veda* (p. 72). Zöllner also outlines its development in Asia (pp. 74–76).

47. Ibid., p. 69. See also Dirk Blasius and Eckart Pankoke, *Lorenz von Stein: Geschichts- und gesellschaftswissenschaftliche Perspektiven* (Darmstadt: Wissenschaftliche Buchgesellschaft, 1977), pp. 72–76, 120–131.

48. Harry R. Sullivan, *Walter Bagehot* (Boston: G. K. Hall, 1975), p. 138.

49. Gluck, *Japan's Modern Myths,* p. 79. Gluck quotes *Ōsaka Asahi Shimbun,* 2 February 1910.

50. Ibid., p. 58.

51. "The Imperial Rescript Ending the War," in Robert J. C. Butow, *Japan's Decision to Surrender* (Stanford: Stanford University Press, 1954), p. 248.

52. Senda Kakō, *Tennō to chokugo to Shōwashi* (The emperor, imperial rescripts, and the history of the Shōwa era) (Tokyo: Sekibunsha, 1983), pp. 327–330. For a translation see Robert A. Fearey, "My Year with Ambassador Joseph C. Grew, 1941–1942: A Personal Account," *Journal of American–East Asian Relations* 1(1) (1992): 134–135. Fearey translates this phrase slightly differently: "It has been truly unavoidable and far from Our wishes that Our Empire has now been brought to cross swords with America and Britain."

53. Tokutomi Iichirō, "The Imperial Rescript Declaring War on the United States and British Empire," trans. Hanama Tasaki, in Tsunoda et al., *Sources,* pp. 798–799.

54. Makino Nobuaki, *Makino Nobuaki nikki* (Makino Nobuaki's diary) (Tokyo: Chūōkōronsha, 1990), pp. 21–23; cited hereafter as Makino Diary.

55. Takeo Doi, *The Anatomy of Dependence,* trans. John Bester (Tokyo: Kodansha International, 1973).

56. Ibid., pp. 44–47, for this discussion.

57. Ibid., pp. 40–41.

58. For other factors see Peter Wetzler, "Kaiser Hirohito und der Krieg im

Pazifik," *Vierteljahrshefte für Zeitgeschichte* 4 (1989): 611–644, especially pp. 615–624.

59. Ideals about racial equality were not consistently put into practice in the West, of course. (Professor Haro von Senger, University of Freiburg, pointed this out emphatically upon reading an earlier version of this book.) An example of the great impression this made on the Japanese can be seen in the spring of 1924 when the U.S. Congress was debating the immigration law designed to exclude further Japanese immigration to the United States. The imperial household minister, Makino Nobuaki, noted the "Japan-America problem" in his diary and on 15 May wrote in heavy black characters that the law had passed Congress (and was signed by the president on 26 May); Makino Diary, pp. 126–130.

60. Leonard Mosley, *Hirohito, Emperor of Japan* (Englewood Cliffs, N.J.: Prentice-Hall, 1966), pp. 32–34, says Hirohito was encouraged to take up biology and not history because of his misgivings about the ancient myths. Ernst Lokowandt, "Das Japanische Kaisertum—religiöse Fundierung und politische Realität" (Tokyo: OAG, 1989), OAG aktuell No. 35, p. 5, also refers to Hirohito's early interest in Japanese history. He says Hirohito was steered away from history and toward marine biology because history was too sensitive politically. I have not been able to find such a comment in any primary sources; likewise Mikiso Hane, trans., *Emperor Hirohito and His Chief Aide-de-Camp: The Honjō Diary, 1933–36* (Tokyo: University of Tokyo Press, 1982), p. 249, n. 4, found no such source.

61. Stefan Tanaka, *Japan's Orient: Rendering Pasts into History* (Berkeley: University of California Press, 1993), p. 21.

62. *Shiratori Kurakichi zenshū* (Collected works of Shiratori Kurakichi), ed. Shiratori Kiyoshi (Tokyo: Iwanami Shoten, 1969–1971), vol. 10, "Nihon ni okeru Jukyō no junnōsei" (The adaptability of Confucianism in Japan), p. 236; Tanaka, *Japan's Orient*, pp. 92–93; Tanaka's translation. This statement confirms Nakamura's thesis about the acceptance of foreign religions and Doi's "takeover" of foreign cultures for Japanese purposes.

63. Tanaka, *Japan's Orient*, pp. 155–156.

64. Minobe Tatsukichi (1873–1948) actually proposed his theory in the early 1900s, but it aroused no controversy outside of academic circles until the 1930s. The theory was influenced by the works of a German legal theorist, Georg Jellinek. For Lorenz von Stein's contribution to this development in Japan see Zöllner, "Lorenz von Stein," passim. Briefly summarized: the state is a corporate entity; functions such as justice, administration, and the authority of the ruler are organs of that corporate state; the emperor as chief executive is the highest of the many organs constituting the modern state. See Frank O. Miller, *Minobe Tatsukichi: Interpreter of Constitutionalism in Japan* (Berkeley: University of California Press, 1965), pp. 196–253. For Hirohito's reaction to the controversy surrounding this theory see Harada Kumao, *Saionjikō to seikyoku* (Prince Saionji and the political developments) (Tokyo: Iwa-nami Shoten, 1950–1956), vol. 4, pp. 238 and 265–266; in English see Toshiaki Kawahara, *Hirohito and His Times* (Tokyo: Kodansha, 1990), pp. 67–68.

65. Tanaka, *Japan's Orient*, p. 33, points out the same trend in the early

Meiji period: "Seemingly 'Western' aspects might have been adopted, but the purpose was to effect Japan's regeneration; constitutionalism, modernity, rationality, and capitalism were merely tools for that regeneration."

Chapter 7: Hirohito's First Adviser

1. Lesley Connors, *The Emperor's Adviser: Saionji Kinmochi and Prewar Japanese Politics* (London: Croom Helm, 1987), p. 67 and passim.

2. David Anson Titus, *Palace and Politics in Prewar Japan* (New York: Columbia University Press, 1974), pp. 190–191.

3. Titus' study *Palace and Politics,* is based on Kido's diary; see Connors, *Emperor's Adviser,* for Saionji. For a reliable translation of the first volume of Harada's memoirs see Thomas Mayer-Oakes, ed. and trans., *Fragile Victory: Saionji-Harada Memoirs* (Detroit: Wayne State University Press, 1968).

4. Joseph C. Grew, *Ten Years in Japan* (New York: Simon & Schuster, 1944), passim.

5. See Nakamura Masanori, *The Japanese Monarchy, Ambassador Joseph Grew and the Making of the "Symbol Emperor System," 1931–1991,* trans. Herbert P. Bix, Jonathan Baker-Bates, and Derek Bowen (Armonk, N.Y.: M. E. Sharpe, 1992), pp. 43–45, for this and the following.

6. Germaine A. Hoston, "The State, Modernity, and the Fate of Liberalism in Prewar Japan," *Journal of Asian Studies* 51 (1992): 287–316.

7. Ibid., pp. 296–297.

8. Ibid., p. 308.

9. Mikiso Hane, trans., *Emperor Hirohito and His Chief Aide-de-Camp* (Tokyo: University of Tokyo Press, 1982), p. 15. For a similar evaluation see Titus, *Palace and Politics,* pp. 111–112.

10. See Robert J. C. Butow, *Tojo and the Coming of the War* (Stanford: Stanford University Press, 1961), p. 54, n. 18, p. 67, p. 129, n. 44.

11. Makino Nobuaki, *Kaikoroku* (Memoirs) (Tokyo: Chūkōbunko, 1977–1978), vol. 1, p. 17; cited hereafter as Makino Memoirs.

12. The idea of writing his memoirs was first proposed to Makino in 1938. In 1939 a preliminary version of the present work was published, *Shōtō Kandan* (Idle talk under the billowing pines), but the intensifying war caused the project to be postponed. After the war, however, Makino dictated it to a group headed by his grandson; he checked and corrected what they wrote down; and Bungei Shunjūsha published the entire *Memoirs (Kaikoroku)* in three volumes in 1948 and 1949. The present publication is a two-volume edition of the same work; ibid., vol. 2, pp. 229–234. The recollections themselves, which begin when Makino was about ten years old, reveal as much about the character of the memoirs and their author as the events recorded in them. Few would dispute that Iwakura and Sanjō were important men during the restoration, but one might doubt that a ten-year-old boy was filled with thoughts of this sort or could remember them many years later.

13. Ibid., vol. 2, p. 10.

14. Irokawa Daikichi, *Meiji no bunka* (Meiji culture) (Tokyo: Iwanami Shoten, 1970). See also, by the same author, "Freedom and the Concept of People's Rights," *Japan Quarterly* 14(2) (April–June 1967): 175–183.

15. Makino Memoirs, vol. 2, pp. 11–17.

16. Ibid., vol. 2, p. 20; for the preceding synopsis and the following information see pp. 17–24.

17. Ibid., vol. 2, pp. 29–31. The Daishin'in, the supreme court in prewar Japan, decided constitutional issues.

18. Carol Gluck, *Japan's Modern Myths: Ideology in the Late Meiji Period* (Princeton: Princeton University Press, 1985), pp. 169–170. Gluck's quotations are from the original: "Gakusei no shisō fūki torishimari kunrei" (Disciplinary regulations on decadent student thought), in Kyōikushi Hensankai, ed., *Hattatsushi* (History of progress), vol. 5, pp. 7–8.

19. See *Kyōiku jiron* (Education issues) (June–July 1906): 763–765.

20. In a critique of an earlier version of this book, David Titus pointed out the issue of "apprenticeship" in democracy. For de Tocqueville and John Stuart Mill see Hans Fenske, Dieter Mertens, Wolfgang Reinhard, and Klaus Rosen, *Geschichte der politischen Ideen: Von Homer bis zur Gegenwart* (Frankfurt: Fischer Taschenbuch Verlag, 1987), pp. 403–405.

21. Makino Nobuaki, *Makino Nobuaki nikki* (Makino Nobuaki's diary) (Tokyo: Chūōkōronsha, 1990), pp. 143–144; cited hereafter as Makino Diary.

22. Makino Memoirs, vol. 2, pp. 62–64.

23. Ibid., p. 66.

24. Tomoko Masuda, "The Emperor's Right of Supreme Command as Exercised up to 1930: A Study Based Especially on the Takarabe and Kuratomi Diaries," in Junji Banno, ed., *The Emperor System in Modern Japan,* Acta Asiatica, no. 59 (Tokyo: Tōhō Gakkai, 1990), pp. 88–90.

25. Titus, *Palace and Politics,* p. 36. Titus quotes Shimizu Noboru, *Teikoku kempō seitai kaigi* (Imperial constitution conference on the government system), pp. 88–89. See Chapter 5 for Shiratori on the same subject.

26. Fenske et al., *Geschichte,* pp. 245–246. The citation is from Machiavelli's "Discorsi sopra la prima deca di Tito Livio" (I, 11).

27. Makino Diary, pp. 7–115.

28. Titus, *Palace and Politics,* pp. 111–112.

29. Makino Diary, p. 13. For a short description of the affair see Toshiaki Kawahara, *Hirohito and His Times* (Tokyo: Kodansha International, 1990), pp. 26–28. See also Hane, *Honjō Diary,* p. 45; Titus, *Palace and Politics,* pp. 122–125.

30. Meiji Constitution, Article 2: "The Imperial Throne shall be succeeded to by Imperial male descendants, according to the provisions of the Imperial House Law"; *Kodansha Encyclopedia of Japan* (Tokyo: Kodansha, 1983), vol. 2, p. 7. The Imperial Household Law (Kōshitsu Tempan) of 1889 designated the order of succession. Normally the next in line was the eldest son, but not necessarily. The law also allowed children of concubines to succeed to the throne. In times of uncertainty, decisions were made by the Imperial Family Council (Kōzoku Kaigi) with the advice of the Privy Council (Sūmitsu komon). See *Kokushi daijiten* (Great dictionary of national history) (Tokyo: Yoshikawa Kōbunkan, 1979–1993), vol. 5, pp. 370–371.

31. Makino Diary, pp. 13–21, 25–26.

32. This is essentially true for the way the LDP ruled in the postwar era as well.

33. Makino Diary, p. 26.

34. Kishida Hideo, *Jijūchō no Shōwashi* (Shōwa history as seen by the grand chamberlains) (Tokyo: Asahi Shimbunsha, 1982), pp. 16–17.

35. Makino Diary, p. 26, quotes a statement by Hirohito to a high official in the Foreign Ministry, Sawada Setsuzō (1884–1976); Titus, *Palace and Politics,* passim.

36. Makino Diary, p. 29; same page for the empress' request to Makino noted below.

37. Ibid., p. 31.

38. Ibid., p. 32, for Imperial Prince Kuni; p. 37 for Prince Fushimi.

39. See Chapter 3, note 36, for documentation. See also Stephen S. Large, *Emperor Hirohito and Shōwa Japan: A Political Biography* (London: Routledge, 1992), pp. 67–68; Hane, *Honjō Diary,* p. 254, n. 30.

40. Makino Diary, p. 34.

41. Ibid., p. 37.

42. For a supporter see Kawahara, *Hirohito and His Times,* pp. 40–41; for a critic see Peter Crome, *Der Tenno: Japan hinter dem Chrysanthemenvorhang* (Cologne: Kiepenheuer & Witsch, 1988), pp. 74–75. Although Crome's book is seriously flawed and seldom cited due to its many errors, Crome may certainly be counted among Hirohito's critics.

43. Makino Diary, pp. 44–45, quoting Hirohito. Numazu is on the upper end of the Izu peninsula and is some 80 kilometers further west from Tokyo than Hayama-machi, which is on the upper end of the Miura peninsula.

44. This position seems to parallel what Sugiura had advocated with his scientism prior to becoming Hirohito's teacher of imperial ethics: modern science was employed (in a wrong-headed manner) to prove the sublime nature of Japan's national polity.

45. Makino Diary, p. 46.

46. Ibid., p. 64.

47. Ibid., pp. 88–90 and 92.

48. Ibid., pp. 91–101, for this and the following.

49. Makino's date for this notation, 23 November, reveals an important aspect of this diary. The day of the ceremony, 17 October, was a national holiday and Makino made no notation on this day; ibid., pp. 94 and 99. Obviously some of the events recorded in the diary were noted some time after their occurrence. See also the "Japan-America problem" noted earlier.

50. Ibid., pp. 107–108.

51. Makino Diary, p. 108.

52. Richard H. Mitchell, *Thought Control in Prewar Japan* (Ithaca: Cornell University Press, 1976), pp. 51–57; Elise Tipton, *Japanese Police State: Tokkō in Interwar Japan* (Honolulu: University of Hawai'i Press, 1990), pp. 21–22.

53. W. G. Beasley, *The Modern History of Japan* (New York: Praeger, 1963), pp. 114–115.

54. Ivan Morris, *The Nobility of Failure: Tragic Heroes in the History of Japan* (New York: New American Library, 1975), pp. 217–275.

55. Makino Diary, pp. 109–110.

56. "Shōwa tennō no dokuhaku hachi-jikan" (The Shōwa emperor's eight-hour monologue), *Bungei shunjū* (December 1990): 101; cited hereafter as Hirohito Monologue; later published in Terasaki Hidenari and Mariko Tera-

saki-Miller, *Shōwa tennō no dokuhakuroku: Terasaki Hidenari, goyōkakari nikki* (The Shōwa emperor monologue and the diary of the liaison officer of the imperial household Terasaki Hidenari) (Tokyo: Bungei Shunjūsha, 1991); references are to the original article. For a critique see Fujiwara Akira, Awaya Kentarō, Yoshida Yutaka, and Yamada Akira, *Tettei kenshō, Shōwa tennō "dokuhakuroku"* (A thorough examination of the Shōwa emperor monologue) (Tokyo: Daigetsu Shoten, 1991). For an English analysis see Herbert Bix, "The Showa Emperor's 'Monologue' and the Problem of War Responsibility," *Journal of Japanese Studies* 18(2) (Summer 1992): 295–363, especially pp. 338–342 for Tanaka Giichi. Bix' interpretation—"although the young emperor had no prior knowledge of Chang Tso-lin's assassination, once he learned that his Kwantung Army had planned it in order to create an opportunity to seize by force the territory of another state, he showed no anger at what his officers had done"—is misleading. Perhaps he displayed no anger, but he did emphasize that discipline in the army should be maintained. See Harada Kumao, *Saionjikō to seikyoku* (Prince Saionji and the political developments) (Tokyo: Iwanami Shoten, 1950–1956), vol. 1, p. 5. For an interpretation different from Bix see Stephen Large, "Emperor Hirohito and Early Showa Japan," *Monumenta Nipponica* 46(3) (Autumn 1991): 349–368. For a study of Tanaka see William Fitch Morton, *Tanaka Giichi and Japan's China Policy* (Folkestone, Kent: William Dawson, 1980); one must note this work is dated, however, due to the newly revealed information. Compare Harada, vol. 1, pp. 3–6, Morton, pp. 130–135, with the Hirohito Monologue, p. 101.

57. Makino Diary, pp. 271–272.

58. Ibid., p. 350, for this and what immediately follows. As Makino did not record in his diary what he did there, one can only speculate about his opinion on the new situation and what he undertook at the palace.

59. This is not to say that discipline was lax in the Imperial Army and Navy. Discipline was very important to the officers not preoccupied with "higher" political concerns. See, for example, Hirose Yutaka (Capt. Imperial Navy), *Nihon no gunki* (Japanese military discipline) (Tokyo: Kaigun Hōjutsu Gakkō, 1926). This essay, prepared for use at the Imperial Navy Gunnery School, contains a history of military discipline in Japan and presents citations from German and Austrian works on the same topic.

The question of discipline with respect to army officers of radical political persuasions is quite another matter. See Leonard A. Humphreys, *The Way of the Heavenly Sword: The Japanese Army in the 1920's* (Stanford: Stanford University Press), 1995, especially chaps. 2 and 5.

60. Makino Diary, pp. 377–378.

61. Compare Harada, *Saionjikō*, vol. 1, pp. 3–6.

62. Makino Diary, p. 379.

63. Fujiwara Akira, *Tennōsei to guntai* (The emperor system and the military) (Tokyo: Aoki Shoten, 1978), p. 116.

64. Ibid.; Fujiwara quotes the original regulations.

65. Minobe Tatsukichi, *Kempō satsuyō* (Important aspects of the constitution) (Tokyo, 1923), p. 225; see Frank O. Miller, *Minobe Tatsukichi: Interpreter of Constitutionalism in Japan* (Berkeley: University of California Press, 1965), p. 100.

66. Makino Diary, p. 112. The specific occasion for this notation was the

controversy surrounding Hirohito's pending marriage, but the comment was obviously an expression of Makino's general convictions concerning this matter.

67. See the Introduction, especially "The Imperial Line, Imperial Legitimacy, and the Imperial Will."

68. Large, *Hirohito and Shōwa Japan*, pp. 46–55. Large is cited here not as a straw man but as the ablest of Hirohito's supporters.

69. James W. Morley, ed., *Japan's Road to the Pacific War: Japan Erupts: The London Naval Conference and the Manchurian Incident, 1928–1932* (New York: Columbia University Press, 1984), p. 177.

70. See Harada, *Saionjikō*, vol. 2, pp. 61–65, for this and the following.

71. See Bōeichō Bōei Kenshūjo, Senshishitsu (NIDS), *Daihonei Rikugunbu (1), Shōwa jū-go nen go gatsu made* (Imperial Headquarters, Army, up to May 1940) (Tokyo: Asagumo Shimbunsha, 1967), *Senshi sōsho*, vol. 8, p. 313, for this and the following report from Shidehara.

72. Kido Diary, vol. 1, pp. 99–100.

73. See Makino Diary, pp. 474–475, for this and the following.

74. Kido Diary, vol. 1, p. 106; Makino Diary, p. 475, reports this discussion also.

75. Makino Diary, p. 476.

76. Morley, *Japan Erupts*, p. 248. Honjō was appointed commander of the Kwantung Army in the beginning of August 1931 and arrived in Manchuria on 20 August. He immediately visited various units under his command and emphasized the importance of protecting the Manchurian railway and the Japanese citizens there. If he mentioned troop discipline, this was not noted by his colleagues and subordinates. Some would further point out that on 1 September he said in his general instructions to the army: "I shall act resolutely. ... The Kwantung Army faces truly heavy responsibilities [in Manchuria and Mongolia]." But what else could the new commander of a military unit say? This quote is from Katakura Chū (Brig. Gen.), "Manshū Jihen ni okeru gun no tōsui" (Army supreme command during the Manchurian Incident), dai go maki, dai ni shō, vol. 1, pp. 1–3. This is the contemporary manuscript used to write *Manshū Jihen shi* (History of the Manchurian Incident) edited by the Army General Staff. These two volumes, which cover the time from the outbreak of the incident to the end of October 1931, may be seen in the NIDS Library in Tokyo. See Morley, *Japan Erupts*, pp. 216–217, for the citation; Morley cites Nihon Kokusai Seiji Gakkai Taiheiyō Sensō Gen'in Kenkyūbu (Japan Association on International Relations, Study Group on the Causes of the Pacific War), ed., *Taiheiyō Sensō e no michi: Bekkan shiryō hen* (Road to the Pacific War: Supplementary volume of documents) (Tokyo: Asahi Shimbunsha, 1963), pp. 111–112.

77. Katakura, *Manshū Jihen*, vol. 1, p. 43.

78. Morley, *Japan Erupts*, pp. 248–250.

79. See Katakura, *Manshū Jihen*, vol. 2, pp. 114, 118, 127, for Minami's telegram and Honjō's response immediately below. See Harada, *Saionjikō*, vol. 2, p. 67, for the chief of staff's statement.

80. Morley, *Japan Erupts*, p. 274.

81. *Nara Takeji Jijū Bukanchō nikki* (Chief Aide-de-Camp Nara Takeji's diary), excerpted in *Chūōkōron* (September and October 1990), No. 1262, pp.

324–346; No. 1263, pp. 338–352; cited hereafter as Nara Diary. See also Large, *Hirohito and Shōwa Japan*, p. 48.

82. Nara Diary (Sept.), p. 338. See also Morley, *Japan Erupts*, pp. 201–202.

83. Nara Diary (Sept.), pp. 330–337.

84. Makino Diary, pp. 473–477.

85. Large, *Hirohito and Shōwa Japan*, pp. 46–49. Large emphasizes the emperor's concern about protecting the constitution.

86. Hirohito Monologue, passim.

87. Yamada Akira, *Daigensui Shōwa tennō* (The Shōwa emperor as commander in chief) (Tokyo: Shin-Nihon Shuppansha, 1994), pp. 45–46. Yamada cites Nara Diary, 9 October 1931; see Nara Diary (Sept.), p. 344. Chang Hsueh-liang was the son of Chang Tso-lin, whose assassination had sparked the Tanaka Affair.

88. Large, *Hirohito and Shōwa Japan*, p. 48; Large cites Nara Diary (Sept.), pp. 344–345. Large also notes that Hirohito was worried about intervention by the Western powers, "for which contingency the military was completely unprepared."

89. Makino Diary, p. 474.

90. Nara Diary (Sept.), pp. 341–342.

91. Large, *Hirohito and Shōwa Japan*, p. 47.

92. Makino Diary, p. 472.

93. Large, *Hirohito and Shōwa Japan*, p. 53, citing Kido.

94. Makino Diary, p. 548. Compare my interpretation with that of Large, *Hirohito and Shōwa Japan*, p. 53. Large again overstates the emperor's position by making him a peace advocate.

95. Titus, *Palace and Politics*, p. 328.

96. Humphreys, *Way of the Heavenly Sword*, p. 119.

97. Yoshitake Oka, *Five Political Leaders of Modern Japan: Itō Hirobumi, Ōkuma Shigenobu, Hara Takashi, Inukai Tsuyoshi, Saionji Kimmochi*, trans. Andrew Fraser and Patricia Murray (Tokyo: University of Tokyo Press, 1986), pp. 186–187, 191.

98. See Hoston, "The State, Modernity, and the Fate of Liberalism," pp. 296–297, for this and the following statement.

99. Harada, *Saionjikō*, vol. 2, p. 377; cited in Connors, *Emperor's Adviser*, p. 132; this is Connors' translation.

100. Harada, *Saionjikō*, vol. 2, pp. 275–276; cited in Connors, *Emperor's Adviser*, p. 132; this is Connors' translation.

101. Makino Memoirs, vol. 2, pp. 170–183. Makino was asked to head the Japanese delegation but refused because of the difficulties he anticipated in gaining acceptance of Japan's conditions for joining the League of Nations. He refers extensively to the foreign policy differences between Japan and its new "allies." Not only were Japan's objectives not realizable, but someone of Saionji's stature was necessary at home and abroad to salvage the situation.

102. Grew, *Ten Years in Japan*, p. 60. Other leading liberals (Shidehara Kijūrō, Saitō Makoto, and Takahashi Korekiyo) joined this opposition.

103. Connors, *Emperor's Adviser*, p. 133.

104. Ibid., p. 68; Connors cites Saionji Kinmochi, *Plenipotentiary Report*, 27 August 1919. The basic principles of French liberalism included freedom of the individual and equality of all before the law. Moreover, the king was sup-

posed to exercise his powers through his ministers as stipulated in the constitution and rule only according to the law. Freedom, property, security, and resisting oppression were inalienable rights. See Fenske et al., *Geschichte*, pp. 381–382.

105. Connors, *Emperor's Adviser*, p. 212.

Chapter 8: Conclusion

1. Stephen S. Large, *Emperor Hirohito and Shōwa Japan* (London: Routledge, 1992), p. 205; Charles D. Sheldon, "Japanese Aggression and the Emperor, 1931–1941, from Contemporary Diaries," *Modern Asian Studies* 10(1) (1976):2.

2. Ibid., p. 216. Large underestimates Hirohito here: the emperor was extremely intelligent and adept at extracting what he could from the social-political situation before the war.

3. Herbert P. Bix, "The Showa Emperor's 'Monologue' and the Problem of War Responsibility," *Journal of Japanese Studies* 18(2) (Summer 1992):352–354.

4. According to the *Kodansha Encyclopedia of Japan* (Tokyo: Kodansha, 1983), vol. 2, pp. 7–9:

Article 2: The Imperial Throne shall be succeeded to by Imperial male descendants, according to the provisions of the Imperial House Law. [p. 7]

Article 4: The Emperor is the head of the Empire, combining in Himself the rights of sovereignty, and exercises them, according to the provisions of the present Constitution. [p. 7]

Article 6: The Emperor gives sanction to laws, and orders them to be promulgated and executed. [p. 7]

Article 11: The Emperor has the supreme command of the Army and Navy. [p. 8]

For the Imperial Household Law see Chapter 7, note 30.

5. Harada Kumao, *Saionjikō to seikyoku* (Prince Saionji and the political developments) (Tokyo: Iwanami Shoten, 1950–1956), vol. 6, p. 297; Large's translation (p. 67).

6. The Minamoto, Taira, Ashikaga, Tokugawa, and other important military families all claimed descent from former emperors or high-ranking nobles. Moreover, the first *"seiitai shōgun,"* Sakanoue no Tamuramaro (758–811), was rewarded for his services with high military and civil posts. In the year of his death he became minister of war *(hyōbukyō)* and great counselor *(dainagon)*. Generally speaking, however, posts dealing with military affairs, and those outside of Kyoto, were not highly regarded among the nobility, especially in the Heian period (794–1185). See Ivan Morris, *The World of the Shining Prince: Court Life in Ancient Japan* (New York: Knopf, 1969), p. 180, n. 1. Morris cites the *Kagerō nikki*, by the "Mother of Michitsuna" and "wife" of Fujiwara Kaneie, written 954 to 974. It was the younger sons, with no prospect of high rank and office in the capital, who sought to improve their lot in the provinces. They were not highly respected by the Fujiwaras, Sugawara, Tachibana, and the like. Later the lack of respect between nobles in the capital and samurai was mutual. See H. Paul Varley, *Imperial Restoration in Medieval Japan* (New York: Columbia University Press, 1971), p. 130; Varley cites the *Taiheiki*, compiled in the fourteenth century.

7. Fujiwara Akira, *Shōwa tennō no jū-go nen sensō* (The Shōwa emperor's fifteen-year war) (Tokyo: Aoki Shoten, 1991), pp. 35–36.

8. Edward Behr, *Hirohito: Behind the Myth* (London: Hamish Hamilton, 1989), p. 38.

9. Large, *Hirohito and Shōwa Japan*, p. 17; Yamamoto Shichihei, *Shōwa tennō no kenkyū: Sono jitsuzō o saguru* (Research on the Shōwa emperor: In search of the real image) (Tokyo: Shōdensha, 1989), pp. 49–50.

10. For a discussion see Bix, "The Showa Emperor's 'Monologue,' " pp. 320–321. Bix quotes Kinoshita Michio, *Sokkin nisshi* (Shorthand diary) (Tokyo: Bungei Shunjūsha, 1990), pp. 89–90.

11. For citations supporting this conclusion and the foregoing information see Chapters 5 and 6 of this study. For a contrary opinion see Large, *Hirohito and Shōwa Japan*, pp. 17–19. Large, however, bases his conclusions about Sugiura and Shiratori on reports about them, not their own writings.

12. Bernd Martin, "Deutsche Geschichtswissenschaft als Instrument nationaler Selbstfindung in Japan," in *Universalgeschichte und Nationalgeschichten*, ed. Gangolf Hübinger et al. (Freiburg: Rombach Verlag, 1994), p. 215.

13. Nakamura Masanori, *The Japanese Monarchy, Ambassador Joseph Grew and the Making of the "Symbol Emperor System," 1931–1991*, trans. Herbert P. Bix, Jonathan Baker-Bates, and Derek Bowen (Armonk, N.Y.: M. E. Sharpe, 1992), pp. 43–45.

14. For a short clear description of the persons and political issues pertaining to the Shōwa Restoration, the February 26 Incident, and its aftermath see Large, *Hirohito and Shōwa Japan*, pp. 57–75. For a full-length study see Ben-Ami Shillony, *Revolt in Japan: The Young Officers and the February 26, 1936 Incident* (Princeton: Princeton University Press, 1973). There are many works in Japanese about this incident: Kono Osamu, *Tennō to Niniroku Jiken* (The emperor and the February 26 Incident) (Tokyo: Kawaide Shobō Shinsha, 1985); Matsumoto Seichō and Fujii Yasue, eds., *Niniroku Jiken, kenkyū shiryō* (The February 26 Incident: Research documents), 3 vols. (Tokyo: Bungei Shunjūsha, 1976, 1986, 1993); Nakano Masao, *Tennō to Niniroku Jiken* (The emperor and the February 26 Incident) (Tokyo: Kōdansha, 1975); Takahashi Masae, *Niniroku Jiken* (The February 26 Incident) (Tokyo: Iwanami Shoten, 1965).

15. The Imperial Way faction was a group of ultranationalist officers headed by General Mazaki and General Araki Sadao. Among others they were active in pursuing the militarization of Manchuria and opposing Minobe's organ theory of imperial government. The Control faction was not really a faction. They opposed the foregoing policies, and *"tōseiha"* was a pejorative applied to them by the ultranationalists. See James B. Crowley, "Japanese Army Factionalism in the Early 1930's," *Journal of Asian Studies* 21(3) (1962): 309–326.

16. Harada, *Saionjikō*, vol. 5, pp. 6–7; same source for the suppression order discussed below.

17. Honjō Shigeru, *Honjō nikki* (Honjō diary) (Tokyo: Hara Shobō, 1975), p. 235.

18. Large, *Hirohito and Shōwa Japan*, pp. 212–215.

19. Ibid., pp. 69–70; Sheldon, "Japanese Aggression and the Emperor," pp. 1–40.

20. Ernst Lokowandt, "Das Japanische Kaisertum—religiöse Fundierung und politische Realität" (Tokyo: OAG, 1989), OAG aktuell No. 35. p. 3.

21. This has been illustrated in Chapters 2 and 3 of this study and will be discussed shortly.

22. Lokowandt, "Japanische Kaisertum," p. 13. For an elaboration of this thesis see Ernst Lokowandt, "Die Stellung der Tennō in der Staatsführung— Die rechtliche Reglung der Herrschaftsbefugnisse des Kaisers unter der Meiji-Verfassung," *Oriens Extremus* 33(1): 49–64.

23. Kido Kōichi, *Kido Kōichi nikki* (Kido Kōichi diary) (Tokyo: Tokyo Daigaku Shuppankai, 1966), vol. 2, p. 1220. Daikichi Irokawa, *The Age of Hirohito: In Search of Modern Japan,* trans. Mikiso Hane and John K. Urda (New York: Free Press, 1995), pp. 30–33, maintains that the emperor was instrumental in not bringing the war to an earlier end.

24. See, for example, Large, *Hirohito and Shōwa Japan,* p. 101 and passim. The only extensive treatment of Tōjō in a Western language, Robert J. C. Butow, *Tojo and the Coming of the War* (Stanford: Stanford University Press, 1961), is an exception to this statement. See the latter part of Chapter 3 for a discussion and citations.

25. See the latter part of Chapter 3 for a discussion and citations.

26. "Shōwa tennō no dokuhaku hachi-jikan" (The Shōwa emperor's eight-hour monologue), *Bungei shunjū,* Dec. 1990, pp. 111–114; cited hereafter as Hirohito Monologue. See Bix, "The Showa Emperor's 'Monologue,' " p. 352, for a discussion.

27. "The Imperial Rescript Ending the War," in Robert J. C. Butow, *Japan's Decision to Surrender* (Stanford: Stanford University Press, 1954), p. 248.

28. Large, *Hirohito and Shōwa Japan,* p. 150.

29. Nakamura, *The Japanese Monarchy,* pp. 87–106, "Origins of the 'Symbol.' "

30. Ibid., pp. 168–170.

31. See Nijō Yoshimoto, *Sakaki no ha nikki* (Evergreen leaf diary, 1366), in Hanawa Hōkiichi, ed., *Gunsho Ruijū* (Tokyo: Heibunsha, 1979), vol. 2, pp. 66–72, for Nijō's thesis. I am indebted to Professor Ishida Ichirō for pointing this out to me during a presentation for his research seminar. See Ishida Ichirō, *Nihon no bunkashi* (Japanese culture history) (Tōkyo: Tōkai Daigaku Shuppankai, 1989), pp. 133–134. My thanks to Professor Tashiro Kazuhisa, too, for the "symbol emperor" suggestion. See *Kodansha Encyclopedia of Japan,* vol. 4, pp. 59–60, for the translation of "Jinnō Shōtōki" and a short discussion of the text.

32. Large, *Hirohito and Shōwa Japan,* pp. 2–3, 55, and passim.

33. Ibid., p. 114; the statement by the Japanese expert, Katō Shūichi, also is found on this page; I have used Large's translation.

34. Ibid., p. 113.

35. Hirohito Monologue, p. 145. Grammatically the original Japanese is broken up into two sentences at an unusual point. One must remember that this was an oral presentation.

Appendix 3

1. This appendix illustrates two things: Tōjō's autocratic handling of government affairs and the difficulty of determining Tōjō's actual stance due to contrasting source materials. The appendix is my paraphrase, not a translation. For this comparison of sources see Itō Takashi, Hirohashi Tadamitsu, and Katashima Norio, eds., *Tōjō naikaku sōridaijin kimitsu kiroku* (The prime minis-

ter's secret agenda during the Tōjō cabinet) (Tokyo: Tokyo Daigaku Shuppan-kai, 1990), pp. 276–281. See also Ōtani Keijirō, *Shōwa Kempeishi* (History of the Shōwa Kempeitai) (Tokyo: Misuzu Shobō, 1987), pp. 455–458. The discussion follows the Tōjō Agenda.

Appendix 4

1. This appendix is a translation based on Sugiura's lecture to Crown Prince Hirohito on the imperial regalia. Sugiura Shigetake, *Rinri goshinkō sōan* (Draft of the ethics lectures to the crown prince) (Tokyo: Yamato Bunkō, 1984), vol. 1, pp. 1–4.

2. *Chung Yung*, bk. 20, chap. VIII; see James Legge, trans., *Confucius: Confucian Analects, The Great Learning, and The Doctrine of the Mean* (New York: Dover, 1971), pp. 406–407. Legge's translation: "Knowledge, magnanimity, and energy, these three, are the virtues universally binding." Here and in the following, Sugiura obviously paraphrased from the Chinese original. Reading only Sugiura's text one wonders why he uses the character 知 and not 智. Standard Japanese lexicons, *Kōjien* and Morohashi's *Daikanwa jiten*, indicate that 知 means to know or have knowledge of things. Its opposite would be "uninformed." But 智, on the other hand, means wise, intelligent, the opposite of stupid. The original Chinese indicates that the first character 知 is to be read *"chih"* in the fourth and not the first tone as is normal, in which case it stands for the second one 智. Where the *Chung Yung* speaks of acquiring knowledge, for example (bk. 20, chap. VII), *"chih"* in the first tone is used. Therefore I have chosen the word "wisdom," which seems more suitable in this case. *"Nin"* (Ch. *"jen"*) I have translated as "benevolence" because it is more common now than "magnanimity," which is equally correct. *"Yū"* (Ch. *"yung"*), Legge indicates in a note, means "valiant energy," although he leaves the first word out of the text translation. "Courage" seems a better choice.

3. In recognition of his services, Emperor Tenji granted Kamatari the surname "Fujiwara." Officially the Fujiwara House dates from this time: this is the precedent subsequently cited throughout Japanese history, including Hirohito's reign, establishing them as the most important advisers to the throne. See *Nihon Shoki*, 669, Tenth Month, Fifteenth Day, *NKBT*, vol. 68, pp. 372–373; Aston, *Nihongi*, vol. 2, p. 291.

4. *Nihon Shoki*, 319, Fourth Month, First Day, *NKBT*, vol. 67, pp. 390–391; Aston, *Nihongi*, vol. 1, p. 279. The Japanese editors and Aston remark that this is standard Confucian liturgy.

5. *Nihon Shoki*, 667 B.C., Tenth Month, Fifth Day, marked the beginning of the expedition. Nagasune-hiko was eventually defeated in 663 B.C., Twelfth Month; *NKBT*, vol. 67, pp. 188–210; Aston, *Nihongi*, vol. 1, pp. 110–127. These dates are for reference only; they are totally fictitious.

Appendix 5

1. Here basic differences in Japanese and Chinese religion are outlined. The superiority of Japanese religious culture is emphasized. This is a paraphrase of the main points presented to the crown prince. See Shiratori Kurakichi, "Kokutai to Jukyō" (Our national polity and Confucianism), in Shiratori Kiyoshi, ed., *Shiratori Kurakichi zenshū* (Collected works of Shiratori Kurakichi) (Tokyo: Iwanami Shoten, 1969–1971), vol. 10, pp. 276–289.

2. For a detailed discussion on the meaning of *"li"* in Chinese culture see Joken Kato, "The Meaning of *Li,"* *Philosophical Studies of Japan* 4 (1963): 79–95.

3. See Stefan Tanaka, *Japan's Orient: Rendering Pasts into History* (Berkeley: University of California Press, 1993), pp. 137–138, for a supporting argument.

4. *"Amatsuhitsugi"* (or one of its variants) is a term that appears in the *Kojiki, Nihon Shoki, Manyōshū,* and other ancient texts. Tanaka, *Japan's Orient,* pp. 92–93, supports this interpretation of Shiratori. This should not cause us to lose sight of the fact that protection and not blood descent was emphasized up to the time of Kitabatake Chikafusa in the fourteenth century. See Tanaka, chap. 5, "The *Jinnō Shōtōki,"* and n. 54 in same.

Appendix 6

1. Here the meaning of the imperial regalia according to Shiratori is outlined. This is a paraphrase of the most important part of this presentation to Hirohito. See *Shiratori Kurakichi zenshū,* vol. 10, pp. 249–260.

Appendix 7

1. Sugiura, *Rinri goshinkō sōan,* vol. 2, pp. 453–454.

2. Ibid., vol. 2, p. 452. See *Nihon Shoki,* 645, Sixth Month, Twelfth Day; *NKBT,* vol. 68, pp. 262–263; Aston, *Nihongi,* vol. 2, pp. 191–193.

3. *Nihon Shoki,* 645, Sixth Month, Fourteenth Day; *NKBT,* vol. 68, pp. 268–269; Aston, *Nihongi,* vol. 2, pp. 195–196.

Appendix 8

1. Here Sugiura presents Washington as an ethical model to illustrate to the crown prince that good Japanese morals are found in important persons overseas also. See Sugiura, *Rinri goshinkō sōan,* vol. 2, pp. 478–487.

Appendix 9

1. Sugiura, *Rinri goshinkō sōan,* vol. 2, pp. 565–569.

Bibliography

Primary Sources

Akamatsu Sadao. *Tōjō hishokan kimitsu nikki* (Secret diary of Tōjō's secretary). Tokyo: Bungei Shunjūsha, 1985.

Bōeichō Bōeikenkyūjo Senshibu (National Institute for Defense Studies, NIDS), ed. *Kaigun nendo sakusen keikaku* (Navy annual operations plans). Tokyo: Asagumo Shimbunsha, 1986. (Not part of *Senshi sōsho.*)

Czernin, Ottokar. *Im Weltkriege*. Berlin and Vienna: Ulstein, 1919.

Daihon'ei. *Jōsō kankeisetsu sono ichi*, Ji Shōwa jūroku nen jūgatsu shi jūichi-gatsu (Imperial Headquarters: Writings relating to imperial audiences, no. 1, Oct.–Nov. 1941). Pages handwritten without numbering. In *Shōwa jū-roku nen jōsō kankei shoruisetsu*, kan ichi. Shōwa jū-roku nen ku-gatsu—jū-ni-gatsu (Materials relating to imperial audiences in 1941, vol. 1, Sept.–Dec. 1941). MS in Bōeikenkyūjo Toshokan (NIDS Library), MS Chūō, sakusen shidō, jōsō 1.

"Daihon'ei Rikugunbu: Sanmitsu dai 438–go dai 1" (Imperial Headquarters Army Dept.: Secret proceedings no. 438–1). 8 Nov. 1941.

"Hōtō shiryō, Tai Bei, Ei, Ran sensō ni okeru sakusenteki mitōshi" (Materials in reply to the throne: The operational outlook in a war with America, England, and Holland). Last ten days of Oct. 1941.

"Jōsōan: Nanpō sakusen zempan ni kan suru ken" (Memorial to the throne: Matters relating to all operations to the south). 8 Oct. 1941.

Fujita Hisanori. *Jijūchō no kaisō* (The grand chamberlain's recollections). Tokyo: Chūōkōronsha, 1987.

Grew, Joseph C. *Ten Years in Japan*. New York: Simon & Schuster, 1944.

Harada Kumao. *Saionjikō to seikyoku* (Prince Saionji and the political developments). 8 vols. Tokyo: Iwanami Shoten, 1950–1956.

Hayashi Razan. "Jimmu tennō-ron" (On Emperor Jimmu; written ca. 1600–1650). In *Hayashi Razan bunshū* (Collected writings of Hayashi Razan). Tokyo: Pelikansha, 1979. (First published in the modern era by Heian Kōkogakkai, 1918.)

Higashikuni Naruhiko. *Higashikuni nikki* (Higashikuni diary). Tokyo: Tokuma Shoten, 1968.

Hirose Yutaka. *Nihon no gunki* (Japanese military discipline). Tokyo: Kaigun Hōjutsu Gakkō, 1926.

Ichijō Kaneyoshi. *Nihon Shoki sanso* (Commentary on the *Nihon Shoki*, written 1455–1457). In Tenri Toshokan Zenhonsōsho, vol. 27, *Nihon Shoki sanso, Nihon Shokishō*. Tokyo: Yagi Shoten, 1977.

Inoue Tetsujirō. *Kokumin dōtoku gairon* (Outline of our national ethics). Rev. ed. Tokyo: Sanseidō, 1922.

———. *Nihon kogakuha no tetsugaku* (Philosophy of the ancient learning school in Japan). Tokyo: Fusanbō, 1931. (First published in 1902.)

Itō Takashi, Hirohashi Tadamitsu, and Katashima Norio, eds. *Tōjō naikaku sōridaijin kimitsu kiroku* (The prime minister's secret agenda during the Tōjō cabinet). Tokyo: Tokyo Daigaku Shuppankai, 1990.

Jien. *Gukanshō* (1219). In Okami Masao and Akamatsu Toshihide, eds., *NKBT,* vol. 86, 1967.

Jōhō Yoshio. *Tōjō Hideki.* Tokyo: Fuyō Shobō, 1974.

Katakura Chū (Brig. Gen.). "Manshū jihen ni okeru gun no tōsui" (Army Supreme Command during the Manchurian Incident). Dai go maki, dai ni shō. 2 vols. (MS in the NIDS Library, Tokyo).

Kido Kōichi. *Kido Kōichi nikki* (Kido Kōichi diary). 2 vols. Tokyo: Tokyo Daigaku Shuppankai, 1966.

Kinoshita Michio. *Sokkin nisshi* (Shorthand diary). Tokyo: Bungei Shunjūsha, 1990.

Kishida Hideo. *Jijūchō no Shōwashi* (Shōwa history as seen by the grand chamberlains). Tokyo: Asahi Shimbunsha, 1982.

Kitabatake Chikafusa. *Jinnō Shōtōki* (written 1339–1343). In Iwasa Tadashi et al., eds., *Jinnō Shōtōki; Masukagami, NKBT,* vol. 87, 1975.

Kojiki (712). In Kurano Kenji and Takeda Yūkichi, eds., *Kojiki; Norito, NKBT,* vol. 1, 1958.

Konoe Fumimaro. *Heiwa e no doryoku* (Efforts for peace). Tokyo: Nihon Denshin Tsūshinsha, 1946.

Kuga Katsunan. "Shidōron" (Concerning a profession). In *Kuga Katsunan zenshū,* vol. 2, pp. 749–750. Originally published in the newspaper *Nippon* (3 Nov. 1890).

Kuga Katsunan zenshū (Collected writings of Kuga Katsunan), Nishida Taketoshi and Uete Michinari, eds. 9 vols. Tokyo: Misuzu Shobō, 1968–1975.

Kume Kunitake. "Shintō wa saiten no kozoku" (Shinto is an outmoded custom of worshiping heaven). *Shigakkai zasshi* (1891).

Kyōiku jiron. (June–July 1906): 763–765.

Makino Nobuaki. *Kaikoroku* (Memoirs). 2 vols. Tokyo: Chūkōbunko, 1977–1978.

———. *Makino Nobuaki nikki* (Makino Nobuaki diary). Tokyo: Chūōkōronsha, 1990.

Matsumoto Seichō and Fujii Yasue, eds. *Niniroku jiken: kenkyū shiryō* (The

February 26 Incident: Research documents). 3 vols. Tokyo: Bungei Shun-jūsha, 1976, 1986, 1993.

Miyake Setsurei. "Yohai kokusuishugi o shōdō suru, ani! Gūzen naranya" (Advocating our policy of national essence, ah!, not by chance) (18 May 1889). In Motoyama Yukihiko, ed., *Miyake Setsureishū* (Collection of Miyake Setsurei's writings). *Kindai Nihon shisō taikei* (Great works on modern Japanese thought). Tokyo: Chikuma Shobō, 1975.

Nara Takeji Jijū Bukanchō nikki (Chief Aide-de-Camp Nara Takeji's diary). In *Chūōkōron* 1262 (Sept. 1990): 324–346 and 1263 (Oct. 1990): 338–352.

Nihon koten bungaku taikei (Great collection of classical Japanese literature). 102 vols. Tokyo: Iwanami Shoten, 1957–1968.

Nihon Shoki (720; also "Nihongi"). In Sakamoto Tarō, Ienaga Saburō, Inoue Mitsusada, and Ōno Susumu, eds., *NKBT*, vols. 67 and 68, 1967 and 1965.

Nijō Yoshimoto. *Sakaki no ha nikki* (Evergreen leaf diary; 1366). In Hanawa Hōkiichi, ed., *Gunsho ruiju.* 3rd rev. ed. Vol. 2. Tokyo: Heibunsha, 1979.

Pritchard, John R., and Sonia Magbanna Zaide, eds. *The Tokyo War Crimes Trial.* Complete transcripts of the proceedings of the International Military Tribunal for the Far East. 22 vols. and vols. 26–27. New York: Garland, 1981–.

Sanbōhonbu (General Staff), eds. *Sugiyama memo* (Sugiyama memoranda). 2 vols. Tokyo: Hara Shobō, 1967.

Satō Kenryō. *Daitōa Sensō kaikoroku* (Greater East Asia War memoirs). Tokyo: Tokuma Shoten, 1966.

Shiratori Kurakichi. "Daijōsai no konpongi" (Basic meaning of the enthrone-ment ceremony banquet). In *Shiratori Kurakichi zenshū*, vol. 10, pp. 249–260.

———. "Kokutai to Jukyō" (National polity and Confucianism). In *Shiratori Kurakichi zenshū*, vol. 10, pp. 276–289.

———. "Kōtenhara to tensonkōrin no shō" (Chapter on the plain of high heaven and the descent of the heavenly grandson). In *Shiratori Kurakichi zenshū*, vol. 1, pp. 418–512.

———. "Nihon ni okeru Jukyō no junnōsei" (Adaptability of Confucianism in Japan). In *Shiratori Kurakichi zenshū*, vol. 10, pp. 234–248.

Shiratori Kurakichi zenshū (Collected works of Shiratori Kurakichi). Edited by Kiyoshi Shiratori. 10 vols. Tokyo: Iwanami Shoten, 1969–1971.

Shōkyūki. [Author and date unknown, perhaps from the middle of the Kama-kura period, 1185–1333.] *Kokubun sōsho*, vol. 15. Tokyo: Hakubunkan, 1912–1915.

"Shōwa tennō no dokuhaku hachi-jikan" (The Shōwa emperor's eight-hour monologue). *Bungei shunjū*, Dec. 1990, pp. 94–145.

Sugiura Shigetake. *Rinri goshinkō sōan* (Draft of the ethics lectures to the crown prince). 3 vols. Tokyo: Yamato Bunko, 1984.

Taiheiki (comp. 14th C.). In Iwanami Yūjirō, ed., *NKBT*, vols. 34–36, 1960–1962.

Terasaki Hidenari and Mariko Terasaki-Miller. *Shōwa tennō no dokuhaku-roku: Terasaki Hidenari, goyōkakari nikki* (The Shōwa emperor monologue and the diary of the liaison officer of the imperial household Terasaki Hide-nari). Tokyo: Bungei Shunjūsha, 1991.

Tōjō Hideki. *Guntai naimuryō* (Army internal ordinances), 11 August 1943. Reprint. Tokyo: Ikeda Shoten, 1970.

Tokugawa Mitsukuni et al. *Dainihonshi* (Great history of Japan; comp. 1657–1906). Edited by Gikō Seitan Sambyakunen Kinenkai. Tokyo: Dainihon Yūbenkai, 1928–1929.

Secondary Sources

Agawa, Hiroyuki. *The Reluctant Admiral: Yamamoto and the Imperial Navy.* Translated by John Bester. Tokyo: Kodansha International, 1979.

Akasaka Norio et al. *Tennōsei nyūmon* (Introduction to the imperial system). Tokyo: JICC Shuppankyoku, 1989.

Ambrose, Stephan E. *Rise to Globalism: American Foreign Policy Since 1938.* 4th rev. ed. New York: Penguin Books, 1985.

Anesaki, Masaharu. *History of Japanese Religion,* Tokyo: Tuttle, 1963.

Antoni, Klaus. *Der Himmlische Herrscher und Sein Staat: Essays zur Stellung des Tennō im modernen Japan.* Munich: Judicium, 1991.

———. "Kokutai—Das 'Nationalwesen' als japanische Utopie." *Saeculum* 37 (2–3) (1987): 266–282.

Asai Nobuo. "Nichibei kaisen zenya ni okeru Terasaki Hidenari no yakuwari" (Terasaki Hidenari's role just prior to the outbreak of war between Japan and the U.S.). *Kōbe Gaidai ronsō* 39(7) (1988): 15–34.

Aston, W. G., trans. *Nihongi.* London: Allen & Unwin, 1956.

Awaya Kentarō et al., eds. *Kido Kōichi jinmon chōsho* (Protocol of the interrogation of Kido Kōichi). Tokyo: Daigetsu Shoten, 1987.

Beasley, W. G. *The Modern History of Japan.* New York: Praeger, 1963.

Behr, Edward. *Hirohito: Behind the Myth.* New York: Villard, 1989.

Bergamini, David. *Japan's Imperial Conspiracy.* 2 vols. New York: Morrow, 1971.

Bix, Herbert P. "The Showa Emperor's 'Monologue' and the Problem of War Responsibility." *Journal of Japanese Studies* 18(2) (Summer 1992): 295–363.

Blasius, Dirk, and Eckart Pankoke. *Lorenz von Stein: Geschichts- und gesellschaftswissenschaftliche Perspektiven.* Darmstadt: Wissenschaftliche Buchgesellschaft, 1977.

Bōeichō Bōeikenshūjo Senshishitsu (National Institute for Defense Studies, NIDS). *Daihon'ei Kaigunbu, Rengōkantai (1) kaisen made* (Imperial Headquarters, Navy, Combined Fleet (1) to the beginning of the war). In *Senshi sōsho,* vol. 91, 1975.

———. *Daihon'ei Kaigunbu Daitōa Sensō kaisenkeii* (Imperial Headquarters, Navy, particulars on the beginning of the Greater East Asia War). In *Senshi sōsho,* vols. 100–101, 1979.

———. *Daihon'ei Rikugunbu (1), Shōwa jū-go nen go gatsu made* (Imperial Headquaters, Army, up to May 1940). In *Senshi sōsho,* vol. 8, 1967.

———. *Daihon'ei Rikugunbu (2)* (Imperial Headquarters, Army). In *Senshi sōsho,* vol. 20, 1968.

———. *Daihon'ei Rikugunbu Daitōa Sensō kaisenkeii* (Imperial Headquarters, Army, particulars on the beginning of the Greater East Asia War). In *Senshi sōsho,* vols. 65, 68–70, and 76, 1973–1974. (Vol. 76 in the series is abbreviated "*Kaisenkeii.*")

———. *Hawai sakusen* (Hawai'i attack). In *Senshi sōsho,* vol. 10, 1967.

———. *Nansei hōmen Kaigun sakusen: Dai nidan sakusen iryō* (Navy operations for the push to the southwest: second-stage operations and thereafter). In *Senshi sōsho*, vol. 54, 1972.

Brown, Delmer M., and Ichirō Ishida. *The Future and the Past: A Translation and Study of the Gukanshō, an Interpretive History of Japan Written in 1219.* Berkeley: University of California Press, 1979.

Butow, Robert J. C. *Japan's Decision to Surrender.* Stanford: Stanford University Press, 1954.

———. *Tojo and the Coming of the War.* Stanford: Stanford University Press, 1961.

Chan, Wing-Tsit. *A Source Book in Chinese Philosophy.* Princeton: Princeton University Press, 1963.

Connors, Lesley. *The Emperor's Adviser: Saionji Kinmochi and Prewar Japanese Politics.* London: Croom Helm, 1987.

Crome, Peter. *Der Tenno: Japan hinter dem Chrysanthemenvorhang.* Cologne: Kiepenheuer & Witsch, 1988.

Crowley, James B. "Japanese Army Factionalism in the Early 1930's." *Journal of Asian Studies* 21(3) (1962): 309–326.

———. "Japan's Imperial Conspiracy." *New York Times Book Review,* 24 Oct. 1971.

Doi, Takeo. *The Anatomy of Dependence.* Translated by John Bester. Tokyo: Kodansha International, 1973.

Dore, Ronald P. *Education in Tokugawa Japan.* Berkeley: University of California Press, 1965.

Duke, Benjamin C. *The Japanese School: Lessons for Industrial America.* New York: Praeger, 1986.

Eisenstadt, S. N. "Education and Political Development." In Don C. Piper and Taylor Cole, eds., *Post-Primary Education and Political and Economic Development.* Durham: Duke University Press, 1964.

Erikson, Erik. *Kindheit und Gesellschaft.* Translated by Marianne Eckhardt-Jaffé. Stuttgart: Klett-Cotta Verlag, 1971.

Fearey, Robert A. "My Year with Ambassador Joseph C. Grew, 1941–1942: A Personal Account." *Journal of American–East Asian Relations* 1(1) (1992): 99–136.

Fenske, Hans, Dieter Mertens, Wolfgang Reinhard, and Klaus Rosen. *Geschichte der politischen Ideen: Von Homer bis zur Gegenwart.* Frankfurt: Fischer Taschenbuch Verlag, 1987.

Fest, Joachim C. *Hitler.* Translated by Richard and Clara Winston. London: Weidenfeld & Nicolson, 1974.

Florenz, Karl. *Die historischen Quellen der Shinto-Religion.* Göttingen: Vandenhoeck & Ruprecht, 1919.

Freidell, Wilbur M. "Government Ethics Textbooks in Late Meiji Japan." *Journal of Asian Studies* 29 (1970): 823–834.

Fujiwara Akira. *Jū-go nen sensō to tennō* (The fifteen-year war and the emperor). Tokyo: Azumino Shobō, 1988.

———. *Shōwa tennō no jū-go nen sensō* (The Shōwa emperor's fifteen-year war). Tokyo: Aoki Shoten, 1991.

———. *Tennōsei to guntai* (The emperor system and the military). Tokyo: Aoki Shoten, 1978.

Fujiwara Akira, Awaya Kentarō, Yoshida Yutaka, and Yamada Akira. *Tettei kensho, Shōwa tennō "dokuhakuroku"* (Thorough examination of the Shōwa emperor's "monologue"). Tokyo: Daigetsu Shoten, 1991.

Gluck, Carol. "The Idea of Showa." In Carol Gluck and Stephen R. Graubard, eds., *Showa: The Japan of Hirohito*. New York: Norton, 1992.

———. *Japan's Modern Myths: Ideology in the Late Meiji Period*. Princeton: Princeton University Press, 1985.

Hackett, Robert F. *Yamagata Aritomo in the Rise of Modern Japan, 1838–1922*. Cambridge, Mass.: Harvard University Press, 1971.

Hahlweg, Werner. "Vorrede." In Carl von Clausewitz, *Vom Kriege*. 19th ed. Bonn: Dümmlers Verlag, 1980.

Hall, Ivan P. *Mori Arinori*. Cambridge, Mass.: Harvard University Press, 1973.

Hall, John Whitney. "A Monarch for Modern Japan." In Robert E. Ward, ed., *Political Development in Modern Japan*. Princeton: Princeton University Press, 1968.

Hane, Mikiso, trans. *Emperor Hirohito and His Chief Aide-de-Camp: The Honjō Diary, 1933–36*. Tokyo: University of Tokyo Press, 1982.

Hara Shirō. "Daihon'ei senshi: Daitōa Sensō kaisen gaishi: Kaisen ni itaru seisenryaku shidō" (Imperial Headquarters war history: General history of beginning hostilities in the Greater East Asia War: Leadership and political strategy with respect to the beginning of hostilities). 3 vols. Pages 4617–5837. MS in the author's possession.

———. *Taisenryaku naki kaisen* (Beginning a war with no great strategy). Tokyo: Hara Shobō, 1987.

Hattori Takushirō. *Daitōa Sensō zenshi* (Complete history of the Greater East Asia War). Tokyo: Hara Shobō, 1965.

Hayashi Kentarō. "Jikobengo de wa nai" (Not a self-defense). In "Showa tennō dokuhakuroku—watashitachi no shogeki" (The Shōwa emperor's monologue—our shock). *Bungei shunjū*, Jan. 1991, pp. 94–147.

Headquarters, U.S. Strategic Bombing Survey (Pacific). Interrogation Nos. 373 (9 Nov. 1945), 487 (23 Nov. 1945), 507 (28 Nov. 1945), 531 (26 Dec. 1945), USSBS No. 379 NAV No. 76 (17 Nov. 1945), Tokyo. National Archives Copy.

Herbert, Jean. *Shintō: The Fountainhead of Japan*. New York: Stein & Day, 1967.

Herde, Peter. *Pearl Harbor: 7. Dezember 1941*. Darmstadt: Wissenschaftliche Buchgesellschaft, 1980.

Hocaoğlu (Kaplan), Cemaleddin. "Die islamische Verfassung." Cologne: Veröffentlichung des Khalifatsstaates, 1993.

Holtom, Clarence. *The Japanese Enthronement Ceremonies with an Account of the Imperial Regalia*. Tokyo: Sophia University Press, 1972.

Honan, William H. *Visions of Infamy*. New York: St. Martin's Press, 1991.

Hosaka Masayasu. *Tōjō Hideki to tennō no jidai* (Tōjō Hideki and the era of the emperor). 2 vols. Tokyo: Gendai Jānarisumu, 1979.

Hoston, Germaine A. "The State, Modernity, and the Fate of Liberalism in Prewar Japan." *Journal of Asian Studies* 51 (1992): 287–316.

Humphreys, Leonard A. *The Way of the Heavenly Sword: The Japanese Army in the 1920's*. Stanford: Stanford University Press, 1995.

Hurst, G. Cameron III. *Insei: Abdicated Sovereigns in the Politics of Late Heian Japan 1086–1185*. New York: Columbia University Press, 1976.

Ienaga Saburō. *Kulturgeschichte Japans.* Translated by Karl Friedrich Zahl. Munich: Judicium, 1990.

———. *Nihon bunkashi* (Cultural history of Japan). 2nd ed. Tokyo: Iwanami Shoten, 1982.

———. *The Pacific War, 1931–1945.* Translated by Frank Baldwin. New York: Pantheon, 1978.

Ike, Nobutaka. *Japan's Decision for War.* Stanford: Stanford University Press, 1967.

Imai, Seiichi. "Cabinet, Emperor, and Senior Statesmen." In Dorothy Borg and Shumpei Okamoto, eds., *Pearl Harbor as History: Japanese-American Relations 1931–1942.* New York: Columbia University Press, 1973.

Inoue Kiyoshi. *Tennō no sensōsekinin* (The emperor's war responsibility). Tokyo: Gendai Hyōronsha, 1975.

———. *Tennōsei* (The emperor system). Tokyo: Tokyo Daigaku Shuppankai, 1958.

Irokawa Daikichi. *The Age of Hirohito: In Search of Modern Japan.* Translated by Mikiso Hane and John K. Urda. New York: Free Press, 1995.

———. *The Culture of Meiji.* Princeton: Princeton University Press, 1985.

———. "Freedom and the Concept of People's Rights." *Japan Quarterly* 14(2) (April–June 1967): 175–183.

———. *Meiji no bunka* (Meiji culture). Tokyo: Iwanami Shoten, 1970.

Ishida Ichirō. *Nihon no bunkashi* (Japanese culture history). Tokyo: Tōkai Daigaku Shuppankai, 1989.

Kai, Miwa, and Philip B. Yampolsky. *Political Chronology of Japan 1885–1957.* New York: East Asian Institute of Columbia University, 1957.

Kato, Joken. "The Meaning of *Li*." In Japanese National Commission for UNESCO, comp., *Philosophical Studies of Japan.* Vol. 4. Tokyo: Japan Society for the Promotion of Science, 1963.

Kawahara, Toshiaki. *Hirohito and His Times.* Tokyo: Kodansha, 1990.

Kerst, Georg. *Jacob Meckel, sein Leben, und sein Wirken in Deutschland und Japan.* Göttingen: Musterschmidt, 1970.

Kodansha Encyclopedia of Japan. 9 vols. Tokyo: Kodansha, 1983.

Kohut, Thomas A. *Wilhelm II and the Germans: A Study in Leadership.* New York: Oxford University Press, 1991.

Kokubun, Noriko. *Die Bedeutung der deutschen für die japanische Staatslehre unter der Meiji-Verfassung.* Frankfurt: Peter Lang, 1993.

Kokushi daijiten (Great dictionary of national history). 14 vols. Tokyo: Yoshikawa Kōbunkan, 1979–1993.

Kono Osamu. *Tennō to Niniroku Jiken* (The emperor and the February 26 Incident). Tokyo: Kawaide Shobo Shinsha, 1985.

Kosaka, Masataka. "The Showa Era (1926–1989)." In Carol Gluck and Stephen R. Graubard, eds., *Showa: The Japan of Hirohito.* New York: Norton, 1992.

Krebs, Gerhard. "Das Ende des Shōwa-Tennō oder der Shōwa-Tennō und kein Ende: Die Diskussion in Politik und Literatur." In *Japanstudien: Jahrbuch des Deutschen Instituts für Japanstudien der Philipp-Franz-von-Siebold Stiftung.* Vol. 5. Munich: Judicium, 1993.

———. *Japans Deutschlandpolitik 1935–1941.* 2 vols. Hamburg: Mitteilung der Gesellschaft für Natur- und Völkerkunde Ostasiens, 1984.

————. Review of *Der Tenno: Japan hinter dem Chrysanthemenvorhang* by Peter Crome. *Kagami* (April 1989): 94–101.

————. "The Spy Activities of Diplomat Terasaki Hidenari in the USA and His Role in Japanese-American Relations." In Ian Neary, ed., *Leaders and Leadership in Japan*. Surrey: Japan Library (Curzon Press), 1996.

Ladstätter, Otto, and Sepp Linhart. *China und Japan: Die Kulturen Ostasiens.* Vienna: Carl Ueberreuter Verlag, 1983.

Large, Stephen S. "Emperor Hirohito and Early Showa Japan." *Monumenta Nipponica* 46(3) (Autumn 1991): 349–368.

————. *Emperor Hirohito and Shōwa Japan: A Political Biography.* London: Routledge, 1992.

Legge, James. "Shoo-King." *The Chinese Classics.* Vol. 3. Reprint. Hong Kong: Hong Kong University Press, 1970.

————, trans. *Confucius: Confucian Analects, The Great Learning, and The Doctrine of the Mean.* New York: Dover, 1971.

Lokowandt, Ernst. "Das Japanische Kaisertum—religiöse Fundierung und politische Realität." OAG aktuell no. 35. Tokyo: OAG, 1989.

————. "Der Staat als Selbstzweck—Staatszwecke und -ziele in Japan." OAG aktuell no. 61. Tokyo: OAG, 1994.

————. "Die Stellung der Tennō in der Staatsführung—Die rechtliche Reglung der Herrschaftsbefugnisse des Kaisers unter der Meiji-Verfassung." *Oriens Extremus* 33(1) (1990): 49–64.

Marder, Arthur J. *Old Friends, New Enemies: The Royal Navy and the Imperial Japanese Navy: Strategic Illusions, 1936–1941.* Oxford: Clarendon Press, 1981.

Martin, Bernd. "Aggressionspolitik als Mobilisierungsfaktor: Der militärische und wirtschaftliche Imperialismus Japans 1931–1941." In Fr. Forstmeier and Hans-Erich Volkmann, eds., *Wirtschaft und Rüstung am Vorabend des Zweiten Weltkrieges.* Düsseldorf: Droste Verlag, 1975.

————. "Deutsche Geschichtswissenschaft als Instrument nationaler Selbstfindung in Japan." In Gangolf Hübinger, Jürgen Osterhammel, and Erich Pelzer, eds., *Universalgeschichte und Nationalgeschichten,* Freiburg: Rombach Verlag, 1994.

————. *Japan and Germany in the Modern World.* Providence: Berghahn Books, 1995.

————. "Japan und der Krieg in Ostasien" (Kommentierender Bericht über das Schrifttum). *Historische Zeitschrift,* Sonderheft 8, *Literaturbericht zur Geschichte Chinas und zur japanischen Zeitgeschichte.* Munich: R. Oldenbourg, 1980.

————. "Japans Imperialismus." *Studia Historiae Oeconomicae.* Vol. 18. Poznan: Uniwersytet im. Adama Mickiewicza W Poznaniu, 1985.

————, ed. *Japans Weg in die Moderne: Ein Sonderweg nach deutschen Vorbild?* Frankfurt: Campus Verlag, 1987.

————. "Zur Tauglichkeit eines übergreifenden Faschismusbegriffes: Ein Vergleich zwischen Japan, Italien und Deutschland." *Vierteljahrshefte für Zeitgeschichte* (Munich) 1 (1981): 48–73.

————. "Verhängnisvolle Wahlverwandtschaft: Deutsche Einflüsse auf die Entstehung des modernen Japans." In Jost Düffler et al., eds., *Deutschland in Europa, Kontinuität und Bruch: Gedenkschrift für Andreas Hillgruber.* Berlin: Ulstein Verlag, 1990.

Maruyama, Masao. *Thought and Behaviour in Modern Japanese Politics.* Edited by Ivan Morris. London: Oxford University Press, 1963.

Masuda, Tomoko. "The Emperor's Right of Supreme Command as Exercised up to 1930: A Study Based Especially on the Takarabe and Kuratomi Diaries." In Junji Banno, ed., *The Emperor System in Modern Japan.* Tokyo: Tōhō Gakkai, 1990.

Matsumoto, Shigeru. *Motoori Norinaga, 1730–1801.* Cambridge, Mass.: Harvard University Press, 1970.

Mayer-Oakes, Thomas, ed. and trans. *Fragile Victory: Saionji-Harada Memoirs.* Detroit: Wayne State University Press, 1968.

McCullough, Helen Craig, trans. *Taiheiki: A Chronicle of Medieval Japan.* New York: Columbia University Press, 1959.

McCullough, William, trans. "The Azuma Kagami Account of the Shōkyū War." *Monumenta Nipponica* 23 (1968): 102–155.

———. "Shōkyūki: An Account of the Shōkyū War." *Monumenta Nipponica* 19 (1964): 163–215 and 21 (1966): 420–453.

Miller, Frank O. *Minobe Tatsukichi: Interpreter of Constitutionalism in Japan.* Berkeley: University of California Press, 1965.

Minear, Richard H. *Victor's Justice.* Tokyo: Tuttle, 1972.

Mitchell, Richard H. *Thought Control in Prewar Japan.* Ithaca: Cornell University Press, 1976.

Mommsen, Wolfgang J. *Bürgerstolz und Weltmachtstreben: Deutschland unter Wilhelm II: 1890 bis 1918.* Berlin: Propyläen Verlag, 1995.

Morley, James William, ed. *Japan's Road to the Pacific War: Japan Erupts: The London Naval Conference and the Manchurian Incident, 1928–1932.* New York: Columbia University Press, 1984.

———, ed. *Japan's Road to the Pacific War: The Final Confrontation: Japan's Negotiations with the United States, 1941.* Translated by David A. Titus. New York: Columbia University Press, 1994.

Morris, Ivan. *The Nobility of Failure: Tragic Heroes in the History of Japan.* New York: New American Library, 1975.

———. *The World of the Shining Prince: Court Life in Ancient Japan.* New York: Knopf, 1969.

Morton, William Fitch. *Tanaka Giichi and Japan's China Policy.* Folkestone, Kent: William Dawson, 1980.

Mosley, Leonard. *Hirohito, Emperor of Japan.* Englewood Cliffs, N.J.: Prentice-Hall, 1966.

Müller, Klaus-Jürgen. "Deutsche Militär-Elite in der Vorgeschichte des Zweiten Weltkrieges." In Martin Broszat and Klaus Schwabe, eds., *Die deutschen Eliten und der Weg in den Zweiten Weltkrieg.* Munich: C. H. Beck, 1989.

Nakahara Shigetoshi. *Kokuryoku naki sensōshidō* (Directing a war without national resources). Tokyo: Hara Shobō, 1989.

Nakamura Masanori. *The Japanese Monarchy, Ambassador Joseph Grew and the Making of the "Symbol Emperor System," 1931–1991.* Translated by Herbert P. Bix, Jonathan Baker-Bates, and Derek Bowen. Armonk, N.Y.: M. E. Sharpe, 1992.

Nakano Masao. *Tennō to Niniroku Jiken* (The emperor and the February 26 Incident). Tokyo: Kodansha, 1975.

Nezu Masashi. *Tennō to Shōwashi* (The emperor and Shōwa history). 2 vols. Tokyo: Sanichi Shobō, 1976.

Nipperdey, Thomas. *Deutsche Geschichte 1866–1918*. Vol. 2: *Machtstaat vor der Demokratie*. Munich: C. H. Beck, 1992.

Nomura Minoru. *Tennō, Fushimi-Miya to Nippon Kaigun* (The emperor, Imperial Prince Fushimi, and the Japanese navy). Tokyo: Kōjinsha, 1988.

Numata, Jiro. "Shigeno Yasutsugu and the Modern Tokyo Tradition of Historical Writing." In W. G. Beasley and E. G. Pulleyblank, eds., *Historians of China and Japan*. London: Oxford University Press, 1961.

Oates, Leslie Russell. *Populist Nationalism in Prewar Japan: A Biography of Nakano Seigō*. Sydney: Allen & Unwin, 1985.

Ōe Shinobu. *Tōsuiken* (Authority of supreme command). Tokyo: Nihon Hyōronsha, 1983.

Ohnuki-Tierney, Emiko. "The Emperor of Japan as Diety (Kami)." *Ethnology* 30(3) (1991): 199–215.

Oka, Yoshitake. *Five Political Leaders of Modern Japan: Itō Hirobumi, Ōkuma Shigenobu, Hara Takashi, Inukai Tsuyoshi, Saionji Kimmochi*. Translated by Andrew Fraser and Patricia Murray. Tokyo: University of Tokyo Press, 1986.

Okamoto, Shumpei. "Japan's Imperial Conspiracy." *Journal of Asian Studies* 31 (1971–1972): 414–416.

Ōkita Saburō, Ōgiya Shōzō, and Kusayanagi Taizō, eds. *Tennō Hirohito* (Emperor Hirohito). Tokyo: Kodansha, 1986.

Ōmachi Keigetsu and Ikari Shisan. *Sugiura Shigetake sensei* (Teacher Sugiura Shigetake). Reprint. Kyoto: Shibunkaku Shuppan, 1986.

Ōtake Shūichi. *Tennō no gakkō* (The emperor's school). Tokyo: Bungei Shunjūsha, 1986.

Ōtani Keijirō. *Shōwa Kempeishi* (History of the Shōwa Kempeitai). Tokyo: Misuzu Shobō, 1987.

Ōyama Azusa, ed. *Yamagata Aritomo ikensho* (Yamagata Aritomo opinion papers). Tokyo: Hara Shobō, 1966.

Packard, Jerrold M. *Sons of Heaven*. New York: Scribner's, 1987.

Philippi, Donald, trans. *Kojiki*. Princeton and Tokyo: Princeton and Tokyo University Presses, 1969.

Prange, Gordon W., with Donald M. Goldstein and Katherine V. Dillon. *Pearl Harbor: The Verdict of History*. New York: McGraw-Hill, 1986.

Pretzell, Klaus-Albrecht. "Das Bunmei-ittō-ki und das Shōdan-chiyō: Zwei Lehrschriften des Ichijō Kanera." Dissertation, Hamburg University, 1966.

Rhodes, Richard. *The Making of the Atomic Bomb*. New York: Simon & Schuster, 1986.

Roden, Donald T. *Schooldays in Imperial Japan: A Study of the Culture of a Student Elite*. Berkeley: University of California Press, 1980.

Rohlen, Thomas. *Japan's High Schools*. Berkeley: University of California Press, 1983.

Sakamoto, Tarō. *The Six National Histories* ("Rikkokushi"). Translated by John S. Brownlee. Vancouver: University of British Columbia Press; Tokyo: University of Tokyo Press, 1991.

Sanematsu Yuruzui. *Jōhō Sensō* (Information war). Tokyo: Tosho Shuppansha, 1972.

Sansom, George. *A History of Japan, 1334–1615*, Stanford: Stanford University Press, 1961.

Satō Kazuhiko, ed. *Kusunoki Masashige no subete* (All about Kusunoki Masashige). Tokyo: Shinjinbutsu Ōraisha, 1989.

Satō Kunio. *Tōgō Heihachirō: Gensui no bannen* (Tōgō Heihachirō: The fleet admiral's last years). Tokyo: Asahi Shimbunsha, 1990.

Senda Kakō. *Tennō to chokugo to Shōwashi* (The emperor, imperial rescripts, and the history of the Shōwa era). Tokyo: Sekibunsha, 1983.

Senger, Harro von. "Die japanische Initiative zur völkerrechtlichen Verankerung des Grundsatzes der Rassengleichheit vom Jahre 1919." *Frankfurter Allgemeine Zeitung*, 25 April 1994, p. 13.

Senshi sōsho (War history series). Edited by Bōeichō Bōeikenshūjo Senshishitsu (National Institute for Defense Studies). 102 vols. Tokyo: Asagumo Shimbunsha, 1966–1980.

Severns, Karen. *Hirohito*. With an introductory essay on leadership by Arthur M. Schlesinger, Jr., World Leaders Past and Present Series. New York: Chelsea House, 1988.

Sheldon, Charles D. "Japanese Aggression and the Emperor, 1931–1941, from Contemporary Diaries." *Modern Asian Studies* 10(1) (1976): 1–40.

Shillony, Ben-ami. *Revolt in Japan: The Young Officers and the February 26, 1936 Incident*. Princeton: Princeton University Press, 1973.

Shinoda, Minoru. *The Founding of the Kamakura Shogunate, 1180–1185*. New York: Columbia University Press, 1957.

"Shōwa tennō dokuhakuroku—watashitachi no shōgeki (The Shōwa emperor's monologue—our shock)." *Bungei shunjū*, Jan. 1991, pp. 94–147.

Stephan, John J. *Hawaii Under the Rising Sun*. Honolulu: University of Hawai'i Press, 1984.

Sullivan, Harry R. *Walter Bagehot*. Boston: G. K. Hall, 1975.

Takahashi Masae. *Niniroku Jiken* (February 26 Incident). Tokyo: Iwanami Shoten, 1965.

Tam, Yun-tai. "Rationalism vs. Nationalism: Tsuda Sōkichi." In John S. Brownlee, ed., *History in the Service of the Japanese Nation*. Toronto: Joint Centre on Modern East Asia, 1983.

Tanaka, Stefan. *Japan's Orient: Rendering Pasts into History*. Berkeley: University of California Press, 1993.

Tipton, Elise. *Japanese Police State: Tokkō in Interwar Japan*. Honolulu: University of Hawai'i Press, 1990.

Titus, David A. "Accessing the World: Palace and Foreign Policy in Post-Occupation Japan." In Gerald L. Curtis, ed., *Japan's Foreign Policy*. Armonk, N.Y.: M. E. Sharpe, 1993.

——, trans. "The Idea of Revering the Emperor and Its Heritage." An abridged and condensed translation of Watsuji Tetsurō, *Sonnō Shisō to Sono Dentō*, chaps. 1–3. Unpublished manuscript.

——. "The Making of the 'Symbol Emperor System' in Postwar Japan." *Modern Asian Studies* 14(4) (1980): 529–578.

——. *Palace and Politics in Prewar Japan*. New York: Columbia University Press, 1974.

Toyama Saburō. *Taiheiyō kaisenshi, 1* (History of the beginning of the Pacific War, 1). Tokyo: Kyōiku Shuppan Center, 1985.

Tsuda, Sōkichi. "On the Stages of the Formation of Japan as a Nation and the Origin of the Belief in the Perpetuity of the Imperial Family." In Japanese National Commission for UNESCO, comp., *Philosophical Studies of Japan.* Vol. 4. Tokyo: Japan Society for the Promotion of Science, 1963.

Tsunoda Jun and Fukuda Shigeo. *Nichibei kaisen* (Beginning of the war between Japan and the United States). In Tsunoda Jun, ed., *Taiheiyō Sensō e no michi* (Road to the Pacific War). Vol. 7. Tokyo: Asahi Shimbunsha, 1962–1963.

Tsunoda, Ryusaku, et al. *Sources of Japanese Tradition.* New York: Columbia University Press, 1958.

Varley, H. Paul, trans. *A Chronicle of Gods and Sovereigns.* New York: Columbia University Press, 1980.

———. *Imperial Restoration in Medieval Japan.* New York: Columbia University Press, 1971.

Wajima Yoshio. *Chūsei no Jugaku* (Medieval Confucianism). Tokyo: Yoshikawa Kōbunkan, 1965.

Ward, Robert E. "Presurrender Planning: Treatment of the Emperor and Constitutional Changes." In Robert E. Ward and Yoshikazu Sakamoto, eds., *Democratizing Japan: The Allied Occupation.* Honolulu: University of Hawai'i Press, 1987.

Watson, Burton. *Records of the Grand Historian of China: Translated from the "Shih chi" of Ssu-Ma Ch'ien.* 2 vols. New York: Columbia University Press, 1961.

Wedemeyer, André. *Japanische Frühgeschichte.* Suppl. 11. Tokyo: MOAG, 1930.

Wetzler, Peter. "Kaiser Hirohito und der Krieg im Pazifik." *Vierteljahrshefte für Zeitgeschichte* (Munich) 4 (1989): 611–644.

———. "Yoshishige no Yasutane: Lineage, Learning, Office, and Amida's Pure Land." Ph.D. dissertation, University of California, Berkeley, 1977.

Wray, Harold J. "Changes and Continuity in Japanese Images of the Kokutai and Roles Toward the Outside World: A Content Analysis of Japanese Textbooks, 1903–1945." Ph.D. dissertation, University of Hawai'i, 1971.

Yamada Akira. *Daigensui Shōwa tennō* (The Shōwa emperor as commander in chief). Tokyo: Shin-Nihon Shuppansha, 1994.

———. *Shōwa tennō no sensōshidō* (The Shōwa emperor's war leadership). Tokyo: Shōwa Shuppan, 1990.

Yamaji Yakichi, Yamaji Aizan, and Nishida Keishi. *Yakubun Dainihonshi.* (Translation [into modern Japanese] of the Great History of Japan). Tokyo: Kōraku Shoin, 1912.

Yamamoto Shichihei. *Shōwa tennō no kenkyū: Sono jitsuzō o saguru* (Research on the Shōwa emperor: In search of his real image). Tokyo: Shōdensha, 1989.

Zainichi Beirikugun Senshika (U.S. Army in Japan, War History Section), trans. *Daikaishi Eiyaku 1–2.* Vol. 1: "Imperial General Headquarters Navy Directives," 5 Nov. 1941–12 Sept. 1945, 540 directives and 3 supplements. (Unpublished MS in the NIDS Library, Tokyo.)

Zöllner, Reinhard. "Lorenz von Stein und *kokutai.*" *Oriens Extremus* 33(1) (1990): 65–76.

Index

Abe Nobuyuki, general and prime minister, 26, 192
adapt, to Japan, 114–115, 120–121
adaptation, of foreign cultures, 137
Akamatsu Sadao, colonel, 68, 78, 194; biographical note, 214 n. 15; diary, 65; Tōjō's private secretary, 50
amae, emotional dependency, 134–136
Amaterasu Ōmikami, 95, 96, 99, 183; benevolence, 109–110; guardian of cereals, 109–110. *See also* Sun Goddess
America, 173, 175, 186; plan to eliminate in East Asia, 53; war with, 192. *See also* United States
Analects, 104
ancient history, 112; and Confucian ethics, 184; importance of, 83; and Sugiura, 101–102
Andō Kisaburō, minister of interior, 207
Annual Imperial Navy Operations Plan, 18–19; 1936, 20–21; 1937, 21; 1938, 21–23; 1939, 24–25; 1940, 26–27; 1941, 28–29; chief aide-de-camp, 19; distribution, 19; emperor, 18–19; imperial army and navy, 39
Araki Sadao, general, 264 n. 15
army: influence on emperor, 55; disagreement with navy, 21–23; preservation records, 33. *See also* emperor; Imperial Army
Army Academy *(Rikugun shikan gakkō)*, 63
army minister, compared to chief of staff, 74
Ashikaga Takauji, shogun, 67, 69, 73, 128, 198–199
Asia, expansion throughout, 121
atomic bomb, 191, 244–245 n. 64
Austro-Hungarian emperor, 123. *See also* Karl

Bagehot, Walter, 93–94, 129, 130, 138
bakufu, 127
Basic Tactics Outline, 18
"being Japanese," 121
benevolence, 214, 251 n. 79
Bismarck, Otto von, 125

About the Author

Peter Wetzler is professor of Japanese business, politics, and language at the East Asia Institute of the Ludwigshafen School of Business Administration in Germany. He was born and educated in the United States, studied language and history in Japan, and has a Ph.D. in Far Eastern history from the University of California, Berkeley (1977). He is the author of a number of essays on premodern and modern Japanese history including "Kaiser Hirohito und der Krieg im Pazifik," in the *Vierteljahrshefte für Zeitgeschichte* (Munich, 1989).